— INTRODUCTION TO —
Philosophy

a survey by
Steve Stakland
NOVA—Annadale Campus

Kendall Hunt
publishing company

Cover image © Shutterstock.com

www.kendallhunt.com
Send all inquiries to:
4050 Westmark Drive
Dubuque, IA 52004-1840

Copyright © 2019 by Kendall Hunt Publishing Company

ISBN: 978-1-5249-8863-0

All rights reserved. No part of this publication may be reproduced, stored in a retrieval system, or transmitted, in any form or by any means, electronic, mechanical, photocopying, recording, or otherwise, without the prior written permission of the copyright owner.

Published in the United States of America

"A man lives as many millennia as are embraced by his knowledge of history."
Marsilio Ficino (1433–1499)

"Questioning is the piety of thought."
Martin Heidegger (1889–1776)

"The unexamined life is not worth living for a human being."
Socrates (470–399 BC)

Contents

Preface .... *ix*
Introduction .... *xi*

Plato   1
    Introduction: 1
Euthyphro   3
    Introduction 3
    Euthyphro 6
Apology   20
    Introduction 20
    Apology 27
Crito   43
    Introduction 43
    Crito 45
Meno   54
    Introduction 54
    On the Ideas of Plato 61
    Meno 68
Ion   98
    Introduction 98
    Ion 100
Rebulic (On Justice)   110
    Book I 110
    Excerpts From The *Republic* 137

v

Aristotle — 165

Nicomachean Ethics Excerpts 165
   Book I 165
   Book II 170
   Book X 173

The Enchiridion — 177

   Introduction 177
   The Enchiridion 180

Discourse on The Method of Rightly Conducting The Reason, and Seeking Truth in the Sciences — 195

   Prefatory Note by The Author 195
   Part I 195
   Part II 199
   Part III 204
   Part IV 208
   Part VI 212

Kant's Spectacles — 221

Hegel's Dialectic — 225

Nietzsche — 229

On the Use and Abuse of History for Life 229

The Question Concerning Technology — 277

The Ideology of Machines — 299

Focal Things and Practices — 309

Appendix 1 Images — 323

The Taking of Christ by Caravaggio 323
The School of Athens by Raphael 324

Appendix 2 Timeline 325
Chronological order of major philosophers 325

Appendix 3 Why Major in Philosophy 327
A $75 Million Bet on the Humanities 327

Preface
The Importance of Studying Philosophy at a Community College

When Norway was deciding whom to put in charge of its 200 billion dollar North Sea oil reserve it chose a philosopher. Not a businessperson, investor, politician, or scientist. Norwegian officials established the position of "state philosopher" because they understood that someone trained in philosophy would be most likely to ask the *right* questions. They believed having someone in charge who could ask the right environmental, ethical, and sociological *questions* was essential. Studying philosophy at a community college is vital because the discipline's subject matter is questioning; engagement with questioning teaches students how to understand and interpret diverse ideas, and it gives them a conduit to potential consolation.

Philosophy begins in the human capacity to *wonder*. Philosophy is a field defined by amazement. Philosophers are amazed and stand in wonder at existence, at consciousness, at beauty, and all of the manifestations of the physical and mental worlds. Questioning is emblematic of the astonishment of the human condition, and it forms the field of philosophy. Answers are important, but, unlike science that focuses on answers, philosophy emphasizes the questions. Questioning is a posture that delineates where we focus most of our active attention, and it is a manifestation of our humanity. Questioning is vital to pursuing the wisdom of the *examined life* that philosophy has advocated since at least Socrates. Philosophy *is* human questioning in all of its diverse forms. All of the answers to human questioning eventually coalesce to form the sciences. So to really understand their primarily scientific education, students must be exposed to philosophy, the mother of physics, chemistry, biology, and so on. Through studying philosophy, they can see how the answers of science originated in human wonder and, just as importantly, can breathe new life into their scientific studies as they formulate their own original questions within established scientific domains.

Carefully tracing the history of human questioning through the primary source texts of Plato, Aristotle, Descartes, Kant, Hegel, and so on, is difficult. Students have often never encountered the topics and writing styles of these reading, which are neither textbooks nor novels and often resemble poetry. The ambiguity and abstractness of these books heightens the potential for students' engagement as they embark on their own interpretive quests.

The exposure to this challenging material increases their reading comprehension, arguably the most important educational skill.

Teaching philosophy in a discussion format maximizes its value and impact. By debating and dialoguing about philosophy, students become more genuinely gripped than if they were exposed to the same content on YouTube. Discussing philosophy in a group allows students to encounter worldviews different from their own. Exposure to intellectual diversity is vital to a mature and educated individual, and it allows them to overcome moral naiveté, that is, to maintain their own standard as unquestionably certain and true. Confronting the diversity of opinions and responses to philosophical readings allows students the precious learning experience of being able to evaluate their fundamental assumptions.

Philosophy has the potential to be one of the greatest sources of consolation. Most students at a community college know the suffering requisite for a good life and the difficulties necessitated by the pursuit of worthy goals. The corpus of philosophical readings that students are exposed to in a philosophy class gives them a peek into a domain of conciliatory material that can buoy them up in times of stress, frustration, and grief. For example, as they imbibe the Platonic dialogues, they can come to see the courage of the intellectual hero, Socrates, as he faces execution. Or, as they experience doubts, they can go along with Descartes as he applies his radical but purposive skepticism. As they seek to emulate his purpose in their own lives, they can experience the wonder of seeking the indubitable. Such a quest can lead them to consider what standards indubitable foundations require. As they cast about for tools in this project, they will find in a philosophy class ready implements, for example, dialectic, existentialism, philosophy of religion, transcendental idealism, and phenomenology. These will assist them in a range of capacities be they managing the wealth of a nation, starting a business, raising a family, or serving in government.

Introduction

Philosophy is its own first problem. Which is to say, philosophy is in perpetual identity crisis. That means that the first question a philosopher asks is, "What *is* philosophy?" You might ask that question too, and once you do that makes you a philosopher. However, it might also make you wonder what the point of philosophy is since it can seem so boundless as it is only limited by all of the potential answers to that question. Everyone who wonders about philosophy can come to a different answer or definition. Therefore, there are many conceptions of philosophy. Much of what follows in this book are readings that show the breadth and limits of philosophy. Even though it is exceedingly broad, as broad as our imagination to some extent, it is also not the same as everything. The readings that are found in this survey show how to start to delineate philosophy from other powerful domains of the human mind like science and religion, for example.

The readings in this book are a tiny survey of the vast literary output of those who have wondered about the meaning, purpose, and consolation of philosophy. The purpose of this survey is merely to introduce some of the main conceptions of philosophy. The readings that follow seek to introduce some of the main problems of philosophy: What is reality (metaphysics)? What is knowledge (epistemology)? What is valued (axiology, ethics and aesthetics)?

No understanding of philosophy is complete without an encounter with Socrates, Plato, and Aristotle. Though Socrates, like other great thinkers (Jesus, the Buddha, Confucius), wrote nothing, his student Plato produced masterful dialogues that seem to capture his voice and method. With Socrates we find the epistemological and ethical interests of philosophy. In the dialogues that express more of Plato's own views, even though they still use Socrates as the main character (Plato almost never speaks for himself), we encounter some of the most influential metaphysics the world has ever known. Profoundly influenced by his *intellectual* grandfather (Socrates) and father (Plato), Aristotle turns his powerful systematizing and categorizing mind to similar problems.

Having started with a substantial amount of ancient philosophy, we are well on our way to understanding the trajectory that philosophy has followed and what it is up to even today. After Plato and Aristotle, we are prepared to go wherever we like in the long tradition that follows. Along that way we can examine one of the major schools that comes from Socrates' influence, Stoicism in Epictetus' *Enchiridion*, that is, "handbook." Descartes is a key figure as he is the father of modern philosophy. He shifts the focus of philosophy away from many of the ancient conceptions started with Plato. The modern world sets humanity on a course of vast technological change. Science and causation in particular are vital issues that philosophers like David Hume and Immanuel Kant confront as they also strive to preserve human freedom and morality. Following from them, we hit the deep ethical thinking of Schopenhauer and Nietzsche, both of whom philosophized in a prophetic manner as they saw calamitous times ahead for the history of humanity. Several of the final readings are about the philosophy of technology and how philosophers think we can deal with the changes it makes to us and our world.

Plato

Introduction

Why Does Socrates Question?

In the *Apology* Socrates appeals, in a round about way, to a character witness, the god at Delphi, Apollo, to justify the activities of his life. It is his activity of questioning, engaging in philosophy, which he says has caused him to have enemies. Socrates testifies that a friend went to the oracle and was told that nobody was wiser than Socrates. Assuming the veracity of this, fine. But why does Socrates use this as motivation to set out to question every person who is either purported to be wise or who claims to have wisdom? That is, why doesn't he just accept the dictum of the oracle? It seems an odd response to claim, as Socrates does, that the god was giving him a mission. A curious reaction to such glorious news considering that it bore the stamp of divinity and could thus hardly be thought to be questioned by anybody, even those who most disagreed with the pronouncement. That he should thus take the oracle to be giving him a riddle that *must* be solved and then, in turn, test this solution *ad infinitum* seems patently absurd. However, when we also consider that Socrates' defense speech also characterizes the main accusations against him, that of impiety and corrupting the youth as a "riddle" it is possible to see why he would take the words of the oracle as a command from Apollo to live a life of philosophy.

|

Socrates verifies whether or not he should treat the oracle's pronouncement as a riddle to be answered and then tested, as if it were then a commandment, by reference to his divine sign. If this daemon, the voice he hears in his head, is accepted as being divine, then nobody can really fault him for following it unless they want to risk being called impious themselves. Rather, they might doubt he has such a divine guide at all rather. But be that as it may, it is because this divine sign never opposed him that Socrates gets the force to say that it was a commandment at all, since his divine sign never objected to the pursuit of testing the oracle and pursuing a life of philosophy which has made him so unpopular.

Plato

The fact is the oracle often did give pronouncements in the form of riddles. Depending on how much the supplicant paid determined the clarity or detail of the answer. It is not given how much Socrates' friend offered up but he clearly paid more than was required for a simple 'yes' or 'no' response (which would have sufficed, and for Socrates' case, and the context of this discussion, probably would not have been much ground for claiming to be commanded by the god). Thus, it is completely normal to suppose that someone could seek to interpret or probe the dictum for a deeper meaning.

II

If Socrates had simply accepted the oracle's decree without any work to interpret it or seeking to understanding he probably would have failed to be morally good, at least by his own standards. By the cultural standards of his fellow Greeks he would probably have been completely justified in simply claiming, straightforwardly, that he was the wisest. But in doing so he may have tripped one of his own cords of immorality. He may himself have fallen prey to his own judgment of maintaining contradictory beliefs. Primarily, if the oracles words had led him to inactivity and resting on his laurels he would probably have been similar to Oedipus, who after answering the riddle of the sphinx accepts the rewards of wisdom. Such a concession, even when sanctioned by the gods, is not for mortals to make. Such actions are hubris and are severely punished for their impiety.

III

Is Socrates serious or is he being ironic. Yes and no. His actions seem ironic, if not outright silly as compared to how most people would react in a similar situation with regard to the oracle and the gods. But Socrates is decidedly not most people. He is a character. He seemingly never does what most people would do. The *Apology* is rife with examples to emphasize this point. During his time in the government he gives two examples where he alone was the only one on the side of the law and justice. In battle he was noted as not running away in retreat as everyone else was wont to do. He also, rather shamefully, does not care for his family very well, as most people do. Thus, Socrates' whole life is, in a sense ironic or unique – unique because ironic. Therefore, even if he is being ironic about the was he takes the oracles pronouncement as a commandment to go on a mission for the god that is the only way he could take it if he were to live consistently. Taking it as he does is obviously the only way Socrates can take it since that is how he approaches everything in his life.

Socrates alters the Iliad to say Protoclus was "murdered." But in battle this is not really the case. Killed, certainly, but not murdered. Later Socrates calls the judges who have voted for his execution his murders. But murder is a legal term and if he is condemned to death by the judges and everything is done according to the law he is not murdered but executed. However, one who is unjustly tried, according to trumped up charges to satisfy the need for a scapegoat for the failure of the government to win a war and if such an one has been subjected to great prejudice in the media before the trial (Aristophanes *Clouds* etc.) a guilty verdict with the punishment of death might indeed be murder.

EUTHYPHRO

By Plato
Translated by Benjamin Jowett

Introduction

In the Meno, Anytus had parted from Socrates with the significant words: "That in any city, and particularly in the city of Athens, it is easier to do men harm than to do them good;" and Socrates was anticipating another opportunity of talking with him. In the Euthyphro, Socrates is awaiting his trial for impiety. But before the trial begins, Plato would like to put the world on their trial, and convince them of ignorance in that very matter touching which Socrates is accused. An incident which may perhaps really have occurred in the family of Euthyphro, a learned Athenian diviner and soothsayer, furnishes the occasion of the discussion.

This Euthyphro and Socrates are represented as meeting in the porch of the King Archon. (Compare Theaet.) Both have legal business in hand. Socrates is defendant in a suit for impiety which Meletus has brought against him (it is remarked by the way that he is not a likely man himself to have brought a suit against another); and Euthyphro too is plaintiff in an action for murder, which he has brought against his own father. The latter has originated in the following manner:—A poor dependent of the family had slain one of their domestic slaves in Naxos. The guilty person was bound and thrown into a ditch by the command of Euthyphro's father, who sent to the interpreters of religion at Athens to ask what should be done with him. Before the messenger came back the criminal had died from hunger and exposure.

This is the origin of the charge of murder which Euthyphro brings against his father. Socrates is confident that before he could have undertaken the responsibility of such a prosecution, he must have been perfectly informed of the nature of piety and impiety; and as he is going to be tried for impiety himself, he thinks that he cannot do better than learn of Euthyphro (who will be admitted by everybody, including the judges, to be an unimpeachable authority) what piety is, and what is impiety. What then is piety?

Euthyphro, who, in the abundance of his knowledge, is very willing to undertake all the responsibility, replies: That piety is doing as I do, prosecuting your father (if he is guilty) on a charge of murder; doing as the gods do—as Zeus did to Cronos, and Cronos to Uranus.

Socrates has a dislike to these tales of mythology, and he fancies that this dislike of his may be the reason why he is charged with impiety. 'Are they really true?' 'Yes, they are;' and Euthyphro will gladly tell Socrates some more of them. But Socrates would like first of all to have a more satisfactory answer to the question, 'What is piety?' 'Doing as I do, charging a father with murder,' may be a single instance of piety, but can hardly be regarded as a general definition.

Euthyphro replies, that 'Piety is what is dear to the gods, and impiety is what is not dear to them.' But may there not be differences of opinion, as among men, so also among the gods? Especially, about good and evil, which have no fixed rule; and these are precisely the sort of differences which give rise to quarrels. And therefore what may be dear to one god may not be dear to another, and the same action may be both pious and impious; e.g. your chastisement of your father, Euthyphro, may be dear or pleasing to Zeus (who inflicted a similar chastisement on his own father), but not equally pleasing to Cronos or Uranus (who suffered at the hands of their sons).

Euthyphro answers that there is no difference of opinion, either among gods or men, as to the propriety of punishing a murderer. Yes, rejoins Socrates, when they know him to be a murderer; but you are assuming the point at issue. If all the circumstances of the case are considered, are you able to show that your father was guilty of murder, or that all the gods are agreed in approving of our prosecution of him? And must you not allow that what is hated by one god may be liked by another? Waiving this last, however, Socrates proposes to amend the definition, and say that 'what all the gods love is pious, and what they all hate is impious.' To this Euthyphro agrees.

Socrates proceeds to analyze the new form of the definition. He shows that in other cases the act precedes the state; e.g. the act of being carried, loved, etc. precedes the state of being carried, loved, etc., and therefore that which is dear to the gods is dear to the gods because it is first loved of them, not loved of them because it is dear to them. But the pious or holy is loved by the gods because it is pious or holy, which is equivalent to saying, that it is loved by them because it is dear to them. Here then appears to be a contradiction,—Euthyphro has been giving an attribute or accident of piety only, and not the essence. Euthyphro acknowledges himself that his explanations seem to walk away or go round in a circle, like the moving figures of Daedalus, the ancestor of Socrates, who has communicated his art to his descendants.

Socrates, who is desirous of stimulating the indolent intelligence of Euthyphro, raises the question in another manner: 'Is all the pious just?' 'Yes.' 'Is all the just pious?' 'No.' 'Then what part of justice is piety?' Euthyphro replies that piety is that part of justice which 'attends' to the gods, as there is another part of justice which 'attends' to men. But what is the meaning of 'attending' to the gods? The word 'attending,' when applied to dogs, horses, and men, implies that in some way they are made better. But how do pious or holy acts make the gods any better? Euthyphro explains that he means by pious acts, acts of service or ministration. Yes; but the ministrations of the husbandman, the physician, and the builder have an end. To what end do we serve the gods, and what do we help them to accomplish? Euthyphro replies, that all these difficult questions cannot be resolved in a short time; and he would rather say simply that piety is knowing how to please the gods in word and deed, by prayers and sacrifices. In other words, says Socrates, piety is 'a science of asking and giving'—asking what we want and giving what they want; in short, a mode of doing business between gods and men. But although they are the givers of all good, how can we give them any good in return? 'Nay, but we give them honor.' Then we give them not what is beneficial, but what is pleasing or dear to them; and this is the point which has been already disproved.

Socrates, although weary of the subterfuges and evasions of Euthyphro, remains unshaken in his conviction that he must know the nature of piety, or he would never have prosecuted his old father. He is still hoping that he will condescend to instruct him. But Euthyphro is in a hurry and cannot stay. And Socrates' last hope of knowing the nature of piety before he is prosecuted for impiety has disappeared. As in the Euthydemus the irony is carried on to the end.

The Euthyphro is manifestly designed to contrast the real nature of piety and impiety with the popular conceptions of them. But when the popular conceptions of them have been overthrown, Socrates does not offer any definition of his own: as in the Laches and Lysis, he prepares the way for an answer to the question which he has raised; but true to his own character, refuses to answer himself.

Euthyphro is a religionist, and is elsewhere spoken of, if he be the same person, as the author of a philosophy of names, by whose 'prancing steeds' Socrates in the Cratylus is carried away. He has the conceit and self-confidence of a Sophist; no doubt that he is right in prosecuting his father has ever entered into his mind. Like a Sophist too, he is incapable either of framing a general definition or of following the course of an argument. His wrong-headedness, one-sidedness, narrowness, positiveness, are characteristic of his priestly office. His failure to apprehend an argument may be compared to a similar defect which is observable in the rhapsode Ion. But he is not a bad man, and he is friendly to Socrates, whose familiar sign he recognizes with interest. Though unable to follow him he is very willing to be led by him, and eagerly catches at any suggestion which saves him from the trouble of thinking. Moreover he is the enemy of Meletus, who, as he says, is availing himself of the popular dislike to innovations in religion in order to injure Socrates; at the same time he is amusingly confident that he has weapons in his own armory which would be more than a match for him. He is quite sincere in his prosecution of his father, who has accidentally been guilty of homicide, and is not wholly free from blame. To purge away the crime appears to him in the light of a duty, whoever may be the criminal.

Thus begins the contrast between the religion of the letter, or of the narrow and unenlightened conscience, and the higher notion of religion which Socrates vainly endeavors to elicit from him. 'Piety is doing as I do' is the idea of religion which first occurs to him, and to many others who do not say what they think with equal frankness. For men are not easily persuaded that any other religion is better than their own; or that other nations, e.g. the Greeks in the time of Socrates, were equally serious in their religious beliefs and difficulties. The chief difference between us and them is, that they were slowly learning what we are in process of forgetting. Greek mythology hardly admitted of the distinction between accidental homicide and murder: that the pollution of blood was the same in both cases is also the feeling of the Athenian diviner. He had not as yet learned the lesson, which philosophy was teaching, that Homer and Hesiod, if not banished from the state, or whipped out of the assembly, as Heracleitus more rudely proposed, at any rate were not to be appealed to as authorities in religion; and he is ready to defend his conduct by the examples of the gods. These are the very tales which Socrates cannot abide; and his dislike of them, as he suspects, has branded him with the reputation of impiety. Here is one answer to the question, 'Why Socrates was put to death,' suggested by the way. Another is conveyed in the words, 'The Athenians do not care about any man being thought wise until he begins to make other men wise; and then for some reason or other they are angry:' which may be said to be the rule of popular toleration in most other countries, and not at Athens only. In the course of the argument Socrates remarks that the controversial nature of morals and religion arises out of the difficulty of verifying them. There is no measure or standard to which they can be referred.

The next definition, 'Piety is that which is loved of the gods,' is shipwrecked on a refined distinction between the state and the act, corresponding respectively to the adjective (philon) and the participle (philoumenon), or rather perhaps to the participle and the verb (philoumenon and phileitai). The act is prior to the state (as in Aristotle the energeia precedes the dunamis); and the state of being loved is preceded by the act of being loved. But piety or holiness is preceded by the act of being pious, not by the act of being loved; and therefore piety and the state of being loved are different. Through such subtleties of dialectic Socrates is working his way into a deeper region of thought and feeling. He means to say that the words 'loved of the gods' express an attribute only, and not the essence of piety.

Then follows the third and last definition, 'Piety is a part of justice.' Thus far Socrates has proceeded in placing religion on a moral foundation. He is seeking to realize the harmony of religion and morality, which the great poets Aeschylus, Sophocles, and Pindar had unconsciously anticipated, and which is the universal want of all men. To this the soothsayer adds the ceremonial element, 'attending upon the gods.' When further interrogated by Socrates as to the nature of this 'attention to the gods,' he replies, that piety is an affair of business, a science of giving and asking, and the like. Socrates points out the anthropomorphism of these notions, (compare Symp.; Republic; Politicus.) But when we expect him to go on and show that the true service of the gods is the service of the spirit and the co-operation with them in all things true and good, he stops short; this was a lesson which the soothsayer could not have been made to understand, and which every one must learn for himself.

There seem to be altogether three aims or interests in this little Dialogue: (1) the dialectical development of the idea of piety; (2) the antithesis of true and false religion, which is carried to a certain extent only; (3) the defense of Socrates.

The subtle connection with the Apology and the Crito; the holding back of the conclusion, as in the Charmides, Lysis, Laches, Protagoras, and other Dialogues; the deep insight into the religious world; the dramatic power and play of the two characters; the inimitable irony, are reasons for believing that the Euthyphro is a genuine Platonic writing. The spirit in which the popular representations of mythology are denounced recalls Republic II. The virtue of piety has been already mentioned as one of five in the Protagoras, but is not reckoned among the four cardinal virtues of Republic IV. The figure of Daedalus has occurred in the Meno; that of Proteus in the Euthydemus and Io. The kingly science has already appeared in the Euthydemus, and will reappear in the Republic and Statesman. But neither from these nor any other indications of similarity or difference, and still less from arguments respecting the suitableness of this little work to aid Socrates at the time of his trial or the reverse, can any evidence of the date be obtained.

Euthyphro

PERSONS OF THE DIALOGUE: Socrates, Euthyphro.

SCENE: The Porch of the King Archon.

EUTHYPHRO: Why have you left the Lyceum, Socrates? and what are you doing in the Porch of the King Archon? Surely you cannot be concerned in a suit before the King, like myself?

SOCRATES: Not in a suit, Euthyphro; impeachment is the word which the Athenians use.

EUTHYPHRO: What! I suppose that some one has been prosecuting you, for I cannot believe that you are the prosecutor of another.

SOCRATES: Certainly not.

EUTHYPHRO: Then some one else has been prosecuting you?

SOCRATES: Yes.

EUTHYPHRO: And who is he?

SOCRATES: A young man who is little known, Euthyphro; and I hardly know him: his name is Meletus, and he is of the deme of Pitthis. Perhaps you may remember his appearance; he has a beak, and long straight hair, and a beard which is ill grown.

EUTHYPHRO: No, I do not remember him, Socrates. But what is the charge which he brings against you?

SOCRATES: What is the charge? Well, a very serious charge, which shows a good deal of character in the young man, and for which he is certainly not to be despised. He says he knows how the youth are corrupted and who are their corruptors. I fancy that he must be a wise man, and seeing that I am the reverse of a wise man, he has found me out, and is going to accuse me of corrupting his young friends. And of this our mother the state is to be the judge. Of all our political men he is the only one who seems to me to begin in the right way, with the cultivation of virtue in youth; like a good husbandman, he makes the young shoots his first care, and clears away us who are the destroyers of them. This is only the first step; he will afterwards attend to the elder branches; and if he goes on as he has begun, he will be a very great public benefactor.

EUTHYPHRO: I hope that he may; but I rather fear, Socrates, that the opposite will turn out to be the truth. My opinion is that in attacking you he is simply aiming a blow at the foundation of the state. But in what way does he say that you corrupt the young?

SOCRATES: He brings a wonderful accusation against me, which at first hearing excites surprise: he says that I am a poet or maker of gods, and that I invent new gods and deny the existence of old ones; this is the ground of his indictment.

EUTHYPHRO: I understand, Socrates; he means to attack you about the familiar sign which occasionally, as you say, comes to you. He thinks that you are a neologian, and he is going to have you up before the court for this. He knows that such a charge is readily received by the world, as I myself know too well; for when I speak in the assembly about divine things, and foretell the future to them, they laugh at me and think me a madman. Yet every word that I say is true. But they are jealous of us all; and we must be brave and go at them.

SOCRATES: Their laughter, friend Euthyphro, is not a matter of much consequence. For a man may be thought wise; but the Athenians, I suspect, do not much trouble themselves about him until he begins to impart his wisdom to others, and then for some reason or other, perhaps, as you say, from jealousy, they are angry.

EUTHYPHRO: I am never likely to try their temper in this way.

SOCRATES: I dare say not, for you are reserved in your behavior, and seldom impart your wisdom. But I have a benevolent habit of pouring out myself to everybody, and would even pay for a listener, and I am afraid that the Athenians may think me too talkative. Now if, as I was saying, they would only laugh at me, as you say that they laugh at you, the time might pass gaily enough in the court; but perhaps they may be in earnest, and then what the end will be you soothsayers only can predict.

EUTHYPHRO: I dare say that the affair will end in nothing, Socrates, and that you will win your cause; and I think that I shall win my own.

SOCRATES: And what is your suit, Euthyphro? are you the pursuer or the defendant?

EUTHYPHRO: I am the pursuer.

SOCRATES: Of whom?

EUTHYPHRO: You will think me mad when I tell you.

SOCRATES: Why, has the fugitive wings?

EUTHYPHRO: Nay, he is not very volatile at his time of life.

SOCRATES: Who is he?

EUTHYPHRO: My father.

SOCRATES: Your father! my good man?

EUTHYPHRO: Yes.

SOCRATES: And of what is he accused?

EUTHYPHRO: Of murder, Socrates.

SOCRATES: By the powers, Euthyphro! how little does the common herd know of the nature of right and truth. A man must be an extraordinary man, and have made great strides in wisdom, before he could have seen his way to bring such an action.

EUTHYPHRO: Indeed, Socrates, he must.

SOCRATES: I suppose that the man whom your father murdered was one of your relatives—clearly he was; for if he had been a stranger you would never have thought of prosecuting him.

EUTHYPHRO: I am amused, Socrates, at your making a distinction between one who is a relation and one who is not a relation; for surely the pollution is the same in either case, if you knowingly associate with the murderer when you ought to clear yourself and him by proceeding against him. The real question is whether the murdered man has been justly slain. If justly, then your duty is to let the matter alone; but if unjustly, then even if the murderer lives under the same roof with you and eats at the same table, proceed against him. Now the man who is dead was a poor dependent of mine who worked for us as a field laborer on our farm in Naxos, and one day in a fit of drunken passion he got into a quarrel with one of our domestic servants and slew him. My father bound him hand and foot and threw him into a ditch, and then sent to Athens to ask of a diviner what he should do with him. Meanwhile he never attended to him and took no care about him, for he regarded him as a murderer; and thought that no great harm would be done even if he did die. Now this was just what happened. For such was the effect of cold and hunger and chains upon him, that before the messenger returned from the diviner, he was dead. And my father and family are angry with me for taking the part of the murderer and prosecuting my father. They say that he did not kill him, and that if he did, the dead man was but a murderer, and I ought not to take any notice, for that a son is impious who prosecutes a father. Which shows, Socrates, how little they know what the gods think about piety and impiety.

SOCRATES: Good heavens, Euthyphro! and is your knowledge of religion and of things pious and impious so very exact, that, supposing the circumstances to be as you state them, you are not afraid lest you too may be doing an impious thing in bringing an action against your father?

EUTHYPHRO: The best of Euthyphro, and that which distinguishes him, Socrates, from other men, is his exact knowledge of all such matters. What should I be good for without it?

SOCRATES: Rare friend! I think that I cannot do better than be your disciple. Then before the trial with Meletus comes on I shall challenge him, and say that I have always had a great interest in religious questions, and now, as he charges me with rash imaginations and innovations in religion, I have become your disciple. You, Meletus, as I shall say to him, acknowledge Euthyphro to be a great theologian, and sound in his opinions; and if you approve of him you ought to approve of me, and not have me into court; but if you disapprove, you should begin by indicting him who is my teacher, and who will be the ruin, not of the young, but of the old; that is to say, of myself whom he instructs, and of his old father whom he admonishes and chastises. And if Meletus refuses to listen to me, but will go on, and will not shift the indictment from me to you, I cannot do better than repeat this challenge in the court.

EUTHYPHRO: Yes, indeed, Socrates; and if he attempts to indict me I am mistaken if I do not find a flaw in him; the court shall have a great deal more to say to him than to me.

SOCRATES: And I, my dear friend, knowing this, am desirous of becoming your disciple. For I observe that no one appears to notice you—not even this Meletus; but his sharp eyes have found me out at once, and he has indicted me for impiety. And therefore, I adjure you to tell me the nature of piety and impiety, which you said that you knew so well, and of murder, and of other offences against the gods. What are they? Is not piety in every action always the same? and impiety, again—is it not always the opposite of piety, and also the same with itself, having, as impiety, one notion which includes whatever is impious?

EUTHYPHRO: To be sure, Socrates.

SOCRATES: And what is piety, and what is impiety?

EUTHYPHRO: Piety is doing as I am doing; that is to say, prosecuting any one who is guilty of murder, sacrilege, or of any similar crime—whether he be your father or mother, or whoever he may be—that makes no difference; and not to prosecute them is impiety. And please to consider, Socrates, what a notable proof I will give you of the truth of my words, a proof which I have already given to others:—of the principle, I mean, that the impious, whoever he may be, ought not to go unpunished. For do not men regard Zeus as the best and most righteous of the gods?—and yet they admit that he bound his father (Cronos) because he wickedly devoured his sons, and that he too had punished his own father (Uranus) for a similar reason, in a nameless manner. And yet when I proceed against my father, they are angry with me. So inconsistent are they in their way of talking when the gods are concerned, and when I am concerned.

SOCRATES: May not this be the reason, Euthyphro, why I am charged with impiety—that I cannot away with these stories about the gods? and therefore I suppose that people think me wrong. But, as you who are well informed about them approve of them, I cannot do better than assent to your superior wisdom. What else can I say, confessing as I do, that I know nothing about them? Tell me, for the love of Zeus, whether you really believe that they are true.

EUTHYPHRO: Yes, Socrates; and things more wonderful still, of which the world is in ignorance.

SOCRATES: And do you really believe that the gods fought with one another, and had dire quarrels, battles, and the like, as the poets say, and as you may see represented in the works of great artists? The temples are full of them; and notably the robe of Athene, which is carried up to the Acropolis at the great Panathenaea, is embroidered with them. Are all these tales of the gods true, Euthyphro?

EUTHYPHRO: Yes, Socrates; and, as I was saying, I can tell you, if you would like to hear them, many other things about the gods which would quite amaze you.

SOCRATES: I dare say; and you shall tell me them at some other time when I have leisure. But just at present I would rather hear from you a more precise answer, which you have not as yet given, my friend, to the question, What is 'piety'? When asked, you only replied, Doing as you do, charging your father with murder.

EUTHYPHRO: And what I said was true, Socrates.

SOCRATES: No doubt, Euthyphro; but you would admit that there are many other pious acts?

EUTHYPHRO: There are.

SOCRATES: Remember that I did not ask you to give me two or three examples of piety, but to explain the general idea which makes all pious things to be pious. Do you not recollect that there was one idea which made the impious impious, and the pious pious?

EUTHYPHRO: I remember.

SOCRATES: Tell me what is the nature of this idea, and then I shall have a standard to which I may look, and by which I may measure actions, whether yours or those of any one else, and then I shall be able to say that such and such an action is pious, such another impious.

EUTHYPHRO: I will tell you, if you like.

SOCRATES: I should very much like.

EUTHYPHRO: Piety, then, is that which is dear to the gods, and impiety is that which is not dear to them.

SOCRATES: Very good, Euthyphro; you have now given me the sort of answer which I wanted. But whether what you say is true or not I cannot as yet tell, although I make no doubt that you will prove the truth of your words.

EUTHYPHRO: Of course.

SOCRATES: Come, then, and let us examine what we are saying. That thing or person which is dear to the gods is pious, and that thing or person which is hateful to the gods is impious, these two being the extreme opposites of one another. Was not that said?

EUTHYPHRO: It was.

SOCRATES: And well said?

EUTHYPHRO: Yes, Socrates, I thought so; it was certainly said.

SOCRATES: And further, Euthyphro, the gods were admitted to have enmities and hatreds and differences?

EUTHYPHRO: Yes, that was also said.

SOCRATES: And what sort of difference creates enmity and anger? Suppose for example that you and I, my good friend, differ about a number; do differences of this sort make us enemies and set us at variance with one another? Do we not go at once to arithmetic, and put an end to them by a sum?

EUTHYPHRO: True.

SOCRATES: Or suppose that we differ about magnitudes, do we not quickly end the differences by measuring?

EUTHYPHRO: Very true.

SOCRATES: And we end a controversy about heavy and light by resorting to a weighing machine?

EUTHYPHRO: To be sure.

SOCRATES: But what differences are there which cannot be thus decided, and which therefore make us angry and set us at enmity with one another? I dare say the answer does not occur to you at the moment, and therefore I will suggest that these enmities arise when the matters of difference are the just and unjust, good and evil, honorable and dishonorable. Are not these the points about which men differ, and about which when we are unable satisfactorily to decide our differences, you and I and all of us quarrel, when we do quarrel? (Compare Alcib.)

EUTHYPHRO: Yes, Socrates, the nature of the differences about which we quarrel is such as you describe.

SOCRATES: And the quarrels of the gods, noble Euthyphro, when they occur, are of a like nature?

EUTHYPHRO: Certainly they are.

SOCRATES: They have differences of opinion, as you say, about good and evil, just and unjust, honorable and dishonorable: there would have been no quarrels among them, if there had been no such differences—would there now?

EUTHYPHRO: You are quite right.

SOCRATES: Does not every man love that which he deems noble and just and good, and hate the opposite of them?

EUTHYPHRO: Very true.

SOCRATES: But, as you say, people regard the same things, some as just and others as unjust,—about these they dispute; and so there arise wars and fightings among them.

EUTHYPHRO: Very true.

SOCRATES: Then the same things are hated by the gods and loved by the gods, and are both hateful and dear to them?

EUTHYPHRO: True.

SOCRATES: And upon this view the same things, Euthyphro, will be pious and also impious?

EUTHYPHRO: So I should suppose.

SOCRATES: Then, my friend, I remark with surprise that you have not answered the question which I asked. For I certainly did not ask you to tell me what action is both pious and impious: but now it would seem that what is loved by the gods is also hated by them. And therefore, Euthyphro, in thus chastising your father you may very likely be doing what is agreeable to Zeus but disagreeable to Cronos or Uranus, and what is acceptable to Hephaestus but unacceptable to Here, and there may be other gods who have similar differences of opinion.

EUTHYPHRO: But I believe, Socrates, that all the gods would be agreed as to the propriety of punishing a murderer: there would be no difference of opinion about that.

SOCRATES: Well, but speaking of men, Euthyphro, did you ever hear any one arguing that a murderer or any sort of evil-doer ought to be let off?

EUTHYPHRO: I should rather say that these are the questions which they are always arguing, especially in courts of law: they commit all sorts of crimes, and there is nothing which they will not do or say in their own defense.

SOCRATES: But do they admit their guilt, Euthyphro, and yet say that they ought not to be punished?

EUTHYPHRO: No; they do not.

SOCRATES: Then there are some things which they do not venture to say and do: for they do not venture to argue that the guilty are to be unpunished, but they deny their guilt, do they not?

EUTHYPHRO: Yes.

SOCRATES: Then they do not argue that the evil-doer should not be punished, but they argue about the fact of who the evil-doer is, and what he did and when?

EUTHYPHRO: True.

SOCRATES: And the gods are in the same case, if as you assert they quarrel about just and unjust, and some of them say while others deny that injustice is done among them. For surely neither God nor man will ever venture to say that the doer of injustice is not to be punished?

EUTHYPHRO: That is true, Socrates, in the main.

SOCRATES: But they join issue about the particulars—gods and men alike; and, if they dispute at all, they dispute about some act which is called in question, and which by some is affirmed to be just, by others to be unjust. Is not that true?

EUTHYPHRO: Quite true.

SOCRATES: Well then, my dear friend Euthyphro, do tell me, for my better instruction and information, what proof have you that in the opinion of all the gods a servant who is guilty of murder, and is put in chains by the master of the dead man, and dies because he is put in chains before he who bound him can learn from the interpreters of the gods what he ought to do with him, dies unjustly; and that on behalf of such an one a son ought to proceed against his father and accuse him of murder. How would you show that all the gods absolutely agree in approving of his act? Prove to me that they do, and I will applaud your wisdom as long as I live.

EUTHYPHRO: It will be a difficult task; but I could make the matter very clear indeed to you.

SOCRATES: I understand; you mean to say that I am not so quick of apprehension as the judges: for to them you will be sure to prove that the act is unjust, and hateful to the gods.

EUTHYPHRO: Yes indeed, Socrates; at least if they will listen to me.

SOCRATES: But they will be sure to listen if they find that you are a good speaker. There was a notion that came into my mind while you were speaking; I said to myself: 'Well, and what if Euthyphro does prove to me that all the gods regarded the death of the serf as unjust, how do I know anything more of the nature of piety and impiety? for granting that this action may be hateful to the gods, still piety and impiety are not adequately defined by these distinctions, for that which is hateful to the gods has been shown to be also pleasing and dear to them.' And therefore, Euthyphro, I do not ask you to prove this; I will suppose, if you like, that all the gods condemn and abominate such an action. But I will amend the definition so far as to say that what all the gods hate is impious, and what they love pious or holy; and what some of them love and others hate is both or neither. Shall this be our definition of piety and impiety?

EUTHYPHRO: Why not, Socrates?

SOCRATES: Why not! certainly, as far as I am concerned, Euthyphro, there is no reason why not. But whether this admission will greatly assist you in the task of instructing me as you promised, is a matter for you to consider.

EUTHYPHRO: Yes, I should say that what all the gods love is pious and holy, and the opposite which they all hate, impious.

SOCRATES: Ought we to enquire into the truth of this, Euthyphro, or simply to accept the mere statement on our own authority and that of others? What do you say?

EUTHYPHRO: We should enquire; and I believe that the statement will stand the test of enquiry.

SOCRATES: We shall know better, my good friend, in a little while. The point which I should first wish to understand is whether the pious or holy is beloved by the gods because it is holy, or holy because it is beloved of the gods.

EUTHYPHRO: I do not understand your meaning, Socrates.

SOCRATES: I will endeavor to explain: we, speak of carrying and we speak of being carried, of leading and being led, seeing and being seen. You know that in all such cases there is a difference, and you know also in what the difference lies?

EUTHYPHRO: I think that I understand.

SOCRATES: And is not that which is beloved distinct from that which loves?

EUTHYPHRO: Certainly.

SOCRATES: Well; and now tell me, is that which is carried in this state of carrying because it is carried, or for some other reason?

EUTHYPHRO: No; that is the reason.

SOCRATES: And the same is true of what is led and of what is seen?

EUTHYPHRO: True.

SOCRATES: And a thing is not seen because it is visible, but conversely, visible because it is seen; nor is a thing led because it is in the state of being led, or carried because it is in the state of being carried, but the converse of this. And now I think, Euthyphro, that my meaning will be intelligible; and my meaning is, that any state of action or passion implies previous action or passion. It does not become because it is becoming, but it is in a state of becoming because it becomes; neither does it suffer because it is in a state of suffering, but it is in a state of suffering because it suffers. Do you not agree?

EUTHYPHRO: Yes.

SOCRATES: Is not that which is loved in some state either of becoming or suffering?

EUTHYPHRO: Yes.

SOCRATES: And the same holds as in the previous instances; the state of being loved follows the act of being loved, and not the act the state.

EUTHYPHRO: Certainly.

SOCRATES: And what do you say of piety, Euthyphro: is not piety, according to your definition, loved by all the gods?

EUTHYPHRO: Yes.

SOCRATES: Because it is pious or holy, or for some other reason?

EUTHYPHRO: No, that is the reason.

SOCRATES: It is loved because it is holy, not holy because it is loved?

EUTHYPHRO: Yes.

SOCRATES: And that which is dear to the gods is loved by them, and is in a state to be loved of them because it is loved of them?

EUTHYPHRO: Certainly.

SOCRATES: Then that which is dear to the gods, Euthyphro, is not holy, nor is that which is holy loved of God, as you affirm; but they are two different things.

EUTHYPHRO: How do you mean, Socrates?

SOCRATES: I mean to say that the holy has been acknowledged by us to be loved of God because it is holy, not to be holy because it is loved.

EUTHYPHRO: Yes.

SOCRATES: But that which is dear to the gods is dear to them because it is loved by them, not loved by them because it is dear to them.

EUTHYPHRO: True.

SOCRATES: But, friend Euthyphro, if that which is holy is the same with that which is dear to God, and is loved because it is holy, then that which is dear to God would have been loved as being dear to God; but if that which is dear to God is dear to him because loved by him, then that which is holy would have been holy because loved by him. But now you see that the reverse is the case, and that they are quite different from one another. For one (theophiles) is of a kind to be loved cause it is loved, and the other (osion) is loved because it is of a kind to be loved. Thus you appear to me, Euthyphro, when I ask you what is the essence of holiness, to offer an attribute only, and not the essence—the attribute of being loved by all the gods. But you still refuse to explain to me the nature of holiness. And therefore, if you please, I will ask you not to hide your treasure, but to tell me once more what holiness or piety really is, whether dear to the gods or not (for that is a matter about which we will not quarrel); and what is impiety?

EUTHYPHRO: I really do not know, Socrates, how to express what I mean. For somehow or other our arguments, on whatever ground we rest them, seem to turn round and walk away from us.

SOCRATES: Your words, Euthyphro, are like the handiwork of my ancestor Daedalus; and if I were the sayer or propounder of them, you might say that my arguments walk away and will not remain fixed where they are placed because I am a descendant of his. But now, since these notions are your own, you must find some other gibe, for they certainly, as you yourself allow, show an inclination to be on the move.

EUTHYPHRO: Nay, Socrates, I shall still say that you are the Daedalus who sets arguments in motion; not I, certainly, but you make them move or go round, for they would never have stirred, as far as I am concerned.

SOCRATES: Then I must be a greater than Daedalus: for whereas he only made his own inventions to move, I move those of other people as well. And the beauty of it is, that I would rather not. For I would give the wisdom of Daedalus, and the wealth of Tantalus, to be able to detain them and keep them fixed. But enough of this. As I perceive that you are lazy, I will myself endeavor to show you how you might instruct me in the nature of piety; and I hope that you will not grudge your labor. Tell me, then—Is not that which is pious necessarily just?

EUTHYPHRO: Yes.

SOCRATES: And is, then, all which is just pious? or, is that which is pious all just, but that which is just, only in part and not all, pious?

EUTHYPHRO: I do not understand you, Socrates.

SOCRATES: And yet I know that you are as much wiser than I am, as you are younger. But, as I was saying, revered friend, the abundance of your wisdom makes you lazy. Please to exert yourself, for there is no real difficulty in understanding me. What I mean I may explain by an illustration of what I do not mean. The poet (Stasinus) sings—

'Of Zeus, the author and creator of all these things, You will not tell: for where there is fear there is also reverence.'

Now I disagree with this poet. Shall I tell you in what respect?

EUTHYPHRO: By all means.

SOCRATES: I should not say that where there is fear there is also reverence; for I am sure that many persons fear poverty and disease, and the like evils, but I do not perceive that they reverence the objects of their fear.

EUTHYPHRO: Very true.

SOCRATES: But where reverence is, there is fear; for he who has a feeling of reverence and shame about the commission of any action, fears and is afraid of an ill reputation.

EUTHYPHRO: No doubt.

SOCRATES: Then we are wrong in saying that where there is fear there is also reverence; and we should say, where there is reverence there is also fear. But there is not always reverence where there is fear; for fear is a more extended notion, and reverence is a part of fear, just as the odd is a part of number, and number is a more extended notion than the odd. I suppose that you follow me now?

EUTHYPHRO: Quite well.

SOCRATES: That was the sort of question which I meant to raise when I asked whether the just is always the pious, or the pious always the just; and whether there may not be justice where there is not piety; for justice is the more extended notion of which piety is only a part. Do you dissent?

EUTHYPHRO: No, I think that you are quite right.

SOCRATES: Then, if piety is a part of justice, I suppose that we should enquire what part? If you had pursued the enquiry in the previous cases; for instance, if you had asked me what is an even number, and what part of number the even is, I should have had no difficulty in replying, a number which represents a figure having two equal sides. Do you not agree?

EUTHYPHRO: Yes, I quite agree.

SOCRATES: In like manner, I want you to tell me what part of justice is piety or holiness, that I may be able to tell Meletus not to do me injustice, or indict me for impiety, as I am now adequately instructed by you in the nature of piety or holiness, and their opposites.

EUTHYPHRO: Piety or holiness, Socrates, appears to me to be that part of justice which attends to the gods, as there is the other part of justice which attends to men.

SOCRATES: That is good, Euthyphro; yet still there is a little point about which I should like to have further information, What is the meaning of 'attention'? For attention can hardly be used in the same sense when applied to the gods as when applied to other things. For instance, horses are said to require attention, and not every person is able to attend to them, but only a person skilled in horsemanship. Is it not so?

EUTHYPHRO: Certainly.

SOCRATES: I should suppose that the art of horsemanship is the art of attending to horses?

EUTHYPHRO: Yes.

SOCRATES: Nor is every one qualified to attend to dogs, but only the huntsman?

EUTHYPHRO: True.

SOCRATES: And I should also conceive that the art of the huntsman is the art of attending to dogs?

EUTHYPHRO: Yes.

SOCRATES: As the art of the oxherd is the art of attending to oxen?

EUTHYPHRO: Very true.

SOCRATES: In like manner holiness or piety is the art of attending to the gods?—that would be your meaning, Euthyphro?

EUTHYPHRO: Yes.

SOCRATES: And is not attention always designed for the good or benefit of that to which the attention is given? As in the case of horses, you may observe that when attended to by the horseman's art they are benefited and improved, are they not?

EUTHYPHRO: True.

SOCRATES: As the dogs are benefited by the huntsman's art, and the oxen by the art of the oxherd, and all other things are tended or attended for their good and not for their hurt?

EUTHYPHRO: Certainly, not for their hurt.

SOCRATES: But for their good?

EUTHYPHRO: Of course.

SOCRATES: And does piety or holiness, which has been defined to be the art of attending to the gods, benefit or improve them? Would you say that when you do a holy act you make any of the gods better?

EUTHYPHRO: No, no; that was certainly not what I meant.

SOCRATES: And I, Euthyphro, never supposed that you did. I asked you the question about the nature of the attention, because I thought that you did not.

EUTHYPHRO: You do me justice, Socrates; that is not the sort of attention which I mean.

SOCRATES: Good: but I must still ask what is this attention to the gods which is called piety?

EUTHYPHRO: It is such, Socrates, as servants show to their masters.

SOCRATES: I understand—a sort of ministration to the gods.

EUTHYPHRO: Exactly.

SOCRATES: Medicine is also a sort of ministration or service, having in view the attainment of some object—would you not say of health?

EUTHYPHRO: I should.

SOCRATES: Again, there is an art which ministers to the ship-builder with a view to the attainment of some result?

EUTHYPHRO: Yes, Socrates, with a view to the building of a ship.

SOCRATES: As there is an art which ministers to the house-builder with a view to the building of a house?

EUTHYPHRO: Yes.

SOCRATES: And now tell me, my good friend, about the art which ministers to the gods: what work does that help to accomplish? For you must surely know if, as you say, you are of all men living the one who is best instructed in religion.

EUTHYPHRO: And I speak the truth, Socrates.

SOCRATES: Tell me then, oh tell me—what is that fair work which the gods do by the help of our ministrations?

EUTHYPHRO: Many and fair, Socrates, are the works which they do.

SOCRATES: Why, my friend, and so are those of a general. But the chief of them is easily told. Would you not say that victory in war is the chief of them?

EUTHYPHRO: Certainly.

SOCRATES: Many and fair, too, are the works of the husbandman, if I am not mistaken; but his chief work is the production of food from the earth?

EUTHYPHRO: Exactly.

SOCRATES: And of the many and fair things done by the gods, which is the chief or principal one?

EUTHYPHRO: I have told you already, Socrates, that to learn all these things accurately will be very tiresome. Let me simply say that piety or holiness is learning how to please the gods in word and deed, by prayers and sacrifices. Such piety is the salvation of families and states, just as the impious, which is unpleasing to the gods, is their ruin and destruction.

SOCRATES: I think that you could have answered in much fewer words the chief question which I asked, Euthyphro, if you had chosen. But I see plainly that you are not disposed to instruct me—clearly not: else why, when we reached the point, did you turn aside? Had you only answered me I should have truly learned of you by this time the nature of piety. Now, as the asker of a question is necessarily dependent on the answerer, whither he leads I must follow; and can only ask again, what is the pious, and what is piety? Do you mean that they are a sort of science of praying and sacrificing?

EUTHYPHRO: Yes, I do.

SOCRATES: And sacrificing is giving to the gods, and prayer is asking of the gods?

EUTHYPHRO: Yes, Socrates.

SOCRATES: Upon this view, then, piety is a science of asking and giving?

EUTHYPHRO: You understand me capitally, Socrates.

SOCRATES: Yes, my friend; the reason is that I am a votary of your science, and give my mind to it, and therefore nothing which you say will be thrown away upon me. Please then to tell me, what is the nature of this service to the gods? Do you mean that we prefer requests and give gifts to them?

EUTHYPHRO: Yes, I do.

SOCRATES: Is not the right way of asking to ask of them what we want?

EUTHYPHRO: Certainly.

SOCRATES: And the right way of giving is to give to them in return what they want of us. There would be no meaning in an art which gives to any one that which he does not want.

EUTHYPHRO: Very true, Socrates.

SOCRATES: Then piety, Euthyphro, is an art which gods and men have of doing business with one another?

EUTHYPHRO: That is an expression which you may use, if you like.

SOCRATES: But I have no particular liking for anything but the truth. I wish, however, that you would tell me what benefit accrues to the gods from our gifts. There is no doubt about what they give to us; for there is no good thing which they do not give; but how we can give any good thing to them in return is far from being equally clear. If they give everything and we give nothing, that must be an affair of business in which we have very greatly the advantage of them.

EUTHYPHRO: And do you imagine, Socrates, that any benefit accrues to the gods from our gifts?

SOCRATES: But if not, Euthyphro, what is the meaning of gifts which are conferred by us upon the gods?

EUTHYPHRO: What else, but tributes of honor; and, as I was just now saying, what pleases them?

SOCRATES: Piety, then, is pleasing to the gods, but not beneficial or dear to them?

EUTHYPHRO: I should say that nothing could be dearer.

SOCRATES: Then once more the assertion is repeated that piety is dear to the gods?

EUTHYPHRO: Certainly.

SOCRATES: And when you say this, can you wonder at your words not standing firm, but walking away? Will you accuse me of being the Daedalus who makes them walk away, not perceiving that there is another and far greater artist than Daedalus who makes them go round in a circle, and he is yourself; for the argument, as you will perceive, comes round to the same point. Were we not saying that the holy or pious was not the same with that which is loved of the gods? Have you forgotten?

EUTHYPHRO: I quite remember.

SOCRATES: And are you not saying that what is loved of the gods is holy; and is not this the same as what is dear to them—do you see?

EUTHYPHRO: True.

SOCRATES: Then either we were wrong in our former assertion; or, if we were right then, we are wrong now.

EUTHYPHRO: One of the two must be true.

SOCRATES: Then we must begin again and ask, What is piety? That is an enquiry which I shall never be weary of pursuing as far as in me lies; and I entreat you not to scorn me, but to apply your mind to the utmost, and tell me the truth. For, if any man knows, you are he; and therefore I must detain you, like Proteus, until you tell. If you had not certainly known the nature of piety and impiety, I am confident that you would never, on behalf of a serf, have charged your aged father with murder. You would not have run such a risk of doing wrong in the sight of the gods, and you would have had too much respect for the opinions of men. I am sure, therefore, that you know the nature of piety and impiety. Speak out then, my dear Euthyphro, and do not hide your knowledge.

EUTHYPHRO: Another time, Socrates; for I am in a hurry, and must go now.

SOCRATES: Alas! my companion, and will you leave me in despair? I was hoping that you would instruct me in the nature of piety and impiety; and then I might have cleared myself of Meletus and his indictment. I would have told him that I had been enlightened by Euthyphro, and had given up rash innovations and speculations, in which I indulged only through ignorance, and that now I am about to lead a better life.

APOLOGY

By Plato
Translated by Benjamin Jowett

Introduction

In what relation the Apology of Plato stands to the real defense of Socrates, there are no means of determining. It certainly agrees in tone and character with the description of Xenophon, who says in the Memorabilia that Socrates might have been acquitted 'if in any moderate degree he would have conciliated the favor of the dicasts;' and who informs us in another passage, on the testimony of Hermogenes, the friend of Socrates, that he had no wish to live; and that the divine sign refused to allow him to prepare a defense, and also that Socrates himself declared this to be unnecessary, on the ground that all his life long he had been preparing against that hour. For the speech breathes throughout a spirit of defiance, (ut non supplex aut reus sed magister aut dominus videretur esse judicum', Cic. de Orat.); and the loose and desultory style is an imitation of the 'accustomed manner' in which Socrates spoke in 'the agora and among the tables of the money-changers.' The allusion in the Crito may, perhaps, be adduced as a further evidence of the literal accuracy of some parts. But in the main it must be regarded as the ideal of Socrates, according to Plato's conception of him, appearing in the greatest and most public scene of his life, and in the height of his triumph, when he is weakest, and yet his mastery over mankind is greatest, and his habitual irony acquires a new meaning and a sort of tragic pathos in the face of death. The facts of his life are summed up, and the features of his character are brought out as if by accident in the course of the defense. The conversational manner, the seeming want of arrangement, the ironical simplicity, are found to result in a perfect work of art, which is the portrait of Socrates.

Yet some of the topics may have been actually used by Socrates; and the recollection of his very words may have rung in the ears of his disciple. The Apology of Plato may be compared generally with those speeches of Thucydides in which he has embodied his conception of the lofty character and policy of the great Pericles, and which at the same time furnish a commentary on the situation of affairs from the point of view of the historian. So in the Apology there is an ideal rather than a literal truth; much is said which was not said, and is only Plato's view of the situation. Plato was not, like Xenophon, a chronicler of facts; he does not appear in any of his writings to have aimed at literal accuracy. He is not therefore to be supplemented from the Memorabilia and Symposium of Xenophon, who belongs to an entirely different class of writers. The Apology of Plato is not the report of what Socrates said, but an elaborate composition, quite as much so in fact as one of the Dialogues. And we may perhaps even indulge in the fancy that the actual defense of Socrates was as much greater than the Platonic defense as the master was greater than the disciple. But in any case, some of the words used by him must have been remembered, and some of the facts recorded must have actually occurred. It is significant that Plato is said to have been present at the defense (Apol.), as he is also said to have been absent at the last scene in the Phaedo. Is it fanciful to suppose that he meant to give the stamp of authenticity to the one and not to the other?—especially when we consider that these two passages are the only ones in which Plato makes mention of himself. The circumstance that Plato was to be one of his sureties for the payment of the fine which he proposed has the appearance of truth. More suspicious is the statement that Socrates received the first impulse to his favorite calling of cross-examining the world from the Oracle of Delphi; for he must already have been famous before Chaerephon went to consult the Oracle (Riddell), and the story is of a kind which is very likely to have been invented. On the whole we arrive at the conclusion that the Apology is true to the character of Socrates, but we cannot show that any single sentence in it was actually spoken by him. It breathes the spirit of Socrates, but has been cast anew in the mold of Plato.

There is not much in the other Dialogues which can be compared with the Apology. The same recollection of his master may have been present to the mind of Plato when depicting the sufferings of the Just in the Republic. The Crito may also be regarded as a sort of appendage to the Apology, in which Socrates, who has defied the judges, is nevertheless represented as scrupulously obedient to the laws. The idealization of the sufferer is carried still further in the Gorgias, in which the thesis is maintained, that 'to suffer is better than to do evil;' and the art of rhetoric is described as only useful for the purpose of self-accusation. The parallelisms which occur in the so-called Apology of Xenophon are not worth noticing, because the writing in which they are contained is manifestly spurious. The statements of the Memorabilia respecting the trial and death of Socrates agree generally with Plato; but they have lost the flavor of Socratic irony in the narrative of Xenophon.

The Apology or Platonic defense of Socrates is divided into three parts: 1st. The defense properly so called; 2nd. The shorter address in mitigation of the penalty; 3rd. The last words of prophetic rebuke and exhortation.

The first part commences with an apology for his colloquial style; he is, as he has always been, the enemy of rhetoric, and knows of no rhetoric but truth; he will not falsify his character by making a speech. Then he proceeds to divide his accusers into two classes; first, there is the nameless accuser—public opinion. All the world from their earliest years had heard that he was a corrupter of youth, and had seen him caricatured in the Clouds of Aristophanes. Secondly, there are the professed accusers, who are but the mouth-piece of the others. The accusations of both might be summed up in a formula. The first say, 'Socrates is an evil-doer and a curious person, searching into things under the earth and above the heaven; and making the worse appear the better cause, and teaching all this to others.' The second, 'Socrates is an evil-doer and corrupter of the youth, who does not receive the gods whom the state receives, but introduces other new divinities.' These last words appear to have been the actual indictment (compare Xen. Mem.); and the previous formula, which is a summary of public opinion, assumes the same legal style.

The answer begins by clearing up a confusion. In the representations of the Comic poets, and in the opinion of the multitude, he had been identified with the teachers of physical science and with the Sophists. But this was an error. For both of them he professes a respect in the open court, which contrasts with his manner of speaking about them in other places. (Compare for Anaxagoras, Phaedo, Laws; for the Sophists, Meno, Republic, Tim., Theaet., Soph., etc.) But at the same time he shows that he is not one of them. Of natural philosophy he knows nothing; not that he despises such pursuits, but the fact is that he is ignorant of them, and never says a word about them. Nor is he paid for giving instruction—that is another mistaken notion:—he has nothing to teach. But he commends Evenus for teaching virtue at such a 'moderate' rate as five minae. Something of the 'accustomed irony,' which may perhaps be expected to sleep in the ear of the multitude, is lurking here.

He then goes on to explain the reason why he is in such an evil name. That had arisen out of a peculiar mission which he had taken upon himself. The enthusiastic Chaerephon (probably in anticipation of the answer which he received) had gone to Delphi and asked the oracle if there was any man wiser than Socrates; and the answer was, that there was no man wiser. What could be the meaning of this—that he who knew nothing, and knew that he knew nothing, should be declared by the oracle to be the wisest of men? Reflecting upon the answer, he determined to refute it by finding 'a wiser;' and first he went to the politicians, and then to the poets, and then to the craftsmen, but always with the same result—he found that they knew nothing, or hardly anything more than himself; and that the little advantage which in some cases they possessed was more than counter-balanced by their conceit of knowledge. He knew nothing, and knew that he knew nothing: they knew little or nothing, and imagined that they knew all things. Thus he had passed his life as a sort of missionary in detecting the pretended wisdom of mankind; and this occupation had quite absorbed him and taken him away both from public and private affairs. Young men of the richer sort had made a pastime of the same pursuit, 'which was not unamusing.' And hence bitter enmities had arisen; the professors of knowledge had revenged themselves by calling him a villainous corrupter of youth, and by repeating the commonplaces about atheism and materialism and sophistry, which are the stock-accusations against all philosophers when there is nothing else to be said of them.

The second accusation he meets by interrogating Meletus, who is present and can be interrogated. 'If he is the corrupter, who is the improver of the citizens?' (Compare Meno.) 'All men everywhere.' But how absurd, how contrary to analogy is this! How inconceivable too, that he should make the citizens worse when he has to live with them. This surely cannot be intentional; and if unintentional, he ought to have been instructed by Meletus, and not accused in the court.

But there is another part of the indictment which says that he teaches men not to receive the gods whom the city receives, and has other new gods. 'Is that the way in which he is supposed to corrupt the youth?' 'Yes, it is.' 'Has he only new gods, or none at all?' 'None at all.' 'What, not even the sun and moon?' 'No; why, he says that the sun is a stone, and the moon earth.' That, replies Socrates, is the old confusion about Anaxagoras; the Athenian people are not so ignorant as to attribute to the influence of Socrates notions which have found their way into the drama, and may be learned at the theatre. Socrates undertakes to show that Meletus (rather unjustifiably) has been compounding a riddle in this part of the indictment: 'There are no gods, but Socrates believes in the existence of the sons of gods, which is absurd.'

Leaving Meletus, who has had enough words spent upon him, he returns to the original accusation. The question may be asked, Why will he persist in following a profession which leads him to death? Why?—because he must remain at his post where the god has placed him, as he remained at Potidaea, and Amphipolis, and Delium, where the generals placed him. Besides, he is not so overwise as to imagine that he knows whether death is a good or an evil; and he is certain that desertion of his duty is an evil. Anytus is quite right in saying that they should never have indicted him if they meant to let him go. For he will certainly obey God rather than man; and will continue to preach to all men of all ages the necessity of virtue and improvement; and if they refuse to listen to him he will still persevere and reprove them. This is his way of corrupting the youth, which he will not cease to follow in obedience to the god, even if a thousand deaths await him.

He is desirous that they should let him live—not for his own sake, but for theirs; because he is their heaven-sent friend (and they will never have such another), or, as he may be ludicrously described, he is the gadfly who stirs the generous steed into motion. Why then has he never taken part in public affairs? Because the familiar divine voice has hindered him; if he had been a public man, and had fought for the right, as he would certainly have fought against the many, he would not have lived, and could therefore have done no good. Twice in public matters he has risked his life for the sake of justice—once at the trial of the generals; and again in resistance to the tyrannical commands of the Thirty.

But, though not a public man, he has passed his days in instructing the citizens without fee or reward—this was his mission. Whether his disciples have turned out well or ill, he cannot justly be charged with the result, for he never promised to teach them anything. They might come if they liked, and they might stay away if they liked: and they did come, because they found an amusement in hearing the pretenders to wisdom detected. If they have been corrupted, their elder relatives (if not themselves) might surely come into court and witness against him, and there is an opportunity still for them to appear. But their fathers and brothers all appear in court (including 'this' Plato), to witness on his behalf; and if their relatives are corrupted, at least they are uncorrupted; 'and they are my witnesses. For they know that I am speaking the truth, and that Meletus is lying.'

This is about all that he has to say. He will not entreat the judges to spare his life; neither will he present a spectacle of weeping children, although he, too, is not made of 'rock or oak.' Some of the judges themselves may have complied with this practice on similar occasions, and he trusts that they will not be angry with him for not following their example. But he feels that such conduct brings discredit on the name of Athens: he feels too, that the judge has sworn not to give away justice; and he cannot be guilty of the impiety of asking the judge to break his oath, when he is himself being tried for impiety.

As he expected, and probably intended, he is convicted. And now the tone of the speech, instead of being more conciliatory, becomes more lofty and commanding. Anytus proposes death as the penalty: and what counter-proposition shall he make? He, the benefactor of the Athenian people, whose whole life has been spent in doing them good, should at least have the Olympic victor's reward of maintenance in the Prytaneum. Or why should he propose any counter-penalty when he does not know whether death, which Anytus proposes, is a good or an evil? And he is certain that imprisonment is an evil, exile is an evil. Loss of money might be an evil, but then he has none to give; perhaps he can make up a mina. Let that be the penalty, or, if his friends wish, thirty minae; for which they will be excellent securities.

(He is condemned to death.)

He is an old man already, and the Athenians will gain nothing but disgrace by depriving him of a few years of life. Perhaps he could have escaped, if he had chosen to throw down his arms and entreat for his life. But he does not at all repent of the manner of his defense; he would rather die in his own fashion than live in theirs. For the penalty of unrighteousness is swifter than death; that penalty has already overtaken his accusers as death will soon overtake him.

And now, as one who is about to die, he will prophesy to them. They have put him to death in order to escape the necessity of giving an account of their lives. But his death 'will be the seed' of many disciples who will convince them of their evil ways, and will come forth to reprove them in harsher terms, because they are younger and more inconsiderate.

He would like to say a few words, while there is time, to those who would have acquitted him. He wishes them to know that the divine sign never interrupted him in the course of his defense; the reason of which, as he conjectures, is that the death to which he is going is a good and not an evil. For either death is a long sleep, the best of sleeps, or a journey to another world in which the souls of the dead are gathered together, and in which there may be a hope of seeing the heroes of old—in which, too, there are just judges; and as all are immortal, there can be no fear of any one suffering death for his opinions.

Nothing evil can happen to the good man either in life or death, and his own death has been permitted by the gods, because it was better for him to depart; and therefore he forgives his judges because they have done him no harm, although they never meant to do him any good.

He has a last request to make to them—that they will trouble his sons as he has troubled them, if they appear to prefer riches to virtue, or to think themselves something when they are nothing.

* * * * *

'Few persons will be found to wish that Socrates should have defended himself otherwise,'—if, as we must add, his defense was that with which Plato has provided him. But leaving this question, which does not admit of a precise solution, we may go on to ask what was the impression which Plato in the Apology intended to give of the character and conduct of his master in the last great scene? Did he intend to represent him (1) as employing sophistries; (2) as designedly irritating the judges? Or are these sophistries to be regarded as belonging to the age in which he lived and to his personal character, and this apparent haughtiness as flowing from the natural elevation of his position?

For example, when he says that it is absurd to suppose that one man is the corrupter and all the rest of the world the improvers of the youth; or, when he argues that he never could have corrupted the men with whom he had to live; or, when he proves his belief in the gods because he believes in the sons of gods, is he serious or jesting? It may be observed that these sophisms all occur in his cross-examination of Meletus, who is easily foiled and mastered in the hands of the great dialectician. Perhaps he regarded these answers as good enough for his accuser, of whom he makes very light. Also there is a touch of irony in them, which takes them out of the category of sophistry. (Compare Euthyph.)

That the manner in which he defends himself about the lives of his disciples is not satisfactory, can hardly be denied. Fresh in the memory of the Athenians, and detestable as they deserved to be to the newly restored democracy, were the names of Alcibiades, Critias, Charmides. It is obviously not a sufficient answer that Socrates had never professed to teach them anything, and is therefore not justly chargeable with their crimes. Yet the defense, when taken out of this ironical form, is doubtless sound: that his teaching had nothing to do with their evil lives. Here, then, the sophistry is rather in form than in substance, though we might desire that to such a serious charge Socrates had given a more serious answer.

Truly characteristic of Socrates is another point in his answer, which may also be regarded as sophistical. He says that 'if he has corrupted the youth, he must have corrupted them involuntarily.' But if, as Socrates argues, all evil is involuntary, then all criminals ought to be admonished and not punished. In these words the Socratic doctrine of the involuntariness of evil is clearly intended to be conveyed. Here again, as in the former instance, the defense of Socrates is untrue practically, but may be true in some ideal or transcendental sense. The commonplace reply, that if he had been guilty of corrupting the youth their relations would surely have witnessed against him, with which he concludes this part of his defense, is more satisfactory.

Again, when Socrates argues that he must believe in the gods because he believes in the sons of gods, we must remember that this is a refutation not of the original indictment, which is consistent enough—'socrates does not receive the gods whom the city receives, and has other new divinities'—but of the interpretation put upon the words by Meletus, who has affirmed that he is a downright atheist. To this Socrates fairly answers, in accordance with the ideas of the time, that a downright atheist cannot believe in the sons of gods or in divine things. The notion that demons or lesser divinities are the sons of gods is not to be regarded as ironical or skeptical. He is arguing 'ad hominem' according to the notions of mythology current in his age. Yet he abstains from saying that he believed in the gods whom the State approved. He does not defend himself, as Xenophon has defended him, by appealing to his practice of religion. Probably he neither wholly believed, nor disbelieved, in the existence of the popular gods; he had no means of knowing about them. According to Plato (compare Phaedo; Symp.), as well as Xenophon (Memor.), he was punctual in the performance of the least religious duties; and he must have believed in his own oracular sign, of which he seemed to have an internal witness. But the existence of Apollo or Zeus, or the other gods whom the State approves, would have appeared to him both uncertain and unimportant in comparison of the duty of self-examination, and of those principles of truth and right which he deemed to be the foundation of religion. (Compare Phaedr.; Euthyph.; Republic.)

The second question, whether Plato meant to represent Socrates as braving or irritating his judges, must also be answered in the negative. His irony, his superiority, his audacity, 'regarding not the person of man,' necessarily flow out of the loftiness of his situation. He is not acting a part upon a great occasion, but he is what he has been all his life long, 'a king of men.' He would rather not appear insolent, if he could avoid it (ouch os authadizomenos touto lego). Neither is he desirous of hastening his own end, for life and death are simply indifferent to him. But such a defense as would be acceptable to his judges and might procure an acquittal, it is not in his nature to make. He will not say or do anything that might pervert the course of justice; he cannot have his tongue bound even 'in the throat of death.' With his accusers he will only fence and play, as he had fenced with other 'improvers of youth,' answering the Sophist according to his sophistry all his life long. He is serious when he is speaking of his own mission, which seems to distinguish him from all other reformers of mankind, and originates in an accident. The dedication of himself to the improvement of his fellow-citizens is not so remarkable as the ironical spirit in which he goes about doing good only in vindication of the credit of the oracle, and in the vain hope of finding a wiser man than himself. Yet this singular and almost accidental character of his mission agrees with the divine sign which, according to our notions, is equally accidental and irrational, and is nevertheless accepted by him as the guiding principle of his life. Socrates is nowhere represented to us as a freethinker or skeptic. There is no reason to doubt his sincerity when he speculates on the possibility of seeing and knowing the heroes of the Trojan war in another world. On the other hand, his hope of immortality is uncertain;—he also conceives of death as a long sleep (in this respect differing from the Phaedo), and at last falls back on resignation to the divine will, and the certainty that no evil can happen to the good man either in life or death. His absolute truthfulness seems to hinder him from asserting positively more than this; and he makes no attempt to veil his ignorance in mythology and figures of speech. The gentleness of the first part of the speech contrasts with the aggravated, almost threatening, tone of the conclusion. He characteristically remarks that he will not speak as a rhetorician, that is to say, he will not make a regular defense such as Lysias or one of the orators might have composed for him, or, according to some accounts, did compose for him. But he first procures himself a hearing by conciliatory words. He does not attack the Sophists; for they were open to the same charges as himself; they were equally ridiculed by the Comic poets, and almost equally hateful to Anytus and Meletus. Yet incidentally the antagonism between Socrates and the Sophists is allowed to appear. He is poor and they are rich; his profession that he teaches nothing is opposed to their readiness to teach all things; his talking in the marketplace to their private instructions; his tarry-at-home life to their wandering from city to city. The tone which he assumes towards them is one of real friendliness, but also of concealed irony. Towards Anaxagoras, who had disappointed him in his hopes of learning about mind and nature, he shows a less kindly feeling, which is also the feeling of Plato in other passages (Laws). But Anaxagoras had been dead thirty years, and was beyond the reach of persecution.

It has been remarked that the prophecy of a new generation of teachers who would rebuke and exhort the Athenian people in harsher and more violent terms was, as far as we know, never fulfillled. No inference can be drawn from this circumstance as to the probability of the words attributed to him having been actually uttered. They express the aspiration of the first martyr of philosophy, that he would leave behind him many followers, accompanied by the not unnatural feeling that they would be fiercer and more inconsiderate in their words when emancipated from his control.

The above remarks must be understood as applying with any degree of certainty to the Platonic Socrates only. For, although these or similar words may have been spoken by Socrates himself, we cannot exclude the possibility, that like so much else, e.g. the wisdom of Critias, the poem of Solon, the virtues of Charmides, they may have been due only to the imagination of Plato. The arguments of those who maintain that the Apology was composed during the process, resting on no evidence, do not require a serious refutation. Nor are the reasonings of Schleiermacher, who argues that the Platonic defense is an exact or nearly exact reproduction of the words of Socrates, partly because Plato would not have been guilty of the impiety of altering them, and also because many points of the defense might have been improved and strengthened, at all more conclusive. (See English Translation.) What effect the death of Socrates produced on the mind of Plato, we cannot certainly determine; nor can we say how he would or must have written under the circumstances. We observe that the enmity of Aristophanes to Socrates does not prevent Plato from introducing them together in the Symposium engaged in friendly intercourse. Nor is there any trace in the Dialogues of an attempt to make Anytus or Meletus personally odious in the eyes of the Athenian public.

Apology

How you, O Athenians, have been affected by my accusers, I cannot tell; but I know that they almost made me forget who I was—so persuasively did they speak; and yet they have hardly uttered a word of truth. But of the many falsehoods told by them, there was one which quite amazed me;—I mean when they said that you should be upon your guard and not allow yourselves to be deceived by the force of my eloquence. To say this, when they were certain to be detected as soon as I opened my lips and proved myself to be anything but a great speaker, did indeed appear to me most shameless—unless by the force of eloquence they mean the force of truth; for if such is their meaning, I admit that

I am eloquent. But in how different a way from theirs! Well, as I was saying, they have scarcely spoken the truth at all; but from me you shall hear the whole truth: not, however, delivered after their manner in a set oration duly ornamented with words and phrases. No, by heaven! but I shall use the words and arguments which occur to me at the moment; for I am confident in the justice of my cause (Or, I am certain that I am right in taking this course.): at my time of life I ought not to be appearing before you, O men of Athens, in the character of a juvenile orator—let no one expect it of me. And I must beg of you to grant me a favor:—If I defend myself in my accustomed manner, and you hear me using the words which I have been in the habit of using in the agora, at the tables of the money-changers, or anywhere else, I would ask you not to be surprised, and not to interrupt me on this account. For I am more than seventy years of age, and appearing now for the first time in a court of law, I am quite a stranger to the language of the place; and therefore I would have you regard me as if I were really a stranger, whom you would excuse if he spoke in his native tongue, and after the fashion of his country:—Am I making an unfair request of you? Never mind the manner, which may or may not be good; but think only of the truth of my words, and give heed to that: let the speaker speak truly and the judge decide justly.

And first, I have to reply to the older charges and to my first accusers, and then I will go on to the later ones. For of old I have had many accusers, who have accused me falsely to you during many years; and I am more afraid of them than of Anytus and his associates, who are dangerous, too, in their own way. But far more dangerous are the others, who began when you were children, and took possession of your minds with their falsehoods, telling of one Socrates, a wise man, who speculated about the heaven above, and searched into the earth beneath, and made the worse appear the better cause. The disseminators of this tale are the accusers whom I dread; for their hearers are apt to fancy that such enquirers do not believe in the existence of the gods. And they are many, and their charges against me are of ancient date, and they were made by them in the days when you were more impressible than you are now—in childhood, or it may have been in youth—and the cause when heard went by default, for there was none to answer. And hardest of all, I do not know and cannot tell the names of my accusers; unless in the chance case of a Comic poet. All who from envy and malice have persuaded you—some of them having first convinced themselves—all this class of men are most difficult to deal with; for I cannot have them up here, and cross-examine them, and therefore I must simply fight with shadows in my own defense, and argue when there is no one who answers. I will ask you then to assume with me, as I was saying, that my opponents are of two kinds; one recent, the other ancient: and I hope that you will see the propriety of my answering the latter first, for these accusations you heard long before the others, and much oftener.

Well, then, I must make my defense, and endeavor to clear away in a short time, a slander which has lasted a long time. May I succeed, if to succeed be for my good and yours, or likely to avail me in my cause! The task is not an easy one; I quite understand the nature of it. And so leaving the event with God, in obedience to the law I will now make my defense.

I will begin at the beginning, and ask what is the accusation which has given rise to the slander of me, and in fact has encouraged Meletus to proof this charge against me. Well, what do the slanderers say? They shall be my prosecutors, and I will sum up their words in an affidavit: 'socrates is an evil-doer, and a curious person, who searches into things under the earth and in heaven, and he makes the worse appear the better cause; and he teaches the aforesaid doctrines to others.' Such is the nature of the accusation: it is just what you have yourselves seen in the comedy of Aristophanes (Aristoph., Clouds.), who has introduced a man whom he calls Socrates, going about and saying that he walks in air, and talking a deal of nonsense concerning matters of which I do not pretend to know either much or little—not that I mean to speak disparagingly of any one who is a student of natural philosophy. I should be very sorry if Meletus could bring so grave a charge against me. But the simple truth is, O Athenians, that I have nothing to do with physical speculations. Very many of those here present are witnesses to the truth of this, and to them I appeal. Speak then, you who have heard me, and tell your neighbors whether any of you have ever known me hold forth in few words or in many upon such matters . . . You hear their answer. And from what they say of this part of the charge you will be able to judge of the truth of the rest.

As little foundation is there for the report that I am a teacher, and take money; this accusation has no more truth in it than the other. Although, if a man were really able to instruct mankind, to receive money for giving instruction would, in my opinion, be an honor to him. There is Gorgias of Leontium, and Prodicus of Ceos, and Hippias of Elis, who go the round of the cities, and are able to persuade the young men to leave their own citizens by whom they might be taught for nothing, and come to them whom they not only pay, but are thankful if they may be allowed to pay them. There is at this time a Parian philosopher residing in Athens, of whom I have heard; and I came to hear of him in this way:—I came across a man who has spent a world of money on the Sophists, Callias, the son of Hipponicus, and knowing that he had sons, I asked him: 'Callias,' I said, 'if your two sons were foals or calves, there would be no difficulty in finding some one to put over them; we should hire a trainer of horses, or a farmer probably, who would improve and perfect them in their own proper virtue and excellence; but as they are human beings, whom are you thinking of placing over them? Is there any one who understands human and political virtue? You must have thought about the matter, for you have sons; is there any one?' 'There is,' he said. 'Who is he?' said I; 'and of what country? and what does he charge?' 'Evenus the Parian,' he replied; 'he is the man, and his charge is five minae.' Happy is Evenus, I said to myself, if he really has this wisdom, and teaches at such a moderate charge. Had I the same, I should have been very proud and conceited; but the truth is that I have no knowledge of the kind.

I dare say, Athenians, that some one among you will reply, 'Yes, Socrates, but what is the origin of these accusations which are brought against you; there must have been something strange which you have been doing? All these rumors and this talk about you would never have arisen if you had been like other men: tell us, then, what is the cause of them, for we should be sorry to judge hastily of you.' Now I regard this as a fair challenge, and I will endeavor to explain to you the reason why I am called wise and have such an evil fame. Please to attend then. And although some of you may think that I am joking, I declare that I will tell you the entire truth. Men of Athens, this reputation of mine has come of a certain sort of wisdom which I possess. If you ask me what kind of wisdom, I reply, wisdom such as may perhaps be attained by man, for to that extent I am inclined to believe that I am wise; whereas the persons of whom I was speaking have a superhuman wisdom which I may fail to describe, because I have it not myself; and he who says that I have, speaks falsely, and is taking away my character. And here, O men of Athens, I must beg you not to interrupt me, even if I seem to say something extravagant. For the word which I will speak is not mine. I will refer you to a witness who is worthy of credit; that witness shall be the God of Delphi—he will tell you about my wisdom, if I have any, and of what sort it is. You must have known Chaerephon; he was early a friend of mine, and also a friend of yours, for he shared in the recent exile of the people, and returned with you. Well, Chaerephon, as you know, was very impetuous in all his doings, and he went to Delphi and boldly asked the oracle to tell him whether—as I was saying, I must beg you not to interrupt—he asked the oracle to tell him whether anyone was wiser than I was, and the Pythian prophetess answered, that there was no man wiser. Chaerephon is dead himself; but his brother, who is in court, will confirm the truth of what I am saying.

Why do I mention this? Because I am going to explain to you why I have such an evil name. When I heard the answer, I said to myself, What can the god mean? and what is the interpretation of his riddle? for I know that I have no wisdom, small or great. What then can he mean when he says that I am the wisest of men? And yet he is a god, and cannot lie; that would be against his nature. After long consideration, I thought of a method of trying the question. I reflected that if I could only find a man wiser than myself, then I might go to the god with a refutation in my hand. I should say to him, 'Here is a man who is wiser than I am; but you said that I was the wisest.' Accordingly I went to one who had the reputation of wisdom, and observed him—his name I need not mention; he was a politician whom I selected for examination—and the result was as follows: When I began to talk with him, I could not help thinking that he was not really wise, although he was thought wise by many, and still wiser by himself; and thereupon I tried to explain to him that he thought himself wise, but was not really wise; and the consequence was that he hated me, and his enmity was shared by several who were present and heard me. So I left him, saying to myself, as I went away: Well, although I do not suppose that either of us knows anything really beautiful and good, I am better off than he is,—for he knows nothing, and thinks that he knows; I neither know nor think that I know. In this latter particular, then, I seem to have slightly the advantage of him. Then I went to another who had still higher pretensions to wisdom, and my conclusion was exactly the same. Whereupon I made another enemy of him, and of many others besides him.

Then I went to one man after another, being not unconscious of the enmity which I provoked, and I lamented and feared this: but necessity was laid upon me,—the word of God, I thought, ought to be considered first. And I said to myself, Go I must to all who appear to know, and find out the meaning of the oracle. And I swear to you, Athenians, by the dog I swear!—for I must tell you the truth—the result of my mission was just this: I found that the men most in repute were all but the most foolish; and that others less esteemed were really wiser and better. I will tell you the tale of my wanderings and of the 'Herculean' labors, as I may call them, which I endured only to find at last the oracle irrefutable. After the politicians, I went to the poets; tragic, dithyrambic, and all sorts. And there, I said to myself, you will be instantly detected; now you will find out that you are more ignorant than they are. Accordingly, I took them some of the most elaborate passages in their own writings, and asked what was the meaning of them—thinking that they would teach me something. Will you believe me? I am almost ashamed to confess the truth, but I must say that there is hardly a person present who would not have talked better about their poetry than they did themselves. Then I knew that not by wisdom do poets write poetry, but by a sort of genius and inspiration; they are like diviners or soothsayers who also say many fine things, but do not understand the meaning of them. The poets appeared to me to be much in the same case; and I further observed that upon the strength of their poetry they believed themselves to be the wisest of men in other things in which they were not wise. So I departed, conceiving myself to be superior to them for the same reason that I was superior to the politicians.

At last I went to the artisans. I was conscious that I knew nothing at all, as I may say, and I was sure that they knew many fine things; and here I was not mistaken, for they did know many things of which I was ignorant, and in this they certainly were wiser than I was. But I observed that even the good artisans fell into the same error as the poets;—because they were good workmen they thought that they also knew all sorts of high matters, and this defect in them overshadowed their wisdom; and therefore I asked myself on behalf of the oracle, whether I would like to be as I was, neither having their knowledge nor their ignorance, or like them in both; and I made answer to myself and to the oracle that I was better off as I was.

This inquisition has led to my having many enemies of the worst and most dangerous kind, and has given occasion also to many calumnies. And I am called wise, for my hearers always imagine that I myself possess the wisdom which I find wanting in others: but the truth is, O men of Athens, that God only is wise; and by his answer he intends to show that the wisdom of men is worth little or nothing; he is not speaking of Socrates, he is only using my name by way of illustration, as if he said, He, O men, is the wisest, who, like Socrates, knows that his wisdom is in truth worth nothing. And so I go about the world, obedient to the god, and search and make enquiry into the wisdom of any one, whether citizen or stranger, who appears to be wise; and if he is not wise, then in vindication of the oracle I show him that he is not wise; and my occupation quite absorbs me, and I have no time to give either to any public matter of interest or to any concern of my own, but I am in utter poverty by reason of my devotion to the god.

There is another thing:—young men of the richer classes, who have not much to do, come about me of their own accord; they like to hear the pretenders examined, and they often imitate me, and proceed to examine others; there are plenty of persons, as they quickly discover, who think that they know something, but really know little or nothing; and then those who are examined by them instead of being angry with themselves are angry with me: This confounded Socrates, they say; this villainous misleader of youth!—and then if somebody asks them, Why, what evil does he practice or teach? they do not know, and cannot tell; but in order that they may not appear to be at a loss, they repeat the ready-made charges which are used against all philosophers about teaching things up in the clouds and under the earth, and having no gods, and making the worse appear the better cause; for they do not like to confess that their pretense of knowledge has been detected—which is the truth; and as they are numerous and ambitious and energetic, and are drawn up in battle array and have persuasive tongues, they have filled your ears with their loud and inveterate calumnies. And this is the reason why my three accusers, Meletus and Anytus and Lycon, have set upon me; Meletus, who has a quarrel with me on behalf of the poets; Anytus, on behalf of the craftsmen and politicians; Lycon, on behalf of the rhetoricians: and as I said at the beginning, I cannot expect to get rid of such a mass of calumny all in a moment. And this, O men of Athens, is the truth and the whole truth; I have concealed nothing, I have dissembled nothing. And yet, I know that my plainness of speech makes them hate me, and what is their hatred but a proof that I am speaking the truth?—Hence has arisen the prejudice against me; and this is the reason of it, as you will find out either in this or in any future enquiry.

I have said enough in my defense against the first class of my accusers; I turn to the second class. They are headed by Meletus, that good man and true lover of his country, as he calls himself. Against these, too, I must try to make a defense:—Let their affidavit be read: it contains something of this kind: It says that Socrates is a doer of evil, who corrupts the youth; and who does not believe in the gods of the state, but has other new divinities of his own. Such is the charge; and now let us examine the particular counts. He says that I am a doer of evil, and corrupt the youth; but I say, O men of Athens, that Meletus is a doer of evil, in that he pretends to be in earnest when he is only in jest, and is so eager to bring men to trial from a pretended zeal and interest about matters in which he really never had the smallest interest. And the truth of this I will endeavor to prove to you.

Come hither, Meletus, and let me ask a question of you. You think a great deal about the improvement of youth?

Yes, I do.

Tell the judges, then, who is their improver; for you must know, as you have taken the pains to discover their corrupter, and are citing and accusing me before them. Speak, then, and tell the judges who their improver is.—Observe, Meletus, that you are silent, and have nothing to say. But is not this rather disgraceful, and a very considerable proof of what I was saying, that you have no interest in the matter? Speak up, friend, and tell us who their improver is.

The laws.

But that, my good sir, is not my meaning. I want to know who the person is, who, in the first place, knows the laws.

The judges, Socrates, who are present in court.

What, do you mean to say, Meletus, that they are able to instruct and improve youth?

Certainly they are.

What, all of them, or some only and not others?

All of them.

By the goddess Here, that is good news! There are plenty of improvers, then. And what do you say of the audience,—do they improve them?

Yes, they do.

And the senators?

Yes, the senators improve them.

But perhaps the members of the assembly corrupt them?—or do they too improve them?

They improve them.

Then every Athenian improves and elevates them; all with the exception of myself; and I alone am their corrupter? Is that what you affirm?

That is what I stoutly affirm.

I am very unfortunate if you are right. But suppose I ask you a question: How about horses? Does one man do them harm and all the world good? Is not the exact opposite the truth? One man is able to do them good, or at least not many;—the trainer of horses, that is to say, does them good, and others who have to do with them rather injure them? Is not that true, Meletus, of horses, or of any other animals? Most assuredly it is; whether you and Anytus say yes or no. Happy indeed would be the condition of youth if they had one corrupter only, and all the rest of the world were their improvers. But you, Meletus, have sufficiently shown that you never had a thought about the young: your carelessness is seen in your not caring about the very things which you bring against me.

And now, Meletus, I will ask you another question—by Zeus I will:

Which is better, to live among bad citizens, or among good ones? Answer, friend, I say; the question is one which may be easily answered. Do not the good do their neighbors good, and the bad do them evil?

Certainly.

And is there anyone who would rather be injured than benefited by those who live with him? Answer, my good friend, the law requires you to answer—does any one like to be injured?

Certainly not.

And when you accuse me of corrupting and deteriorating the youth, do you allege that I corrupt them intentionally or unintentionally?

Intentionally, I say.

But you have just admitted that the good do their neighbors good, and the evil do them evil. Now, is that a truth which your superior wisdom has recognized thus early in life, and am I, at my age, in such darkness and ignorance as not to know that if a man with whom I have to live is corrupted by me, I am very likely to be harmed by him; and yet I corrupt him, and intentionally, too—so you say, although neither I nor any other human being is ever likely to be convinced by you. But either I do not corrupt them, or I corrupt them unintentionally; and on either view of the case you lie. If my offence is unintentional, the law has no cognizance of unintentional offences: you ought to have taken me privately, and warned and admonished me; for if I had been better advised, I should have left off doing what I only did unintentionally—no doubt I should; but you would have nothing to say to me and refused to teach me. And now you bring me up in this court, which is a place not of instruction, but of punishment.

It will be very clear to you, Athenians, as I was saying, that Meletus has no care at all, great or small, about the matter. But still I should like to know, Meletus, in what I am affirmed to corrupt the young. I suppose you mean, as I infer from your indictment, that I teach them not to acknowledge the gods which the state acknowledges, but some other new divinities or spiritual agencies in their stead. These are the lessons by which I corrupt the youth, as you say.

Yes, that I say emphatically.

Then, by the gods, Meletus, of whom we are speaking, tell me and the court, in somewhat plainer terms, what you mean! for I do not as yet understand whether you affirm that I teach other men to acknowledge some gods, and therefore that I do believe in gods, and am not an entire atheist—this you do not lay to my charge,—but only you say that they are not the same gods which the city recognizes—the charge is that they are different gods. Or, do you mean that I am an atheist simply, and a teacher of atheism?

I mean the latter—that you are a complete atheist.

What an extraordinary statement! Why do you think so, Meletus? Do you mean that I do not believe in the godhead of the sun or moon, like other men?

I assure you, judges, that he does not: for he says that the sun is stone, and the moon earth.

Friend Meletus, you think that you are accusing Anaxagoras: and you have but a bad opinion of the judges, if you fancy them illiterate to such a degree as not to know that these doctrines are found in the books of Anaxagoras the Clazomenian, which are full of them. And so, forsooth, the youth are said to be taught them by Socrates, when there are not infrequently exhibitions of them at the theatre (Probably in allusion to Aristophanes who caricatured, and to Euripides who borrowed the notions of Anaxagoras, as well as to other dramatic poets.) (price of admission one drachma at the most); and they might pay their money, and laugh at Socrates if he pretends to father these extraordinary views. And so, Meletus, you really think that I do not believe in any god?

I swear by Zeus that you believe absolutely in none at all.

Nobody will believe you, Meletus, and I am pretty sure that you do not believe yourself. I cannot help thinking, men of Athens, that Meletus is reckless and impudent, and that he has written this indictment in a spirit of mere wantonness and youthful bravado. Has he not compounded a riddle, thinking to try me? He said to himself:—I shall see whether the wise Socrates will discover my facetious contradiction, or whether I shall be able to deceive him and the rest of them. For he certainly does appear to me to contradict himself in the indictment as much as if he said that Socrates is guilty of not believing in the gods, and yet of believing in them—but this is not like a person who is in earnest.

I should like you, O men of Athens, to join me in examining what I conceive to be his inconsistency; and do you, Meletus, answer. And I must remind the audience of my request that they would not make a disturbance if I speak in my accustomed manner:

Did ever man, Meletus, believe in the existence of human things, and not of human beings? . . . I wish, men of Athens, that he would answer, and not be always trying to get up an interruption. Did ever any man believe in horsemanship, and not in horses? or in flute-playing, and not in flute-players? No, my friend; I will answer to you and to the court, as you refuse to answer for yourself. There is no man who ever did. But now please to answer the next question: Can a man believe in spiritual and divine agencies, and not in spirits or demigods?

He cannot.

How lucky I am to have extracted that answer, by the assistance of the court! But then you swear in the indictment that I teach and believe in divine or spiritual agencies (new or old, no matter for that); at any rate, I believe in spiritual agencies,—so you say and swear in the affidavit; and yet if I believe in divine beings, how can I help believing in spirits or demigods;—must I not? To be sure I must; and therefore I may assume that your silence gives consent. Now what are spirits or demigods? Are they not either gods or the sons of gods?

Certainly they are.

But this is what I call the facetious riddle invented by you: the demigods or spirits are gods, and you say first that I do not believe in gods, and then again that I do believe in gods; that is, if I believe in demigods. For if the demigods are the illegitimate sons of gods, whether by the nymphs or by any other mothers, of whom they are said to be the sons—what human being will ever believe that there are no gods if they are the sons of gods? You might as well affirm the existence of mules, and deny that of horses and asses. Such nonsense, Meletus, could only have been intended by you to make trial of me. You have put this into the indictment because you had nothing real of which to accuse me. But no one who has a particle of understanding will ever be convinced by you that the same men can believe in divine and superhuman things, and yet not believe that there are gods and demigods and heroes.

I have said enough in answer to the charge of Meletus: any elaborate defense is unnecessary, but I know only too well how many are the enmities which I have incurred, and this is what will be my destruction if I am destroyed;—not Meletus, nor yet Anytus, but the envy and detraction of the world, which has been the death of many good men, and will probably be the death of many more; there is no danger of my being the last of them.

Some one will say: And are you not ashamed, Socrates, of a course of life which is likely to bring you to an untimely end? To him I may fairly answer: There you are mistaken: a man who is good for anything ought not to calculate the chance of living or dying; he ought only to consider whether in doing anything he is doing right or wrong—acting the part of a good man or of a bad. Whereas, upon your view, the heroes who fell at Troy were not good for much, and the son of Thetis above all, who altogether despised danger in comparison with disgrace; and when he was so eager to slay Hector, his goddess mother said to him, that if he avenged his companion Patroclus, and slew Hector, he would die himself—'Fate,' she said, in these or the like words, 'waits for you next after Hector;' he, receiving this warning, utterly despised danger and death, and instead of fearing them, feared rather to live in dishonor, and not to avenge his friend. 'Let me die forthwith,' he replies, 'and be avenged of my enemy, rather than abide here by the beaked ships, a laughing-stock and a burden of the earth.' Had Achilles any thought of death and danger? For wherever a man's place is, whether the place which he has chosen or that in which he has been placed by a commander, there he ought to remain in the hour of danger; he should not think of death or of anything but of disgrace. And this, O men of Athens, is a true saying.

Strange, indeed, would be my conduct, O men of Athens, if I who, when I was ordered by the generals whom you chose to command me at Potidaea and Amphipolis and Delium, remained where they placed me, like any other man, facing death—if now, when, as I conceive and imagine, God orders me to fulfill the philosopher's mission of searching into myself and other men, I were to desert my post through fear of death, or any other fear; that would indeed be strange, and I might justly be arraigned in court for denying the existence of the gods, if I disobeyed the oracle because I was afraid of death, fancying that I was wise when I was not wise. For the fear of death is indeed the pretense of wisdom, and not real wisdom, being a pretense of knowing the unknown; and no one knows whether death, which men in their fear apprehend to be the greatest evil, may not be the greatest good. Is not this ignorance of a disgraceful sort, the ignorance which is the conceit that a man knows what he does not know? And in this respect only I believe myself to differ from men in general, and may perhaps claim to be wiser than they are:—that whereas I know but little of the world below, I do not suppose that I know: but I do know that injustice and disobedience to a better, whether God or man, is evil and dishonorable, and I will never fear or avoid a possible good rather than a certain evil. And therefore if you let me go now, and are not convinced by Anytus, who said that since I had been prosecuted I must be put to death; (or if not that I ought never to have been prosecuted at all); and that if I escape now, your sons will all be utterly ruined by listening to my words—if you say to me, Socrates, this time we will not mind Anytus, and you shall be let off, but upon one condition, that you are not to enquire and speculate in this way any more, and that if you are caught doing so again you shall die;—if this was the condition on which you let me go, I should reply: Men of Athens, I honor and love you; but I shall obey God rather than you, and while I have life and strength I shall never cease from the practice and teaching of philosophy, exhorting any one whom I meet and saying to him after my manner: You, my friend,—a citizen of the great and mighty and wise city of Athens,—are you not ashamed of heaping up the greatest amount of money and honor and reputation, and caring so little about wisdom and truth and the greatest improvement of the soul, which you never regard or heed at all? And if the person with whom I am arguing, says: Yes, but I do care; then I do not leave him or let him go at once; but I proceed to interrogate and examine and cross-examine him, and if I think that he has no virtue in him, but only says that he has, I reproach him with undervaluing the greater, and overvaluing the less. And I shall repeat the same words to every one whom I meet, young and old, citizen and alien, but especially to the citizens, inasmuch as they are my brethren. For know that this is the command of God; and I believe that no greater good has ever happened in the state than my service to the God. For I do nothing but go about persuading you all, old and young alike, not to take thought for your persons or your properties, but first and chiefly to care about the greatest improvement of the soul. I tell you that virtue is not given by money, but that from virtue comes money and every other good of man, public as well as private. This is my teaching, and if this is the doctrine which corrupts the youth, I am a mischievous person. But if any one says that this is not my teaching, he is speaking an untruth. Wherefore, O men of Athens, I say to you, do as Anytus bids or not as Anytus bids, and either acquit me or not; but whichever you do, understand that I shall never alter my ways, not even if I have to die many times.

Men of Athens, do not interrupt, but hear me; there was an understanding between us that you should hear me to the end: I have something more to say, at which you may be inclined to cry out; but I believe that to hear me will be good for you, and therefore I beg that you will not cry out. I would have you know, that if you kill such an one as I am, you will injure yourselves more than you will injure me. Nothing will injure me, not Meletus nor yet Anytus—they cannot, for a bad man is not permitted to injure a better than himself. I do not deny that Anytus may, perhaps, kill him, or drive him into exile, or deprive him of civil rights; and he may imagine, and others may imagine, that he is inflicting a great injury upon him: but there I do not agree. For the evil of doing as he is doing—the evil of unjustly taking away the life of another—is greater far.

And now, Athenians, I am not going to argue for my own sake, as you may think, but for yours, that you may not sin against the God by condemning me, who am his gift to you. For if you kill me you will not easily find a successor to me, who, if I may use such a ludicrous figure of speech, am a sort of gadfly, given to the state by God; and the state is a great and noble steed who is tardy in his motions owing to his very size, and requires to be stirred into life. I am that gadfly which God has attached to the state, and all day long and in all places am always fastening upon you, arousing and persuading and reproaching you. You will not easily find another like me, and therefore I would advise you to spare me. I dare say that you may feel out of temper (like a person who is suddenly awakened from sleep), and you think that you might easily strike me dead as Anytus advises, and then you would sleep on for the remainder of your lives, unless God in his care of you sent you another gadfly. When I say that I am given to you by God, the proof of my mission is this:—if I had been like other men, I should not have neglected all my own concerns or patiently seen the neglect of them during all these years, and have been doing yours, coming to you individually like a father or elder brother, exhorting you to regard virtue; such conduct, I say, would be unlike human nature. If I had gained anything, or if my exhortations had been paid, there would have been some sense in my doing so; but now, as you will perceive, not even the impudence of my accusers dares to say that I have ever exacted or sought pay of any one; of that they have no witness. And I have a sufficient witness to the truth of what I say—my poverty.

Some one may wonder why I go about in private giving advice and busying myself with the concerns of others, but do not venture to come forward in public and advise the state. I will tell you why. You have heard me speak at sundry times and in divers places of an oracle or sign which comes to me, and is the divinity which Meletus ridicules in the indictment. This sign, which is a kind of voice, first began to come to me when I was a child; it always forbids but never commands me to do anything which I am going to do. This is what deters me from being a politician. And rightly, as I think. For I am certain, O men of Athens, that if I had engaged in politics, I should have perished long ago, and done no good either to you or to myself. And do not be offended at my telling you the truth: for the truth is, that no man who goes to war with you or any other multitude, honestly striving against the many lawless and unrighteous deeds which are done in a state, will save his life; he who will fight for the right, if he would live even for a brief space, must have a private station and not a public one.

I can give you convincing evidence of what I say, not words only, but what you value far more—actions. Let me relate to you a passage of my own life which will prove to you that I should never have yielded to injustice from any fear of death, and that 'as I should have refused to yield' I must have died at once. I will tell you a tale of the courts, not very interesting perhaps, but nevertheless true. The only office of state which I ever held, O men of Athens, was that of senator: the tribe Antiochis, which is my tribe, had the presidency at the trial of the generals who had not taken up the bodies of the slain after the battle of Arginusae; and you proposed to try them in a body, contrary to law, as you all thought afterwards; but at the time I was the only one of the Prytanes who was opposed to the illegality, and I gave my vote against you; and when the orators threatened to impeach and arrest me, and you called and shouted, I made up my mind that I would run the risk, having law and justice with me, rather than take part in your injustice because I feared imprisonment and death. This happened in the days of the democracy. But when the oligarchy of the Thirty was in power, they sent for me and four others into the rotunda, and bade us bring Leon the Salaminian from Salamis, as they wanted to put him to death. This was a specimen of the sort of commands which they were always giving with the view of implicating as many as possible in their crimes; and then I showed, not in word only but in deed, that, if I may be allowed to use such an expression, I cared not a straw for death, and that my great and only care was lest I should do an unrighteous or unholy thing. For the strong arm of that oppressive power did not frighten me into doing wrong; and when we came out of the rotunda the other four went to Salamis and fetched Leon, but I went quietly home. For which I might have lost my life, had not the power of the Thirty shortly afterwards come to an end. And many will witness to my words.

Now do you really imagine that I could have survived all these years, if I had led a public life, supposing that like a good man I had always maintained the right and had made justice, as I ought, the first thing? No indeed, men of Athens, neither I nor any other man. But I have been always the same in all my actions, public as well as private, and never have I yielded any base compliance to those who are slanderously termed my disciples, or to any other. Not that I have any regular disciples. But if any one likes to come and hear me while I am pursuing my mission, whether he be young or old, he is not excluded. Nor do I converse only with those who pay; but any one, whether he be rich or poor, may ask and answer me and listen to my words; and whether he turns out to be a bad man or a good one, neither result can be justly imputed to me; for I never taught or professed to teach him anything. And if any one says that he has ever learned or heard anything from me in private which all the world has not heard, let me tell you that he is lying.

But I shall be asked, Why do people delight in continually conversing with you? I have told you already, Athenians, the whole truth about this matter: they like to hear the cross-examination of the pretenders to wisdom; there is amusement in it. Now this duty of cross-examining other men has been imposed upon me by God; and has been signified to me by oracles, visions, and in every way in which the will of divine power was ever intimated to any one. This is true, O Athenians, or, if not true, would be soon refuted. If I am or have been corrupting the youth, those of them who are now grown up and have become sensible that I gave them bad advice in the days of their youth should come forward as accusers, and take their revenge; or if they do not like to come themselves, some of their relatives, fathers, brothers, or other kinsmen, should say what evil their families have suffered at my hands. Now is their time. Many of them I see in the court. There is Crito, who is of the same age and of the same deme with myself, and there is Critobulus his son, whom I also see. Then again there is Lysanias of Sphettus, who is the father of Aeschines—he is present; and also there is Antiphon of Cephisus, who is the father of Epigenes; and there are the brothers of several who have associated with me. There is Nicostratus the son of Theosdotides, and the brother of Theodotus (now Theodotus himself is dead, and therefore he, at any rate, will not seek to stop him); and there is Paralus the son of Demodocus, who had a brother Theages; and Adeimantus the son of Ariston, whose brother Plato is present; and Aeantodorus, who is the brother of Apollodorus, whom I also see. I might mention a great many others, some of whom Meletus should have produced as witnesses in the course of his speech; and let him still produce them, if he has forgotten—I will make way for him. And let him say, if he has any testimony of the sort which he can produce. Nay, Athenians, the very opposite is the truth. For all these are ready to witness on behalf of the corrupter, of the injurer of their kindred, as Meletus and Anytus call me; not the corrupted youth only—there might have been a motive for that—but their uncorrupted elder relatives. Why should they too support me with their testimony? Why, indeed, except for the sake of truth and justice, and because they know that I am speaking the truth, and that Meletus is a liar.

Well, Athenians, this and the like of this is all the defense which I have to offer. Yet a word more. Perhaps there may be some one who is offended at me, when he calls to mind how he himself on a similar, or even a less serious occasion, prayed and entreated the judges with many tears, and how he produced his children in court, which was a moving spectacle, together with a host of relations and friends; whereas I, who am probably in danger of my life, will do none of these things. The contrast may occur to his mind, and he may be set against me, and vote in anger because he is displeased at me on this account. Now if there be such a person among you,—mind, I do not say that there is,—to him I may fairly reply: My friend, I am a man, and like other men, a creature of flesh and blood, and not 'of wood or stone,' as Homer says; and I have a family, yes, and sons, O Athenians, three in number, one almost a man, and two others who are still young; and yet I will not bring any of them hither in order to petition you for an acquittal. And why not? Not from any self-assertion or want of respect for you. Whether I am or am not afraid of death is another question, of which I will not now speak. But, having regard to public opinion, I feel that such conduct would be discreditable to myself, and to you, and to the whole state. One who has reached my years, and who has a name for wisdom, ought not to demean himself. Whether this opinion of me be deserved or not, at any rate the world has decided that Socrates is in some way superior to other men. And if those among you who are said to be superior in wisdom and courage, and any other virtue, demean themselves in this way, how shameful is their conduct! I have seen men of reputation, when they have been condemned, behaving in the strangest manner: they seemed to fancy that they were going to suffer something dreadful if they died, and that they could be immortal if you only allowed them to live; and I think that such are a dishonor to the state, and that any stranger coming in would have said of them that the most eminent men of Athens, to whom the Athenians themselves give honor and command, are no better than women. And I say that these things ought not to be done by those of us who have a reputation; and if they are done, you ought not to permit them; you ought rather to show that you are far more disposed to condemn the man who gets up a doleful scene and makes the city ridiculous, than him who holds his peace.

But, setting aside the question of public opinion, there seems to be something wrong in asking a favor of a judge, and thus procuring an acquittal, instead of informing and convincing him. For his duty is, not to make a present of justice, but to give judgment; and he has sworn that he will judge according to the laws, and not according to his own good pleasure; and we ought not to encourage you, nor should you allow yourselves to be encouraged, in this habit of perjury—there can be no piety in that. Do not then require me to do what I consider dishonorable and impious and wrong, especially now, when I am being tried for impiety on the indictment of Meletus. For if, O men of Athens, by force of persuasion and entreaty I could overpower your oaths, then I should be teaching you to believe that there are no gods, and in defending should simply convict myself of the charge of not believing in them. But that is not so—far otherwise. For I do believe that there are gods, and in a sense higher than that in which any of my accusers believe in them. And to you and to God I commit my cause, to be determined by you as is best for you and me.

* * * * *

There are many reasons why I am not grieved, O men of Athens, at the vote of condemnation. I expected it, and am only surprised that the votes are so nearly equal; for I had thought that the majority against me would have been far larger; but now, had thirty votes gone over to the other side, I should have been acquitted. And I may say, I think, that I have escaped Meletus. I may say more; for without the assistance of Anytus and Lycon, any one may see that he would not have had a fifth part of the votes, as the law requires, in which case he would have incurred a fine of a thousand drachmae.

And so he proposes death as the penalty. And what shall I propose on my part, O men of Athens? Clearly that which is my due. And what is my due? What return shall be made to the man who has never had the wit to be idle during his whole life; but has been careless of what the many care for—wealth, and family interests, and military offices, and speaking in the assembly, and magistracies, and plots, and parties. Reflecting that I was really too honest a man to be a politician and live, I did not go where I could do no good to you or to myself; but where I could do the greatest good privately to every one of you, thither I went, and sought to persuade every man among you that he must look to himself, and seek virtue and wisdom before he looks to his private interests, and look to the state before he looks to the interests of the state; and that this should be the order which he observes in all his actions. What shall be done to such an one? Doubtless some good thing, O men of Athens, if he has his reward; and the good should be of a kind suitable to him. What would be a reward suitable to a poor man who is your benefactor, and who desires leisure that he may instruct you? There can be no reward so fitting as maintenance in the Prytaneum, O men of Athens, a reward which he deserves far more than the citizen who has won the prize at Olympia in the horse or chariot race, whether the chariots were drawn by two horses or by many. For I am in want, and he has enough; and he only gives you the appearance of happiness, and I give you the reality. And if I am to estimate the penalty fairly, I should say that maintenance in the Prytaneum is the just return.

Perhaps you think that I am braving you in what I am saying now, as in what I said before about the tears and prayers. But this is not so. I speak rather because I am convinced that I never intentionally wronged any one, although I cannot convince you—the time has been too short; if there were a law at Athens, as there is in other cities, that a capital cause should not be decided in one day, then I believe that I should have convinced you. But I cannot in a moment refute great slanders; and, as I am convinced that I never wronged another, I will assuredly not wrong myself. I will not say of myself that I deserve any evil, or propose any penalty. Why should I? because I am afraid of the penalty of death which Meletus proposes? When I do not know whether death is a good or an evil, why should I propose a penalty which would certainly be an evil? Shall I say imprisonment? And why should I live in prison, and be the slave of the magistrates of the year—of the Eleven? Or shall the penalty be a fine, and imprisonment until the fine is paid? There is the same objection. I should have to lie in prison, for money I have none, and cannot pay. And if I say exile (and this may possibly be the penalty which you will affix), I must indeed be blinded by the love of life, if I am so irrational as to expect that when you, who are my own citizens, cannot endure my discourses and words, and have found them so grievous and odious that you will have no more of them, others are likely to endure me. No indeed, men of Athens, that is not very likely. And what a life should I lead, at my age, wandering from city to city, ever changing my place of exile, and always being driven out! For I am quite sure that wherever I go, there, as here, the young men will flock to me; and if I drive them away, their elders will drive me out at their request; and if I let them come, their fathers and friends will drive me out for their sakes.

Some one will say: Yes, Socrates, but cannot you hold your tongue, and then you may go into a foreign city, and no one will interfere with you? Now I have great difficulty in making you understand my answer to this. For if I tell you that to do as you say would be a disobedience to the God, and therefore that I cannot hold my tongue, you will not believe that I am serious; and if I say again that daily to discourse about virtue, and of those other things about which you hear me examining myself and others, is the greatest good of man, and that the unexamined life is not worth living, you are still less likely to believe me. Yet I say what is true, although a thing of which it is hard for me to persuade you. Also, I have never been accustomed to think that I deserve to suffer any harm. Had I money I might have estimated the offence at what I was able to pay, and not have been much the worse. But I have none, and therefore I must ask you to proportion the fine to my means. Well, perhaps I could afford a mina, and therefore I propose that penalty: Plato, Crito, Critobulus, and Apollodorus, my friends here, bid me say thirty minae, and they will be the sureties. Let thirty minae be the penalty; for which sum they will be ample security to you.

* * * * *

Not much time will be gained, O Athenians, in return for the evil name which you will get from the detractors of the city, who will say that you killed Socrates, a wise man; for they will call me wise, even although I am not wise, when they want to reproach you. If you had waited a little while, your desire would have been fulfilled in the course of nature. For I am far advanced in years, as you may perceive, and not far from death. I am speaking now not to all of you, but only to those who have condemned me to death. And I have another thing to say to them: you think that I was convicted because I had no words of the sort which would have procured my acquittal—I mean, if I had thought fit to leave nothing undone or unsaid. Not so; the deficiency which led to my conviction was not of words—certainly not. But I had not the boldness or impudence or inclination to address you as you would have liked me to do, weeping and wailing and lamenting, and saying and doing many things which you have been accustomed to hear from others, and which, as I maintain, are unworthy of me. I thought at the time that I ought not to do anything common or mean when in danger: nor do I now repent of the style of my defense; I would rather die having spoken after my manner, than speak in your manner and live. For neither in war nor yet at law ought I or any man to use every way of escaping death. Often in battle there can be no doubt that if a man will throw away his arms, and fall on his knees before his pursuers, he may escape death; and in other dangers there are other ways of escaping death, if a man is willing to say and do anything. The difficulty, my friends, is not to avoid death, but to avoid unrighteousness; for that runs faster than death. I am old and move slowly, and the slower runner has overtaken me, and my accusers are keen and quick, and the faster runner, who is unrighteousness, has overtaken them. And now I depart hence condemned by you to suffer the penalty of death,—they too go their ways condemned by the truth to suffer the penalty of villainy and wrong; and I must abide by my award—let them abide by theirs. I suppose that these things may be regarded as fated,—and I think that they are well.

And now, O men who have condemned me, I would fain prophesy to you; for I am about to die, and in the hour of death men are gifted with prophetic power. And I prophesy to you who are my murderers, that immediately after my departure punishment far heavier than you have inflicted on me will surely await you. Me you have killed because you wanted to escape the accuser, and not to give an account of your lives. But that will not be as you suppose: far otherwise. For I say that there will be more accusers of you than there are now; accusers whom hitherto I have restrained: and as they are younger they will be more inconsiderate with you, and you will be more offended at them. If you think that by killing men you can prevent some one from censuring your evil lives, you are mistaken; that is not a way of escape which is either possible or honorable; the easiest and the noblest way is not to be disabling others, but to be improving yourselves. This is the prophecy which I utter before my departure to the judges who have condemned me.

Friends, who would have acquitted me, I would like also to talk with you about the thing which has come to pass, while the magistrates are busy, and before I go to the place at which I must die. Stay then a little, for we may as well talk with one another while there is time. You are my friends, and I should like to show you the meaning of this event which has happened to me. O my judges—for you I may truly call judges—I should like to tell you of a wonderful circumstance. Hitherto the divine faculty of which the internal oracle is the source has constantly been in the habit of opposing me even about trifles, if I was going to make a slip or error in any matter; and now as you see there has come upon me that which may be thought, and is generally believed to be, the last and worst evil. But the oracle made no sign of opposition, either when I was leaving my house in the morning, or when I was on my way to the court, or while I was speaking, at anything which I was going to say; and yet I have often been stopped in the middle of a speech, but now in nothing I either said or did touching the matter in hand has the oracle opposed me. What do I take to be the explanation of this silence? I will tell you. It is an intimation that what has happened to me is a good, and that those of us who think that death is an evil are in error. For the customary sign would surely have opposed me had I been going to evil and not to good.

Let us reflect in another way, and we shall see that there is great reason to hope that death is a good; for one of two things—either death is a state of nothingness and utter unconsciousness, or, as men say, there is a change and migration of the soul from this world to another. Now if you suppose that there is no consciousness, but a sleep like the sleep of him who is undisturbed even by dreams, death will be an unspeakable gain. For if a person were to select the night in which his sleep was undisturbed even by dreams, and were to compare with this the other days and nights of his life, and then were to tell us how many days and nights he had passed in the course of his life better and more pleasantly than this one, I think that any man, I will not say a private man, but even the great king will not find many such days or nights, when compared with the others. Now if death be of such a nature, I say that to die is gain; for eternity is then only a single night. But if death is the journey to another place, and there, as men say, all the dead abide, what good, O my friends and judges, can be greater than this? If indeed when the pilgrim arrives in the world below, he is delivered from the professors of justice in this world, and finds the true judges who are said to give judgment there, Minos and Rhadamanthus and Aeacus and Triptolemus, and other sons of God who were righteous in their own life, that pilgrimage will be worth making. What would not a man give if he might converse with Orpheus and Musaeus and Hesiod and Homer? Nay, if this be true, let me die again and again. I myself, too, shall have a wonderful interest in there meeting and conversing with Palamedes, and Ajax the son of Telamon, and any other ancient hero who has suffered death through an unjust judgment; and there will be no small pleasure, as I think, in comparing my own sufferings with theirs. Above all, I shall then be able to continue my search into true and false knowledge; as in this world, so also in the next; and I shall find out who is wise, and who pretends to be wise, and is not. What would not a man give, O judges, to be able to examine the leader of the great Trojan expedition; or Odysseus or Sisyphus, or numberless others, men and women too! What infinite delight would there be in conversing with them and asking them questions! In another world they do not put a man to death for asking questions: assuredly not. For besides being happier than we are, they will be immortal, if what is said is true.

Wherefore, O judges, be of good cheer about death, and know of a certainty, that no evil can happen to a good man, either in life or after death. He and his are not neglected by the gods; nor has my own approaching end happened by mere chance. But I see clearly that the time had arrived when it was better for me to die and be released from trouble; wherefore the oracle gave no sign. For which reason, also, I am not angry with my condemners, or with my accusers; they have done me no harm, although they did not mean to do me any good; and for this I may gently blame them.

Still I have a favor to ask of them. When my sons are grown up, I would ask you, O my friends, to punish them; and I would have you trouble them, as I have troubled you, if they seem to care about riches, or anything, more than about virtue; or if they pretend to be something when they are really nothing,—then reprove them, as I have reproved you, for not caring about that for which they ought to care, and thinking that they are something when they are really nothing. And if you do this, both I and my sons will have received justice at your hands.

The hour of departure has arrived, and we go our ways—I to die, and you to live. Which is better God only knows.

CRITO

By Plato
Translated by Benjamin Jowett

Introduction

The Crito seems intended to exhibit the character of Socrates in one light only, not as the philosopher, fulfilling a divine mission and trusting in the will of heaven, but simply as the good citizen, who having been unjustly condemned is willing to give up his life in obedience to the laws of the state . . .

Plato

The days of Socrates are drawing to a close; the fatal ship has been seen off Sunium, as he is informed by his aged friend and contemporary Crito, who visits him before the dawn has broken; he himself has been warned in a dream that on the third day he must depart. Time is precious, and Crito has come early in order to gain his consent to a plan of escape. This can be easily accomplished by his friends, who will incur no danger in making the attempt to save him, but will be disgraced for ever if they allow him to perish. He should think of his duty to his children, and not play into the hands of his enemies. Money is already provided by Crito as well as by Simmias and others, and he will have no difficulty in finding friends in Thessaly and other places.

Socrates is afraid that Crito is but pressing upon him the opinions of the many: whereas, all his life long he has followed the dictates of reason only and the opinion of the one wise or skilled man. There was a time when Crito himself had allowed the propriety of this. And although some one will say 'the many can kill us,' that makes no difference; but a good life, in other words, a just and honorable life, is alone to be valued. All considerations of loss of reputation or injury to his children should be dismissed: the only question is whether he would be right in attempting to escape. Crito, who is a disinterested person not having the fear of death before his eyes, shall answer this for him. Before he was condemned they had often held discussions, in which they agreed that no man should either do evil, or return evil for evil, or betray the right. Are these principles to be altered because the circumstances of Socrates are altered? Crito admits that they remain the same. Then is his escape consistent with the maintenance of them? To this Crito is unable or unwilling to reply.

Socrates proceeds:—Suppose the Laws of Athens to come and remonstrate with him: they will ask 'Why does he seek to overturn them?' and if he replies, 'they have injured him,' will not the Laws answer, 'Yes, but was that the agreement? Has he any objection to make to them which would justify him in overturning them? Was he not brought into the world and educated by their help, and are they not his parents? He might have left Athens and gone where he pleased, but he has lived there for seventy years more constantly than any other citizen.' Thus he has clearly shown that he acknowledged the agreement, which he cannot now break without dishonor to himself and danger to his friends. Even in the course of the trial he might have proposed exile as the penalty, but then he declared that he preferred death to exile. And whither will he direct his footsteps? In any well-ordered state the Laws will consider him as an enemy. Possibly in a land of misrule like Thessaly he may be welcomed at first, and the unseemly narrative of his escape will be regarded by the inhabitants as an amusing tale. But if he offends them he will have to learn another sort of lesson. Will he continue to give lectures in virtue? That would hardly be decent. And how will his children be the gainers if he takes them into Thessaly, and deprives them of Athenian citizenship? Or if he leaves them behind, does he expect that they will be better taken care of by his friends because he is in Thessaly? Will not true friends care for them equally whether he is alive or dead?

Finally, they exhort him to think of justice first, and of life and children afterwards. He may now depart in peace and innocence, a sufferer and not a doer of evil. But if he breaks agreements, and returns evil for evil, they will be angry with him while he lives; and their brethren the Laws of the world below will receive him as an enemy. Such is the mystic voice which is always murmuring in his ears.

That Socrates was not a good citizen was a charge made against him during his lifetime, which has been often repeated in later ages. The crimes of Alcibiades, Critias, and Charmides, who had been his pupils, were still recent in the memory of the now restored democracy. The fact that he had been neutral in the death-struggle of Athens was not likely to conciliate popular good-will. Plato, writing probably in the next generation, undertakes the defense of his friend and master in this particular, not to the Athenians of his day, but to posterity and the world at large.

Whether such an incident ever really occurred as the visit of Crito and the proposal of escape is uncertain: Plato could easily have invented far more than that (Phaedr.); and in the selection of Crito, the aged friend, as the fittest person to make the proposal to Socrates, we seem to recognize the hand of the artist. Whether any one who has been subjected by the laws of his country to an unjust judgment is right in attempting to escape, is a thesis about which casuists might disagree. Shelley (Prose Works) is of opinion that Socrates 'did well to die,' but not for the 'sophistical' reasons which Plato has put into his mouth. And there would be no difficulty in arguing that Socrates should have lived and preferred to a glorious death the good which he might still be able to perform. 'A rhetorician would have had much to say upon that point.' It may be observed however that Plato never intended to answer the question of casuistry, but only to exhibit the ideal of patient virtue which refuses to do the least evil in order to avoid the greatest, and to show his master maintaining in death the opinions which he had professed in his life. Not 'the world,' but the 'one wise man,' is still the paradox of Socrates in his last hours. He must be guided by reason, although her conclusions may be fatal to him. The remarkable sentiment that the wicked can do neither good nor evil is true, if taken in the sense, which he means, of moral evil; in his own words, 'they cannot make a man wise or foolish.' This little dialogue is a perfect piece of dialectic, in which granting the 'common principle,' there is no escaping from the conclusion. It is anticipated at the beginning by the dream of Socrates and the parody of Homer. The personification of the Laws, and of their brethren the Laws in the world below, is one of the noblest and boldest figures of speech which occur in Plato.

Crito

PERSONS OF THE DIALOGUE: Socrates, Crito.

SCENE: The Prison of Socrates.

SOCRATES: Why have you come at this hour, Crito? it must be quite early.

CRITO: Yes, certainly.

SOCRATES: What is the exact time?

CRITO: The dawn is breaking.

SOCRATES: I wonder that the keeper of the prison would let you in.

CRITO: He knows me because I often come, Socrates; moreover. I have done him a kindness.

SOCRATES: And are you only just arrived?

CRITO: No, I came some time ago.

SOCRATES: Then why did you sit and say nothing, instead of at once awakening me?

CRITO: I should not have liked myself, Socrates, to be in such great trouble and unrest as you are—indeed I should not: I have been watching with amazement your peaceful slumbers; and for that reason I did not awake you, because I wished to minimize the pain. I have always thought you to be of a happy disposition; but never did I see anything like the easy, tranquil manner in which you bear this calamity.

SOCRATES: Why, Crito, when a man has reached my age he ought not to be repining at the approach of death.

CRITO: And yet other old men find themselves in similar misfortunes, and age does not prevent them from repining.

SOCRATES: That is true. But you have not told me why you come at this early hour.

CRITO: I come to bring you a message which is sad and painful; not, as I believe, to yourself, but to all of us who are your friends, and saddest of all to me.

SOCRATES: What? Has the ship come from Delos, on the arrival of which I am to die?

CRITO: No, the ship has not actually arrived, but she will probably be here to-day, as persons who have come from Sunium tell me that they have left her there; and therefore to-morrow, Socrates, will be the last day of your life.

SOCRATES: Very well, Crito; if such is the will of God, I am willing; but my belief is that there will be a delay of a day.

CRITO: Why do you think so?

SOCRATES: I will tell you. I am to die on the day after the arrival of the ship?

CRITO: Yes; that is what the authorities say.

SOCRATES: But I do not think that the ship will be here until to-morrow; this I infer from a vision which I had last night, or rather only just now, when you fortunately allowed me to sleep.

CRITO: And what was the nature of the vision?

SOCRATES: There appeared to me the likeness of a woman, fair and comely, clothed in bright raiment, who called to me and said: O Socrates,

'The third day hence to fertile Phthia shalt thou go.' (Homer, Il.)

CRITO: What a singular dream, Socrates!

SOCRATES: There can be no doubt about the meaning, Crito, I think.

CRITO: Yes; the meaning is only too clear. But, oh! my beloved Socrates, let me entreat you once more to take my advice and escape. For if you die I shall not only lose a friend who can never be replaced, but there is another evil: people who do not know you and me will believe that I might have saved you if I had been willing to give money, but that I did not care. Now, can there be a worse disgrace than this—that I should be thought to value money more than the life of a friend? For the many will not be persuaded that I wanted you to escape, and that you refused.

SOCRATES: But why, my dear Crito, should we care about the opinion of the many? Good men, and they are the only persons who are worth considering, will think of these things truly as they occurred.

CRITO: But you see, Socrates, that the opinion of the many must be regarded, for what is now happening shows that they can do the greatest evil to any one who has lost their good opinion.

SOCRATES: I only wish it were so, Crito; and that the many could do the greatest evil; for then they would also be able to do the greatest good— and what a fine thing this would be! But in reality they can do neither; for they cannot make a man either wise or foolish; and whatever they do is the result of chance.

CRITO: Well, I will not dispute with you; but please to tell me, Socrates, whether you are not acting out of regard to me and your other friends: are you not afraid that if you escape from prison we may get into trouble with the informers for having stolen you away, and lose either the whole or a great part of our property; or that even a worse evil may happen to us? Now, if you fear on our account, be at ease; for in order to save you, we ought surely to run this, or even a greater risk; be persuaded, then, and do as I say.

SOCRATES: Yes, Crito, that is one fear which you mention, but by no means the only one.

CRITO: Fear not—there are persons who are willing to get you out of prison at no great cost; and as for the informers they are far from being exorbitant in their demands—a little money will satisfy them. My means, which are certainly ample, are at your service, and if you have a scruple about spending all mine, here are strangers who will give you the use of theirs; and one of them, Simmias the Theban, has brought a large sum of money for this very purpose; and Cebes and many others are prepared to spend their money in helping you to escape. I say, therefore, do not hesitate on our account, and do not say, as you did in the court (compare Apol.), that you will have a difficulty in knowing what to do with yourself anywhere else. For men will love you in other places to which you may go, and not in Athens only; there are friends of mine in Thessaly, if you like to go to them, who will value and protect you, and no Thessalian will give you any trouble. Nor can I think that you are at all justified, Socrates, in betraying your own life when you might be saved; in acting thus you are playing into the hands of your enemies, who are hurrying on your destruction. And further I should say that you are deserting your own children; for you might bring them up and educate them; instead of which you go away and leave them, and they will have to take their chance; and if they do not meet with the usual fate of orphans, there will be small thanks to you. No man should bring children into the world who is unwilling to persevere to the end in their nurture and education. But you appear to be choosing the easier part, not the better and manlier, which would have been more becoming in one who professes to care for virtue in all his actions, like yourself. And indeed, I am ashamed not only of you, but of us who are your friends, when I reflect that the whole business will be attributed entirely to our want of courage. The trial need never have come on, or might have been managed differently; and this last act, or crowning folly, will seem to have occurred through our negligence and cowardice, who might have saved you, if we had been good for anything; and you might have saved yourself, for there was no difficulty at all. See now, Socrates, how sad and discreditable are the consequences, both to us and you. Make up your mind then, or rather have your mind already made up, for the time of deliberation is over, and there is only one thing to be done, which must be done this very night, and if we delay at all will be no longer practicable or possible; I beseech you therefore, Socrates, be persuaded by me, and do as I say.

SOCRATES: Dear Crito, your zeal is invaluable, if a right one; but if wrong, the greater the zeal the greater the danger; and therefore we ought to consider whether I shall or shall not do as you say. For I am and always have been one of those natures who must be guided by reason, whatever the reason may be which upon reflection appears to me to be the best; and now that this chance has befallen me, I cannot repudiate my own words: the principles which I have hitherto honored and revered I still honor, and unless we can at once find other and better principles, I am certain not to agree with you; no, not even if the power of the multitude could inflict many more imprisonments, confiscations, deaths, frightening us like children with hobgoblin terrors (compare Apol.). What will be the fairest way of considering the question? Shall I return to your old argument about the opinions of men?—we were saying that some of them are to be regarded, and others not. Now were we right in maintaining this before I was condemned? And has the argument which was once good now proved to be talk for the sake of talking—mere childish nonsense? That is what I want to consider with your help, Crito:—whether, under my present circumstances, the argument appears to be in any way different or not; and is to be allowed by me or disallowed. That argument, which, as I believe, is maintained by many persons of authority, was to the effect, as I was saying, that the opinions of some men are to be regarded, and of other men not to be regarded. Now you, Crito, are not going to die to-morrow—at least, there is no human probability of this, and therefore you are disinterested and not liable to be deceived by the circumstances in which you are placed. Tell me then, whether I am right in saying that some opinions, and the opinions of some men only, are to be valued, and that other opinions, and the opinions of other men, are not to be valued. I ask you whether I was right in maintaining this?

CRITO: Certainly.

SOCRATES: The good are to be regarded, and not the bad?

CRITO: Yes.

SOCRATES: And the opinions of the wise are good, and the opinions of the unwise are evil?

CRITO: Certainly.

SOCRATES: And what was said about another matter? Is the pupil who devotes himself to the practice of gymnastics supposed to attend to the praise and blame and opinion of every man, or of one man only—his physician or trainer, whoever he may be?

CRITO: Of one man only.

SOCRATES: And he ought to fear the censure and welcome the praise of that one only, and not of the many?

CRITO: Clearly so.

SOCRATES: And he ought to act and train, and eat and drink in the way which seems good to his single master who has understanding, rather than according to the opinion of all other men put together?

CRITO: True.

SOCRATES: And if he disobeys and disregards the opinion and approval of the one, and regards the opinion of the many who have no understanding, will he not suffer evil?

CRITO: Certainly he will.

SOCRATES: And what will the evil be, whither tending and what affecting, in the disobedient person?

CRITO: Clearly, affecting the body; that is what is destroyed by the evil.

SOCRATES: Very good; and is not this true, Crito, of other things which we need not separately enumerate? In questions of just and unjust, fair and foul, good and evil, which are the subjects of our present consultation, ought we to follow the opinion of the many and to fear them; or the opinion of the one man who has understanding? ought we not to fear and reverence him more than all the rest of the world: and if we desert him shall we not destroy and injure that principle in us which may be assumed to be improved by justice and deteriorated by injustice;—there is such a principle?

CRITO: Certainly there is, Socrates.

SOCRATES: Take a parallel instance:—if, acting under the advice of those who have no understanding, we destroy that which is improved by health and is deteriorated by disease, would life be worth having? And that which has been destroyed is—the body?

CRITO: Yes.

SOCRATES: Could we live, having an evil and corrupted body?

CRITO: Certainly not.

SOCRATES: And will life be worth having, if that higher part of man be destroyed, which is improved by justice and depraved by injustice? Do we suppose that principle, whatever it may be in man, which has to do with justice and injustice, to be inferior to the body?

CRITO: Certainly not.

SOCRATES: More honorable than the body?

CRITO: Far more.

SOCRATES: Then, my friend, we must not regard what the many say of us: but what he, the one man who has understanding of just and unjust, will say, and what the truth will say. And therefore you begin in error when you advise that we should regard the opinion of the many about just and unjust, good and evil, honorable and dishonorable.—'Well,' some one will say, 'but the many can kill us.'

CRITO: Yes, Socrates; that will clearly be the answer.

SOCRATES: And it is true; but still I find with surprise that the old argument is unshaken as ever. And I should like to know whether I may say the same of another proposition—that not life, but a good life, is to be chiefly valued?

CRITO: Yes, that also remains unshaken.

SOCRATES: And a good life is equivalent to a just and honorable one—that holds also?

CRITO: Yes, it does.

SOCRATES: From these premises I proceed to argue the question whether I ought or ought not to try and escape without the consent of the Athenians: and if I am clearly right in escaping, then I will make the attempt; but if not, I will abstain. The other considerations which you mention, of money and loss of character and the duty of educating one's children, are, I fear, only the doctrines of the multitude, who would be as ready to restore people to life, if they were able, as they are to put them to death—and with as little reason. But now, since the argument has thus far prevailed, the only question which remains to be considered is, whether we shall do rightly either in escaping or in suffering others to aid in our escape and paying them in money and thanks, or whether in reality we shall not do rightly; and if the latter, then death or any other calamity which may ensue on my remaining here must not be allowed to enter into the calculation.

CRITO: I think that you are right, Socrates; how then shall we proceed?

SOCRATES: Let us consider the matter together, and do you either refute me if you can, and I will be convinced; or else cease, my dear friend, from repeating to me that I ought to escape against the wishes of the Athenians: for I highly value your attempts to persuade me to do so, but I may not be persuaded against my own better judgment. And now please to consider my first position, and try how you can best answer me.

CRITO: I will.

SOCRATES: Are we to say that we are never intentionally to do wrong, or that in one way we ought and in another way we ought not to do wrong, or is doing wrong always evil and dishonorable, as I was just now saying, and as has been already acknowledged by us? Are all our former admissions which were made within a few days to be thrown away? And have we, at our age, been earnestly discoursing with one another all our life long only to discover that we are no better than children? Or, in spite of the opinion of the many, and in spite of consequences whether better or worse, shall we insist on the truth of what was then said, that injustice is always an evil and dishonor to him who acts unjustly? Shall we say so or not?

CRITO: Yes.

SOCRATES: Then we must do no wrong?

CRITO: Certainly not.

SOCRATES: Nor when injured injure in return, as the many imagine; for we must injure no one at all? (E.g. compare Rep.)

CRITO: Clearly not.

SOCRATES: Again, Crito, may we do evil?

CRITO: Surely not, Socrates.

SOCRATES: And what of doing evil in return for evil, which is the morality of the many—is that just or not?

CRITO: Not just.

SOCRATES: For doing evil to another is the same as injuring him?

CRITO: Very true.

SOCRATES: Then we ought not to retaliate or render evil for evil to any one, whatever evil we may have suffered from him. But I would have you consider, Crito, whether you really mean what you are saying. For this opinion has never been held, and never will be held, by any considerable number of persons; and those who are agreed and those who are not agreed upon this point have no common ground, and can only despise one another when they see how widely they differ. Tell me, then, whether you agree with and assent to my first principle, that neither injury nor retaliation nor warding off evil by evil is ever right. And shall that be the premise of our argument? Or do you decline and dissent from this? For so I have ever thought, and continue to think; but, if you are of another opinion, let me hear what you have to say. If, however, you remain of the same mind as formerly, I will proceed to the next step.

CRITO: You may proceed, for I have not changed my mind.

SOCRATES: Then I will go on to the next point, which may be put in the form of a question:—Ought a man to do what he admits to be right, or ought he to betray the right?

CRITO: He ought to do what he thinks right.

SOCRATES: But if this is true, what is the application? In leaving the prison against the will of the Athenians, do I wrong any? or rather do I not wrong those whom I ought least to wrong? Do I not desert the principles which were acknowledged by us to be just—what do you say?

CRITO: I cannot tell, Socrates, for I do not know.

SOCRATES: Then consider the matter in this way:—Imagine that I am about to play truant (you may call the proceeding by any name which you like), and the laws and the government come and interrogate me: 'Tell us, Socrates,' they say; 'what are you about? are you not going by an act of yours to overturn us—the laws, and the whole state, as far as in you lies? Do you imagine that a state can subsist and not be overthrown, in which the decisions of law have no power, but are set aside and trampled upon by individuals?' What will be our answer, Crito, to these and the like words? Any one, and especially a rhetorician, will have a good deal to say on behalf of the law which requires a sentence to be carried out. He will argue that this law should not be set aside; and shall we reply, 'Yes; but the state has injured us and given an unjust sentence.' Suppose I say that?

CRITO: Very good, Socrates.

SOCRATES: 'And was that our agreement with you?' the law would answer; 'or were you to abide by the sentence of the state?' And if I were to express my astonishment at their words, the law would probably add: 'Answer, Socrates, instead of opening your eyes—you are in the habit of asking and answering questions. Tell us,—What complaint have you to make against us which justifies you in attempting to destroy us and the state? In the first place did we not bring you into existence? Your father married your mother by our aid and begat you. Say whether you have any objection to urge against those of us who regulate marriage?' None, I should reply. 'Or against those of us who after birth regulate the nurture and education of children, in which you also were trained? Were not the laws, which have the charge of education, right in commanding your father to train you in music and gymnastic?' Right, I should reply. 'Well then, since you were brought into the world and nurtured and educated by us, can you deny in the first place that you are our child and slave, as your fathers were before you? And if this is true you are not on equal terms with us; nor can you think that you have a right to do to us what we are doing to you. Would you have any right to strike or revile or do any other evil to your father or your master, if you had one, because you have been struck or reviled by him, or received some other evil at his hands?—you would not say this? And because we think right to destroy you, do you think that you have any right to destroy us in return, and your country as far as in you lies? Will you, O professor of true virtue, pretend that you are justified in this? Has a philosopher like you failed to discover that our country is more to be valued and higher and holier far than mother or father or any ancestor, and more to be regarded in the eyes of the gods and of men of understanding? also to be soothed, and gently and reverently entreated when angry, even more than a father, and either to be persuaded, or if not persuaded, to be obeyed? And when we are punished by her, whether with imprisonment or stripes, the punishment is to be endured in silence; and if she lead us to wounds or death in battle, thither we follow as is right; neither may any one yield or retreat or leave his rank, but whether in battle or in a court of law, or in any other place, he must do what his city and his country order him; or he must change their view of what is just: and if he may do no violence to his father or mother, much less may he do violence to his country.' What answer shall we make to this, Crito? Do the laws speak truly, or do they not?

CRITO: I think that they do.

SOCRATES: Then the laws will say: 'Consider, Socrates, if we are speaking truly that in your present attempt you are going to do us an injury. For, having brought you into the world, and nurtured and educated you, and given you and every other citizen a share in every good which we had to give, we further proclaim to any Athenian by the liberty which we allow him, that if he does not like us when he has become of age and has seen the ways of the city, and made our acquaintance, he may go where he pleases and take his goods with him. None of us laws will forbid him or interfere with him. Any one who does not like us and the city, and who wants to emigrate to a colony or to any other city, may go where he likes, retaining his property. But he who has experience of the manner in which we order justice and administer the state, and still remains, has entered into an implied contract that he will do as we command him. And he who disobeys us is, as we maintain, thrice wrong: first, because in disobeying us he is disobeying his parents; secondly, because we are the authors of his education; thirdly, because he has made an agreement with us that he will duly obey our commands; and he neither obeys them nor convinces us that our commands are unjust; and we do not rudely impose them, but give him the alternative of obeying or convincing us;—that is what we offer, and he does neither.

'These are the sort of accusations to which, as we were saying, you, Socrates, will be exposed if you accomplish your intentions; you, above all other Athenians.' Suppose now I ask, why I rather than anybody else? they will justly retort upon me that I above all other men have acknowledged the agreement. 'There is clear proof,' they will say, 'Socrates, that we and the city were not displeasing to you. Of all Athenians you have been the most constant resident in the city, which, as you never leave, you may be supposed to love (compare Phaedr.). For you never went out of the city either to see the games, except once when you went to the Isthmus, or to any other place unless when you were on military service; nor did you travel as other men do. Nor had you any curiosity to know other states or their laws: your affections did not go beyond us and our state; we were your especial favorites, and you acquiesced in our government of you; and here in this city you begat your children, which is a proof of your satisfaction. Moreover, you might in the course of the trial, if you had liked, have fixed the penalty at banishment; the state which refuses to let you go now would have let you go then. But you pretended that you preferred death to exile (compare Apol.), and that you were not unwilling to die. And now you have forgotten these fine sentiments, and pay no respect to us the laws, of whom you are the destroyer; and are doing what only a miserable slave would do, running away and turning your back upon the compacts and agreements which you made as a citizen. And first of all answer this very question: Are we right in saying that you agreed to be governed according to us in deed, and not in word only? Is that true or not?' How shall we answer, Crito? Must we not assent?

CRITO: We cannot help it, Socrates.

SOCRATES: Then will they not say: 'You, Socrates, are breaking the covenants and agreements which you made with us at your leisure, not in any haste or under any compulsion or deception, but after you have had seventy years to think of them, during which time you were at liberty to leave the city, if we were not to your mind, or if our covenants appeared to you to be unfair. You had your choice, and might have gone either to Lacedaemon or Crete, both which states are often praised by you for their good government, or to some other Hellenic or foreign state. Whereas you, above all other Athenians, seemed to be so fond of the state, or, in other words, of us her laws (and who would care about a state which has no laws?), that you never stirred out of her; the halt, the blind, the maimed, were not more stationary in her than you were. And now you run away and forsake your agreements. Not so, Socrates, if you will take our advice; do not make yourself ridiculous by escaping out of the city.

'For just consider, if you transgress and err in this sort of way, what good will you do either to yourself or to your friends? That your friends will be driven into exile and deprived of citizenship, or will lose their property, is tolerably certain; and you yourself, if you fly to one of the neighboring cities, as, for example, Thebes or Megara, both of which are well governed, will come to them as an enemy, Socrates, and their government will be against you, and all patriotic citizens will cast an evil eye upon you as a subverter of the laws, and you will confirm in the minds of the judges the justice of their own condemnation of you. For he who is a corrupter of the laws is more than likely to be a corrupter of the young and foolish portion of mankind. Will you then flee from well-ordered cities and virtuous men? and is existence worth having on these terms? Or will you go to them without shame, and talk to them, Socrates? And what will you say to them? What you say here about virtue and justice and institutions and laws being the best things among men? Would that be decent of you? Surely not. But if you go away from well-governed states to Crito's friends in Thessaly, where there is great disorder and license, they will be charmed to hear the tale of your escape from prison, set off with ludicrous particulars of the manner in which you were wrapped in a goatskin or some other disguise, and metamorphosed as the manner is of runaways; but will there be no one to remind you that in your old age you were not ashamed to violate the most sacred laws from a miserable desire of a little more life? Perhaps not, if you keep them in a good temper; but if they are out of temper you will hear many degrading things; you will live, but how?—as the flatterer of all men, and the servant of all men; and doing what?—eating and drinking in Thessaly, having gone abroad in order that you may get a dinner. And where will be your fine sentiments about justice and virtue?

Say that you wish to live for the sake of your children—you want to bring them up and educate them—will you take them into Thessaly and deprive them of Athenian citizenship? Is this the benefit which you will confer upon them? Or are you under the impression that they will be better cared for and educated here if you are still alive, although absent from them; for your friends will take care of them? Do you fancy that if you are an inhabitant of Thessaly they will take care of them, and if you are an inhabitant of the other world that they will not take care of them? Nay; but if they who call themselves friends are good for anything, they will—to be sure they will.

'Listen, then, Socrates, to us who have brought you up. Think not of life and children first, and of justice afterwards, but of justice first, that you may be justified before the princes of the world below. For neither will you nor any that belong to you be happier or holier or juster in this life, or happier in another, if you do as Crito bids. Now you depart in innocence, a sufferer and not a doer of evil; a victim, not of the laws, but of men. But if you go forth, returning evil for evil, and injury for injury, breaking the covenants and agreements which you have made with us, and wronging those whom you ought least of all to wrong, that is to say, yourself, your friends, your country, and us, we shall be angry with you while you live, and our brethren, the laws in the world below, will receive you as an enemy; for they will know that you have done your best to destroy us. Listen, then, to us and not to Crito.'

This, dear Crito, is the voice which I seem to hear murmuring in my ears, like the sound of the flute in the ears of the mystic; that voice, I say, is humming in my ears, and prevents me from hearing any other. And I know that anything more which you may say will be vain. Yet speak, if you have anything to say.

CRITO: I have nothing to say, Socrates.

SOCRATES: Leave me then, Crito, to fulfill the will of God, and to follow whither he leads.

MENO

By Plato
Translated by Benjamin Jowett

Introduction

This Dialogue begins abruptly with a question of Meno, who asks, 'whether virtue can be taught.' Socrates replies that he does not as yet know what virtue is, and has never known anyone who did. 'Then he cannot have met Gorgias when he was at Athens.' Yes, Socrates had met him, but he has a bad memory, and has forgotten what Gorgias said. Will Meno tell him his own notion, which is probably not very different from that of Gorgias?
'O yes—nothing easier: there is the virtue of a man, of a woman, of an old man, and of a child; there is a virtue of every age and state of life, all of which may be easily described.' Socrates reminds Meno that this is only an enumeration of the virtues and not a definition of the notion which is common to them all. In a second attempt Meno defines virtue to be 'the power of command.' But to this, again, exceptions are taken. For there must be a virtue

of those who obey, as well as of those who command; and the power of command must be justly or not unjustly exercised. Meno is very ready to admit that justice is virtue: 'Would you say virtue or a virtue, for there are other virtues, such as courage, temperance, and the like; just as round is a figure, and black and white are colors, and yet there are other figures and other colors. Let Meno take the examples of figure and color, and try to define them.' Meno confesses his inability, and after a process of interrogation, in which Socrates explains to him the nature of a 'simile in multis,' Socrates himself defines figure as 'the accompaniment of color.' But some one may object that he does not know the meaning of the word 'color;' and if he is a candid friend, and not a mere disputant, Socrates is willing to furnish him with a simpler and more philosophical definition, into which no disputed word is allowed to intrude: 'Figure is the limit of form.' Meno imperiously insists that he must still have a definition of color. Some raillery follows; and at length Socrates is induced to reply, 'that color is the effluence of form, sensible, and in due proportion to the sight.' This definition is exactly suited to the taste of Meno, who welcomes the familiar language of Gorgias and Empedocles. Socrates is of opinion that the more abstract or dialectical definition of figure is far better.

Now that Meno has been made to understand the nature of a general definition, he answers in the spirit of a Greek gentleman, and in the words of a poet, 'that virtue is to delight in things honorable, and to have the power of getting them.' This is a nearer approximation than he has yet made to a complete definition, and, regarded as a piece of proverbial or popular morality, is not far from the truth. But the objection is urged, 'that the honorable is the good,' and as every one equally desires the good, the point of the definition is contained in the words, 'the power of getting them.' 'And they must be got justly or with justice.' The definition will then stand thus: 'Virtue is the power of getting good with justice.' But justice is a part of virtue, and therefore virtue is the getting of good with a part of virtue. The definition repeats the word defined.

Meno complains that the conversation of Socrates has the effect of a torpedo's shock upon him. When he talks with other persons he has plenty to say about virtue; in the presence of Socrates, his thoughts desert him. Socrates replies that he is only the cause of perplexity in others, because he is himself perplexed. He proposes to continue the enquiry. But how, asks Meno, can he enquire either into what he knows or into what he does not know? This is a sophistical puzzle, which, as Socrates remarks, saves a great deal of trouble to him who accepts it. But the puzzle has a real difficulty latent under it, to which Socrates will endeavor to find a reply. The difficulty is the origin of knowledge:—

He has heard from priests and priestesses, and from the poet Pindar, of an immortal soul which is born again and again in successive periods of existence, returning into this world when she has paid the penalty of ancient crime, and, having wandered over all places of the upper and under world, and seen and known all things at one time or other, is by association out of one thing capable of recovering all. For nature is of one kindred; and every soul has a seed or germ which may be developed into all knowledge. The existence of this latent knowledge is further proved by the interrogation of one of Meno's slaves, who, in the skillful hands of Socrates, is made to acknowledge some elementary relations of geometrical figures. The theorem that the square of the diagonal is double the square of the side—that famous discovery of primitive mathematics, in honor of which the legendary Pythagoras is said to have sacrificed a hecatomb—is elicited from him. The first step in the process of teaching has made him conscious of his own ignorance. He has had the 'torpedo's shock' given him, and is the better for the operation. But whence had the uneducated man this knowledge? He had never learnt geometry in this world; nor was it born with him; he must therefore have had it when he was not a man. And as he always either was or was not a man, he must have always had it. (Compare Phaedo.)

After Socrates has given this specimen of the true nature of teaching, the original question of the teachableness of virtue is renewed. Again he professes a desire to know 'what virtue is' first. But he is willing to argue the question, as mathematicians say, under an hypothesis. He will assume that if virtue is knowledge, then virtue can be taught. (This was the stage of the argument at which the Protagoras concluded.)

Socrates has no difficulty in showing that virtue is a good, and that goods, whether of body or mind, must be under the direction of knowledge. Upon the assumption just made, then, virtue is teachable. But where are the teachers? There are none to be found. This is extremely discouraging. Virtue is no sooner discovered to be teachable, than the discovery follows that it is not taught. Virtue, therefore, is and is not teachable.

In this dilemma an appeal is made to Anytus, a respectable and well-to-do citizen of the old school, and a family friend of Meno, who happens to be present. He is asked 'whether Meno shall go to the Sophists and be taught.' The suggestion throws him into a rage. 'To whom, then, shall Meno go?' asks Socrates. To any Athenian gentleman—to the great Athenian statesmen of past times. Socrates replies here, as elsewhere (Laches, Prot.), that Themistocles, Pericles, and other great men, had sons to whom they would surely, if they could have done so, have imparted their own political wisdom; but no one ever heard that these sons of theirs were remarkable for anything except riding and wrestling and similar accomplishments. Anytus is angry at the imputation which is cast on his favorite statesmen, and on a class to which he supposes himself to belong; he breaks off with a significant hint. The mention of another opportunity of talking with him, and the suggestion that Meno may do the Athenian people a service by pacifying him, are evident allusions to the trial of Socrates.

Socrates returns to the consideration of the question 'whether virtue is teachable,' which was denied on the ground that there are no teachers of it: (for the Sophists are bad teachers, and the rest of the world do not profess to teach). But there is another point which we failed to observe, and in which Gorgias has never instructed Meno, nor Prodicus Socrates. This is the nature of right opinion. For virtue may be under the guidance of right opinion as well as of knowledge; and right opinion is for practical purposes as good as knowledge, but is incapable of being taught, and is also liable, like the images of Daedalus, to 'walk off,' because not bound by the tie of the cause. This is the sort of instinct which is possessed by statesmen, who are not wise or knowing persons, but only inspired or divine. The higher virtue, which is identical with knowledge, is an ideal only. If the statesman had this knowledge, and could teach what he knew, he would be like Tiresias in the world below,— 'he alone has wisdom, but the rest flit like shadows.'

This Dialogue is an attempt to answer the question, Can virtue be taught? No one would either ask or answer such a question in modern times. But in the age of Socrates it was only by an effort that the mind could rise to a general notion of virtue as distinct from the particular virtues of courage, liberality, and the like. And when a hazy conception of this ideal was attained, it was only by a further effort that the question of the teachableness of virtue could be resolved.

The answer which is given by Plato is paradoxical enough, and seems rather intended to stimulate than to satisfy enquiry. Virtue is knowledge, and therefore virtue can be taught. But virtue is not taught, and therefore in this higher and ideal sense there is no virtue and no knowledge. The teaching of the Sophists is confessedly inadequate, and Meno, who is their pupil, is ignorant of the very nature of general terms. He can only produce out of their armory the sophism, 'that you can neither enquire into what you know nor into what you do not know;' to which Socrates replies by his theory of reminiscence.

To the doctrine that virtue is knowledge, Plato has been constantly tending in the previous Dialogues. But the new truth is no sooner found than it vanishes away. 'If there is knowledge, there must be teachers; and where are the teachers?' There is no knowledge in the higher sense of systematic, connected, reasoned knowledge, such as may one day be attained, and such as Plato himself seems to see in some far off vision of a single science. And there are no teachers in the higher sense of the word; that is to say, no real teachers who will arouse the spirit of enquiry in their pupils, and not merely instruct them in rhetoric or impart to them ready-made information for a fee of 'one' or of 'fifty drachms.' Plato is desirous of deepening the notion of education, and therefore he asserts the paradox that there are no educators. This paradox, though different in form, is not really different from the remark which is often made in modern times by those who would depreciate either the methods of education commonly employed, or the standard attained—that 'there is no true education among us.'

There remains still a possibility which must not be overlooked. Even if there be no true knowledge, as is proved by 'the wretched state of education,' there may be right opinion, which is a sort of guessing or divination resting on no knowledge of causes, and incommunicable to others. This is the gift which our statesmen have, as is proved by the circumstance that they are unable to impart their knowledge to their sons. Those who are possessed of it cannot be said to be men of science or philosophers, but they are inspired and divine.

There may be some trace of irony in this curious passage, which forms the concluding portion of the Dialogue. But Plato certainly does not mean to intimate that the supernatural or divine is the true basis of human life. To him knowledge, if only attainable in this world, is of all things the most divine. Yet, like other philosophers, he is willing to admit that 'probability is the guide of life (Butler's Analogy.);' and he is at the same time desirous of contrasting the wisdom which governs the world with a higher wisdom. There are many instincts, judgments, and anticipations of the human mind which cannot be reduced to rule, and of which the grounds cannot always be given in words. A person may have some skill or latent experience which he is able to use himself and is yet unable to teach others, because he has no principles, and is incapable of collecting or arranging his ideas. He has practice, but not theory; art, but not science. This is a true fact of psychology, which is recognized by Plato in this passage. But he is far from saying, as some have imagined, that inspiration or divine grace is to be regarded as higher than knowledge. He would not have preferred the poet or man of action to the philosopher, or the virtue of custom to the virtue based upon ideas.

Also here, as in the Ion and Phaedrus, Plato appears to acknowledge an unreasoning element in the higher nature of man. The philosopher only has knowledge, and yet the statesman and the poet are inspired. There may be a sort of irony in regarding in this way the gifts of genius. But there is no reason to suppose that he is deriding them, any more than he is deriding the phenomena of love or of enthusiasm in the Symposium, or of oracles in the Apology, or of divine intimations when he is speaking of the daemonium of Socrates. He recognizes the lower form of right opinion, as well as the higher one of science, in the spirit of one who desires to include in his philosophy every aspect of human life; just as he recognizes the existence of popular opinion as a fact, and the Sophists as the expression of it.

This Dialogue contains the first intimation of the doctrine of reminiscence and of the immortality of the soul. The proof is very slight, even slighter than in the Phaedo and Republic. Because men had abstract ideas in a previous state, they must have always had them, and their souls therefore must have always existed. For they must always have been either men or not men. The fallacy of the latter words is transparent. And Socrates himself appears to be conscious of their weakness; for he adds immediately afterwards, 'I have said some things of which I am not altogether confident.' (Compare Phaedo.) It may be observed, however, that the fanciful notion of pre-existence is combined with a true but partial view of the origin and unity of knowledge, and of the association of ideas. Knowledge is prior to any particular knowledge, and exists not in the previous state of the individual, but of the race. It is potential, not actual, and can only be appropriated by strenuous exertion.

The idealism of Plato is here presented in a less developed form than in the Phaedo and Phaedrus. Nothing is said of the pre-existence of ideas of justice, temperance, and the like. Nor is Socrates positive of anything but the duty of enquiry. The doctrine of reminiscence too is explained more in accordance with fact and experience as arising out of the affinities of nature (ate tes thuseos oles suggenous ouses). Modern philosophy says that all things in nature are dependent on one another; the ancient philosopher had the same truth latent in his mind when he affirmed that out of one thing all the rest may be recovered. The subjective was converted by him into an objective; the mental phenomenon of the association of ideas (compare Phaedo) became a real chain of existences. The germs of two valuable principles of education may also be gathered from the 'words of priests and priestesses:' (1) that true knowledge is a knowledge of causes (compare Aristotle's theory of episteme); and (2) that the process of learning consists not in what is brought to the learner, but in what is drawn out of him.

Some lesser points of the dialogue may be noted, such as (1) the acute observation that Meno prefers the familiar definition, which is embellished with poetical language, to the better and truer one; or (2) the shrewd reflection, which may admit of an application to modern as well as to ancient teachers, that the Sophists having made large fortunes; this must surely be a criterion of their powers of teaching, for that no man could get a living by shoemaking who was not a good shoemaker; or (3) the remark conveyed, almost in a word, that the verbal skeptic is saved the labor of thought and enquiry (ouden dei to toiouto zeteseos). Characteristic also of the temper of the Socratic enquiry is, (4) the proposal to discuss the teachableness of virtue under an hypothesis, after the manner of the mathematicians; and (5) the repetition of the favorite doctrine which occurs so frequently in the earlier and more Socratic Dialogues, and gives a color to all of them—that mankind only desire evil through ignorance; (6) the experiment of eliciting from the slave-boy the mathematical truth which is latent in him, and (7) the remark that he is all the better for knowing his ignorance.

The character of Meno, like that of Critias, has no relation to the actual circumstances of his life. Plato is silent about his treachery to the ten thousand Greeks, which Xenophon has recorded, as he is also silent about the crimes of Critias. He is a Thessalian Alcibiades, rich and luxurious—a spoilt child of fortune, and is described as the hereditary friend of the great king. Like Alcibiades he is inspired with an ardent desire of knowledge, and is equally willing to learn of Socrates and of the Sophists. He may be regarded as standing in the same relation to Gorgias as Hippocrates in the Protagoras to the other great Sophist. He is the sophisticated youth on whom Socrates tries his cross-examining powers, just as in the Charmides, the Lysis, and the Euthydemus, ingenuous boyhood is made the subject of a similar experiment. He is treated by Socrates in a half-playful manner suited to his character; at the same time he appears not quite to understand the process to which he is being subjected. For he is exhibited as ignorant of the very elements of dialectics, in which the Sophists have failed to instruct their disciple. His definition of virtue as 'the power and desire of attaining things honorable,' like the first definition of justice in the Republic, is taken from a poet. His answers have a sophistical ring, and at the same time show the sophistical incapacity to grasp a general notion.

Anytus is the type of the narrow-minded man of the world, who is indignant at innovation, and equally detests the popular teacher and the true philosopher. He seems, like Aristophanes, to regard the new opinions, whether of Socrates or the Sophists, as fatal to Athenian greatness. He is of the same class as Callicles in the Gorgias, but of a different variety; the immoral and sophistical doctrines of Callicles are not attributed to him. The moderation with which he is described is remarkable, if he be the accuser of Socrates, as is apparently indicated by his parting words. Perhaps Plato may have been desirous of showing that the accusation of Socrates was not to be attributed to badness or malevolence, but rather to a tendency in men's minds. Or he may have been regardless of the historical truth of the characters of his dialogue, as in the case of Meno and Critias. Like Chaerephon (Apol.) the real Anytus was a democrat, and had joined Thrasybulus in the conflict with the thirty.

The Protagoras arrived at a sort of hypothetical conclusion, that if 'virtue is knowledge, it can be taught.' In the Euthydemus, Socrates himself offered an example of the manner in which the true teacher may draw out the mind of youth; this was in contrast to the quibbling follies of the Sophists. In the Meno the subject is more developed; the foundations of the enquiry are laid deeper, and the nature of knowledge is more distinctly explained. There is a progression by antagonism of two opposite aspects of philosophy. But at the moment when we approach nearest, the truth doubles upon us and passes out of our reach. We seem to find that the ideal of knowledge is irreconcilable with experience. In human life there is indeed the profession of knowledge, but right opinion is our actual guide. There is another sort of progress from the general notions of Socrates, who asked simply, 'what is friendship?' 'what is temperance?' 'what is courage?' as in the Lysis, Charmides, Laches, to the transcendentalism of Plato, who, in the second stage of his philosophy, sought to find the nature of knowledge in a prior and future state of existence.

The difficulty in framing general notions which has appeared in this and in all the previous Dialogues recurs in the Gorgias and Theaetetus as well as in the Republic. In the Gorgias too the statesmen reappear, but in stronger opposition to the philosopher. They are no longer allowed to have a divine insight, but, though acknowledged to have been clever men and good speakers, are denounced as 'blind leaders of the blind.' The doctrine of the immortality of the soul is also carried further, being made the foundation not only of a theory of knowledge, but of a doctrine of rewards and punishments. In the Republic the relation of knowledge to virtue is described in a manner more consistent with modern distinctions. The existence of the virtues without the possession of knowledge in the higher or philosophical sense is admitted to be possible. Right opinion is again introduced in the Theaetetus as an account of knowledge, but is rejected on the ground that it is irrational (as here, because it is not bound by the tie of the cause), and also because the conception of false opinion is given up as hopeless. The doctrines of Plato are necessarily different at different times of his life, as new distinctions are realized, or new stages of thought attained by him. We are not therefore justified, in order to take away the appearance of inconsistency, in attributing to him hidden meanings or remote allusions.

There are no external criteria by which we can determine the date of the Meno. There is no reason to suppose that any of the Dialogues of Plato were written before the death of Socrates; the Meno, which appears to be one of the earliest of them, is proved to have been of a later date by the allusion of Anytus.

We cannot argue that Plato was more likely to have written, as he has done, of Meno before than after his miserable death; for we have already seen, in the examples of Charmides and Critias, that the characters in Plato are very far from resembling the same characters in history. The repulsive picture which is given of him in the Anabasis of Xenophon, where he also appears as the friend of Aristippus 'and a fair youth having lovers,' has no other trait of likeness to the Meno of Plato.

The place of the Meno in the series is doubtfully indicated by internal evidence. The main character of the Dialogue is Socrates; but to the 'general definitions' of Socrates is added the Platonic doctrine of reminiscence. The problems of virtue and knowledge have been discussed in the Lysis, Laches, Charmides, and Protagoras; the puzzle about knowing and learning has already appeared in the Euthydemus. The doctrines of immortality and pre-existence are carried further in the Phaedrus and Phaedo; the distinction between opinion and knowledge is more fully developed in the Theaetetus. The lessons of Prodicus, whom he facetiously calls his master, are still running in the mind of Socrates. Unlike the later Platonic Dialogues, the Meno arrives at no conclusion. Hence we are led to place the Dialogue at some point of time later than the Protagoras, and earlier than the Phaedrus and Gorgias. The place which is assigned to it in this work is due mainly to the desire to bring together in a single volume all the Dialogues which contain allusions to the trial and death of Socrates.

* * * * *

On the Ideas of Plato

Plato's doctrine of ideas has attained an imaginary clearness and definiteness which is not to be found in his own writings. The popular account of them is partly derived from one or two passages in his Dialogues interpreted without regard to their poetical environment. It is due also to the misunderstanding of him by the Aristotelian school; and the erroneous notion has been further narrowed and has become fixed by the realism of the schoolmen. This popular view of the Platonic ideas may be summed up in some such formula as the following: 'Truth consists not in particulars, but in universals, which have a place in the mind of God, or in some far-off heaven. These were revealed to men in a former state of existence, and are recovered by reminiscence (anamnesis) or association from sensible things. The sensible things are not realities, but shadows only, in relation to the truth.' These unmeaning propositions are hardly suspected to be a caricature of a great theory of knowledge, which Plato in various ways and under many figures of speech is seeking to unfold. Poetry has been converted into dogma; and it is not remarked that the Platonic ideas are to be found only in about a third of Plato's writings and are not confined to him. The forms which they assume are numerous, and if taken literally, inconsistent with one another. At one time we are in the clouds of mythology, at another among the abstractions of mathematics or metaphysics; we pass imperceptibly from one to the other. Reason and fancy are mingled in the same passage. The ideas are sometimes described as many, coextensive with the universals of sense and also with the first principles of ethics; or again they are absorbed into the single idea of good, and subordinated to it. They are not more certain than facts, but they are equally certain (Phaedo). They are both personal and impersonal. They are abstract terms: they are also the causes of things; and they are even transformed into the demons or spirits by whose help God made the world. And the idea of good (Republic) may without violence be converted into the Supreme Being, who 'because He was good' created all things (Tim.).

It would be a mistake to try and reconcile these differing modes of thought. They are not to be regarded seriously as having a distinct meaning. They are parables, prophecies, myths, symbols, revelations, aspirations after an unknown world. They derive their origin from a deep religious and contemplative feeling, and also from an observation of curious mental phenomena. They gather up the elements of the previous philosophies, which they put together in a new form. Their great diversity shows the tentative character of early endeavors to think. They have not yet settled down into a single system. Plato uses them, though he also criticizes them; he acknowledges that both he and others are always talking about them, especially about the Idea of Good; and that they are not peculiar to himself (Phaedo; Republic; Soph.). But in his later writings he seems to have laid aside the old forms of them. As he proceeds he makes for himself new modes of expression more akin to the Aristotelian logic.

Yet amid all these varieties and incongruities, there is a common meaning or spirit which pervades his writings, both those in which he treats of the ideas and those in which he is silent about them. This is the spirit of idealism, which in the history of philosophy has had many names and taken many forms, and has in a measure influenced those who seemed to be most averse to it. It has often been charged with inconsistency and fancifulness, and yet has had an elevating effect on human nature, and has exercised a wonderful charm and interest over a few spirits who have been lost in the thought of it. It has been banished again and again, but has always returned. It has attempted to leave the earth and soar heavenwards, but soon has found that only in experience could any solid foundation of knowledge be laid. It has degenerated into pantheism, but has again emerged. No other knowledge has given an equal stimulus to the mind. It is the science of sciences, which are also ideas, and under either aspect require to be defined. They can only be thought of in due proportion when conceived in relation to one another. They are the glasses through which the kingdoms of science are seen, but at a distance. All the greatest minds, except when living in an age of reaction against them, have unconsciously fallen under their power.

The account of the Platonic ideas in the Meno is the simplest and clearest, and we shall best illustrate their nature by giving this first and then comparing the manner in which they are described elsewhere, e.g. in the Phaedrus, Phaedo, Republic; to which may be added the criticism of them in the Parmenides, the personal form which is attributed to them in the Timaeus, the logical character which they assume in the Sophist and Philebus, and the allusion to them in the Laws. In the Cratylus they dawn upon him with the freshness of a newly-discovered thought.

The Meno goes back to a former state of existence, in which men did and suffered good and evil, and received the reward or punishment of them until their sin was purged away and they were allowed to return to earth. This is a tradition of the olden time, to which priests and poets bear witness. The souls of men returning to earth bring back a latent memory of ideas, which were known to them in a former state. The recollection is awakened into life and consciousness by the sight of the things which resemble them on earth. The soul evidently possesses such innate ideas before she has had time to acquire them. This is proved by an experiment tried on one of Meno's slaves, from whom Socrates elicits truths of arithmetic and geometry, which he had never learned in this world. He must therefore have brought them with him from another.

The notion of a previous state of existence is found in the verses of Empedocles and in the fragments of Heracleitus. It was the natural answer to two questions, 'Whence came the soul? What is the origin of evil?' and prevailed far and wide in the east. It found its way into Hellas probably through the medium of Orphic and Pythagorean rites and mysteries. It was easier to think of a former than of a future life, because such a life has really existed for the race though not for the individual, and all men come into the world, if not 'trailing clouds of glory,' at any rate able to enter into the inheritance of the past. In the Phaedrus, as well as in the Meno, it is this former rather than a future life on which Plato is disposed to dwell. There the Gods, and men following in their train, go forth to contemplate the heavens, and are borne round in the revolutions of them. There they see the divine forms of justice, temperance, and the like, in their unchangeable beauty, but not without an effort more than human. The soul of man is likened to a charioteer and two steeds, one mortal, the other immortal. The charioteer and the mortal steed are in fierce conflict; at length the animal principle is finally overpowered, though not extinguished, by the combined energies of the passionate and rational elements. This is one of those passages in Plato which, partaking both of a philosophical and poetical character, is necessarily indistinct and inconsistent. The magnificent figure under which the nature of the soul is described has not much to do with the popular doctrine of the ideas. Yet there is one little trait in the description which shows that they are present to Plato's mind, namely, the remark that the soul, which had seen truths in the form of the universal, cannot again return to the nature of an animal.

In the Phaedo, as in the Meno, the origin of ideas is sought for in a previous state of existence. There was no time when they could have been acquired in this life, and therefore they must have been recovered from another. The process of recovery is no other than the ordinary law of association, by which in daily life the sight of one thing or person recalls another to our minds, and by which in scientific enquiry from any part of knowledge we may be led on to infer the whole. It is also argued that ideas, or rather ideals, must be derived from a previous state of existence because they are more perfect than the sensible forms of them which are given by experience. But in the Phaedo the doctrine of ideas is subordinate to the proof of the immortality of the soul. 'If the soul existed in a previous state, then it will exist in a future state, for a law of alternation pervades all things.' And, 'If the ideas exist, then the soul exists; if not, not.' It is to be observed, both in the Meno and the Phaedo, that Socrates expresses himself with diffidence. He speaks in the Phaedo of the words with which he has comforted himself and his friends, and will not be too confident that the description which he has given of the soul and her mansions is exactly true, but he 'ventures to think that something of the kind is true.' And in the Meno, after dwelling upon the immortality of the soul, he adds, 'Of some things which I have said I am not altogether confident' (compare Apology; Gorgias). From this class of uncertainties he exempts the difference between truth and appearance, of which he is absolutely convinced.

In the Republic the ideas are spoken of in two ways, which though not contradictory are different. In the tenth book they are represented as the genera or general ideas under which individuals having a common name are contained. For example, there is the bed which the carpenter makes, the picture of the bed which is drawn by the painter, the bed existing in nature of which God is the author. Of the latter all visible beds are only the shadows or reflections. This and similar illustrations or explanations are put forth, not for their own sake, or as an exposition of Plato's theory of ideas, but with a view of showing that poetry and the mimetic arts are concerned with an inferior part of the soul and a lower kind of knowledge. On the other hand, in the 6th and 7th books of the Republic we reach the highest and most perfect conception, which Plato is able to attain, of the nature of knowledge. The ideas are now finally seen to be one as well as many, causes as well as ideas, and to have a unity which is the idea of good and the cause of all the rest. They seem, however, to have lost their first aspect of universals under which individuals are contained, and to have been converted into forms of another kind, which are inconsistently regarded from the one side as images or ideals of justice, temperance, holiness and the like; from the other as hypotheses, or mathematical truths or principles.

In the Timaeus, which in the series of Plato's works immediately follows the Republic, though probably written some time afterwards, no mention occurs of the doctrine of ideas. Geometrical forms and arithmetical ratios furnish the laws according to which the world is created. But though the conception of the ideas as genera or species is forgotten or laid aside, the distinction of the visible and intellectual is as firmly maintained as ever. The IDEA of good likewise disappears and is superseded by the conception of a personal God, who works according to a final cause or principle of goodness which he himself is. No doubt is expressed by Plato, either in the Timaeus or in any other dialogue, of the truths which he conceives to be the first and highest. It is not the existence of God or the idea of good which he approaches in a tentative or hesitating manner, but the investigations of physiology. These he regards, not seriously, as a part of philosophy, but as an innocent recreation (Tim.).

Passing on to the Parmenides, we find in that dialogue not an exposition or defense of the doctrine of ideas, but an assault upon them, which is put into the mouth of the veteran Parmenides, and might be ascribed to Aristotle himself, or to one of his disciples. The doctrine which is assailed takes two or three forms, but fails in any of them to escape the dialectical difficulties which are urged against it. It is admitted that there are ideas of all things, but the manner in which individuals partake of them, whether of the whole or of the part, and in which they become like them, or how ideas can be either within or without the sphere of human knowledge, or how the human and divine can have any relation to each other, is held to be incapable of explanation. And yet, if there are no universal ideas, what becomes of philosophy? (Parmenides.) In the Sophist the theory of ideas is spoken of as a doctrine held not by Plato, but by another sect of philosophers, called 'the Friends of Ideas,' probably the Megarians, who were very distinct from him, if not opposed to him (Sophist). Nor in what may be termed Plato's abridgement of the history of philosophy (Soph.), is any mention made such as we find in the first book of Aristotle's Metaphysics, of the derivation of such a theory or of any part of it from the Pythagoreans, the Eleatics, the Heracleiteans, or even from Socrates. In the Philebus, probably one of the latest of the Platonic Dialogues, the conception of a personal or semi-personal deity expressed under the figure of mind, the king of all, who is also the cause, is retained. The one and many of the Phaedrus and Theaetetus is still working in the mind of Plato, and the correlation of ideas, not of 'all with all,' but of 'some with some,' is asserted and explained. But they are spoken of in a different manner, and are not supposed to be recovered from a former state of existence. The metaphysical conception of truth passes into a psychological one, which is continued in the Laws, and is the final form of the Platonic philosophy, so far as can be gathered from his own writings (see especially Laws). In the Laws he harps once more on the old string, and returns to general notions:—these he acknowledges to be many, and yet he insists that they are also one. The guardian must be made to recognize the truth, for which he has contended long ago in the Protagoras, that the virtues are four, but they are also in some sense one (Laws; compare Protagoras).

So various, and if regarded on the surface only, inconsistent, are the statements of Plato respecting the doctrine of ideas. If we attempted to harmonize or to combine them, we should make out of them, not a system, but the caricature of a system. They are the ever-varying expression of Plato's Idealism. The terms used in them are in their substance and general meaning the same, although they seem to be different. They pass from the subject to the object, from earth (diesseits) to heaven (jenseits) without regard to the gulf which later theology and philosophy have made between them. They are also intended to supplement or explain each other. They relate to a subject of which Plato himself would have said that 'he was not confident of the precise form of his own statements, but was strong in the belief that something of the kind was true.' It is the spirit, not the letter, in which they agree—the spirit which places the divine above the human, the spiritual above the material, the one above the many, the mind before the body.

The stream of ancient philosophy in the Alexandrian and Roman times widens into a lake or sea, and then disappears underground to reappear after many ages in a distant land. It begins to flow again under new conditions, at first confined between high and narrow banks, but finally spreading over the continent of Europe. It is and is not the same with ancient philosophy. There is a great deal in modern philosophy which is inspired by ancient.

There is much in ancient philosophy which was 'born out of due time; and before men were capable of understanding it. To the fathers of modern philosophy, their own thoughts appeared to be new and original, but they carried with them an echo or shadow of the past, coming back by recollection from an elder world. Of this the enquirers of the seventeenth century, who to themselves appeared to be working out independently the enquiry into all truth, were unconscious. They stood in a new relation to theology and natural philosophy, and for a time maintained towards both an attitude of reserve and separation. Yet the similarities between modern and ancient thought are greater far than the differences. All philosophy, even that part of it which is said to be based upon experience, is really ideal; and ideas are not only derived from facts, but they are also prior to them and extend far beyond them, just as the mind is prior to the senses.

Early Greek speculation culminates in the ideas of Plato, or rather in the single idea of good. His followers, and perhaps he himself, having arrived at this elevation, instead of going forwards went backwards from philosophy to psychology, from ideas to numbers. But what we perceive to be the real meaning of them, an explanation of the nature and origin of knowledge, will always continue to be one of the first problems of philosophy.

Plato also left behind him a most potent instrument, the forms of logic—arms ready for use, but not yet taken out of their armory. They were the late birth of the early Greek philosophy, and were the only part of it which has had an uninterrupted hold on the mind of Europe. Philosophies come and go; but the detection of fallacies, the framing of definitions, the invention of methods still continue to be the main elements of the reasoning process.

Modern philosophy, like ancient, begins with very simple conceptions. It is almost wholly a reflection on self. It might be described as a quickening into life of old words and notions latent in the semi-barbarous Latin, and putting a new meaning into them. Unlike ancient philosophy, it has been unaffected by impressions derived from outward nature: it arose within the limits of the mind itself. From the time of Descartes to Hume and Kant it has had little or nothing to do with facts of science. On the other hand, the ancient and mediaeval logic retained a continuous influence over it, and a form like that of mathematics was easily impressed upon it; the principle of ancient philosophy which is most apparent in it is skepticism; we must doubt nearly every traditional or received notion, that we may hold fast one or two. The being of God in a personal or impersonal form was a mental necessity to the first thinkers of modern times: from this alone all other ideas could be deduced. There had been an obscure presentiment of 'cognito, ergo sum' more than 2000 years previously. The Eleatic notion that being and thought were the same was revived in a new form by Descartes. But now it gave birth to consciousness and self-reflection: it awakened the 'ego' in human nature. The mind naked and abstract has no other certainty but the conviction of its own existence. 'I think, therefore I am;' and this thought is God thinking in me, who has also communicated to the reason of man his own attributes of thought and extension—these are truly imparted to him because God is true (compare Republic). It has been often remarked that Descartes, having begun by dismissing all presuppositions, introduces several: he passes almost at once from skepticism to dogmatism. It is more important for the illustration of Plato to observe that he, like Plato, insists that God is true and incapable of deception (Republic)—that he proceeds from general ideas, that many elements of mathematics may be found in him. A certain influence of mathematics both on the form and substance of their philosophy is discernible in both of them. After making the greatest opposition between thought and extension, Descartes, like Plato, supposes them to be reunited for a time, not in their own nature but by a special divine act (compare Phaedrus), and he also supposes all the parts of the human body to meet in the pineal gland, that alone affording a principle of unity in the material frame of man. It is characteristic of the first period of modern philosophy, that having begun (like the Presocratics) with a few general notions, Descartes first falls absolutely under their influence, and then quickly discards them. At the same time he is less able to observe facts, because they are too much magnified by the glasses through which they are seen. The common logic says 'the greater the extension, the less the comprehension,' and we may put the same thought in another way and say of abstract or general ideas, that the greater the abstraction of them, the less are they capable of being applied to particular and concrete natures.

Not very different from Descartes in his relation to ancient philosophy is his successor Spinoza, who lived in the following generation. The system of Spinoza is less personal and also less dualistic than that of Descartes. In this respect the difference between them is like that between Xenophanes and Parmenides. The teaching of Spinoza might be described generally as the Jewish religion reduced to an abstraction and taking the form of the Eleatic philosophy. Like Parmenides, he is overpowered and intoxicated with the idea of Being or God. The greatness of both philosophies consists in the immensity of a thought which excludes all other thoughts; their weakness is the necessary separation of this thought from actual existence and from practical life. In neither of them is there any clear opposition between the inward and outward world. The substance of Spinoza has two attributes, which alone are cognizable by man, thought and extension; these are in extreme opposition to one another, and also in inseparable identity. They may be regarded as the two aspects or expressions under which God or substance is unfolded to man. Here a step is made beyond the limits of the Eleatic philosophy. The famous theorem of Spinoza, 'Omnis determinatio est negatio,' is already contained in the 'negation is relation' of Plato's Sophist. The grand description of the philosopher in Republic VI, as the spectator of all time and all existence, may be paralleled with another famous expression of Spinoza, 'Contemplatio rerum sub specie eternitatis.' According to Spinoza finite objects are unreal, for they are conditioned by what is alien to them, and by one another. Human beings are included in the number of them. Hence there is no reality in human action and no place for right and wrong. Individuality is accident. The boasted freedom of the will is only a consciousness of necessity. Truth, he says, is the direction of the reason towards the infinite, in which all things repose; and herein lies the secret of man's well-being. In the exaltation of the reason or intellect, in the denial of the voluntariness of evil (Timaeus; Laws) Spinoza approaches nearer to Plato than in his conception of an infinite substance. As Socrates said that virtue is knowledge, so Spinoza would have maintained that knowledge alone is good, and what contributes to knowledge useful. Both are equally far from any real experience or observation of nature. And the same difficulty is found in both when we seek to apply their ideas to life and practice. There is a gulf fixed between the infinite substance and finite objects or individuals of Spinoza, just as there is between the ideas of Plato and the world of sense.

Removed from Spinoza by less than a generation is the philosopher Leibnitz, who after deepening and intensifying the opposition between mind and matter, reunites them by his preconcerted harmony (compare again Phaedrus). To him all the particles of matter are living beings which reflect on one another, and in the least of them the whole is contained. Here we catch a reminiscence both of the omoiomere, or similar particles of Anaxagoras, and of the world-animal of the Timaeus.

In Bacon and Locke we have another development in which the mind of man is supposed to receive knowledge by a new method and to work by observation and experience. But we may remark that it is the idea of experience, rather than experience itself, with which the mind is filled. It is a symbol of knowledge rather than the reality which is vouchsafed to us. The Organon of Bacon is not much nearer to actual facts than the Organon of Aristotle or the Platonic idea of good. Many of the old rags and ribbons which defaced the garment of philosophy have been stripped off, but some of them still adhere. A crude conception of the ideas of Plato survives in the 'forms' of Bacon. And on the other hand, there are many passages of Plato in which the importance of the investigation of facts is as much insisted upon as by Bacon. Both are almost equally superior to the illusions of language, and are constantly crying out against them, as against other idols.

Locke cannot be truly regarded as the author of sensationalism any more than of idealism. His system is based upon experience, but with him experience includes reflection as well as sense. His analysis and construction of ideas has no foundation in fact; it is only the dialectic of the mind 'talking to herself.' The philosophy of Berkeley is but the transposition of two words. For objects of sense he would substitute sensations. He imagines himself to have changed the relation of the human mind towards God and nature; they remain the same as before, though he has drawn the imaginary line by which they are divided at a different point. He has annihilated the outward world, but it instantly reappears governed by the same laws and described under the same names.

A like remark applies to David Hume, of whose philosophy the central principle is the denial of the relation of cause and effect. He would deprive men of a familiar term which they can ill afford to lose; but he seems not to have observed that this alteration is merely verbal and does not in any degree affect the nature of things. Still less did he remark that he was arguing from the necessary imperfection of language against the most certain facts. And here, again, we may find a parallel with the ancients. He goes beyond facts in his skepticism, as they did in their idealism. Like the ancient Sophists, he relegates the more important principles of ethics to custom and probability. But crude and unmeaning as this philosophy is, it exercised a great influence on his successors, not unlike that which Locke exercised upon Berkeley and Berkeley upon Hume himself. All three were both skeptical and ideal in almost equal degrees. Neither they nor their predecessors had any true conception of language or of the history of philosophy. Hume's paradox has been forgotten by the world, and did not any more than the skepticism of the ancients require to be seriously refuted. Like some other philosophical paradoxes, it would have been better left to die out. It certainly could not be refuted by a philosophy such as Kant's, in which, no less than in the previously mentioned systems, the history of the human mind and the nature of language are almost wholly ignored, and the certainty of objective knowledge is transferred to the subject; while absolute truth is reduced to a figment, more abstract and narrow than Plato's ideas, of 'thing in itself,' to which, if we reason strictly, no predicate can be applied.

The question which Plato has raised respecting the origin and nature of ideas belongs to the infancy of philosophy; in modern times it would no longer be asked. Their origin is only their history, so far as we know it; there can be no other. We may trace them in language, in philosophy, in mythology, in poetry, but we cannot argue a priori about them. We may attempt to shake them off, but they are always returning, and in every sphere of science and human action are tending to go beyond facts. They are thought to be innate, because they have been familiar to us all our lives, and we can no longer dismiss them from our mind. Many of them express relations of terms to which nothing exactly or nothing at all in rerum natura corresponds. We are not such free agents in the use of them as we sometimes imagine. Fixed ideas have taken the most complete possession of some thinkers who have been most determined to renounce them, and have been vehemently affirmed when they could be least explained and were incapable of proof. The world has often been led away by a word to which no distinct meaning could be attached. Abstractions such as 'authority,' 'equality,' 'utility,' 'liberty,' 'pleasure,' 'experience,' 'consciousness,' 'chance,' 'substance,' 'matter,' 'atom,' and a heap of other metaphysical and theological terms, are the source of quite as much error and illusion and have as little relation to actual facts as the ideas of Plato. Few students of theology or philosophy have sufficiently reflected how quickly the bloom of a philosophy passes away; or how hard it is for one age to understand the writings of another; or how nice a judgment is required of those who are seeking to express the philosophy of one age in the terms of another. The 'eternal truths' of which metaphysicians speak have hardly ever lasted more than a generation. In our own day schools or systems of philosophy which have once been famous have died before the founders of them. We are still, as in Plato's age, groping about for a new method more comprehensive than any of those which now prevail; and also more permanent. And we seem to see at a distance the promise of such a method, which can hardly be any other than the method of idealized experience, having roots which strike far down into the history of philosophy. It is a method which does not divorce the present from the past, or the part from the whole, or the abstract from the concrete, or theory from fact, or the divine from the human, or one science from another, but labors to connect them. Along such a road we have proceeded a few steps, sufficient, perhaps, to make us reflect on the want of method which prevails in our own day. In another age, all the branches of knowledge, whether relating to God or man or nature, will become the knowledge of 'the revelation of a single science' (Symp.), and all things, like the stars in heaven, will shed their light upon one another.

Meno

PERSONS OF THE DIALOGUE: Meno, Socrates, A Slave of Meno (Boy), Anytus.

MENO: Can you tell me, Socrates, whether virtue is acquired by teaching or by practice; or if neither by teaching nor by practice, then whether it comes to man by nature, or in what other way?

SOCRATES: O Meno, there was a time when the Thessalians were famous among the other Hellenes only for their riches and their riding; but now, if I am not mistaken, they are equally famous for their wisdom, especially at Larisa, which is the native city of your friend Aristippus. And this is Gorgias' doing; for when he came there, the flower of the Aleuadae, among them your admirer Aristippus, and the other chiefs of the Thessalians, fell in love with his wisdom. And he has taught you the habit of answering questions in a grand and bold style, which becomes those who know, and is the style in which he himself answers all comers; and any Hellene who likes may ask him anything. How different is our lot! my dear Meno. Here at Athens there is a dearth of the commodity, and all wisdom seems to have emigrated from us to you. I am certain that if you were to ask any Athenian whether virtue was natural or acquired, he would laugh in your face, and say: 'Stranger, you have far too good an opinion of me, if you think that I can answer your question. For I literally do not know what virtue is, and much less whether it is acquired by teaching or not.' And I myself, Meno, living as I do in this region of poverty, am as poor as the rest of the world; and I confess with shame that I know literally nothing about virtue; and when I do not know the 'quid' of anything how can I know the 'quale'? How, if I knew nothing at all of Meno, could I tell if he was fair, or the opposite of fair; rich and noble, or the reverse of rich and noble? Do you think that I could?

MENO: No, indeed. But are you in earnest, Socrates, in saying that you do not know what virtue is? And am I to carry back this report of you to Thessaly?

SOCRATES: Not only that, my dear boy, but you may say further that I have never known of any one else who did, in my judgment.

MENO: Then you have never met Gorgias when he was at Athens?

SOCRATES: Yes, I have.

MENO: And did you not think that he knew?

SOCRATES: I have not a good memory, Meno, and therefore I cannot now tell what I thought of him at the time. And I dare say that he did know, and that you know what he said: please, therefore, to remind me of what he said; or, if you would rather, tell me your own view; for I suspect that you and he think much alike.

MENO: Very true.

SOCRATES: Then as he is not here, never mind him, and do you tell me: By the gods, Meno, be generous, and tell me what you say that virtue is; for I shall be truly delighted to find that I have been mistaken, and that you and Gorgias do really have this knowledge; although I have been just saying that I have never found anybody who had.

MENO: There will be no difficulty, Socrates, in answering your question. Let us take first the virtue of a man—he should know how to administer the state, and in the administration of it to benefit his friends and harm his enemies; and he must also be careful not to suffer harm himself. A woman's virtue, if you wish to know about that, may also be easily described: her duty is to order her house, and keep what is indoors, and obey her husband. Every age, every condition of life, young or old, male or female, bond or free, has a different virtue: there are virtues numberless, and no lack of definitions of them; for virtue is relative to the actions and ages of each of us in all that we do. And the same may be said of vice, Socrates (Compare Arist. Pol.).

SOCRATES: How fortunate I am, Meno! When I ask you for one virtue, you present me with a swarm of them (Compare Theaet.), which are in your keeping. Suppose that I carry on the figure of the swarm, and ask of you, What is the nature of the bee? and you answer that there are many kinds of bees, and I reply: But do bees differ as bees, because there are many and different kinds of them; or are they not rather to be distinguished by some other quality, as for example beauty, size, or shape? How would you answer me?

MENO: I should answer that bees do not differ from one another, as bees.

SOCRATES: And if I went on to say: That is what I desire to know, Meno; tell me what is the quality in which they do not differ, but are all alike;—would you be able to answer?

MENO: I should.

SOCRATES: And so of the virtues, however many and different they may be, they have all a common nature which makes them virtues; and on this he who would answer the question, 'What is virtue?' would do well to have his eye fixed: Do you understand?

MENO: I am beginning to understand; but I do not as yet take hold of the question as I could wish.

SOCRATES: When you say, Meno, that there is one virtue of a man, another of a woman, another of a child, and so on, does this apply only to virtue, or would you say the same of health, and size, and strength? Or is the nature of health always the same, whether in man or woman?

MENO: I should say that health is the same, both in man and woman.

SOCRATES: And is not this true of size and strength? If a woman is strong, she will be strong by reason of the same form and of the same strength subsisting in her which there is in the man. I mean to say that strength, as strength, whether of man or woman, is the same. Is there any difference?

MENO: I think not.

SOCRATES: And will not virtue, as virtue, be the same, whether in a child or in a grown-up person, in a woman or in a man?

MENO: I cannot help feeling, Socrates, that this case is different from the others.

SOCRATES: But why? Were you not saying that the virtue of a man was to order a state, and the virtue of a woman was to order a house?

MENO: I did say so.

SOCRATES: And can either house or state or anything be well ordered without temperance and without justice?

MENO: Certainly not.

SOCRATES: Then they who order a state or a house temperately or justly order them with temperance and justice?

MENO: Certainly.

SOCRATES: Then both men and women, if they are to be good men and women, must have the same virtues of temperance and justice?

MENO: True.

SOCRATES: And can either a young man or an elder one be good, if they are intemperate and unjust?

MENO: They cannot.

SOCRATES: They must be temperate and just?

MENO: Yes.

SOCRATES: Then all men are good in the same way, and by participation in the same virtues?

MENO: Such is the inference.

SOCRATES: And they surely would not have been good in the same way, unless their virtue had been the same?

MENO: They would not.

SOCRATES: Then now that the sameness of all virtue has been proven, try and remember what you and Gorgias say that virtue is.

MENO: Will you have one definition of them all?

SOCRATES: That is what I am seeking.

MENO: If you want to have one definition of them all, I know not what to say, but that virtue is the power of governing mankind.

SOCRATES: And does this definition of virtue include all virtue? Is virtue the same in a child and in a slave, Meno? Can the child govern his father, or the slave his master; and would he who governed be any longer a slave?

MENO: I think not, Socrates.

SOCRATES: No, indeed; there would be small reason in that. Yet once more, fair friend; according to you, virtue is 'the power of governing;' but do you not add 'justly and not unjustly'?

MENO: Yes, Socrates; I agree there; for justice is virtue.

SOCRATES: Would you say 'virtue,' Meno, or 'a virtue'?

MENO: What do you mean?

SOCRATES: I mean as I might say about anything; that a round, for example, is 'a figure' and not simply 'figure,' and I should adopt this mode of speaking, because there are other figures.

MENO: Quite right; and that is just what I am saying about virtue—that there are other virtues as well as justice.

SOCRATES: What are they? tell me the names of them, as I would tell you the names of the other figures if you asked me.

MENO: Courage and temperance and wisdom and magnanimity are virtues; and there are many others.

SOCRATES: Yes, Meno; and again we are in the same case: in searching after one virtue we have found many, though not in the same way as before; but we have been unable to find the common virtue which runs through them all.

MENO: Why, Socrates, even now I am not able to follow you in the attempt to get at one common notion of virtue as of other things.

SOCRATES: No wonder; but I will try to get nearer if I can, for you know that all things have a common notion. Suppose now that some one asked you the question which I asked before: Meno, he would say, what is figure? And if you answered 'roundness,' he would reply to you, in my way of speaking, by asking whether you would say that roundness is 'figure' or 'a figure;' and you would answer 'a figure.'

MENO: Certainly.

SOCRATES: And for this reason—that there are other figures?

MENO: Yes.

SOCRATES: And if he proceeded to ask, What other figures are there? you would have told him.

MENO: I should.

SOCRATES: And if he similarly asked what color is, and you answered whiteness, and the questioner rejoined, Would you say that whiteness is color or a color? you would reply, A color, because there are other colors as well.

MENO: I should.

SOCRATES: And if he had said, Tell me what they are?—you would have told him of other colors which are colors just as much as whiteness.

MENO: Yes.

SOCRATES: And suppose that he were to pursue the matter in my way, he would say: Ever and anon we are landed in particulars, but this is not what I want; tell me then, since you call them by a common name, and say that they are all figures, even when opposed to one another, what is that common nature which you designate as figure—which contains straight as well as round, and is no more one than the other—that would be your mode of speaking?

MENO: Yes.

SOCRATES: And in speaking thus, you do not mean to say that the round is round any more than straight, or the straight any more straight than round?

MENO: Certainly not.

SOCRATES: You only assert that the round figure is not more a figure than the straight, or the straight than the round?

MENO: Very true.

SOCRATES: To what then do we give the name of figure? Try and answer. Suppose that when a person asked you this question either about figure or color, you were to reply, Man, I do not understand what you want, or know what you are saying; he would look rather astonished and say: Do you not understand that I am looking for the 'simile in multis'? And then he might put the question in another form: Meno, he might say, what is that 'simile in multis' which you call figure, and which includes not only round and straight figures, but all? Could you not answer that question, Meno? I wish that you would try; the attempt will be good practice with a view to the answer about virtue.

MENO: I would rather that you should answer, Socrates.

SOCRATES: Shall I indulge you?

MENO: By all means.

SOCRATES: And then you will tell me about virtue?

MENO: I will.

SOCRATES: Then I must do my best, for there is a prize to be won.

MENO: Certainly.

SOCRATES: Well, I will try and explain to you what figure is. What do you say to this answer?—Figure is the only thing which always follows color. Will you be satisfied with it, as I am sure that I should be, if you would let me have a similar definition of virtue?

MENO: But, Socrates, it is such a simple answer.

SOCRATES: Why simple?

MENO: Because, according to you, figure is that which always follows color.

(SOCRATES: Granted.)

MENO: But if a person were to say that he does not know what color is, any more than what figure is—what sort of answer would you have given him?

SOCRATES: I should have told him the truth. And if he were a philosopher of the eristic and antagonistic sort, I should say to him: You have my answer, and if I am wrong, your business is to take up the argument and refute me. But if we were friends, and were talking as you and I are now, I should reply in a milder strain and more in the dialectician's vein; that is to say, I should not only speak the truth, but I should make use of premises which the person interrogated would be willing to admit. And this is the way in which I shall endeavor to approach you. You will acknowledge, will you not, that there is such a thing as an end, or termination, or extremity?—all which words I use in the same sense, although I am aware that Prodicus might draw distinctions about them: but still you, I am sure, would speak of a thing as ended or terminated—that is all which I am saying—not anything very difficult.

MENO: Yes, I should; and I believe that I understand your meaning.

SOCRATES: And you would speak of a surface and also of a solid, as for example in geometry.

MENO: Yes.

SOCRATES: Well then, you are now in a condition to understand my definition of figure. I define figure to be that in which the solid ends; or, more concisely, the limit of solid.

MENO: And now, Socrates, what is color?

SOCRATES: You are outrageous, Meno, in thus plaguing a poor old man to give you an answer, when you will not take the trouble of remembering what is Gorgias' definition of virtue.

MENO: When you have told me what I ask, I will tell you, Socrates.

SOCRATES: A man who was blindfolded has only to hear you talking, and he would know that you are a fair creature and have still many lovers.

MENO: Why do you think so?

SOCRATES: Why, because you always speak in imperatives: like all beauties when they are in their prime, you are tyrannical; and also, as I suspect, you have found out that I have weakness for the fair, and therefore to humour you I must answer.

MENO: Please do.

SOCRATES: Would you like me to answer you after the manner of Gorgias, which is familiar to you?

MENO: I should like nothing better.

SOCRATES: Do not he and you and Empedocles say that there are certain effluences of existence?

MENO: Certainly.

SOCRATES: And passages into which and through which the effluences pass?

MENO: Exactly.

SOCRATES: And some of the effluences fit into the passages, and some of them are too small or too large?

MENO: True.

SOCRATES: And there is such a thing as sight?

MENO: Yes.

SOCRATES: And now, as Pindar says, 'read my meaning:'—color is an effluence of form, commensurate with sight, and palpable to sense.

MENO: That, Socrates, appears to me to be an admirable answer.

SOCRATES: Why, yes, because it happens to be one which you have been in the habit of hearing: and your wit will have discovered, I suspect, that you may explain in the same way the nature of sound and smell, and of many other similar phenomena.

MENO: Quite true.

SOCRATES: The answer, Meno, was in the orthodox solemn vein, and therefore was more acceptable to you than the other answer about figure.

MENO: Yes.

SOCRATES: And yet, O son of Alexidemus, I cannot help thinking that the other was the better; and I am sure that you would be of the same opinion, if you would only stay and be initiated, and were not compelled, as you said yesterday, to go away before the mysteries.

MENO: But I will stay, Socrates, if you will give me many such answers.

SOCRATES: Well then, for my own sake as well as for yours, I will do my very best; but I am afraid that I shall not be able to give you very many as good: and now, in your turn, you are to fulfill your promise, and tell me what virtue is in the universal; and do not make a singular into a plural, as the facetious say of those who break a thing, but deliver virtue to me whole and sound, and not broken into a number of pieces: I have given you the pattern.

MENO: Well then, Socrates, virtue, as I take it, is when he, who desires the honorable, is able to provide it for himself; so the poet says, and I say too—

'Virtue is the desire of things honorable and the power of attaining them.'

SOCRATES: And does he who desires the honorable also desire the good?

MENO: Certainly.

SOCRATES: Then are there some who desire the evil and others who desire the good? Do not all men, my dear sir, desire good?

MENO: I think not.

SOCRATES: There are some who desire evil?

MENO: Yes.

SOCRATES: Do you mean that they think the evils which they desire, to be good; or do they know that they are evil and yet desire them?

MENO: Both, I think.

SOCRATES: And do you really imagine, Meno, that a man knows evils to be evils and desires them notwithstanding?

MENO: Certainly I do.

SOCRATES: And desire is of possession?

MENO: Yes, of possession.

SOCRATES: And does he think that the evils will do good to him who possesses them, or does he know that they will do him harm?

MENO: There are some who think that the evils will do them good, and others who know that they will do them harm.

SOCRATES: And, in your opinion, do those who think that they will do them good know that they are evils?

MENO: Certainly not.

SOCRATES: Is it not obvious that those who are ignorant of their nature do not desire them; but they desire what they suppose to be goods although they are really evils; and if they are mistaken and suppose the evils to be goods they really desire goods?

MENO: Yes, in that case.

SOCRATES: Well, and do those who, as you say, desire evils, and think that evils are hurtful to the possessor of them, know that they will be hurt by them?

MENO: They must know it.

SOCRATES: And must they not suppose that those who are hurt are miserable in proportion to the hurt which is inflicted upon them?

MENO: How can it be otherwise?

SOCRATES: But are not the miserable ill-fated?

MENO: Yes, indeed.

SOCRATES: And does any one desire to be miserable and ill-fated?

MENO: I should say not, Socrates.

SOCRATES: But if there is no one who desires to be miserable, there is no one, Meno, who desires evil; for what is misery but the desire and possession of evil?

MENO: That appears to be the truth, Socrates, and I admit that nobody desires evil.

SOCRATES: And yet, were you not saying just now that virtue is the desire and power of attaining good?

MENO: Yes, I did say so.

SOCRATES: But if this be affirmed, then the desire of good is common to all, and one man is no better than another in that respect?

MENO: True.

SOCRATES: And if one man is not better than another in desiring good, he must be better in the power of attaining it?

MENO: Exactly.

SOCRATES: Then, according to your definition, virtue would appear to be the power of attaining good?

MENO: I entirely approve, Socrates, of the manner in which you now view this matter.

SOCRATES: Then let us see whether what you say is true from another point of view; for very likely you may be right:—You affirm virtue to be the power of attaining goods?

MENO: Yes.

SOCRATES: And the goods which you mean are such as health and wealth and the possession of gold and silver, and having office and honor in the state—those are what you would call goods?

MENO: Yes, I should include all those.

SOCRATES: Then, according to Meno, who is the hereditary friend of the great king, virtue is the power of getting silver and gold; and would you add that they must be gained piously, justly, or do you deem this to be of no consequence? And is any mode of acquisition, even if unjust and dishonest, equally to be deemed virtue?

MENO: Not virtue, Socrates, but vice.

SOCRATES: Then justice or temperance or holiness, or some other part of virtue, as would appear, must accompany the acquisition, and without them the mere acquisition of good will not be virtue.

MENO: Why, how can there be virtue without these?

SOCRATES: And the non-acquisition of gold and silver in a dishonest manner for oneself or another, or in other words the want of them, may be equally virtue?

MENO: True.

SOCRATES: Then the acquisition of such goods is no more virtue than the non-acquisition and want of them, but whatever is accompanied by justice or honesty is virtue, and whatever is devoid of justice is vice.

MENO: It cannot be otherwise, in my judgment.

SOCRATES: And were we not saying just now that justice, temperance, and the like, were each of them a part of virtue?

MENO: Yes.

SOCRATES: And so, Meno, this is the way in which you mock me.

MENO: Why do you say that, Socrates?

SOCRATES: Why, because I asked you to deliver virtue into my hands whole and unbroken, and I gave you a pattern according to which you were to frame your answer; and you have forgotten already, and tell me that virtue is the power of attaining good justly, or with justice; and justice you acknowledge to be a part of virtue.

MENO: Yes.

SOCRATES: Then it follows from your own admissions, that virtue is doing what you do with a part of virtue; for justice and the like are said by you to be parts of virtue.

MENO: What of that?

SOCRATES: What of that! Why, did not I ask you to tell me the nature of virtue as a whole? And you are very far from telling me this; but declare every action to be virtue which is done with a part of virtue; as though you had told me and I must already know the whole of virtue, and this too when frittered away into little pieces. And, therefore, my dear Meno, I fear that I must begin again and repeat the same question: What is virtue? for otherwise, I can only say, that every action done with a part of virtue is virtue; what else is the meaning of saying that every action done with justice is virtue? Ought I not to ask the question over again; for can any one who does not know virtue know a part of virtue?

MENO: No; I do not say that he can.

SOCRATES: Do you remember how, in the example of figure, we rejected any answer given in terms which were as yet unexplained or unadmitted?

MENO: Yes, Socrates; and we were quite right in doing so.

SOCRATES: But then, my friend, do not suppose that we can explain to any one the nature of virtue as a whole through some unexplained portion of virtue, or anything at all in that fashion; we should only have to ask over again the old question, What is virtue? Am I not right?

MENO: I believe that you are.

SOCRATES: Then begin again, and answer me, What, according to you and your friend Gorgias, is the definition of virtue?

MENO: O Socrates, I used to be told, before I knew you, that you were always doubting yourself and making others doubt; and now you are casting your spells over me, and I am simply getting bewitched and enchanted, and am at my wits' end. And if I may venture to make a jest upon you, you seem to me both in your appearance and in your power over others to be very like the flat torpedo fish, who torpifies those who come near him and touch him, as you have now torpified me, I think. For my soul and my tongue are really torpid, and I do not know how to answer you; and though I have been delivered of an infinite variety of speeches about virtue before now, and to many persons—and very good ones they were, as I thought—at this moment I cannot even say what virtue is. And I think that you are very wise in not voyaging and going away from home, for if you did in other places as you do in Athens, you would be cast into prison as a magician.

SOCRATES: You are a rogue, Meno, and had all but caught me.

MENO: What do you mean, Socrates?

SOCRATES: I can tell why you made a simile about me.

MENO: Why?

SOCRATES: In order that I might make another simile about you. For I know that all pretty young gentlemen like to have pretty similes made about them—as well they may—but I shall not return the compliment. As to my being a torpedo, if the torpedo is torpid as well as the cause of torpidity in others, then indeed I am a torpedo, but not otherwise; for I perplex others, not because I am clear, but because I am utterly perplexed myself. And now I know not what virtue is, and you seem to be in the same case, although you did once perhaps know before you touched me. However, I have no objection to join with you in the enquiry.

MENO: And how will you enquire, Socrates, into that which you do not know? What will you put forth as the subject of enquiry? And if you find what you want, how will you ever know that this is the thing which you did not know?

SOCRATES: I know, Meno, what you mean; but just see what a tiresome dispute you are introducing. You argue that a man cannot enquire either about that which he knows, or about that which he does not know; for if he knows, he has no need to enquire; and if not, he cannot; for he does not know the very subject about which he is to enquire (Compare Aristot. Post. Anal.).

MENO: Well, Socrates, and is not the argument sound?

SOCRATES: I think not.

MENO: Why not?

SOCRATES: I will tell you why: I have heard from certain wise men and women who spoke of things divine that—

MENO: What did they say?

SOCRATES: They spoke of a glorious truth, as I conceive.

MENO: What was it? and who were they?

SOCRATES: Some of them were priests and priestesses, who had studied how they might be able to give a reason of their profession: there have been poets also, who spoke of these things by inspiration, like Pindar, and many others who were inspired. And they say—mark, now, and see whether their words are true—they say that the soul of man is immortal, and at one time has an end, which is termed dying, and at another time is born again, but is never destroyed. And the moral is, that a man ought to live always in perfect holiness. 'For in the ninth year Persephone sends the souls of those from whom she has received the penalty of ancient crime back again from beneath into the light of the sun above, and these are they who become noble kings and mighty men and great in wisdom and are called saintly heroes in after ages.' The soul, then, as being immortal, and having been born again many times, and having seen all things that exist, whether in this world or in the world below, has knowledge of them all; and it is no wonder that she should be able to call to remembrance all that she ever knew about virtue, and about everything; for as all nature is akin, and the soul has learned all things; there is no difficulty in her eliciting or as men say learning, out of a single recollection all the rest, if a man is strenuous and does not faint; for all enquiry and all learning is but recollection. And therefore we ought not to listen to this sophistical argument about the impossibility of enquiry: for it will make us idle; and is sweet only to the sluggard; but the other saying will make us active and inquisitive. In that confiding, I will gladly enquire with you into the nature of virtue.

MENO: Yes, Socrates; but what do you mean by saying that we do not learn, and that what we call learning is only a process of recollection? Can you teach me how this is?

SOCRATES: I told you, Meno, just now that you were a rogue, and now you ask whether I can teach you, when I am saying that there is no teaching, but only recollection; and thus you imagine that you will involve me in a contradiction.

MENO: Indeed, Socrates, I protest that I had no such intention. I only asked the question from habit; but if you can prove to me that what you say is true, I wish that you would.

SOCRATES: It will be no easy matter, but I will try to please you to the utmost of my power. Suppose that you call one of your numerous attendants, that I may demonstrate on him.

MENO: Certainly. Come hither, boy.

SOCRATES: He is Greek, and speaks Greek, does he not?

MENO: Yes, indeed; he was born in the house.

SOCRATES: Attend now to the questions which I ask him, and observe whether he learns of me or only remembers.

MENO: I will.

SOCRATES: Tell me, boy, do you know that a figure like this is a square?

BOY: I do.

SOCRATES: And you know that a square figure has these four lines equal?

BOY: Certainly.

SOCRATES: And these lines which I have drawn through the middle of the square are also equal?

BOY: Yes.

SOCRATES: A square may be of any size?

BOY: Certainly.

SOCRATES: And if one side of the figure be of two feet, and the other side be of two feet, how much will the whole be? Let me explain: if in one direction the space was of two feet, and in the other direction of one foot, the whole would be of two feet taken once?

BOY: Yes.

SOCRATES: But since this side is also of two feet, there are twice two feet?

BOY: There are.

SOCRATES: Then the square is of twice two feet?

BOY: Yes.

SOCRATES: And how many are twice two feet? count and tell me.

BOY: Four, Socrates.

SOCRATES: And might there not be another square twice as large as this, and having like this the lines equal?

BOY: Yes.

SOCRATES: And of how many feet will that be?

BOY: Of eight feet.

SOCRATES: And now try and tell me the length of the line which forms the side of that double square: this is two feet—what will that be?

BOY: Clearly, Socrates, it will be double.

SOCRATES: Do you observe, Meno, that I am not teaching the boy anything, but only asking him questions; and now he fancies that he knows how long a line is necessary in order to produce a figure of eight square feet; does he not?

MENO: Yes.

SOCRATES: And does he really know?

MENO: Certainly not.

SOCRATES: He only guesses that because the square is double, the line is double.

MENO: True.

SOCRATES: Observe him while he recalls the steps in regular order. (To the Boy:) Tell me, boy, do you assert that a double space comes from a double line? Remember that I am not speaking of an oblong, but of a figure equal every way, and twice the size of this—that is to say of eight feet; and I want to know whether you still say that a double square comes from double line?

BOY: Yes.

SOCRATES: But does not this line become doubled if we add another such line here?

BOY: Certainly.

SOCRATES: And four such lines will make a space containing eight feet?

BOY: Yes.

SOCRATES: Let us describe such a figure: Would you not say that this is the figure of eight feet?

BOY: Yes.

SOCRATES: And are there not these four divisions in the figure, each of which is equal to the figure of four feet?

BOY: True.

SOCRATES: And is not that four times four?

BOY: Certainly.

SOCRATES: And four times is not double?

BOY: No, indeed.

SOCRATES: But how much?

BOY: Four times as much.

SOCRATES: Therefore the double line, boy, has given a space, not twice, but four times as much.

BOY: True.

SOCRATES: Four times four are sixteen—are they not?

BOY: Yes.

SOCRATES: What line would give you a space of eight feet, as this gives one of sixteen feet;—do you see?

BOY: Yes.

SOCRATES: And the space of four feet is made from this half line?

BOY: Yes.

SOCRATES: Good; and is not a space of eight feet twice the size of this, and half the size of the other?

BOY: Certainly.

SOCRATES: Such a space, then, will be made out of a line greater than this one, and less than that one?

BOY: Yes; I think so.

SOCRATES: Very good; I like to hear you say what you think. And now tell me, is not this a line of two feet and that of four?

BOY: Yes.

SOCRATES: Then the line which forms the side of eight feet ought to be more than this line of two feet, and less than the other of four feet?

BOY: It ought.

SOCRATES: Try and see if you can tell me how much it will be.

BOY: Three feet.

SOCRATES: Then if we add a half to this line of two, that will be the line of three. Here are two and there is one; and on the other side, here are two also and there is one: and that makes the figure of which you speak?

BOY: Yes.

SOCRATES: But if there are three feet this way and three feet that way, the whole space will be three times three feet?

BOY: That is evident.

SOCRATES: And how much are three times three feet?

BOY: Nine.

SOCRATES: And how much is the double of four?

BOY: Eight.

SOCRATES: Then the figure of eight is not made out of a line of three?

BOY: No.

SOCRATES: But from what line?—tell me exactly; and if you would rather not reckon, try and show me the line.

BOY: Indeed, Socrates, I do not know.

SOCRATES: Do you see, Meno, what advances he has made in his power of recollection? He did not know at first, and he does not know now, what is the side of a figure of eight feet: but then he thought that he knew, and answered confidently as if he knew, and had no difficulty; now he has a difficulty, and neither knows nor fancies that he knows.

MENO: True.

SOCRATES: Is he not better off in knowing his ignorance?

MENO: I think that he is.

SOCRATES: If we have made him doubt, and given him the 'torpedo's shock,' have we done him any harm?

MENO: I think not.

SOCRATES: We have certainly, as would seem, assisted him in some degree to the discovery of the truth; and now he will wish to remedy his ignorance, but then he would have been ready to tell all the world again and again that the double space should have a double side.

MENO: True.

SOCRATES: But do you suppose that he would ever have enquired into or learned what he fancied that he knew, though he was really ignorant of it, until he had fallen into perplexity under the idea that he did not know, and had desired to know?

MENO: I think not, Socrates.

SOCRATES: Then he was the better for the torpedo's touch?

MENO: I think so.

SOCRATES: Mark now the farther development. I shall only ask him, and not teach him, and he shall share the enquiry with me: and do you watch and see if you find me telling or explaining anything to him, instead of eliciting his opinion. Tell me, boy, is not this a square of four feet which I have drawn?

BOY: Yes.

SOCRATES: And now I add another square equal to the former one?

BOY: Yes.

SOCRATES: And a third, which is equal to either of them?

BOY: Yes.

SOCRATES: Suppose that we fill up the vacant corner?

BOY: Very good.

SOCRATES: Here, then, there are four equal spaces?

BOY: Yes.

SOCRATES: And how many times larger is this space than this other?

BOY: Four times.

SOCRATES: But it ought to have been twice only, as you will remember.

BOY: True.

SOCRATES: And does not this line, reaching from corner to corner, bisect each of these spaces?

BOY: Yes.

SOCRATES: And are there not here four equal lines which contain this space?

BOY: There are.

SOCRATES: Look and see how much this space is.

BOY: I do not understand.

SOCRATES: Has not each interior line cut off half of the four spaces?

BOY: Yes.

SOCRATES: And how many spaces are there in this section?

BOY: Four.

SOCRATES: And how many in this?

BOY: Two.

SOCRATES: And four is how many times two?

BOY: Twice.

SOCRATES: And this space is of how many feet?

BOY: Of eight feet.

SOCRATES: And from what line do you get this figure?

BOY: From this.

SOCRATES: That is, from the line which extends from corner to corner of the figure of four feet?

BOY: Yes.

SOCRATES: And that is the line which the learned call the diagonal. And if this is the proper name, then you, Meno's slave, are prepared to affirm that the double space is the square of the diagonal?

BOY: Certainly, Socrates.

SOCRATES: What do you say of him, Meno? Were not all these answers given out of his own head?

MENO: Yes, they were all his own.

SOCRATES: And yet, as we were just now saying, he did not know?

MENO: True.

SOCRATES: But still he had in him those notions of his—had he not?

MENO: Yes.

SOCRATES: Then he who does not know may still have true notions of that which he does not know?

MENO: He has.

SOCRATES: And at present these notions have just been stirred up in him, as in a dream; but if he were frequently asked the same questions, in different forms, he would know as well as any one at last?

MENO: I dare say.

SOCRATES: Without any one teaching him he will recover his knowledge for himself, if he is only asked questions?

MENO: Yes.

SOCRATES: And this spontaneous recovery of knowledge in him is recollection?

MENO: True.

SOCRATES: And this knowledge which he now has must he not either have acquired or always possessed?

MENO: Yes.

SOCRATES: But if he always possessed this knowledge he would always have known; or if he has acquired the knowledge he could not have acquired it in this life, unless he has been taught geometry; for he may be made to do the same with all geometry and every other branch of knowledge. Now, has any one ever taught him all this? You must know about him, if, as you say, he was born and bred in your house.

MENO: And I am certain that no one ever did teach him.

SOCRATES: And yet he has the knowledge?

MENO: The fact, Socrates, is undeniable.

SOCRATES: But if he did not acquire the knowledge in this life, then he must have had and learned it at some other time?

MENO: Clearly he must.

SOCRATES: Which must have been the time when he was not a man?

MENO: Yes.

SOCRATES: And if there have been always true thoughts in him, both at the time when he was and was not a man, which only need to be awakened into knowledge by putting questions to him, his soul must have always possessed this knowledge, for he always either was or was not a man?

MENO: Obviously.

SOCRATES: And if the truth of all things always existed in the soul, then the soul is immortal. Wherefore be of good cheer, and try to recollect what you do not know, or rather what you do not remember.

MENO: I feel, somehow, that I like what you are saying.

SOCRATES: And I, Meno, like what I am saying. Some things I have said of which I am not altogether confident. But that we shall be better and braver and less helpless if we think that we ought to enquire, than we should have been if we indulged in the idle fancy that there was no knowing and no use in seeking to know what we do not know;—that is a theme upon which I am ready to fight, in word and deed, to the utmost of my power.

MENO: There again, Socrates, your words seem to me excellent.

SOCRATES: Then, as we are agreed that a man should enquire about that which he does not know, shall you and I make an effort to enquire together into the nature of virtue?

MENO: By all means, Socrates. And yet I would much rather return to my original question, Whether in seeking to acquire virtue we should regard it as a thing to be taught, or as a gift of nature, or as coming to men in some other way?

SOCRATES: Had I the command of you as well as of myself, Meno, I would not have enquired whether virtue is given by instruction or not, until we had first ascertained 'what it is.' But as you think only of controlling me who am your slave, and never of controlling yourself,—such being your notion of freedom, I must yield to you, for you are irresistible. And therefore I have now to enquire into the qualities of a thing of which I do not as yet know the nature. At any rate, will you condescend a little, and allow the question 'Whether virtue is given by instruction, or in any other way,' to be argued upon hypothesis? As the geometrician, when he is asked whether a certain triangle is capable being inscribed in a certain circle (Or, whether a certain area is capable of being inscribed as a triangle in a certain circle.), will reply: 'I cannot tell you as yet; but I will offer a hypothesis which may assist us in forming a conclusion: If the figure be such that when you have produced a given side of it (Or, when you apply it to the given line, i.e. the diameter of the circle (autou).), the given area of the triangle falls short by an area corresponding to the part produced (Or, similar to the area so applied.), then one consequence follows, and if this is impossible then some other; and therefore I wish to assume a hypothesis before I tell you whether this triangle is capable of being inscribed in the circle':—that is a geometrical hypothesis. And we too, as we know not the nature and qualities of virtue, must ask, whether virtue is or is not taught, under a hypothesis: as thus, if virtue is of such a class of mental goods, will it be taught or not? Let the first hypothesis be that virtue is or is not knowledge,—in that case will it be taught or not? or, as we were just now saying, 'remembered'? For there is no use in disputing about the name. But is virtue taught or not? or rather, does not every one see that knowledge alone is taught?

MENO: I agree.

SOCRATES: Then if virtue is knowledge, virtue will be taught?

MENO: Certainly.

SOCRATES: Then now we have made a quick end of this question: if virtue is of such a nature, it will be taught; and if not, not?

MENO: Certainly.

SOCRATES: The next question is, whether virtue is knowledge or of another species?

MENO: Yes, that appears to be the question which comes next in order.

SOCRATES: Do we not say that virtue is a good?—This is a hypothesis which is not set aside.

MENO: Certainly.

SOCRATES: Now, if there be any sort of good which is distinct from knowledge, virtue may be that good; but if knowledge embraces all good, then we shall be right in thinking that virtue is knowledge?

MENO: True.

SOCRATES: And virtue makes us good?

MENO: Yes.

SOCRATES: And if we are good, then we are profitable; for all good things are profitable?

MENO: Yes.

SOCRATES: Then virtue is profitable?

MENO: That is the only inference.

SOCRATES: Then now let us see what are the things which severally profit us. Health and strength, and beauty and wealth—these, and the like of these, we call profitable?

MENO: True.

SOCRATES: And yet these things may also sometimes do us harm: would you not think so?

MENO: Yes.

SOCRATES: And what is the guiding principle which makes them profitable or the reverse? Are they not profitable when they are rightly used, and hurtful when they are not rightly used?

MENO: Certainly.

SOCRATES: Next, let us consider the goods of the soul: they are temperance, justice, courage, quickness of apprehension, memory, magnanimity, and the like?

MENO: Surely.

SOCRATES: And such of these as are not knowledge, but of another sort, are sometimes profitable and sometimes hurtful; as, for example, courage wanting prudence, which is only a sort of confidence? When a man has no sense he is harmed by courage, but when he has sense he is profited?

MENO: True.

SOCRATES: And the same may be said of temperance and quickness of apprehension; whatever things are learned or done with sense are profitable, but when done without sense they are hurtful?

MENO: Very true.

SOCRATES: And in general, all that the soul attempts or endures, when under the guidance of wisdom, ends in happiness; but when she is under the guidance of folly, in the opposite?

MENO: That appears to be true.

SOCRATES: If then virtue is a quality of the soul, and is admitted to be profitable, it must be wisdom or prudence, since none of the things of the soul are either profitable or hurtful in themselves, but they are all made profitable or hurtful by the addition of wisdom or of folly; and therefore if virtue is profitable, virtue must be a sort of wisdom or prudence?

MENO: I quite agree.

SOCRATES: And the other goods, such as wealth and the like, of which we were just now saying that they are sometimes good and sometimes evil, do not they also become profitable or hurtful, accordingly as the soul guides and uses them rightly or wrongly; just as the things of the soul herself are benefited when under the guidance of wisdom and harmed by folly?

MENO: True.

SOCRATES: And the wise soul guides them rightly, and the foolish soul wrongly.

MENO: Yes.

SOCRATES: And is not this universally true of human nature? All other things hang upon the soul, and the things of the soul herself hang upon wisdom, if they are to be good; and so wisdom is inferred to be that which profits—and virtue, as we say, is profitable?

MENO: Certainly.

SOCRATES: And thus we arrive at the conclusion that virtue is either wholly or partly wisdom?

MENO: I think that what you are saying, Socrates, is very true.

SOCRATES: But if this is true, then the good are not by nature good?

MENO: I think not.

SOCRATES: If they had been, there would assuredly have been discerners of characters among us who would have known our future great men; and on their showing we should have adopted them, and when we had got them, we should have kept them in the citadel out of the way of harm, and set a stamp upon them far rather than upon a piece of gold, in order that no one might tamper with them; and when they grew up they would have been useful to the state?

MENO: Yes, Socrates, that would have been the right way.

SOCRATES: But if the good are not by nature good, are they made good by instruction?

MENO: There appears to be no other alternative, Socrates. On the supposition that virtue is knowledge, there can be no doubt that virtue is taught.

SOCRATES: Yes, indeed; but what if the supposition is erroneous?

MENO: I certainly thought just now that we were right.

SOCRATES: Yes, Meno; but a principle which has any soundness should stand firm not only just now, but always.

MENO: Well; and why are you so slow of heart to believe that knowledge is virtue?

SOCRATES: I will try and tell you why, Meno. I do not retract the assertion that if virtue is knowledge it may be taught; but I fear that I have some reason in doubting whether virtue is knowledge: for consider now and say whether virtue, and not only virtue but anything that is taught, must not have teachers and disciples?

MENO: Surely.

SOCRATES: And conversely, may not the art of which neither teachers nor disciples exist be assumed to be incapable of being taught?

MENO: True; but do you think that there are no teachers of virtue?

SOCRATES: I have certainly often enquired whether there were any, and taken great pains to find them, and have never succeeded; and many have assisted me in the search, and they were the persons whom I thought the most likely to know. Here at the moment when he is wanted we fortunately have sitting by us Anytus, the very person of whom we should make enquiry; to him then let us repair. In the first place, he is the son of a wealthy and wise father, Anthemion, who acquired his wealth, not by accident or gift, like Ismenias the Theban (who has recently made himself as rich as Polycrates), but by his own skill and industry, and who is a well-conditioned, modest man, not insolent, or overbearing, or annoying; moreover, this son of his has received a good education, as the Athenian people certainly appear to think, for they choose him to fill the highest offices. And these are the sort of men from whom you are likely to learn whether there are any teachers of virtue, and who they are. Please, Anytus, to help me and your friend Meno in answering our question, Who are the teachers? Consider the matter thus: If we wanted Meno to be a good physician, to whom should we send him? Should we not send him to the physicians?

ANYTUS: Certainly.

SOCRATES: Or if we wanted him to be a good cobbler, should we not send him to the cobblers?

ANYTUS: Yes.

SOCRATES: And so forth?

ANYTUS: Yes.

SOCRATES: Let me trouble you with one more question. When we say that we should be right in sending him to the physicians if we wanted him to be a physician, do we mean that we should be right in sending him to those who profess the art, rather than to those who do not, and to those who demand payment for teaching the art, and profess to teach it to any one who will come and learn? And if these were our reasons, should we not be right in sending him?

ANYTUS: Yes.

SOCRATES: And might not the same be said of flute-playing, and of the other arts? Would a man who wanted to make another a flute-player refuse to send him to those who profess to teach the art for money, and be plaguing other persons to give him instruction, who are not professed teachers and who never had a single disciple in that branch of knowledge which he wishes him to acquire—would not such conduct be the height of folly?

ANYTUS: Yes, by Zeus, and of ignorance too.

SOCRATES: Very good. And now you are in a position to advise with me about my friend Meno. He has been telling me, Anytus, that he desires to attain that kind of wisdom and virtue by which men order the state or the house, and honor their parents, and know when to receive and when to send away citizens and strangers, as a good man should. Now, to whom should he go in order that he may learn this virtue? Does not the previous argument imply clearly that we should send him to those who profess and avouch that they are the common teachers of all Hellas, and are ready to impart instruction to any one who likes, at a fixed price?

ANYTUS: Whom do you mean, Socrates?

SOCRATES: You surely know, do you not, Anytus, that these are the people whom mankind call Sophists?

ANYTUS: By Heracles, Socrates, forbear! I only hope that no friend or kinsman or acquaintance of mine, whether citizen or stranger, will ever be so mad as to allow himself to be corrupted by them; for they are a manifest pest and corrupting influence to those who have to do with them.

SOCRATES: What, Anytus? Of all the people who profess that they know how to do men good, do you mean to say that these are the only ones who not only do them no good, but positively corrupt those who are entrusted to them, and in return for this disservice have the face to demand money? Indeed, I cannot believe you; for I know of a single man, Protagoras, who made more out of his craft than the illustrious Pheidias, who created such noble works, or any ten other statuaries. How could that be? A mender of old shoes, or patcher up of clothes, who made the shoes or clothes worse than he received them, could not have remained thirty days undetected, and would very soon have starved; whereas during more than forty years, Protagoras was corrupting all Hellas, and sending his disciples from him worse than he received them, and he was never found out. For, if I am not mistaken, he was about seventy years old at his death, forty of which were spent in the practice of his profession; and during all that time he had a good reputation, which to this day he retains: and not only Protagoras, but many others are well spoken of; some who lived before him, and others who are still living. Now, when you say that they deceived and corrupted the youth, are they to be supposed to have corrupted them consciously or unconsciously? Can those who were deemed by many to be the wisest men of Hellas have been out of their minds?

ANYTUS: Out of their minds! No, Socrates; the young men who gave their money to them were out of their minds, and their relations and guardians who entrusted their youth to the care of these men were still more out of their minds, and most of all, the cities who allowed them to come in, and did not drive them out, citizen and stranger alike.

SOCRATES: Has any of the Sophists wronged you, Anytus? What makes you so angry with them?

ANYTUS: No, indeed, neither I nor any of my belongings has ever had, nor would I suffer them to have, anything to do with them.

SOCRATES: Then you are entirely unacquainted with them?

ANYTUS: And I have no wish to be acquainted.

SOCRATES: Then, my dear friend, how can you know whether a thing is good or bad of which you are wholly ignorant?

ANYTUS: Quite well; I am sure that I know what manner of men these are, whether I am acquainted with them or not.

SOCRATES: You must be a diviner, Anytus, for I really cannot make out, judging from your own words, how, if you are not acquainted with them, you know about them. But I am not enquiring of you who are the teachers who will corrupt Meno (let them be, if you please, the Sophists); I only ask you to tell him who there is in this great city who will teach him how to become eminent in the virtues which I was just now describing. He is the friend of your family, and you will oblige him.

ANYTUS: Why do you not tell him yourself?

SOCRATES: I have told him whom I supposed to be the teachers of these things; but I learn from you that I am utterly at fault, and I dare say that you are right. And now I wish that you, on your part, would tell me to whom among the Athenians he should go. Whom would you name?

ANYTUS: Why single out individuals? Any Athenian gentleman, taken at random, if he will mind him, will do far more good to him than the Sophists.

SOCRATES: And did those gentlemen grow of themselves; and without having been taught by any one, were they nevertheless able to teach others that which they had never learned themselves?

ANYTUS: I imagine that they learned of the previous generation of gentlemen. Have there not been many good men in this city?

SOCRATES: Yes, certainly, Anytus; and many good statesmen also there always have been and there are still, in the city of Athens. But the question is whether they were also good teachers of their own virtue;—not whether there are, or have been, good men in this part of the world, but whether virtue can be taught, is the question which we have been discussing. Now, do we mean to say that the good men of our own and of other times knew how to impart to others that virtue which they had themselves; or is virtue a thing incapable of being communicated or imparted by one man to another? That is the question which I and Meno have been arguing. Look at the matter in your own way: Would you not admit that Themistocles was a good man?

ANYTUS: Certainly; no man better.

SOCRATES: And must not he then have been a good teacher, if any man ever was a good teacher, of his own virtue?

ANYTUS: Yes certainly,—if he wanted to be so.

SOCRATES: But would he not have wanted? He would, at any rate, have desired to make his own son a good man and a gentleman; he could not have been jealous of him, or have intentionally abstained from imparting to him his own virtue. Did you never hear that he made his son Cleophantus a famous horseman; and had him taught to stand upright on horseback and hurl a javelin, and to do many other marvellous things; and in anything which could be learned from a master he was well trained? Have you not heard from our elders of him?

ANYTUS: I have.

SOCRATES: Then no one could say that his son showed any want of capacity?

ANYTUS: Very likely not.

SOCRATES: But did any one, old or young, ever say in your hearing that Cleophantus, son of Themistocles, was a wise or good man, as his father was?

ANYTUS: I have certainly never heard any one say so.

SOCRATES: And if virtue could have been taught, would his father Themistocles have sought to train him in these minor accomplishments, and allowed him who, as you must remember, was his own son, to be no better than his neighbors in those qualities in which he himself excelled?

ANYTUS: Indeed, indeed, I think not.

SOCRATES: Here was a teacher of virtue whom you admit to be among the best men of the past. Let us take another,—Aristides, the son of Lysimachus: would you not acknowledge that he was a good man?

ANYTUS: To be sure I should.

SOCRATES: And did not he train his son Lysimachus better than any other Athenian in all that could be done for him by the help of masters? But what has been the result? Is he a bit better than any other mortal? He is an acquaintance of yours, and you see what he is like. There is Pericles, again, magnificent in his wisdom; and he, as you are aware, had two sons, Paralus and Xanthippus.

ANYTUS: I know.

SOCRATES: And you know, also, that he taught them to be unrivalled horsemen, and had them trained in music and gymnastics and all sorts of arts—in these respects they were on a level with the best—and had he no wish to make good men of them? Nay, he must have wished it. But virtue, as I suspect, could not be taught. And that you may not suppose the incompetent teachers to be only the meaner sort of Athenians and few in number, remember again that Thucydides had two sons, Melesias and Stephanus, whom, besides giving them a good education in other things, he trained in wrestling, and they were the best wrestlers in Athens: one of them he committed to the care of Xanthias, and the other of Eudorus, who had the reputation of being the most celebrated wrestlers of that day. Do you remember them?

ANYTUS: I have heard of them.

SOCRATES: Now, can there be a doubt that Thucydides, whose children were taught things for which he had to spend money, would have taught them to be good men, which would have cost him nothing, if virtue could have been taught? Will you reply that he was a mean man, and had not many friends among the Athenians and allies? Nay, but he was of a great family, and a man of influence at Athens and in all Hellas, and, if virtue could have been taught, he would have found out some Athenian or foreigner who would have made good men of his sons, if he could not himself spare the time from cares of state. Once more, I suspect, friend Anytus, that virtue is not a thing which can be taught?

ANYTUS: Socrates, I think that you are too ready to speak evil of men: and, if you will take my advice, I would recommend you to be careful. Perhaps there is no city in which it is not easier to do men harm than to do them good, and this is certainly the case at Athens, as I believe that you know.

SOCRATES: O Meno, think that Anytus is in a rage. And he may well be in a rage, for he thinks, in the first place, that I am defaming these gentlemen; and in the second place, he is of opinion that he is one of them himself. But some day he will know what is the meaning of defamation, and if he ever does, he will forgive me. Meanwhile I will return to you, Meno; for I suppose that there are gentlemen in your region too?

MENO: Certainly there are.

SOCRATES: And are they willing to teach the young? and do they profess to be teachers? and do they agree that virtue is taught?

MENO: No indeed, Socrates, they are anything but agreed; you may hear them saying at one time that virtue can be taught, and then again the reverse.

SOCRATES: Can we call those teachers who do not acknowledge the possibility of their own vocation?

MENO: I think not, Socrates.

SOCRATES: And what do you think of these Sophists, who are the only professors? Do they seem to you to be teachers of virtue?

MENO: I often wonder, Socrates, that Gorgias is never heard promising to teach virtue: and when he hears others promising he only laughs at them; but he thinks that men should be taught to speak.

SOCRATES: Then do you not think that the Sophists are teachers?

MENO: I cannot tell you, Socrates; like the rest of the world, I am in doubt, and sometimes I think that they are teachers and sometimes not.

SOCRATES: And are you aware that not you only and other politicians have doubts whether virtue can be taught or not, but that Theognis the poet says the very same thing?

MENO: Where does he say so?

SOCRATES: In these elegiac verses (Theog.):

'Eat and drink and sit with the mighty, and make yourself agreeable to them; for from the good you will learn what is good, but if you mix with the bad you will lose the intelligence which you already have.'

Do you observe that here he seems to imply that virtue can be taught?

MENO: Clearly.

SOCRATES: But in some other verses he shifts about and says (Theog.):

'If understanding could be created and put into a man, then they' (who were able to perform this feat) 'would have obtained great rewards.'

And again:—

'Never would a bad son have sprung from a good sire, for he would have heard the voice of instruction; but not by teaching will you ever make a bad man into a good one.'

And this, as you may remark, is a contradiction of the other.

MENO: Clearly.

SOCRATES: And is there anything else of which the professors are affirmed not only not to be teachers of others, but to be ignorant themselves, and bad at the knowledge of that which they are professing to teach? or is there anything about which even the acknowledged 'gentlemen' are sometimes saying that 'this thing can be taught,' and sometimes the opposite? Can you say that they are teachers in any true sense whose ideas are in such confusion?

MENO: I should say, certainly not.

SOCRATES: But if neither the Sophists nor the gentlemen are teachers, clearly there can be no other teachers?

MENO: No.

SOCRATES: And if there are no teachers, neither are there disciples?

MENO: Agreed.

SOCRATES: And we have admitted that a thing cannot be taught of which there are neither teachers nor disciples?

MENO: We have.

SOCRATES: And there are no teachers of virtue to be found anywhere?

MENO: There are not.

SOCRATES: And if there are no teachers, neither are there scholars?

MENO: That, I think, is true.

SOCRATES: Then virtue cannot be taught?

MENO: Not if we are right in our view. But I cannot believe, Socrates, that there are no good men: And if there are, how did they come into existence?

SOCRATES: I am afraid, Meno, that you and I are not good for much, and that Gorgias has been as poor an educator of you as Prodicus has been of me. Certainly we shall have to look to ourselves, and try to find some one who will help in some way or other to improve us. This I say, because I observe that in the previous discussion none of us remarked that right and good action is possible to man under other guidance than that of knowledge (episteme);—and indeed if this be denied, there is no seeing how there can be any good men at all.

MENO: How do you mean, Socrates?

SOCRATES: I mean that good men are necessarily useful or profitable. Were we not right in admitting this? It must be so.

MENO: Yes.

SOCRATES: And in supposing that they will be useful only if they are true guides to us of action—there we were also right?

MENO: Yes.

SOCRATES: But when we said that a man cannot be a good guide unless he have knowledge (phrhonesis), this we were wrong.

MENO: What do you mean by the word 'right'?

SOCRATES: I will explain. If a man knew the way to Larisa, or anywhere else, and went to the place and led others thither, would he not be a right and good guide?

MENO: Certainly.

SOCRATES: And a person who had a right opinion about the way, but had never been and did not know, might be a good guide also, might he not?

MENO: Certainly.

SOCRATES: And while he has true opinion about that which the other knows, he will be just as good a guide if he thinks the truth, as he who knows the truth?

MENO: Exactly.

SOCRATES: Then true opinion is as good a guide to correct action as knowledge; and that was the point which we omitted in our speculation about the nature of virtue, when we said that knowledge only is the guide of right action; whereas there is also right opinion.

MENO: True.

SOCRATES: Then right opinion is not less useful than knowledge?

MENO: The difference, Socrates, is only that he who has knowledge will always be right; but he who has right opinion will sometimes be right, and sometimes not.

SOCRATES: What do you mean? Can he be wrong who has right opinion, so long as he has right opinion?

MENO: I admit the cogency of your argument, and therefore, Socrates, I wonder that knowledge should be preferred to right opinion—or why they should ever differ.

SOCRATES: And shall I explain this wonder to you?

MENO: Do tell me.

SOCRATES: You would not wonder if you had ever observed the images of Daedalus (Compare Euthyphro); but perhaps you have not got them in your country?

MENO: What have they to do with the question?

SOCRATES: Because they require to be fastened in order to keep them, and if they are not fastened they will play truant and run away.

MENO: Well, what of that?

SOCRATES: I mean to say that they are not very valuable possessions if they are at liberty, for they will walk off like runaway slaves; but when fastened, they are of great value, for they are really beautiful works of art. Now this is an illustration of the nature of true opinions: while they abide with us they are beautiful and fruitful, but they run away out of the human soul, and do not remain long, and therefore they are not of much value until they are fastened by the tie of the cause; and this fastening of them, friend Meno, is recollection, as you and I have agreed to call it. But when they are bound, in the first place, they have the nature of knowledge; and, in the second place, they are abiding. And this is why knowledge is more honorable and excellent than true opinion, because fastened by a chain.

MENO: What you are saying, Socrates, seems to be very like the truth.

SOCRATES: I too speak rather in ignorance; I only conjecture. And yet that knowledge differs from true opinion is no matter of conjecture with me. There are not many things which I profess to know, but this is most certainly one of them.

MENO: Yes, Socrates; and you are quite right in saying so.

SOCRATES: And am I not also right in saying that true opinion leading the way perfects action quite as well as knowledge?

MENO: There again, Socrates, I think you are right.

SOCRATES: Then right opinion is not a whit inferior to knowledge, or less useful in action; nor is the man who has right opinion inferior to him who has knowledge?

MENO: True.

SOCRATES: And surely the good man has been acknowledged by us to be useful?

MENO: Yes.

SOCRATES: Seeing then that men become good and useful to states, not only because they have knowledge, but because they have right opinion, and that neither knowledge nor right opinion is given to man by nature or acquired by him—(do you imagine either of them to be given by nature?

MENO: Not I.)

SOCRATES: Then if they are not given by nature, neither are the good by nature good?

MENO: Certainly not.

SOCRATES: And nature being excluded, then came the question whether virtue is acquired by teaching?

MENO: Yes.

SOCRATES: If virtue was wisdom (or knowledge), then, as we thought, it was taught?

MENO: Yes.

SOCRATES: And if it was taught it was wisdom?

MENO: Certainly.

SOCRATES: And if there were teachers, it might be taught; and if there were no teachers, not?

MENO: True.

SOCRATES: But surely we acknowledged that there were no teachers of virtue?

MENO: Yes.

SOCRATES: Then we acknowledged that it was not taught, and was not wisdom?

MENO: Certainly.

SOCRATES: And yet we admitted that it was a good?

MENO: Yes.

SOCRATES: And the right guide is useful and good?

MENO: Certainly.

SOCRATES: And the only right guides are knowledge and true opinion—these are the guides of man; for things which happen by chance are not under the guidance of man: but the guides of man are true opinion and knowledge.

MENO: I think so too.

SOCRATES: But if virtue is not taught, neither is virtue knowledge.

MENO: Clearly not.

SOCRATES: Then of two good and useful things, one, which is knowledge, has been set aside, and cannot be supposed to be our guide in political life.

MENO: I think not.

SOCRATES: And therefore not by any wisdom, and not because they were wise, did Themistocles and those others of whom Anytus spoke govern states. This was the reason why they were unable to make others like themselves—because their virtue was not grounded on knowledge.

MENO: That is probably true, Socrates.

SOCRATES: But if not by knowledge, the only alternative which remains is that statesmen must have guided states by right opinion, which is in politics what divination is in religion; for diviners and also prophets say many things truly, but they know not what they say.

MENO: So I believe.

SOCRATES: And may we not, Meno, truly call those men 'divine' who, having no understanding, yet succeed in many a grand deed and word?

MENO: Certainly.

SOCRATES: Then we shall also be right in calling divine those whom we were just now speaking of as diviners and prophets, including the whole tribe of poets. Yes, and statesmen above all may be said to be divine and illumined, being inspired and possessed of God, in which condition they say many grand things, not knowing what they say.

MENO: Yes.

SOCRATES: And the women too, Meno, call good men divine—do they not? and the Spartans, when they praise a good man, say 'that he is a divine man.'

MENO: And I think, Socrates, that they are right; although very likely our friend Anytus may take offence at the word.

SOCRATES: I do not care; as for Anytus, there will be another opportunity of talking with him. To sum up our enquiry—the result seems to be, if we are at all right in our view, that virtue is neither natural nor acquired, but an instinct given by God to the virtuous. Nor is the instinct accompanied by reason, unless there may be supposed to be among statesmen some one who is capable of educating statesmen. And if there be such an one, he may be said to be among the living what Homer says that Tiresias was among the dead, 'he alone has understanding; but the rest are flitting shades'; and he and his virtue in like manner will be a reality among shadows.

MENO: That is excellent, Socrates.

SOCRATES: Then, Meno, the conclusion is that virtue comes to the virtuous by the gift of God. But we shall never know the certain truth until, before asking how virtue is given, we enquire into the actual nature of virtue. I fear that I must go away, but do you, now that you are persuaded yourself, persuade our friend Anytus. And do not let him be so exasperated; if you can conciliate him, you will have done good service to the Athenian people.

ION

By Plato
Translated by Benjamin Jowett

Introduction

The Ion is the shortest, or nearly the shortest, of all the writings which bear the name of Plato, and is not authenticated by any early external testimony. The grace and beauty of this little work supply the only, and perhaps a sufficient, proof of its genuineness. The plan is simple; the dramatic interest consists entirely in the contrast between the irony of Socrates and the transparent vanity and childlike enthusiasm of the rhapsode Ion. The theme of the Dialogue may possibly have been suggested by the passage of Xenophon's Memorabilia in which the rhapsodists are described by Euthydemus as 'very precise about the exact words of Homer, but very idiotic themselves.' (Compare Aristotle, Met.)

Ion the rhapsode has just come to Athens; he has been exhibiting in Epidaurus at the festival of Asclepius, and is intending to exhibit at the festival of the Panathenaea. Socrates admires and envies the rhapsode's art; for he is always well dressed and in good company—in the company of good poets and of Homer, who is the prince of them. In the course of conversation the admission is elicited from Ion that his skill is restricted to Homer, and that he knows nothing of inferior poets, such as Hesiod and Archilochus;—he brightens up and is wide awake when Homer is being recited, but is apt to go to sleep at the recitations of any other poet. 'And yet, surely, he who knows the superior ought to know the inferior also;—he who can judge of the good speaker is able to judge of the bad. And poetry is a whole; and he who judges of poetry by rules of art ought to be able to judge of all poetry.' This is confirmed by the analogy of sculpture, painting, flute-playing, and the other arts. The argument is at last brought home to the mind of Ion, who asks how this contradiction is to be solved. The solution given by Socrates is as follows:—

The rhapsode is not guided by rules of art, but is an inspired person who derives a mysterious power from the poet; and the poet, in like manner, is inspired by the God. The poets and their interpreters may be compared to a chain of magnetic rings suspended from one another, and from a magnet. The magnet is the Muse, and the ring which immediately follows is the poet himself; from him are suspended other poets; there is also a chain of rhapsodes and actors, who also hang from the Muses, but are let down at the side; and the last ring of all is the spectator. The poet is the inspired interpreter of the God, and this is the reason why some poets, like Homer, are restricted to a single theme, or, like Tynnichus, are famous for a single poem; and the rhapsode is the inspired interpreter of the poet, and for a similar reason some rhapsodes, like Ion, are the interpreters of single poets.

Ion is delighted at the notion of being inspired, and acknowledges that he is beside himself when he is performing;—his eyes rain tears and his hair stands on end. Socrates is of opinion that a man must be mad who behaves in this way at a festival when he is surrounded by his friends and there is nothing to trouble him. Ion is confident that Socrates would never think him mad if he could only hear his embellishments of Homer. Socrates asks whether he can speak well about everything in Homer. 'Yes, indeed he can.' 'What about things of which he has no knowledge?' Ion answers that he can interpret anything in Homer. But, rejoins Socrates, when Homer speaks of the arts, as for example, of chariot-driving, or of medicine, or of prophecy, or of navigation—will he, or will the charioteer or physician or prophet or pilot be the better judge? Ion is compelled to admit that every man will judge of his own particular art better than the rhapsode. He still maintains, however, that he understands the art of the general as well as any one. 'Then why in this city of Athens, in which men of merit are always being sought after, is he not at once appointed a general?' Ion replies that he is a foreigner, and the Athenians and Spartans will not appoint a foreigner to be their general. 'No, that is not the real reason; there are many examples to the contrary. But Ion has long been playing tricks with the argument; like Proteus, he transforms himself into a variety of shapes, and is at last about to run away in the disguise of a general. Would he rather be regarded as inspired or dishonest?' Ion, who has no suspicion of the irony of Socrates, eagerly embraces the alternative of inspiration.

The Ion, like the other earlier Platonic Dialogues, is a mixture of jest and earnest, in which no definite result is obtained, but some Socratic or Platonic truths are allowed dimly to appear.

The elements of a true theory of poetry are contained in the notion that the poet is inspired. Genius is often said to be unconscious, or spontaneous, or a gift of nature: that 'genius is akin to madness' is a popular aphorism of modern times. The greatest strength is observed to have an element of limitation. Sense or passion are too much for the 'dry light' of intelligence which mingles with them and becomes discolored by them. Imagination is often at war with reason and fact. The concentration of the mind on a single object, or on a single aspect of human nature, overpowers the orderly perception of the whole. Yet the feelings too bring truths home to the minds of many who in the way of reason would be incapable of understanding them. Reflections of this kind may have been passing before Plato's mind when he describes the poet as inspired, or when, as in the Apology, he speaks of poets as the worst critics of their own writings—anybody taken at random from the crowd is a better interpreter of them than they are of themselves. They are sacred persons, 'winged and holy things' who have a touch of madness in their composition (Phaedr.), and should be treated with every sort of respect (Republic), but not allowed to live in a well-ordered state. Like the Statesmen in the Meno, they have a divine instinct, but they are narrow and confused; they do not attain to the clearness of ideas, or to the knowledge of poetry or of any other art as a whole.

In the Protagoras the ancient poets are recognized by Protagoras himself as the original sophists; and this family resemblance may be traced in the Ion. The rhapsode belongs to the realm of imitation and of opinion: he professes to have all knowledge, which is derived by him from Homer, just as the sophist professes to have all wisdom, which is contained in his art of rhetoric. Even more than the sophist he is incapable of appreciating the commonest logical distinctions; he cannot explain the nature of his own art; his great memory contrasts with his inability to follow the steps of the argument. And in his highest moments of inspiration he has an eye to his own gains.

The old quarrel between philosophy and poetry, which in the Republic leads to their final separation, is already working in the mind of Plato, and is embodied by him in the contrast between Socrates and Ion. Yet here, as in the Republic, Socrates shows a sympathy with the poetic nature. Also, the manner in which Ion is affected by his own recitations affords a lively illustration of the power which, in the Republic, Socrates attributes to dramatic performances over the mind of the performer. His allusion to his embellishments of Homer, in which he declares himself to have surpassed Metrodorus of Lampsacus and Stesimbrotus of Thasos, seems to show that, like them, he belonged to the allegorical school of interpreters. The circumstance that nothing more is known of him may be adduced in confirmation of the argument that this truly Platonic little work is not a forgery of later times.

Ion

PERSONS OF THE DIALOGUE: Socrates, Ion.

SOCRATES: Welcome, Ion. Are you from your native city of Ephesus?

ION: No, Socrates; but from Epidaurus, where I attended the festival of Asclepius.

SOCRATES: And do the Epidaurians have contests of rhapsodes at the festival?

ION: O yes; and of all sorts of musical performers.

SOCRATES: And were you one of the competitors—and did you succeed?

ION: I obtained the first prize of all, Socrates.

SOCRATES: Well done; and I hope that you will do the same for us at the Panathenaea.

ION: And I will, please heaven.

SOCRATES: I often envy the profession of a rhapsode, Ion; for you have always to wear fine clothes, and to look as beautiful as you can is a part of your art. Then, again, you are obliged to be continually in the company of many good poets; and especially of Homer, who is the best and most divine of them; and to understand him, and not merely learn his words by rote, is a thing greatly to be envied. And no man can be a rhapsode who does not understand the meaning of the poet. For the rhapsode ought to interpret the mind of the poet to his hearers, but how can he interpret him well unless he knows what he means? All this is greatly to be envied.

ION: Very true, Socrates; interpretation has certainly been the most laborious part of my art; and I believe myself able to speak about Homer better than any man; and that neither Metrodorus of Lampsacus, nor Stesimbrotus of Thasos, nor Glaucon, nor any one else who ever was, had as good ideas about Homer as I have, or as many.

SOCRATES: I am glad to hear you say so, Ion; I see that you will not refuse to acquaint me with them.

ION: Certainly, Socrates; and you really ought to hear how exquisitely I render Homer. I think that the Homeridae should give me a golden crown.

SOCRATES: I shall take an opportunity of hearing your embellishments of him at some other time. But just now I should like to ask you a question: Does your art extend to Hesiod and Archilochus, or to Homer only?

ION: To Homer only; he is in himself quite enough.

SOCRATES: Are there any things about which Homer and Hesiod agree?

ION: Yes; in my opinion there are a good many.

SOCRATES: And can you interpret better what Homer says, or what Hesiod says, about these matters in which they agree?

ION: I can interpret them equally well, Socrates, where they agree.

SOCRATES: But what about matters in which they do not agree?—for example, about divination, of which both Homer and Hesiod have something to say,—

ION: Very true:

SOCRATES: Would you or a good prophet be a better interpreter of what these two poets say about divination, not only when they agree, but when they disagree?

ION: A prophet.

SOCRATES: And if you were a prophet, would you not be able to interpret them when they disagree as well as when they agree?

ION: Clearly.

SOCRATES: But how did you come to have this skill about Homer only, and not about Hesiod or the other poets? Does not Homer speak of the same themes which all other poets handle? Is not war his great argument? and does he not speak of human society and of intercourse of men, good and bad, skilled and unskilled, and of the gods conversing with one another and with mankind, and about what happens in heaven and in the world below, and the generations of gods and heroes? Are not these the themes of which Homer sings?

ION: Very true, Socrates.

SOCRATES: And do not the other poets sing of the same?

ION: Yes, Socrates; but not in the same way as Homer.

SOCRATES: What, in a worse way?

ION: Yes, in a far worse.

SOCRATES: And Homer in a better way?

ION: He is incomparably better.

SOCRATES: And yet surely, my dear friend Ion, in a discussion about arithmetic, where many people are speaking, and one speaks better than the rest, there is somebody who can judge which of them is the good speaker?

ION: Yes.

SOCRATES: And he who judges of the good will be the same as he who judges of the bad speakers?

ION: The same.

SOCRATES: And he will be the arithmetician?

ION: Yes.

SOCRATES: Well, and in discussions about the wholesomeness of food, when many persons are speaking, and one speaks better than the rest, will he who recognizes the better speaker be a different person from him who recognizes the worse, or the same?

ION: Clearly the same.

SOCRATES: And who is he, and what is his name?

ION: The physician.

SOCRATES: And speaking generally, in all discussions in which the subject is the same and many men are speaking, will not he who knows the good know the bad speaker also? For if he does not know the bad, neither will he know the good when the same topic is being discussed.

ION: True.

SOCRATES: Is not the same person skillful in both?

ION: Yes.

SOCRATES: And you say that Homer and the other poets, such as Hesiod and Archilochus, speak of the same things, although not in the same way; but the one speaks well and the other not so well?

ION: Yes; and I am right in saying so.

SOCRATES: And if you knew the good speaker, you would also know the inferior speakers to be inferior?

ION: That is true.

SOCRATES: Then, my dear friend, can I be mistaken in saying that Ion is equally skilled in Homer and in other poets, since he himself acknowledges that the same person will be a good judge of all those who speak of the same things; and that almost all poets do speak of the same things?

ION: Why then, Socrates, do I lose attention and go to sleep and have absolutely no ideas of the least value, when any one speaks of any other poet; but when Homer is mentioned, I wake up at once and am all attention and have plenty to say?

SOCRATES: The reason, my friend, is obvious. No one can fail to see that you speak of Homer without any art or knowledge. If you were able to speak of him by rules of art, you would have been able to speak of all other poets; for poetry is a whole.

ION: Yes.

SOCRATES: And when any one acquires any other art as a whole, the same may be said of them. Would you like me to explain my meaning, Ion?

ION: Yes, indeed, Socrates; I very much wish that you would: for I love to hear you wise men talk.

SOCRATES: O that we were wise, Ion, and that you could truly call us so; but you rhapsodes and actors, and the poets whose verses you sing, are wise; whereas I am a common man, who only speak the truth. For consider what a very commonplace and trivial thing is this which I have said—a thing which any man might say: that when a man has acquired a knowledge of a whole art, the enquiry into good and bad is one and the same. Let us consider this matter; is not the art of painting a whole?

ION: Yes.

SOCRATES: And there are and have been many painters good and bad?

ION: Yes.

SOCRATES: And did you ever know any one who was skillful in pointing out the excellences and defects of Polygnotus the son of Aglaophon, but incapable of criticizing other painters; and when the work of any other painter was produced, went to sleep and was at a loss, and had no ideas; but when he had to give his opinion about Polygnotus, or whoever the painter might be, and about him only, woke up and was attentive and had plenty to say?

ION: No indeed, I have never known such a person.

SOCRATES: Or did you ever know of any one in sculpture, who was skillful in expounding the merits of Daedalus the son of Metion, or of Epeius the son of Panopeus, or of Theodorus the Samian, or of any individual sculptor; but when the works of sculptors in general were produced, was at a loss and went to sleep and had nothing to say?

ION: No indeed; no more than the other.

SOCRATES: And if I am not mistaken, you never met with any one among flute-players or harp-players or singers to the harp or rhapsodes who was able to discourse of Olympus or Thamyras or Orpheus, or Phemius the rhapsode of Ithaca, but was at a loss when he came to speak of Ion of Ephesus, and had no notion of his merits or defects?

ION: I cannot deny what you say, Socrates. Nevertheless I am conscious in my own self, and the world agrees with me in thinking that I do speak better and have more to say about Homer than any other man. But I do not speak equally well about others—tell me the reason of this.

SOCRATES: I perceive, Ion; and I will proceed to explain to you what I imagine to be the reason of this. The gift which you possess of speaking excellently about Homer is not an art, but, as I was just saying, an inspiration; there is a divinity moving you, like that contained in the stone which Euripides calls a magnet, but which is commonly known as the stone of Heraclea. This stone not only attracts iron rings, but also imparts to them a similar power of attracting other rings; and sometimes you may see a number of pieces of iron and rings suspended from one another so as to form quite a long chain: and all of them derive their power of suspension from the original stone. In like manner the Muse first of all inspires men herself; and from these inspired persons a chain of other persons is suspended, who take the inspiration. For all good poets, epic as well as lyric, compose their beautiful poems not by art, but because they are inspired and possessed. And as the Corybantian revellers when they dance are not in their right mind, so the lyric poets are not in their right mind when they are composing their beautiful strains: but when falling under the power of music and metre they are inspired and possessed; like Bacchic maidens who draw milk and honey from the rivers when they are under the influence of Dionysus but not when they are in their right mind. And the soul of the lyric poet does the same, as they themselves say; for they tell us that they bring songs from honeyed fountains, culling them out of the gardens and dells of the Muses; they, like the bees, winging their way from flower to flower. And this is true. For the poet is a light and winged and holy thing, and there is no invention in him until he has been inspired and is out of his senses, and the mind is no longer in him: when he has not attained to this state, he is powerless and is unable to utter his oracles. Many are the noble words in which poets speak concerning the actions of men; but like yourself when speaking about Homer, they do not speak of them by any rules of art: they are simply inspired to utter that to which the Muse impels them, and that only; and when inspired, one of them will make dithyrambs, another hymns of praise, another choral strains, another epic or iambic verses—and he who is good at one is not good at any other kind of verse: for not by art does the poet sing, but by power divine. Had he learned by rules of art, he would have known how to speak not of one theme only, but of all; and therefore God takes away the minds of poets, and uses them as his ministers, as he also uses diviners and holy prophets, in order that we who hear them may know them to be speaking not of themselves who utter these priceless words in a state of unconsciousness, but that God himself is the speaker, and that through them he is conversing with us. And Tynnichus the Chalcidian affords a striking instance of what I am saying: he wrote nothing that any one would care to remember but the famous paean which is in every one's mouth, one of the finest poems ever written, simply an invention of the Muses, as he himself says. For in this way the God would seem to indicate to us and not allow us to doubt that these beautiful poems are not human, or the work of man, but divine and the work of God; and that the poets are only the interpreters of the Gods by whom they are severally possessed. Was not this the lesson which the God intended to teach when by the mouth of the worst of poets he sang the best of songs? Am I not right, Ion?

ION: Yes, indeed, Socrates, I feel that you are; for your words touch my soul, and I am persuaded that good poets by a divine inspiration interpret the things of the Gods to us.

SOCRATES: And you rhapsodists are the interpreters of the poets?

ION: There again you are right.

SOCRATES: Then you are the interpreters of interpreters?

ION: Precisely.

SOCRATES: I wish you would frankly tell me, Ion, what I am going to ask of you: When you produce the greatest effect upon the audience in the recitation of some striking passage, such as the apparition of Odysseus leaping forth on the floor, recognized by the suitors and casting his arrows at his feet, or the description of Achilles rushing at Hector, or the sorrows of Andromache, Hecuba, or Priam,—are you in your right mind? Are you not carried out of yourself, and does not your soul in an ecstasy seem to be among the persons or places of which you are speaking, whether they are in Ithaca or in Troy or whatever may be the scene of the poem?

ION: That proof strikes home to me, Socrates. For I must frankly confess that at the tale of pity my eyes are filled with tears, and when I speak of horrors, my hair stands on end and my heart throbs.

SOCRATES: Well, Ion, and what are we to say of a man who at a sacrifice or festival, when he is dressed in holiday attire, and has golden crowns upon his head, of which nobody has robbed him, appears weeping or panic-stricken in the presence of more than twenty thousand friendly faces, when there is no one despoiling or wronging him;—is he in his right mind or is he not?

ION: No indeed, Socrates, I must say that, strictly speaking, he is not in his right mind.

SOCRATES: And are you aware that you produce similar effects on most of the spectators?

ION: Only too well; for I look down upon them from the stage, and behold the various emotions of pity, wonder, sternness, stamped upon their countenances when I am speaking: and I am obliged to give my very best attention to them; for if I make them cry I myself shall laugh, and if I make them laugh I myself shall cry when the time of payment arrives.

SOCRATES: Do you know that the spectator is the last of the rings which, as I am saying, receive the power of the original magnet from one another? The rhapsode like yourself and the actor are intermediate links, and the poet himself is the first of them. Through all these the God sways the souls of men in any direction which he pleases, and makes one man hang down from another. Thus there is a vast chain of dancers and masters and under-masters of choruses, who are suspended, as if from the stone, at the side of the rings which hang down from the Muse. And every poet has some Muse from whom he is suspended, and by whom he is said to be possessed, which is nearly the same thing; for he is taken hold of. And from these first rings, which are the poets, depend others, some deriving their inspiration from Orpheus, others from Musaeus; but the greater number are possessed and held by Homer. Of whom, Ion, you are one, and are possessed by Homer; and when any one repeats the words of another poet you go to sleep, and know not what to say; but when any one recites a strain of Homer you wake up in a moment, and your soul leaps within you, and you have plenty to say; for not by art or knowledge about Homer do you say what you say, but by divine inspiration and by possession; just as the Corybantian revellers too have a quick perception of that strain only which is appropriated to the God by whom they are possessed, and have plenty of dances and words for that, but take no heed of any other. And you, Ion, when the name of Homer is mentioned have plenty to say, and have nothing to say of others. You ask, 'Why is this?' The answer is that you praise Homer not by art but by divine inspiration.

ION: That is good, Socrates; and yet I doubt whether you will ever have eloquence enough to persuade me that I praise Homer only when I am mad and possessed; and if you could hear me speak of him I am sure you would never think this to be the case.

SOCRATES: I should like very much to hear you, but not until you have answered a question which I have to ask. On what part of Homer do you speak well?—not surely about every part.

ION: There is no part, Socrates, about which I do not speak well: of that I can assure you.

SOCRATES: Surely not about things in Homer of which you have no knowledge?

ION: And what is there in Homer of which I have no knowledge?

SOCRATES: Why, does not Homer speak in many passages about arts? For example, about driving; if I can only remember the lines I will repeat them.

ION: I remember, and will repeat them.

SOCRATES: Tell me then, what Nestor says to Antilochus, his son, where he bids him be careful of the turn at the horserace in honor of Patroclus.

ION: 'Bend gently,' he says, 'in the polished chariot to the left of them, and urge the horse on the right hand with whip and voice; and slacken the rein. And when you are at the goal, let the left horse draw near, yet so that the nave of the well-wrought wheel may not even seem to touch the extremity; and avoid catching the stone (Il.).'

SOCRATES: Enough. Now, Ion, will the charioteer or the physician be the better judge of the propriety of these lines?

ION: The charioteer, clearly.

SOCRATES: And will the reason be that this is his art, or will there be any other reason?

ION: No, that will be the reason.

SOCRATES: And every art is appointed by God to have knowledge of a certain work; for that which we know by the art of the pilot we do not know by the art of medicine?

ION: Certainly not.

SOCRATES: Nor do we know by the art of the carpenter that which we know by the art of medicine?

ION: Certainly not.

SOCRATES: And this is true of all the arts;—that which we know with one art we do not know with the other? But let me ask a prior question: You admit that there are differences of arts?

ION: Yes.

SOCRATES: You would argue, as I should, that when one art is of one kind of knowledge and another of another, they are different?

ION: Yes.

SOCRATES: Yes, surely; for if the subject of knowledge were the same, there would be no meaning in saying that the arts were different,—if they both gave the same knowledge. For example, I know that here are five fingers, and you know the same. And if I were to ask whether I and you became acquainted with this fact by the help of the same art of arithmetic, you would acknowledge that we did?

ION: Yes.

SOCRATES: Tell me, then, what I was intending to ask you,—whether this holds universally? Must the same art have the same subject of knowledge, and different arts other subjects of knowledge?

ION: That is my opinion, Socrates.

SOCRATES: Then he who has no knowledge of a particular art will have no right judgment of the sayings and doings of that art?

ION: Very true.

SOCRATES: Then which will be a better judge of the lines which you were reciting from Homer, you or the charioteer?

ION: The charioteer.

SOCRATES: Why, yes, because you are a rhapsode and not a charioteer.

ION: Yes.

SOCRATES: And the art of the rhapsode is different from that of the charioteer?

ION: Yes.

SOCRATES: And if a different knowledge, then a knowledge of different matters?

ION: True.

SOCRATES: You know the passage in which Hecamede, the concubine of Nestor, is described as giving to the wounded Machaon a posset, as he says,

'Made with Pramnian wine; and she grated cheese of goat's milk with a grater of bronze, and at his side placed an onion which gives a relish to drink (Il.).'

Now would you say that the art of the rhapsode or the art of medicine was better able to judge of the propriety of these lines?

ION: The art of medicine.

SOCRATES: And when Homer says,

'And she descended into the deep like a leaden plummet, which, set in the horn of ox that ranges in the fields, rushes along carrying death among the ravenous fishes (Il.),'—

will the art of the fisherman or of the rhapsode be better able to judge whether these lines are rightly expressed or not?

ION: Clearly, Socrates, the art of the fisherman.

SOCRATES: Come now, suppose that you were to say to me: 'Since you, Socrates, are able to assign different passages in Homer to their corresponding arts, I wish that you would tell me what are the passages of which the excellence ought to be judged by the prophet and prophetic art'; and you will see how readily and truly I shall answer you. For there are many such passages, particularly in the Odyssee; as, for example, the passage in which Theoclymenus the prophet of the house of Melampus says to the suitors:—

'Wretched men! what is happening to you? Your heads and your faces and your limbs underneath are shrouded in night; and the voice of lamentation bursts forth, and your cheeks are wet with tears. And the vestibule is full, and the court is full, of ghosts descending into the darkness of Erebus, and the sun has perished out of heaven, and an evil mist is spread abroad (Od.).'

And there are many such passages in the Iliad also; as for example in the description of the battle near the rampart, where he says:—

'As they were eager to pass the ditch, there came to them an omen: a soaring eagle, holding back the people on the left, bore a huge bloody dragon in his talons, still living and panting;

nor had he yet resigned the strife, for he bent back and smote the bird which carried him on the breast by the neck, and he in pain let him fall from him to the ground into the midst of the multitude. And the eagle, with a cry, was borne afar on the wings of the wind (Il.).'

These are the sort of things which I should say that the prophet ought to consider and determine.

ION: And you are quite right, Socrates, in saying so.

SOCRATES: Yes, Ion, and you are right also. And as I have selected from the Iliad and Odyssee for you passages which describe the office of the prophet and the physician and the fisherman, do you, who know Homer so much better than I do, Ion, select for me passages which relate to the rhapsode and the rhapsode's art, and which the rhapsode ought to examine and judge of better than other men.

ION: All passages, I should say, Socrates.

SOCRATES: Not all, Ion, surely. Have you already forgotten what you were saying? A rhapsode ought to have a better memory.

ION: Why, what am I forgetting?

SOCRATES: Do you not remember that you declared the art of the rhapsode to be different from the art of the charioteer?

ION: Yes, I remember.

SOCRATES: And you admitted that being different they would have different subjects of knowledge?

ION: Yes.

SOCRATES: Then upon your own showing the rhapsode, and the art of the rhapsode, will not know everything?

ION: I should exclude certain things, Socrates.

SOCRATES: You mean to say that you would exclude pretty much the subjects of the other arts. As he does not know all of them, which of them will he know?

ION: He will know what a man and what a woman ought to say, and what a freeman and what a slave ought to say, and what a ruler and what a subject.

SOCRATES: Do you mean that a rhapsode will know better than the pilot what the ruler of a sea-tossed vessel ought to say?

ION: No; the pilot will know best.

SOCRATES: Or will the rhapsode know better than the physician what the ruler of a sick man ought to say?

ION: He will not.

SOCRATES: But he will know what a slave ought to say?

ION: Yes.

SOCRATES: Suppose the slave to be a cowherd; the rhapsode will know better than the cowherd what he ought to say in order to soothe the infuriated cows?

ION: No, he will not.

SOCRATES: But he will know what a spinning-woman ought to say about the working of wool?

ION: No.

SOCRATES: At any rate he will know what a general ought to say when exhorting his soldiers?

ION: Yes, that is the sort of thing which the rhapsode will be sure to know.

SOCRATES: Well, but is the art of the rhapsode the art of the general?

ION: I am sure that I should know what a general ought to say.

SOCRATES: Why, yes, Ion, because you may possibly have a knowledge of the art of the general as well as of the rhapsode; and you may also have a knowledge of horsemanship as well as of the lyre: and then you would know when horses were well or ill managed. But suppose I were to ask you: By the help of which art, Ion, do you know whether horses are well managed, by your skill as a horseman or as a performer on the lyre—what would you answer?

ION: I should reply, by my skill as a horseman.

SOCRATES: And if you judged of performers on the lyre, you would admit that you judged of them as a performer on the lyre, and not as a horseman?

ION: Yes.

SOCRATES: And in judging of the general's art, do you judge of it as a general or a rhapsode?

ION: To me there appears to be no difference between them.

SOCRATES: What do you mean? Do you mean to say that the art of the rhapsode and of the general is the same?

ION: Yes, one and the same.

SOCRATES: Then he who is a good rhapsode is also a good general?

ION: Certainly, Socrates.

SOCRATES: And he who is a good general is also a good rhapsode?

ION: No; I do not say that.

SOCRATES: But you do say that he who is a good rhapsode is also a good general.

ION: Certainly.

SOCRATES: And you are the best of Hellenic rhapsodes?

ION: Far the best, Socrates.

SOCRATES: And are you the best general, Ion?

ION: To be sure, Socrates; and Homer was my master.

SOCRATES: But then, Ion, what in the name of goodness can be the reason why you, who are the best of generals as well as the best of rhapsodes in all Hellas, go about as a rhapsode when you might be a general? Do you think that the Hellenes want a rhapsode with his golden crown, and do not want a general?

ION: Why, Socrates, the reason is, that my countrymen, the Ephesians, are the servants and soldiers of Athens, and do not need a general; and you and Sparta are not likely to have me, for you think that you have enough generals of your own.

SOCRATES: My good Ion, did you never hear of Apollodorus of Cyzicus?

ION: Who may he be?

SOCRATES: One who, though a foreigner, has often been chosen their general by the Athenians: and there is Phanosthenes of Andros, and Heraclides of Clazomenae, whom they have also appointed to the command of their armies and to other offices, although aliens, after they had shown their merit. And will they not choose Ion the Ephesian to be their general, and honor him, if he prove himself worthy? Were not the Ephesians originally Athenians, and Ephesus is no mean city? But, indeed, Ion, if you are correct in saying that by art and knowledge you are able to praise Homer, you do not deal fairly with me, and after all your professions of knowing many glorious things about Homer, and promises that you would exhibit them, you are only a deceiver, and so far from exhibiting the art of which you are a master, will not, even after my repeated entreaties, explain to me the nature of it. You have literally as many forms as Proteus; and now you go all manner of ways, twisting and turning, and, like Proteus, become all manner of people at once, and at last slip away from me in the disguise of a general, in order that you may escape exhibiting your Homeric lore. And if you have art, then, as I was saying, in falsifying your promise that you would exhibit Homer, you are not dealing fairly with me. But if, as I believe, you have no art, but speak all these beautiful words about Homer unconsciously under his inspiring influence, then I acquit you of dishonesty, and shall only say that you are inspired. Which do you prefer to be thought, dishonest or inspired?

ION: There is a great difference, Socrates, between the two alternatives; and inspiration is by far the nobler.

SOCRATES: Then, Ion, I shall assume the nobler alternative; and attribute to you in your praises of Homer inspiration, and not art.

REBULIC (ON JUSTICE)

By Plato

Book I

SOCRATES - GLAUCON

I WENT down yesterday to the Piraeus with Glaucon the son of Ariston, that I might offer up my prayers to the goddess; and also because I wanted to see in what manner they would celebrate the festival, which was a new thing. I was delighted with the procession of the inhabitants; but that of the Thracians was equally, if not more, beautiful. When we had finished our prayers and viewed the spectacle, we turned in the direction of the city; and at that instant Polemarchus the son of Cephalus chanced to catch sight of us from a distance as we were starting on our way home, and told his servant to run and bid us wait for him. The servant took hold of me by the cloak behind, and said: Polemarchus desires you to wait.

I turned round, and asked him where his master was.

There he is, said the youth, coming after you, if you will only wait.

Certainly we will, said Glaucon; and in a few minutes Polemarchus appeared, and with him Adeimantus, Glaucon's brother, Niceratus the son of Nicias, and several others who had been at the procession.

SOCRATES - POLEMARCHUS - GLAUCON - ADEIMANTUS

Polemarchus said to me: I perceive, Socrates, that you and our companion are already on your way to the city.

You are not far wrong, I said.

But do you see, he rejoined, how many we are?

Of course.

And are you stronger than all these? for if not, you will have to remain where you are.

May there not be the alternative, I said, that we may persuade you to let us go?

But can you persuade us, if we refuse to listen to you? he said.

Certainly not, replied Glaucon.

Then we are not going to listen; of that you may be assured.

Adeimantus added: Has no one told you of the torch-race on horseback in honor of the goddess which will take place in the evening?

With horses! I replied: That is a novelty. Will horsemen carry torches and pass them one to another during the race?

Yes, said Polemarchus, and not only so, but a festival will he celebrated at night, which you certainly ought to see. Let us rise soon after supper and see this festival; there will be a gathering of young men, and we will have a good talk. Stay then, and do not be perverse.

Glaucon said: I suppose, since you insist, that we must.

Very good, I replied.

GLAUCON - CEPHALUS - SOCRATES

Accordingly we went with Polemarchus to his house; and there we found his brothers Lysias and Euthydemus, and with them Thrasymachus the Chalcedonian, Charmantides the Paeanian, and Cleitophon the son of Aristonymus. There too was Cephalus the father of Polemarchus, whom I had not seen for a long time, and I thought him very much aged. He was seated on a cushioned chair, and had a garland on his head, for he had been sacrificing in the court; and there were some other chairs in the room arranged in a semicircle, upon which we sat down by him. He saluted me eagerly, and then he said:—

You don't come to see me, Socrates, as often as you ought: If I were still able to go and see you I would not ask you to come to me. But at my age I can hardly get to the city, and therefore you should come oftener to the Piraeus. For let me tell you, that the more the pleasures of the body fade away, the greater to me is the pleasure and charm of conversation. Do not then deny my request, but make our house your resort and keep company with these young men; we are old friends, and you will be quite at home with us.

I replied: There is nothing which for my part I like better, Cephalus, than conversing with aged men; for I regard them as travellers who have gone a journey which I too may have to go, and of whom I ought to enquire, whether the way is smooth and easy, or rugged and difficult. And this is a question which I should like to ask of you who have arrived at that time which the poets call the 'threshold of old age'—Is life harder towards the end, or what report do you give of it?

I will tell you, Socrates, he said, what my own feeling is. Men of my age flock together; we are birds of a feather, as the old proverb says; and at our meetings the tale of my acquaintance commonly is—I cannot eat, I cannot drink; the pleasures of youth and love are fled away: there was a good time once, but now that is gone, and life is no longer life. Some complain of the slights which are put upon them by relations, and they will tell you sadly of how many evils their old age is the cause. But to me, Socrates, these complainers seem to blame that which is not really in fault. For if old age were the cause, I too being old, and every other old man, would have felt as they do. But this is not my own experience, nor that of others whom I have known. How well I remember the aged poet Sophocles, when in answer to the question, How does love suit with age, Sophocles,—are you still the man you were? Peace, he replied; most gladly have I escaped the thing of which you speak; I feel as if I had escaped from a mad and furious master. His words have often occurred to my mind since, and they seem as good to me now as at the time when he uttered them. For certainly old age has a great sense of calm and freedom; when the passions relax their hold, then, as Sophocles says, we are freed from the grasp not of one mad master only, but of many. The truth is, Socrates, that these regrets, and also the complaints about relations, are to be attributed to the same cause, which is not old age, but men's characters and tempers; for he who is of a calm and happy nature will hardly feel the pressure of age, but to him who is of an opposite disposition youth and age are equally a burden.

I listened in admiration, and wanting to draw him out, that he might go on—Yes, Cephalus, I said: but I rather suspect that people in general are not convinced by you when you speak thus; they think that old age sits lightly upon you, not because of your happy disposition, but because you are rich, and wealth is well known to be a great comforter.

You are right, he replied; they are not convinced: and there is something in what they say; not, however, so much as they imagine. I might answer them as Themistocles answered the Seriphian who was abusing him and saying that he was famous, not for his own merits but because he was an Athenian: 'If you had been a native of my country or I of yours, neither of us would have been famous.' And to those who are not rich and are impatient of old age, the same reply may be made; for to the good poor man old age cannot be a light burden, nor can a bad rich man ever have peace with himself.

May I ask, Cephalus, whether your fortune was for the most part inherited or acquired by you?

Acquired! Socrates; do you want to know how much I acquired? In the art of making money I have been midway between my father and grandfather: for my grandfather, whose name I bear, doubled and trebled the value of his patrimony, that which he inherited being much what I possess now; but my father Lysanias reduced the property below what it is at present: and I shall be satisfied if I leave to these my sons not less but a little more than I received.

That was why I asked you the question, I replied, because I see that you are indifferent about money, which is a characteristic rather of those who have inherited their fortunes than of those who have acquired them; the makers of fortunes have a second love of money as a creation of their own, resembling the affection of authors for their own poems, or of parents for their children, besides that natural love of it for the sake of use and profit which is common to them and all men. And hence they are very bad company, for they can talk about nothing but the praises of wealth. That is true, he said.

Yes, that is very true, but may I ask another question? What do you consider to be the greatest blessing which you have reaped from your wealth?

One, he said, of which I could not expect easily to convince others. For let me tell you, Socrates, that when a man thinks himself to be near death, fears and cares enter into his mind which he never had before; the tales of a world below and the punishment which is exacted there of deeds done here were once a laughing matter to him, but now he is tormented with the thought that they may be true: either from the weakness of age, or because he is now drawing nearer to that other place, he has a clearer view of these things; suspicions and alarms crowd thickly upon him, and he begins to reflect and consider what wrongs he has done to others. And when he finds that the sum of his transgressions is great he will many a time like a child start up in his sleep for fear, and he is filled with dark forebodings. But to him who is conscious of no sin, sweet hope, as Pindar charmingly says, is the kind nurse of his age:

> Hope, he says, cherishes the soul of him who lives in justice and holiness and is the nurse of his age and the companion of his journey;—hope which is mightiest to sway the restless soul of man.

How admirable are his words! And the great blessing of riches, I do not say to every man, but to a good man, is, that he has had no occasion to deceive or to defraud others, either intentionally or unintentionally; and when he departs to the world below he is not in any apprehension about offerings due to the gods or debts which he owes to men. Now to this peace of mind the possession of wealth greatly contributes; and therefore I say, that, setting one thing against another, of the many advantages which wealth has to give, to a man of sense this is in my opinion the greatest.

Well said, Cephalus, I replied; but as concerning justice, what is it?—to speak the truth and to pay your debts—no more than this? And even to this are there not exceptions? Suppose that a friend when in his right mind has deposited arms with me and he asks for them when he is not in his right mind, ought I to give them back to him? No one would say that I ought or that I should be right in doing so, any more than they would say that I ought always to speak the truth to one who is in his condition.

You are quite right, he replied.

But then, I said, speaking the truth and paying your debts is not a correct definition of justice.

CEPHALUS - SOCRATES - POLEMARCHUS

Quite correct, Socrates, if Simonides is to be believed, said Polemarchus interposing.

I fear, said Cephalus, that I must go now, for I have to look after the sacrifices, and I hand over the argument to Polemarchus and the company.

Is not Polemarchus your heir? I said.

To be sure, he answered, and went away laughing to the sacrifices.

SOCRATES - POLEMARCHUS

Tell me then, O thou heir of the argument, what did Simonides say, and according to you truly say, about justice?

He said that the repayment of a debt is just, and in saying so he appears to me to be right.

I should be sorry to doubt the word of such a wise and inspired man, but his meaning, though probably clear to you, is the reverse of clear to me. For he certainly does not mean, as we were now saying that I ought to return a return a deposit of arms or of anything else to one who asks for it when he is not in his right senses; and yet a deposit cannot be denied to be a debt.

True.

Then when the person who asks me is not in his right mind I am by no means to make the return?

Certainly not.

When Simonides said that the repayment of a debt was justice, he did not mean to include that case?

Certainly not; for he thinks that a friend ought always to do good to a friend and never evil.

You mean that the return of a deposit of gold which is to the injury of the receiver, if the two parties are friends, is not the repayment of a debt,—that is what you would imagine him to say?

Yes.

And are enemies also to receive what we owe to them?

To be sure, he said, they are to receive what we owe them, and an enemy, as I take it, owes to an enemy that which is due or proper to him—that is to say, evil.

Simonides, then, after the manner of poets, would seem to have spoken darkly of the nature of justice; for he really meant to say that justice is the giving to each man what is proper to him, and this he termed a debt.

That must have been his meaning, he said.

By heaven! I replied; and if we asked him what due or proper thing is given by medicine, and to whom, what answer do you think that he would make to us?

He would surely reply that medicine gives drugs and meat and drink to human bodies.

And what due or proper thing is given by cookery, and to what?

Seasoning to food.

And what is that which justice gives, and to whom?

If, Socrates, we are to be guided at all by the analogy of the preceding instances, then justice is the art which gives good to friends and evil to enemies.

That is his meaning then?

I think so.

And who is best able to do good to his friends and evil to his enemies in time of sickness?

The physician.

Or when they are on a voyage, amid the perils of the sea?

The pilot.

And in what sort of actions or with a view to what result is the just man most able to do harm to his enemy and good to his friends?

In going to war against the one and in making alliances with the other.

But when a man is well, my dear Polemarchus, there is no need of a physician?

No.

And he who is not on a voyage has no need of a pilot?

No.

Then in time of peace justice will be of no use?

I am very far from thinking so.

You think that justice may be of use in peace as well as in war?

Yes.

Like husbandry for the acquisition of corn?

Yes.

Or like shoemaking for the acquisition of shoes,—that is what you mean?

Yes.

And what similar use or power of acquisition has justice in time of peace?

In contracts, Socrates, justice is of use.

And by contracts you mean partnerships?

Exactly.

But is the just man or the skillful player a more useful and better partner at a game of draughts?

The skillful player.

And in the laying of bricks and stones is the just man a more useful or better partner than the builder?

Quite the reverse.

Then in what sort of partnership is the just man a better partner than the harp-player, as in playing the harp the harp-player is certainly a better partner than the just man?

In a money partnership.

Yes, Polemarchus, but surely not in the use of money; for you do not want a just man to be your counsellor the purchase or sale of a horse; a man who is knowing about horses would be better for that, would he not?

Certainly.

And when you want to buy a ship, the shipwright or the pilot would be better?

True.

Then what is that joint use of silver or gold in which the just man is to be preferred?

When you want a deposit to be kept safely.

You mean when money is not wanted, but allowed to lie?

Precisely.

That is to say, justice is useful when money is useless?

That is the inference.

And when you want to keep a pruning-hook safe, then justice is useful to the individual and to the state; but when you want to use it, then the art of the vine-dresser?

Clearly.

And when you want to keep a shield or a lyre, and not to use them, you would say that justice is useful; but when you want to use them, then the art of the soldier or of the musician?

Certainly.

And so of all the other things;—justice is useful when they are useless, and useless when they are useful?

That is the inference.

Then justice is not good for much. But let us consider this further point: Is not he who can best strike a blow in a boxing match or in any kind of fighting best able to ward off a blow?

Certainly.

And he who is most skillful in preventing or escaping from a disease is best able to create one?

True.

And he is the best guard of a camp who is best able to steal a march upon the enemy?

Certainly.

Then he who is a good keeper of anything is also a good thief?

That, I suppose, is to be inferred.

Then if the just man is good at keeping money, he is good at stealing it.

That is implied in the argument.

Then after all the just man has turned out to be a thief. And this is a lesson which I suspect you must have learnt out of Homer; for he, speaking of Autolycus, the maternal grandfather of Odysseus, who is a favorite of his, affirms that

> He was excellent above all men in theft and perjury.

And so, you and Homer and Simonides are agreed that justice is an art of theft; to be practiced however 'for the good of friends and for the

No, certainly not that, though I do not now know what I did say; but I still stand by the latter words.

Well, there is another question: By friends and enemies do we mean those who are so really, or only in seeming?

Surely, he said, a man may be expected to love those whom he thinks good, and to hate those whom he thinks evil.

Yes, but do not persons often err about good and evil: many who are not good seem to be so, and conversely?

That is true.

Then to them the good will be enemies and the evil will be their friends? True.

And in that case they will be right in doing good to the evil and evil to the good?

Clearly.

But the good are just and would not do an injustice?

True.

Then according to your argument it is just to injure those who do no wrong?

Nay, Socrates; the doctrine is immoral.

Then I suppose that we ought to do good to the just and harm to the unjust?

I like that better.

But see the consequence:—Many a man who is ignorant of human nature has friends who are bad friends, and in that case he ought to do harm to them; and he has good enemies whom he ought to benefit; but, if so, we shall be saying the very opposite of that which we affirmed to be the meaning of Simonides.

Very true, he said: and I think that we had better correct an error into which we seem to have fallen in the use of the words 'friend' and 'enemy.'

What was the error, Polemarchus? I asked.

We assumed that he is a friend who seems to be or who is thought good.

And how is the error to be corrected?

We should rather say that he is a friend who is, as well as seems, good; and that he who seems only, and is not good, only seems to be and is not a friend; and of an enemy the same may be said.

You would argue that the good are our friends and the bad our enemies?

Yes.

And instead of saying simply as we did at first, that it is just to do good to our friends and harm to our enemies, we should further say: It is just to do good to our friends when they are good and harm to our enemies when they are evil?

Yes, that appears to me to be the truth.

But ought the just to injure any one at all?

Undoubtedly he ought to injure those who are both wicked and his enemies.

When horses are injured, are they improved or deteriorated?

The latter.

Deteriorated, that is to say, in the good qualities of horses, not of dogs?

Yes, of horses.

And dogs are deteriorated in the good qualities of dogs, and not of horses?

Of course.

And will not men who are injured be deteriorated in that which is the proper virtue of man?

Certainly.

And that human virtue is justice?

To be sure.

Then men who are injured are of necessity made unjust?

That is the result.

But can the musician by his art make men unmusical?

Certainly not.

Or the horseman by his art make them bad horsemen?

Impossible.

And can the just by justice make men unjust, or speaking general can the good by virtue make them bad?

Assuredly not.

Any more than heat can produce cold?

It cannot.

Or drought moisture?

Clearly not.

Nor can the good harm any one?

Impossible.

And the just is the good?

Certainly.

Then to injure a friend or any one else is not the act of a just man, but of the opposite, who is the unjust?

I think that what you say is quite true, Socrates.

Then if a man says that justice consists in the repayment of debts, and that good is the debt which a man owes to his friends, and evil the debt which he owes to his enemies,—to say this is not wise; for it is not true, if, as has been clearly shown, the injuring of another can be in no case just.

I agree with you, said Polemarchus.

Then you and I are prepared to take up arms against any one who attributes such a saying to Simonides or Bias or Pittacus, or any other wise man or seer?

I am quite ready to do battle at your side, he said.

Shall I tell you whose I believe the saying to be?

Whose?

I believe that Periander or Perdiccas or Xerxes or Ismenias the Theban, or some other rich and mighty man, who had a great opinion of his own power, was the first to say that justice is 'doing good to your friends and harm to your enemies.'

Most true, he said.

Yes, I said; but if this definition of justice also breaks down, what other can be offered?

Several times in the course of the discussion Thrasymachus had made an attempt to get the argument into his own hands, and had been put down by the rest of the company, who wanted to hear the end. But when Polemarchus and I had done speaking and there was a pause, he could no longer hold his peace; and, gathering himself up, he came at us like a wild beast, seeking to devour us. We were quite panic-stricken at the sight of him.

SOCRATES - POLEMARCHUS - THRASYMACHUS

He roared out to the whole company: What folly. Socrates, has taken possession of you all? And why, sillybillies, do you knock under to one another? I say that if you want really to know what justice is, you should not only ask but answer, and you should not seek honor to yourself from the refutation of an opponent, but have your own answer; for there is many a one who can ask and cannot answer. And now I will not have you say that justice is duty or advantage or profit or gain or interest, for this sort of nonsense will not do for me; I must have clearness and accuracy.

I was panic-stricken at his words, and could not look at him without trembling. Indeed I believe that if I had not fixed my eye upon him, I should have been struck dumb: but when I saw his fury rising, I looked at him first, and was therefore able to reply to him.

Thrasymachus, I said, with a quiver, don't be hard upon us. Polemarchus and I may have been guilty of a little mistake in the argument, but I can assure you that the error was not intentional. If we were seeking for a piece of gold, you would not imagine that we were 'knocking under to one another,' and so losing our chance of finding it. And why, when we are seeking for justice, a thing more precious than many pieces of gold, do you say that we are weakly yielding to one another and not doing our utmost to get at the truth? Nay, my good friend, we are most willing and anxious to do so, but the fact is that we cannot. And if so, you people who know all things should pity us and not be angry with us.

How characteristic of Socrates! he replied, with a bitter laugh;—that's your ironical style! Did I not foresee—have I not already told you, that whatever he was asked he would refuse to answer, and try irony or any other shuffle, in order that he might avoid answering?

You are a philosopher, Thrasymachus, I replied, and well know that if you ask a person what numbers make up twelve, taking care to prohibit him whom you ask from answering twice six, or three times four, or six times two, or four times three, 'for this sort of nonsense will not do for me,'—then obviously, that is your way of putting the question, no one can answer you. But suppose that he were to retort, 'Thrasymachus, what do you mean? If one of these numbers which you interdict be the true answer to the question, am I falsely to say some other number which is not the right one?—is that your meaning?'—How would you answer him?

Just as if the two cases were at all alike! he said.

Why should they not be? I replied; and even if they are not, but only appear to be so to the person who is asked, ought he not to say what he thinks, whether you and I forbid him or not?

I presume then that you are going to make one of the interdicted answers?

I dare say that I may, notwithstanding the danger, if upon reflection I approve of any of them.

But what if I give you an answer about justice other and better, he said, than any of these? What do you deserve to have done to you?

Done to me!—as becomes the ignorant, I must learn from the wise—that is what I deserve to have done to me.

What, and no payment! a pleasant notion!

I will pay when I have the money, I replied.

SOCRATES - THRASYMACHUS - GLAUCON

But you have, Socrates, said Glaucon: and you, Thrasymachus, need be under no anxiety about money, for we will all make a contribution for Socrates.

Yes, he replied, and then Socrates will do as he always does—refuse to answer himself, but take and pull to pieces the answer of some one else.

Why, my good friend, I said, how can any one answer who knows, and says that he knows, just nothing; and who, even if he has some faint notions of his own, is told by a man of authority not to utter them? The natural thing is, that the speaker should be some one like yourself who professes to know and can tell what he knows. Will you then kindly answer, for the edification of the company and of myself?

Glaucon and the rest of the company joined in my request and Thrasymachus, as any one might see, was in reality eager to speak; for he thought that he had an excellent answer, and would distinguish himself. But at first he to insist on my answering; at length he consented to begin. Behold, he said, the wisdom of Socrates; he refuses to teach himself, and goes about learning of others, to whom he never even says thank you.

That I learn of others, I replied, is quite true; but that I am ungrateful I wholly deny. Money I have none, and therefore I pay in praise, which is all I have: and how ready I am to praise any one who appears to me to speak well you will very soon find out when you answer; for I expect that you will answer well.

Listen, then, he said; I proclaim that justice is nothing else than the interest of the stronger. And now why do you not me? But of course you won't.

Let me first understand you, I replied. Justice, as you say, is the interest of the stronger. What, Thrasymachus, is the meaning of this? You cannot mean to say that because Polydamas, the pancratiast, is stronger than we are, and finds the eating of beef conducive to his bodily strength, that to eat beef is therefore equally for our good who are weaker than he is, and right and just for us?

That's abominable of you, Socrates; you take the words in the sense which is most damaging to the argument.

Not at all, my good sir, I said; I am trying to understand them; and I wish that you would be a little clearer.

Well, he said, have you never heard that forms of government differ; there are tyrannies, and there are democracies, and there are aristocracies?

Yes, I know.

And the government is the ruling power in each state?

Certainly.

And the different forms of government make laws democratical, aristocratical, tyrannical, with a view to their several interests; and these laws, which are made by them for their own interests, are the justice which they deliver to their subjects, and him who transgresses them they punish as a breaker of the law, and unjust. And that is what I mean when I say that in all states there is the same principle of justice, which is the interest of the government; and as the government must be supposed to have power, the only reasonable conclusion is, that everywhere there is one principle of justice, which is the interest of the stronger.

Now I understand you, I said; and whether you are right or not I will try to discover. But let me remark, that in defining justice you have yourself used the word 'interest' which you forbade me to use. It is true, however, that in your definition the words 'of the stronger' are added.

A small addition, you must allow, he said.

Great or small, never mind about that: we must first enquire whether what you are saying is the truth. Now we are both agreed that justice is interest of some sort, but you go on to say 'of the stronger'; about this addition I am not so sure, and must therefore consider further.

Proceed.

I will; and first tell me, Do you admit that it is just or subjects to obey their rulers?

I do.

But are the rulers of states absolutely infallible, or are they sometimes liable to err?

To be sure, he replied, they are liable to err.

Then in making their laws they may sometimes make them rightly, and sometimes not?

True.

When they make them rightly, they make them agreeably to their interest; when they are mistaken, contrary to their interest; you admit that?

Yes.

And the laws which they make must be obeyed by their subjects,—and that is what you call justice?

Doubtless.

Then justice, according to your argument, is not only obedience to the interest of the stronger but the reverse?

What is that you are saying? he asked.

I am only repeating what you are saying, I believe. But let us consider: Have we not admitted that the rulers may be mistaken about their own interest in what they command, and also that to obey them is justice? Has not that been admitted?

Yes.

Then you must also have acknowledged justice not to be for the interest of the stronger, when the rulers unintentionally command things to be done which are to their own injury. For if, as you say, justice is the obedience which the subject renders to their commands, in that case, O wisest of men, is there any escape from the conclusion that the weaker are commanded to do, not what is for the interest, but what is for the injury of the stronger?

Nothing can be clearer, Socrates, said Polemarchus.

SOCRATES - CLEITOPHON - POLEMARCHUS - THRASYMACHUS

Yes, said Cleitophon, interposing, if you are allowed to be his witness.

But there is no need of any witness, said Polemarchus, for Thrasymachus himself acknowledges that rulers may sometimes command what is not for their own interest, and that for subjects to obey them is justice.

Yes, Polemarchus,—Thrasymachus said that for subjects to do what was commanded by their rulers is just.

Yes, Cleitophon, but he also said that justice is the interest of the stronger, and, while admitting both these propositions, he further acknowledged that the stronger may command the weaker who are his subjects to do what is not for his own interest; whence follows that justice is the injury quite as much as the interest of the stronger.

But, said Cleitophon, he meant by the interest of the stronger what the stronger thought to be his interest,—this was what the weaker had to do; and this was affirmed by him to be justice.

Those were not his words, rejoined Polemarchus.

SOCRATES - THRASYMACHUS

Never mind, I replied, if he now says that they are, let us accept his statement. Tell me, Thrasymachus, I said, did you mean by justice what the stronger thought to be his interest, whether really so or not?

Certainly not, he said. Do you suppose that I call him who is mistaken the stronger at the time when he is mistaken?

Yes, I said, my impression was that you did so, when you admitted that the ruler was not infallible but might be sometimes mistaken.

You argue like an informer, Socrates. Do you mean, for example, that he who is mistaken about the sick is a physician in that he is mistaken? or that he who errs in arithmetic or grammar is an arithmetician or grammarian at the me when he is making the mistake, in respect of the mistake? True, we say that the physician or arithmetician or grammarian has made a mistake, but this is only a way of speaking; for the fact is that neither the grammarian nor any other person of skill ever makes a mistake in so far as he is what his name implies; they none of them err unless their skill fails them, and then they cease to be skilled artists. No artist or sage or ruler errs at the time when he is what his name implies; though he is commonly said to err, and I adopted the common mode of speaking. But to be perfectly accurate, since you are such a lover of accuracy, we should say that the ruler, in so far as he is the ruler, is unerring, and, being unerring, always commands that which is for his own interest; and the subject is required to execute his commands; and therefore, as I said at first and now repeat, justice is the interest of the stronger.

Indeed, Thrasymachus, and do I really appear to you to argue like an informer?

Certainly, he replied.

And you suppose that I ask these questions with any design of injuring you in the argument?

Nay, he replied, 'suppose' is not the word—I know it; but you will be found out, and by sheer force of argument you will never prevail.

I shall not make the attempt, my dear man; but to avoid any misunderstanding occurring between us in future, let me ask, in what sense do you speak of a ruler or stronger whose interest, as you were saying, he being the superior, it is just that the inferior should execute—is he a ruler in the popular or in the strict sense of the term?

In the strictest of all senses, he said. And now cheat and play the informer if you can; I ask no quarter at your hands. But you never will be able, never.

And do you imagine, I said, that I am such a madman as to try and cheat, Thrasymachus? I might as well shave a lion.

Why, he said, you made the attempt a minute ago, and you failed.

Enough, I said, of these civilities. It will be better that I should ask you a question: Is the physician, taken in that strict sense of which you are speaking, a healer of the sick or a maker of money? And remember that I am now speaking of the true physician.

A healer of the sick, he replied.

And the pilot—that is to say, the true pilot—is he a captain of sailors or a mere sailor?

A captain of sailors.

The circumstance that he sails in the ship is not to be taken into account; neither is he to be called a sailor; the name pilot by which he is distinguished has nothing to do with sailing, but is significant of his skill and of his authority over the sailors.

Very true, he said.

Now, I said, every art has an interest?

Certainly.

For which the art has to consider and provide?

Yes, that is the aim of art.

And the interest of any art is the perfection of it—this and nothing else?

What do you mean?

I mean what I may illustrate negatively by the example of the body. Suppose you were to ask me whether the body is self-sufficing or has wants, I should reply: Certainly the body has wants; for the body may be ill and require to be cured, and has therefore interests to which the art of medicine ministers; and this is the origin and intention of medicine, as you will acknowledge. Am I not right?

Quite right, he replied.

But is the art of medicine or any other art faulty or deficient in any quality in the same way that the eye may be deficient in sight or the ear fail of hearing, and therefore requires another art to provide for the interests of seeing and hearing—has art in itself, I say, any similar liability to fault or defect, and does every art require another supplementary art to provide for its interests, and that another and another without end? Or have the arts to look only after their own interests? Or have they no need either of themselves or of another?—having no faults or defects, they have no need to correct them, either by the exercise of their own art or of any other; they have only to consider the interest of their subject-matter. For every art remains pure and faultless while remaining true—that is to say, while perfect and unimpaired. Take the words in your precise sense, and tell me whether I am not right.

Yes, clearly.

Then medicine does not consider the interest of medicine, but the interest of the body?

True, he said.

Nor does the art of horsemanship consider the interests of the art of horsemanship, but the interests of the horse; neither do any other arts care for themselves, for they have no needs; they care only for that which is the subject of their art?

True, he said.

But surely, Thrasymachus, the arts are the superiors and rulers of their own subjects?

To this he assented with a good deal of reluctance.

Then, I said, no science or art considers or enjoins the interest of the stronger or superior, but only the interest of the subject and weaker?

He made an attempt to contest this proposition also, but finally acquiesced.

Then, I continued, no physician, in so far as he is a physician, considers his own good in what he prescribes, but the good of his patient; for the true physician is also a ruler having the human body as a subject, and is not a mere money-maker; that has been admitted?

Yes.

And the pilot likewise, in the strict sense of the term, is a ruler of sailors and not a mere sailor?

That has been admitted.

And such a pilot and ruler will provide and prescribe for the interest of the sailor who is under him, and not for his own or the ruler's interest?

He gave a reluctant 'Yes.'

Then, I said, Thrasymachus, there is no one in any rule who, in so far as he is a ruler, considers or enjoins what is for his own interest, but always what is for the interest of his subject or suitable to his art; to that he looks, and that alone he considers in everything which he says and does.

When we had got to this point in the argument, and every one saw that the definition of justice had been completely upset, Thrasymachus, instead of replying to me, said: Tell me, Socrates, have you got a nurse?

Why do you ask such a question, I said, when you ought rather to be answering?

Because she leaves you to snivel, and never wipes your nose: she has not even taught you to know the shepherd from the sheep.

What makes you say that? I replied.

Because you fancy that the shepherd or neatherd fattens of tends the sheep or oxen with a view to their own good and not to the good of himself or his master; and you further imagine that the rulers of states, if they are true rulers, never think of their subjects as sheep, and that they are not studying their own advantage day and night. Oh, no; and so entirely astray are you in your ideas about the just and unjust as not even to know that justice and the just are in reality another's good; that is to say, the interest of the ruler and stronger, and the loss of the subject and servant; and injustice the opposite; for the unjust is lord over the truly simple and just: he is the stronger, and his subjects do what is for his interest, and minister to his happiness, which is very far from being their own. Consider further, most foolish Socrates, that the just is always a loser in comparison with the unjust. First of all, in private contracts: wherever the unjust is the partner of the just you will find that, when the partnership is dissolved, the unjust man has always more and the just less. Secondly, in their dealings with the State: when there is an income tax, the just man will pay more and the unjust less on the same amount of income; and when there is anything to be received the one gains nothing and the other much. Observe also what happens when they take an office; there is the just man neglecting his affairs and perhaps suffering other losses, and getting nothing out of the public, because he is just; moreover he is hated by his friends and acquaintance for refusing to serve them in unlawful ways. But all this is reversed in the case of the unjust man. I am speaking, as before, of injustice on a large scale in which the advantage of the unjust is more apparent; and my meaning will be most clearly seen if we turn to that highest form of injustice in which the criminal is the happiest of men, and the sufferers or those who refuse to do injustice are the most miserable—that is to say tyranny, which by fraud and force takes away the property of others, not little by little but wholesale; comprehending in one, things sacred as well as profane, private and public; for which acts of wrong, if he were detected perpetrating any one of them singly, he would be punished and incur great disgrace—they who do such wrong in particular cases are called robbers of temples, and man-stealers and burglars and swindlers and thieves. But when a man besides taking away the money of the citizens has made slaves of them, then, instead of these names of reproach, he is termed happy and blessed, not only by the citizens but by all who hear of his having achieved the consummation of injustice. For mankind censure injustice, fearing that they may be the victims of it and not because they shrink from committing it. And thus, as I have shown, Socrates, injustice, when on a sufficient scale, has more strength and freedom and mastery than justice; and, as I said at first, justice is the interest of the stronger, whereas injustice is a man's own profit and interest.

Thrasymachus, when he had thus spoken, having, like a bathman, deluged our ears with his words, had a mind to go away. But the company would not let him; they insisted that he should remain and defend his position; and I myself added my own humble request that he would not leave us. Thrasymachus, I said to him, excellent man, how suggestive are your remarks! And are you going to run away before you have fairly taught or learned whether they are true or not? Is the attempt to determine the way of man's life so small a matter in your eyes—to determine how life may be passed by each one of us to the greatest advantage?

And do I differ from you, he said, as to the importance of the enquiry?

You appear rather, I replied, to have no care or thought about us, Thrasymachus—whether we live better or worse from not knowing what you say you know, is to you a matter of indifference. Prithee, friend, do not keep your knowledge to yourself; we are a large party; and any benefit which you confer upon us will be amply rewarded. For my own part I openly declare that I am not convinced, and that I do not believe injustice to be more gainful than justice, even if uncontrolled and allowed to have free play. For, granting that there may be an unjust man who is able to commit injustice either by fraud or force, still this does not convince me of the superior advantage of injustice, and there may be others who are in the same predicament with myself. Perhaps we may be wrong; if so, you in your wisdom should convince us that we are mistaken in preferring justice to injustice.

And how am I to convince you, he said, if you are not already convinced by what I have just said; what more can I do for you? Would you have me put the proof bodily into your souls?

Heaven forbid! I said; I would only ask you to be consistent; or, if you change, change openly and let there be no deception. For I must remark, Thrasymachus, if you will recall what was previously said, that although you began by defining the true physician in an exact sense, you did not observe a like exactness when speaking of the shepherd; you thought that the shepherd as a shepherd tends the sheep not with a view to their own good, but like a mere diner or banqueter with a view to the pleasures of the table; or, again, as a trader for sale in the market, and not as a shepherd. Yet surely the art of the shepherd is concerned only with the good of his subjects; he has only to provide the best for them, since the perfection of the art is already ensured whenever all the requirements of it are satisfied. And that was what I was saying just now about the ruler. I conceived that the art of the ruler, considered as ruler, whether in a state or in private life, could only regard the good of his flock or subjects; whereas you seem to think that the rulers in states, that is to say, the true rulers, like being in authority.

Think! Nay, I am sure of it.

Then why in the case of lesser offices do men never take them willingly without payment, unless under the idea that they govern for the advantage not of themselves but of others? Let me ask you a question: Are not the several arts different, by reason of their each having a separate function? And, my dear illustrious friend, do say what you think, that we may make a little progress.

Yes, that is the difference, he replied.

And each art gives us a particular good and not merely a general one—medicine, for example, gives us health; navigation, safety at sea, and so on?

Yes, he said.

And the art of payment has the special function of giving pay: but we do not confuse this with other arts, any more than the art of the pilot is to be confused with the art of medicine, because the health of the pilot may be improved by a sea voyage. You would not be inclined to say, would you, that navigation is the art of medicine, at least if we are to adopt your exact use of language?

Certainly not.

Or because a man is in good health when he receives pay you would not say that the art of payment is medicine?

I should say not.

Nor would you say that medicine is the art of receiving pay because a man takes fees when he is engaged in healing?

Certainly not.

And we have admitted, I said, that the good of each art is specially confined to the art?

Yes.

Then, if there be any good which all artists have in common, that is to be attributed to something of which they all have the common use?

True, he replied.

And when the artist is benefited by receiving pay the advantage is gained by an additional use of the art of pay, which is not the art professed by him?

He gave a reluctant assent to this.

Then the pay is not derived by the several artists from their respective arts. But the truth is, that while the art of medicine gives health, and the art of the builder builds a house, another art attends them which is the art of pay. The various arts may be doing their own business and benefiting that over which they preside, but would the artist receive any benefit from his art unless he were paid as well?

I suppose not.

But does he therefore confer no benefit when he works for nothing?

Certainly, he confers a benefit.

Then now, Thrasymachus, there is no longer any doubt that neither arts nor governments provide for their own interests; but, as we were before saying, they rule and provide for the interests of their subjects who are the weaker and not the stronger—to their good they attend and not to the good of the superior.

And this is the reason, my dear Thrasymachus, why, as I was just now saying, no one is willing to govern; because no one likes to take in hand the reformation of evils which are not his concern without remuneration. For, in the execution of his work, and in giving his orders to another, the true artist does not regard his own interest, but always that of his subjects; and therefore in order that rulers may be willing to rule, they must be paid in one of three modes of payment: money, or honor, or a penalty for refusing.

SOCRATES - GLAUCON

What do you mean, Socrates? said Glaucon. The first two modes of payment are intelligible enough, but what the penalty is I do not understand, or how a penalty can be a payment.

You mean that you do not understand the nature of this payment which to the best men is the great inducement to rule? Of course you know that ambition and avarice are held to be, as indeed they are, a disgrace?

Very true.

And for this reason, I said, money and honor have no attraction for them; good men do not wish to be openly demanding payment for governing and so to get the name of hirelings, nor by secretly helping themselves out of the public revenues to get the name of thieves. And not being ambitious they do not care about honor. Wherefore necessity must be laid upon them, and they must be induced to serve from the fear of punishment. And this, as I imagine, is the reason why the forwardness to take office, instead of waiting to be compelled, has been deemed dishonorable. Now the worst part of the punishment is that he who refuses to rule is liable to be ruled by one who is worse than himself. And the fear of this, as I conceive, induces the good to take office, not because they would, but because they cannot help—not under the idea that they are going to have any benefit or enjoyment themselves, but as a necessity, and because they are not able to commit the task of ruling to any one who is better than themselves, or indeed as good. For there is reason to think that if a city were composed entirely of good men, then to avoid office would be as much an object of contention as to obtain office is at present; then we should have plain proof that the true ruler is not meant by nature to regard his own interest, but that of his subjects; and every one who knew this would choose rather to receive a benefit from another than to have the trouble of conferring one. So far am I from agreeing with Thrasymachus that justice is the interest of the stronger. This latter question need not be further discussed at present; but when Thrasymachus says that the life of the unjust is more advantageous than that of the just, his new statement appears to me to be of a far more serious character. Which of us has spoken truly? And which sort of life, Glaucon, do you prefer?

I for my part deem the life of the just to be the more advantageous, he answered.

Did you hear all the advantages of the unjust which Thrasymachus was rehearsing?

Yes, I heard him, he replied, but he has not convinced me.

Then shall we try to find some way of convincing him, if we can, that he is saying what is not true?

Most certainly, he replied.

If, I said, he makes a set speech and we make another recounting all the advantages of being just, and he answers and we rejoin, there must be a numbering and measuring of the goods which are claimed on either side, and in the end we shall want judges to decide; but if we proceed in our enquiry as we lately did, by making admissions to one another, we shall unite the offices of judge and advocate in our own persons.

Very good, he said.

And which method do I understand you to prefer? I said.

That which you propose.

Well, then, Thrasymachus, I said, suppose you begin at the beginning and answer me. You say that perfect injustice is more gainful than perfect justice?

SOCRATES - GLAUCON - THRASYMACHUS

Yes, that is what I say, and I have given you my reasons.

And what is your view about them? Would you call one of them virtue and the other vice?

Certainly.

I suppose that you would call justice virtue and injustice vice?

What a charming notion! So likely too, seeing that I affirm injustice to be profitable and justice not.

What else then would you say?

The opposite, he replied.

And would you call justice vice?

No, I would rather say sublime simplicity.

Then would you call injustice malignity?

No; I would rather say discretion.

And do the unjust appear to you to be wise and good?

Yes, he said; at any rate those of them who are able to be perfectly unjust, and who have the power of subduing states and nations; but perhaps you imagine me to be talking of cutpurses.

Even this profession if undetected has advantages, though they are not to be compared with those of which I was just now speaking.

I do not think that I misapprehend your meaning, Thrasymachus, I replied; but still I cannot hear without amazement that you class injustice with wisdom and virtue, and justice with the opposite.

Certainly I do so class them.

Now, I said, you are on more substantial and almost unanswerable ground; for if the injustice which you were maintaining to be profitable had been admitted by you as by others to be vice and deformity, an answer might have been given to you on received principles; but now I perceive that you will call injustice honorable and strong, and to the unjust you will attribute all the qualities which were attributed by us before to the just, seeing that you do not hesitate to rank injustice with wisdom and virtue.

You have guessed most infallibly, he replied.

Then I certainly ought not to shrink from going through with the argument so long as I have reason to think that you, Thrasymachus, are speaking your real mind; for I do believe that you are now in earnest and are not amusing yourself at our expense.

I may be in earnest or not, but what is that to you?—to refute the argument is your business.

Very true, I said; that is what I have to do: But will you be so good as answer yet one more question? Does the just man try to gain any advantage over the just?

Far otherwise; if he did would not be the simple, amusing creature which he is.

And would he try to go beyond just action?

He would not.

And how would he regard the attempt to gain an advantage over the unjust; would that be considered by him as just or unjust?

He would think it just, and would try to gain the advantage; but he would not be able.

Whether he would or would not be able, I said, is not to the point. My question is only whether the just man, while refusing to have more than another just man, would wish and claim to have more than the unjust?

Yes, he would.

And what of the unjust—does he claim to have more than the just man and to do more than is just.

Of course, he said, for he claims to have more than all men.

And the unjust man will strive and struggle to obtain more than the unjust man or action, in order that he may have more than all?

True.

We may put the matter thus, I said—the just does not desire more than his like but more than his unlike, whereas the unjust desires more than both his like and his unlike?

Nothing, he said, can be better than that statement.

And the unjust is good and wise, and the just is neither?

Good again, he said.

And is not the unjust like the wise and good and the just unlike them?

Of course, he said, he who is of a certain nature, is like those who are of a certain nature; he who is not, not.

Each of them, I said, is such as his like is?

Certainly, he replied.

Very good, Thrasymachus, I said; and now to take the case of the arts:

you would admit that one man is a musician and another not a musician?

Yes.

And which is wise and which is foolish?

Clearly the musician is wise, and he who is not a musician is foolish.

And he is good in as far as he is wise, and bad in as far as he is foolish?

Yes.

And you would say the same sort of thing of the physician?

Yes.

And do you think, my excellent friend, that a musician when he adjusts the lyre would desire or claim to exceed or go beyond a musician in the tightening and loosening the strings?

I do not think that he would.

But he would claim to exceed the non-musician?

Of course.

And what would you say of the physician? In prescribing meats and drinks would he wish to go beyond another physician or beyond the practice of medicine?

He would not.

But he would wish to go beyond the non-physician?

Yes.

And about knowledge and ignorance in general; see whether you think that any man who has knowledge ever would wish to have the choice of saying or doing more than another man who has knowledge. Would he not rather say or do the same as his like in the same case?

That, I suppose, can hardly be denied.

And what of the ignorant? would he not desire to have more than either the knowing or the ignorant?

I dare say.

And the knowing is wise?

Yes.

And the wise is good?

True.

Then the wise and good will not desire to gain more than his like, but more than his unlike and opposite?

I suppose so.

Whereas the bad and ignorant will desire to gain more than both?

Yes.

But did we not say, Thrasymachus, that the unjust goes beyond both his like and unlike? Were not these your words? They were.

They were.

And you also said that the lust will not go beyond his like but his unlike?

Yes.

Then the just is like the wise and good, and the unjust like the evil and ignorant?

That is the inference.

And each of them is such as his like is?

That was admitted.

Then the just has turned out to be wise and good and the unjust evil and ignorant.

Thrasymachus made all these admissions, not fluently, as I repeat them, but with extreme reluctance; it was a hot summer's day, and the perspiration poured from him in torrents; and then I saw what I had never seen before, Thrasymachus blushing. As we were now agreed that justice was virtue and wisdom, and injustice vice and ignorance, I proceeded to another point:

Well, I said, Thrasymachus, that matter is now settled; but were we not also saying that injustice had strength; do you remember?

Yes, I remember, he said, but do not suppose that I approve of what you are saying or have no answer; if however I were to answer, you would be quite certain to accuse me of haranguing; therefore either permit me to have my say out, or if you would rather ask, do so, and I will answer 'Very good,' as they say to story-telling old women, and will nod 'Yes' and 'No.'

Certainly not, I said, if contrary to your real opinion.

Yes, he said, I will, to please you, since you will not let me speak. What else would you have?

Nothing in the world, I said; and if you are so disposed I will ask and you shall answer.

Proceed.

Then I will repeat the question which I asked before, in order that our examination of the relative nature of justice and injustice may be carried on regularly. A statement was made that injustice is stronger and more powerful than justice, but now justice, having been identified with wisdom and virtue, is easily shown to be stronger than injustice, if injustice is ignorance; this can no longer be questioned by any one. But I want to view the matter, Thrasymachus, in a different way: You would not deny that a state may be unjust and may be unjustly attempting to enslave other states, or may have already enslaved them, and may be holding many of them in subjection?

True, he replied; and I will add the best and perfectly unjust state will be most likely to do so.

I know, I said, that such was your position; but what I would further consider is, whether this power which is possessed by the superior state can exist or be exercised without justice.

If you are right in you view, and justice is wisdom, then only with justice; but if I am right, then without justice.

I am delighted, Thrasymachus, to see you not only nodding assent and dissent, but making answers which are quite excellent.

That is out of civility to you, he replied.

You are very kind, I said; and would you have the goodness also to inform me, whether you think that a state, or an army, or a band of robbers and thieves, or any other gang of evil-doers could act at all if they injured one another?

No indeed, he said, they could not.

But if they abstained from injuring one another, then they might act together better?

Yes.

And this is because injustice creates divisions and hatreds and fighting, and justice imparts harmony and friendship; is not that true, Thrasymachus?

I agree, he said, because I do not wish to quarrel with you.

How good of you, I said; but I should like to know also whether injustice, having this tendency to arouse hatred, wherever existing, among slaves or among freemen, will not make them hate one another and set them at variance and render them incapable of common action?

Certainly.

And even if injustice be found in two only, will they not quarrel and fight, and become enemies to one another and to the just.

They will.

And suppose injustice abiding in a single person, would your wisdom say that she loses or that she retains her natural power?

Let us assume that she retains her power.

Yet is not the power which injustice exercises of such a nature that wherever she takes up her abode, whether in a city, in an army, in a family, or in any other body, that body is, to begin with, rendered incapable of united action by reason of sedition and distraction; and does it not become its own enemy and at variance with all that opposes it, and with the just? Is not this the case?

Yes, certainly.

And is not injustice equally fatal when existing in a single person; in the first place rendering him incapable of action because he is not at unity with himself, and in the second place making him an enemy to himself and the just? Is not that true, Thrasymachus?

Yes.

And O my friend, I said, surely the gods are just?

Granted that they are.

But if so, the unjust will be the enemy of the gods, and the just will be their friend?

Feast away in triumph, and take your fill of the argument; I will not oppose you, lest I should displease the company.

Well then, proceed with your answers, and let me have the remainder of my repast. For we have already shown that the just are clearly wiser and better and abler than the unjust, and that the unjust are incapable of common action; nay ing at more, that to speak as we did of men who are evil acting at any time vigorously together, is not strictly true, for if they had been perfectly evil, they would have laid hands upon one another; but it is evident that there must have been some remnant of justice in them, which enabled them to combine; if there had not been they would have injured one another as well as their victims; they were but half—villains in their enterprises; for had they been whole villains, and utterly unjust, they would have been utterly incapable of action. That, as I believe, is the truth of the matter, and not what you said at first. But whether the just have a better and happier life than the unjust is a further question which we also proposed to consider. I think that they have, and for the reasons which to have given; but still I should like to examine further, for no light matter is at stake, nothing less than the rule of human life.

Proceed.

I will proceed by asking a question: Would you not say that a horse has some end?

I should.

And the end or use of a horse or of anything would be that which could not be accomplished, or not so well accomplished, by any other thing?

I do not understand, he said.

Let me explain: Can you see, except with the eye?

Certainly not.

Or hear, except with the ear?

No.

These then may be truly said to be the ends of these organs?

They may.

But you can cut off a vine-branch with a dagger or with a chisel, and in many other ways?

Of course.

And yet not so well as with a pruning-hook made for the purpose?

True.

May we not say that this is the end of a pruning-hook?

We may.

Then now I think you will have no difficulty in understanding my meaning when I asked the question whether the end of anything would be that which could not be accomplished, or not so well accomplished, by any other thing?

I understand your meaning, he said, and assent.

And that to which an end is appointed has also an excellence? Need I ask again whether the eye has an end?

It has.

And has not the eye an excellence?

Yes.

And the ear has an end and an excellence also?

True.

And the same is true of all other things; they have each of them an end and a special excellence?

That is so.

Well, and can the eyes fulfill their end if they are wanting in their own proper excellence and have a defect instead?

How can they, he said, if they are blind and cannot see?

You mean to say, if they have lost their proper excellence, which is sight; but I have not arrived at that point yet. I would rather ask the question more generally, and only enquire whether the things which fulfill their ends fulfill them by their own proper excellence, and fall of fulfilling them by their own defect?

Certainly, he replied.

I might say the same of the ears; when deprived of their own proper excellence they cannot fulfill their end?

True.

And the same observation will apply to all other things?

I agree.

Well; and has not the soul an end which nothing else can fulfill? for example, to superintend and command and deliberate and the like. Are not these functions proper to the soul, and can they rightly be assigned to any other?

To no other.

And is not life to be reckoned among the ends of the soul?

Assuredly, he said.

And has not the soul an excellence also?

Yes.

And can she or can she not fulfill her own ends when deprived of that excellence?

She cannot.

Then an evil soul must necessarily be an evil ruler and superintendent, and the good soul a good ruler?

Yes, necessarily.

And we have admitted that justice is the excellence of the soul, and injustice the defect of the soul?

That has been admitted.

Then the just soul and the just man will live well, and the unjust man will live ill?

That is what your argument proves.

And he who lives well is blessed and happy, and he who lives ill the reverse of happy?

Certainly.

Then the just is happy, and the unjust miserable?

So be it.

But happiness and not misery is profitable.

Of course.

Then, my blessed Thrasymachus, injustice can never be more profitable than justice.

Let this, Socrates, he said, be your entertainment at the Bendidea.

For which I am indebted to you, I said, now that you have grown gentle towards me and have left off scolding. Nevertheless, I have not been well entertained; but that was my own fault and not yours. As an epicure snatches a taste of every dish which is successively brought to table, he not having allowed himself time to enjoy the one before, so have I gone from one subject to another without having discovered what I sought at first, the nature of justice. I left that enquiry and turned away to consider whether justice is virtue and wisdom or evil and folly; and when there arose a further question about the comparative advantages of justice and injustice, I could not refrain from passing on to that. And the result of the whole discussion has been that I know nothing at all. For I know not what justice is, and therefore I am not likely to know whether it is or is not a virtue, nor can I say whether the just man is happy or unhappy.

EXCERPTS FROM THE *REPUBLIC*

Excerpt 1: The Ring of Gyges: *Republic* 359a–360d

Excerpt 2: The Noble Lie: *Republic* 381e–382d and 414b–415d

Excerpt 3: *Republic* Book V 451c–457c: Equality of the Sexes

Excerpt 4: Forms; the Sun and the Good; the Divided Line: *Republic* Book VI 507b–511e

Excerpt 5: The Cave: *Republic* Book VII 514–527c

The Ring of Gyges: *Republic* 359a–360d

Glaucon (speaking here)

They say that to do injustice is, by nature, good; to suffer injustice, evil; but that the evil is greater than the good. And so when men have both done and suffered injustice and have had experience of both, not being able to avoid the one and obtain the other, they think that they had better agree among themselves to have neither; hence there arise laws and mutual covenants; and that which is ordained by law is termed by them lawful and just. This they affirm to be the origin and nature of justice;—it is a mean or compromise, between the best of all, which is to do injustice and not be punished, and the worst of all, which is to suffer injustice without the power of retaliation; and justice, being at a middle point between the two, is tolerated not as a good, but as the lesser evil, and honored by reason of the inability of men to do injustice. For no man who is worthy to be called a man would ever submit to such an agreement if he were able to resist; he would be mad if he did. Such is the received account, Socrates, of the nature and origin of justice.

Now that those who practice justice do so involuntarily and because they have not the power to be unjust will best appear if we imagine something of this kind: having given both to the just and the unjust power to do what they will, let us watch and see whither desire will lead them; then we shall discover in the very act the just and unjust man to be proceeding along the same road, following their interest, which all natures deem to be their good, and are only diverted into the path of justice by the force of law. The liberty which we are supposing may be most completely given to them in the form of such a power as is said to have been Possessed by Gyges, the ancestor of Croesus the Lydian. The story of Gyges. According to the tradition, Gyges was a shepherd in the service of the king of Lydia; there was a great storm, and an earthquake made an opening in the earth at the place where he was feeding his flock. Amazed at the sight, he 39 descended into the opening, where, among other marvels, he beheld a hollow brazen horse, having doors, at which he stooping and looking in saw a dead body of stature, as appeared to him, more than human, and having nothing on but a gold ring; this he took from the finger of the dead and rescinded. Now the shepherds met together, according to custom, that they might send their monthly report about the flocks to the king; into their assembly he came having the ring on his finger, and as he was sitting among them he chanced to turn the collet of the ring inside his hand, when instantly he became invisible to the rest of the company and they began to speak of him as if he were no longer present. He was astonished at this, and again touching the ring he turned the collet outwards and reappeared; he made several trials of the ring, and always with the same result—when he turned the collet inwards he became invisible, when outwards he reappeared. Whereupon he contrived to be chosen one of the messengers who were sent to the court; where as soon as he arrived he seduced the queen, and with her help conspired against the king and slew him, and took the kingdom. The application of the story of Gyges. Suppose now that there were two such magic rings, and the just put on one of them and the unjust the other; no man can be imagined to be of such an iron nature that he would stand fast in justice. No man would keep his hands off what was not his own when he could safely take what he liked out of the market, or go into houses and lie with any one at his pleasure, or kill or release from prison whom he would, and in all respects be like a God among men. Then the actions of the just would be as the actions of the unjust; they would both come at last to the same point. And this we may truly affirm to be a great proof that a man is just, not willingly or because he thinks that justice is any good to him individually, but of necessity, for wherever any one thinks that he can safely be unjust, there he is unjust. For all men believe in their hearts that injustice is far more profitable to the individual than justice, and he who argues as I have been supposing, will say that they are right. If you could imagine any one obtaining this power of becoming invisible, and never doing any wrong or touching what was another's, he would be thought by the lookers-on to be a most wretched idiot, although they would praise him to one another's faces, and keep up appearances with one another from a fear that they too might suffer injustice. Enough of this.

Now, if we are to form a real judgment of the life of the just and unjust, we must isolate them; there is no other way; and how is the isolation to be effected? I answer: Let the unjust man be entirely unjust, and the just man entirely just; nothing is to be taken away from either of them, and both are to be perfectly furnished for the work of their respective lives. The unjust to be clothed with power and reputation. First, let the unjust be like other distinguished masters of craft; like the skillful pilot or physician, who knows intuitively his own powers and keeps within their limits, and who, if he fails at any point, is able to recover himself. So let the unjust make his unjust attempts in the right way, and lie hidden if he means to be great in his injustice: (he who is found out is nobody:) for the highest reach of injustice is, to be deemed just when you are not. Therefore I say that in the perfectly unjust man we must assume the most perfect injustice; there is to be no deduction, but we must allow him, while doing the most unjust acts, to have acquired the greatest reputation for justice. If he have taken a false step he must be able to recover himself; he must be one who can speak with effect, if any of his deeds come to light, and who can force his way where force is required by his courage and strength, and command of money and friends. And at his side let us place the just man in his nobleness and simplicity, wishing, as Aeschylus says, to be and not to seem good. The just to be unclothed of all but his virtue. There must be no seeming, for if he seem to be just he will be honored and rewarded, and then we shall not know whether he is just for the sake of justice or for the sake of honors and rewards; therefore, let him be clothed in justice only, and have no other covering; and he must be imagined in a state of life the opposite of the former. Let him be the best of men, and let him be thought the worst; then he will have been put to the proof; and we shall see whether he will be affected by the fear of infamy and its consequences. And let him continue thus to the hour of death; being just and seeming to be unjust. When both have reached the uttermost extreme, the one of justice and the other of injustice, let judgment be given which of them is the happier of the two.

The Noble Lie: *Republic* 381e–382d and 414b–415d

—let us have no more lies of that sort. Neither must we have mothers under the influence of the poets scaring their children with a bad version of these myths—telling how certain gods, as they say, 'Go about by night in the likeness of so many strangers and in divers forms;' but let them take heed lest they make cowards of their children, and at the same time speak blasphemy against the gods.

Heaven forbid, he said.

But although the gods are themselves unchangeable, still by witchcraft and deception they may make us think that they appear in various forms?

Perhaps, he replied.

Nor will he make any false representation of himself. Well, but can you imagine that God will be willing to lie, whether in word or deed, or to put forth a phantom of himself?

I cannot say, he replied.

Do you not know, I said, that the true lie, if such an expression may be allowed, is hated of gods and men?

What do you mean? he said.

I mean that no one is willingly deceived in that which is the truest and highest part of himself, or about the truest and highest matters; there, above all, he is most afraid of a lie having possession of him.

Still, he said, I do not comprehend you.

The reason is, I replied, that you attribute some profound meaning to my words; but I am only saying that deception, or being deceived or uninformed about the highest realities in the highest part of themselves, which is the soul, and in that part of them to have and to hold the lie, is what mankind least like;—that, I say, is what they utterly detest.

There is nothing more hateful to them.

And, as I was just now remarking, this ignorance in the soul of him who is deceived may be called the true lie; for the lie in words is only a kind of imitation and shadowy image of a previous affection of the soul, not pure unadulterated falsehood. Am I not right?

Perfectly right.

The true lie is equally hated both by gods and men; the remedial or preventive lie is comparatively innocent, but God can have no need of it. The true lie is hated not only by the gods, but also by men?

Yes.

Whereas the lie in words is in certain cases useful and not hateful; in dealing with enemies—that would be an instance; or again, when those whom we call our friends in a fit of madness or illusion are going to do some harm, then it is useful and is a sort of medicine or preventive; also in the tales of mythology, of which we were just now speaking—because we do not know the truth about ancient times, we make falsehood as much like truth as we can, and so turn it to account.

414b–415d

How then may we devise one of those needful falsehoods of which we lately spoke—just one royal lie which may deceive the rulers, if that be possible, and at any rate the rest of the city?

What sort of lie? he said.

The Phoenician tale. Nothing new, I replied; only an old Phoenician tale of what has often occurred before now in other places, (as the poets say, and have made the world believe) though not in our time, and I do not know whether such an event could ever happen again, or could now even be made probable, if it did.

How your words seem to hesitate on your lips!

You will not wonder, I replied, at my hesitation when you have heard.

Speak, he said, and fear not.

The citizens to be told that they are really autochthonous, sent up out of the earth, Well then, I will speak, although I really know not how to look you in the face, or in what words to utter the audacious fiction, which I propose to communicate gradually, first to the rulers, then to the soldiers, and lastly to the people. They are to be told that their youth was a dream, and the education and training which they received from us, an appearance only; in reality during all that time they were being formed and fed in the womb of the earth, where they themselves and their arms and appurtenances were manufactured; when they were completed, the earth, their mother, sent them up; and so, their country being their mother and also their nurse, they are bound to advise for her good, and to defend her against attacks, and her citizens they are to regard as children of the earth and their own brothers.

You had good reason, he said, to be ashamed of the lie which you were going to tell.

True, I replied, but there is more coming; I have only told you half. Citizens, we shall say to them in our tale, you are brothers, yet God has framed you differently. Some of you have the power of command, and in the composition of these he has mingled gold, wherefore also they have the greatest honor; others he has made of silver, to be auxiliaries; others again who are to be husbandmen and craftsmen he has composed of brass and iron; and the species will generally be preserved in the children. But as all are of the same original stock, a golden parent will sometimes have a silver son, or a silver parent a golden son. And God proclaims as a first principle to the rulers, and above all else, that there is nothing which they should so anxiously guard, or of which they are to be such good guardians, as of the purity of the race. The noble quality to rise in the State, the ignoble to descend. They should observe what elements mingle in their offspring; for if the son of a golden or silver parent has an admixture of brass and iron, then nature orders a transposition of ranks, and the eye of the ruler must not be pitiful towards the child because he has to descend in the scale and become a husbandman or artisan, just as there may be sons of artisans who having an admixture of gold or silver in them are raised to honor, and become guardians or auxiliaries. For an oracle says that when a man of brass or iron guards the State, it will be destroyed. Is such a fiction credible?—Yes, in a future generation; not in the present. Such is the tale; is there any possibility of making our citizens believe in it?

Not in the present generation, he replied; there is no way of accomplishing this; but their sons may be made to believe in the tale, and their sons' sons, and posterity after them.

I see the difficulty, I replied; yet the fostering of such a belief will make them care more for the city and for one another.

Republic Book V 451c–457c: Equality of the Sexes

Well, I replied, I suppose that I must retrace my steps and say what I perhaps ought to have said before in the proper place. The part of the men has been played out, and now properly enough comes the turn of the women. Of them I will proceed to speak, and the more readily since I am invited by you.

For men born and educated like our citizens, the only way, in my opinion, of arriving at a right conclusion about the possession and use of women and children is to follow the path on which we originally started, when we said that the men were to be the guardians and watchdogs of the herd.

True.

Let us further suppose the birth and education of our women to be subject to similar or nearly similar regulations; then we shall see whether the result accords with our design.

What do you mean?

No distinction among the animals such as is made between men and women. What I mean may be put into the form of a question, I said: Are dogs divided into hes and shes, or do they both share equally in hunting and in keeping watch and in the other duties of dogs? or do we entrust to the males the entire and exclusive care of the flocks, while we leave the females at home, under the idea that the bearing and suckling their puppies is labor enough for them?

No, he said, they share alike; the only difference between them is that the males are stronger and the females weaker.

But can you use different animals for the same purpose, unless they are bred and fed in the same way?

You cannot.

Then, if women are to have the same duties as men, they must have the same nurture and education?

Yes.

The education which was assigned to the men was music and gymnastic.

Yes.

Women must be taught music, gymnastic, and military exercises equally with men. Then women must be taught music and gymnastic and also the art of war, which they must practice like the men?

That is the inference, I suppose.

I should rather expect, I said, that several of our proposals, if they are carried out, being unusual, may appear ridiculous.

No doubt of it.

Yes, and the most ridiculous thing of all will be the sight of women naked in the palaestra, exercising with the men, especially when they are no longer young; they certainly will not be a vision of beauty, any more than the enthusiastic old men who in spite of wrinkles and ugliness continue to frequent the gymnasia.

Yes, indeed, he said: according to present notions the proposal would be thought ridiculous.

But then, I said, as we have determined to speak our minds, we must not fear the jests of the wits which will be directed against this sort of innovation; how they will talk of women's attainments both in music and gymnastic, and above all about their wearing armour and riding upon horseback!

Very true, he replied.

Convention should not be permitted to stand in the way of a higher good. Yet having begun we must go forward to the rough places of the law; at the same time begging of these gentlemen for once in their life to be serious. Not long ago, as we shall remind them, the Hellenes were of the opinion, which is still generally received among the barbarians, that the sight of a naked man was ridiculous and improper; and when first the Cretans and then the Lacedaemonians introduced the custom, the wits of that day might equally have ridiculed the innovation.

No doubt.

But when experience showed that to let all things be uncovered was far better than to cover them up, and the ludicrous effect to the outward eye vanished before the better principle which reason asserted, then the man was perceived to be a fool who directs the shafts of his ridicule at any other sight but that of folly and vice, or seriously inclines to weigh the beautiful by any other standard but that of the good.

Very true, he replied.

First, then, whether the question is to be put in jest or in earnest, let us come to an understanding about the nature of woman: Is she capable of sharing either wholly or partially in the actions of men, or not at all? And is the art of war one of those arts in which she can or can not share? That will be the best way of commencing the enquiry, and will probably lead to the fairest conclusion.

That will be much the best way.

Shall we take the other side first and begin by arguing against ourselves; in this manner the adversary's position will not be undefended.

Why not? he said.

Objection: We were saying that every one should do his own work: Have not women and men severally a work of their own? Then let us put a speech into the mouths of our opponents. They will say: 'Socrates and Glaucon, no adversary need convict you, for you yourselves, at the first foundation of the State, admitted the principle that everybody was to do the one work suited to his own nature.' And certainly, if I am not mistaken, such an admission was made by us. 'And do not the natures of men and women differ very much indeed?' And we shall reply: Of course they do. Then we shall be asked, 'Whether the tasks assigned to men and to women should not be different, and such as are agreeable to their different natures?' Certainly they should. 'But if so, have you not fallen into a serious inconsistency in saying that men and women, whose natures are so entirely different, ought to perform the same actions?'—What defense will you make for us, my good Sir, against any one who offers these objections?

That is not an easy question to answer when asked suddenly; and I shall and I do beg of you to draw out the case on our side.

These are the objections, Glaucon, and there are many others of a like kind, which I foresaw long ago; they made me afraid and reluctant to take in hand any law about the possession and nurture of women and children.

By Zeus, he said, the problem to be solved is anything but easy.

Why yes, I said, but the fact is that when a man is out of his depth, whether he has fallen into a little swimming bath or into mid ocean, he has to swim all the same.

Very true.

And must not we swim and try to reach the shore: we will hope that Arion's dolphin or some other miraculous help may save us?

I suppose so, he said.

Well then, let us see if any way of escape can be found. We acknowledged—did we not? that different natures ought to have different pursuits, and that men's and women's natures are different. And now what are we saying?—that different natures ought to have the same pursuits,—this is the inconsistency which is charged upon us.

Precisely.

Verily, Glaucon, I said, glorious is the power of the art of contradiction!

Why do you say so?

The seeming inconsistency arises out of a verbal opposition. Because I think that many a man falls into the practice against his will. When he thinks that he is reasoning he is really disputing, just because he cannot define and divide, and so know that of which he is speaking; and he will pursue a merely verbal opposition in the spirit of contention and not of fair discussion.

Yes, he replied, such is very often the case; but what has that to do with us and our argument?

A great deal; for there is certainly a danger of our getting unintentionally into a verbal opposition.

In what way?

When we assigned to different natures different pursuits, we meant only those differences of nature which affected the pursuits. Why we valiantly and pugnaciously insist upon the verbal truth, that different natures ought to have different pursuits, but we never considered at all what was the meaning of sameness or difference of nature, or why we distinguished them when we assigned different pursuits to different natures and the same to the same natures.

Why, no, he said, that was never considered by us.

I said: Suppose that by way of illustration we were to ask the question whether there is not an opposition in nature between bald men and hairy men; and if this is admitted by us, then, if bald men are cobblers, we should forbid the hairy men to be cobblers, and conversely?

That would be a jest, he said.

Yes, I said, a jest; and why? because we never meant when we constructed the State, that the opposition of natures should extend to every difference, but only to those differences which affected the pursuit in which the individual is engaged; we should have argued, for example, that a physician and one who is in mind a physician may be said to have the same nature.

True.

Whereas the physician and the carpenter have different natures?

Certainly.

And if, I said, the male and female sex appear to differ in their fitness for any art or pursuit, we should say that such pursuit or art ought to be assigned to one or the other of them; but if the difference consists only in women bearing and men begetting children, this does not amount to a proof that a woman differs from a man in respect of the sort of education she should receive; and we shall therefore continue to maintain that our guardians and their wives ought to have the same pursuits.

Very true, he said.

Next, we shall ask our opponent how, in reference to any of the pursuits or arts of civic life, the nature of a woman differs from that of a man?

That will be quite fair.

And perhaps he, like yourself, will reply that to give a sufficient answer on the instant is not easy; but after a little reflection there is no difficulty.

Yes, perhaps.

Suppose then that we invite him to accompany us in the argument, and then we may hope to show him that there is nothing peculiar in the constitution of women which would affect them in the administration of the State.

By all means.

The same natural gifts are found in both sexes, but they are possessed in a higher degree by men than women. Let us say to him: Come now, and we will ask you a question:—when you spoke of a nature gifted or not gifted in any respect, did you mean to say that one man will acquire a thing easily, another with difficulty; a little learning will lead the one to discover a great deal; whereas the other, after much study and application, no sooner learns than he forgets; or again, did you mean, that the one has a body which is a good servant to his mind, while the body of the other is a hindrance to him?—would not these be the sort of differences which distinguish the man gifted by nature from the one who is ungifted?

No one will deny that.

And can you mention any pursuit of mankind in which the male sex has not all these gifts and qualities in a higher degree than the female? Need I waste time in speaking of the art of weaving, and the management of pancakes and preserves, in which womankind does really appear to be great, and in which for her to be beaten by a man is of all things the most absurd?

You are quite right, he replied, in maintaining the general inferiority of the female sex: although many women are in many things superior to many men, yet on the whole what you say is true.

And if so, my friend, I said, there is no special faculty of administration in a state which a woman has because she is a woman, or which a man has by virtue of his sex, but the gifts of nature are alike diffused in both; all the pursuits of men are the pursuits of women also, but in all of them a woman is inferior to a man.

Very true.

Men and women are to be governed by the same laws and to have the same pursuits. Then are we to impose all our enactments on men and none of them on women?

That will never do.

One woman has a gift of healing, another not; one is a musician, and another has no music in her nature?

Very true.

And one woman has a turn for gymnastic and military exercises, and another is unwarlike and hates gymnastics?

Certainly.

And one woman is a philosopher, and another is an enemy of philosophy; one has spirit, and another is without spirit?

That is also true.

Then one woman will have the temper of a guardian, and another not. Was not the selection of the male guardians determined by differences of this sort?

Yes.

Men and women alike possess the qualities which make a guardian; they differ only in their comparative strength or weakness.

Obviously.

And those women who have such qualities are to be selected as the companions and colleagues of men who have similar qualities and whom they resemble in capacity and in character?

Very true.

And ought not the same natures to have the same pursuits?

They ought.

Then, as we were saying before, there is nothing unnatural in assigning music and gymnastic to the wives of the guardians—to that point we come round again.

Certainly not.

The law which we then enacted was agreeable to nature, and therefore not an impossibility or mere aspiration; and the contrary practice, which prevails at present, is in reality a violation of nature.

That appears to be true.

We had to consider, first, whether our proposals were possible, and secondly whether they were the most beneficial?

Yes.

And the possibility has been acknowledged?

Yes.

The very great benefit has next to be established?

Quite so.

There are different degrees of goodness both in women and in men. You will admit that the same education which makes a man a good guardian will make a woman a good guardian; for their original nature is the same?

Yes.

I should like to ask you a question.

What is it?

Would you say that all men are equal in excellence, or is one man better than another?

The latter.

And in the commonwealth which we were founding do you conceive the guardians who have been brought up on our model system to be more perfect men, or the cobblers whose education has been cobbling?

What a ridiculous question!

You have answered me, I replied: Well, and may we not further say that our guardians are the best of our citizens?

By far the best.

And will not their wives be the best women?

Yes, by far the best.

And can there be anything better for the interests of the State than that the men and women of a State should be as good as possible?

There can be nothing better.

And this is what the arts of music and gymnastic, when present in such manner as we have described, will accomplish?

Certainly.

Then we have made an enactment not only possible but in the highest degree beneficial to the State?

True.

Then let the wives of our guardians strip, for their virtue will be their robe, and let them share in the toils of war and the defense of their country; only in the distribution of labors the lighter are to be assigned to the women, who are the weaker natures, but in other respects their duties are to be the same. And as for the man who laughs at naked women exercising their bodies from the best of motives, in his laughter he is plucking

'A fruit of unripe wisdom,'

and he himself is ignorant of what he is laughing at, or what he is about;—for that is, and ever will be, the best of The noble saying.sayings, *That the useful is the noble and the hurtful is the base.*

Very true.

Here, then, is one difficulty in our law about women, which we may say that we have now escaped; the wave has not swallowed us up alive for enacting that the guardians of either sex should have all their pursuits in common; to the utility and also to the possibility of this arrangement the consistency of the argument with itself bears witness.

Forms; the Sun and the Good; the Divided Line: *Republic* Book VI 507b–511e

The old story, that there is a many beautiful and a many good, and so of other things which we describe and define; to all of them the term 'many' is applied.

True, he said.

And there is an absolute beauty and an absolute good, and of other things to which the term 'many' is applied there is an absolute; for they may be brought under a single idea, which is called the essence of each.

Very true.

The many, as we say, are seen but not known, and the ideas are known but not seen.

Exactly.

And what is the organ with which we see the visible things?

The sight, he said.

And with the hearing, I said, we hear, and with the other senses perceive the other objects of sense?

True.

Sight the most complex of the senses, But have you remarked that sight is by far the most costly and complex piece of workmanship which the artificer of the senses ever contrived?

No, I never have, he said.

Then reflect; has the ear or voice need of any third or additional nature in order that the one may be able to hear and the other to be heard?

Nothing of the sort.

No, indeed, I replied; and the same is true of most, if not all, the other senses—you would not say that any of them requires such an addition?

Certainly not.

But you see that without the addition of some other nature there is no seeing or being seen?

How do you mean?

and, unlike the other senses, requires the addition of a third nature before it can be used. This third nature is light. Sight being, as I conceive, in the eyes, and he who has eyes wanting to see; color being also present in them, still Eunless there be a third nature specially adapted to the purpose, the owner of the eyes will see nothing and the colors will be invisible.

Of what nature are you speaking?

Of that which you term light, I replied.

True, he said.

Noble, then, is the bond which links together sight and visibility, and great beyond other bonds by no small difference of nature; for light is their bond, and light is no ignoble thing?

Nay, he said, the reverse of ignoble.

And which, I said, of the gods in heaven would you say was the lord of this element? Whose is that light which makes the eye to see perfectly and the visible to appear?

You mean the sun, as you and all mankind say.

May not the relation of sight to this deity be described as follows?

How?

Neither sight nor the eye in which sight resides is the sun?

No.

The eye like the sun, but not the same with it. Yet of all the organs of sense the eye is the most like the sun?

By far the most like.

And the power which the eye possesses is a sort of effluence which is dispensed from the sun?

Exactly.

Then the sun is not sight, but the author of sight who is recognized by sight?

True, he said.

And this is he whom I call the child of the good, whom the good begat in his own likeness, to be in the visible world, in relation to sight and the things of sight, what the good is in the intellectual world in relation to mind and the things of mind:

Will you be a little more explicit? he said.

Why, you know, I said, that the eyes, when a person directs them towards objects on which the light of day is no longer shining, but the moon and stars only, see dimly, and are nearly blind; they seem to have no clearness of vision in them?

Very true.

Visible objects are to be seen only when the sun shines upon them; truth is only known when illuminated by the idea of good. But when they are directed towards objects on which the sun shines, they see clearly and there is sight in them?

Certainly.

And the soul is like the eye: when resting upon that on which truth and being shine, the soul perceives and understands, and is radiant with intelligence; but when turned towards the twilight of becoming and perishing, then she has opinion only, and goes blinking about, and is first of one opinion and then of another, and seems to have no intelligence?

Just so.

The idea of good higher than science or truth (the objective than the subjective). Now, that which imparts truth to the known and the power of knowing to the knower is what I would have you term the idea of good, and this you will deem to be the cause of science, and of truth in so far as the latter becomes the subject of knowledge; beautiful too, as are both truth and knowledge, you will be right in esteeming this other nature as more beautiful than either; and, as in the previous instance, light and sight may be truly said to be like the sun, and yet not to be the sun, so in this other sphere, science and truth may be deemed to be like the good, but not the good; the good has a place of honor yet higher.

What a wonder of beauty that must be, he said, which is the author of science and truth, and yet surpasses them in beauty; for you surely cannot mean to say that pleasure is the good?

God forbid, I replied; but may I ask you to consider the image in another point of view?

In what point of view?

You would say, would you not, that the sun is not only the author of visibility in all visible things, but of generation and nourishment and growth, though he himself is not generation?

Certainly.

As the sun is the cause of generation, so the good is the cause of being and essence. In like manner the good may be said to be not only the author of knowledge to all things known, but of their being and essence, and yet the good is not essence, but far exceeds essence in dignity and power.

Glaucon said, with a ludicrous earnestness: By the light of heaven, how amazing!

Yes, I said, and the exaggeration may be set down to you; for you made me utter my fancies.

And pray continue to utter them; at any rate let us hear if there is anything more to be said about the similitude of the sun.

Yes, I said, there is a great deal more.

Then omit nothing, however slight.

I will do my best, I said; but I should think that a great deal will have to be omitted.

I hope not, he said.

You have to imagine, then, that there are two ruling powers, and that one of them is set over the intellectual world, the other over the visible. I do not say heaven, lest you should fancy that I am playing upon the name (ουρανος, ορατος). May I suppose that you have this distinction of the visible and intelligible fixed in your mind?

I have.

The two spheres of sight and knowledge are represented by a line which is divided into two unequal parts. Now take a line which has been cut into two unequal parts, and divide each of them again in the same proportion, and suppose the two main divisions to answer, one to the visible and the other to the intelligible, and then compare the subdivisions in respect of their clearness and want of Eclearness, and you will find that the first section in the sphere of the visible consists of images. And by images I mean, in the first place, shadows, and in the second place, reflections in water and in solid, smooth and polished bodies and the like: Do you understand?

Yes, I understand.

Imagine, now, the other section, of which this is only the resemblance, to include the animals which we see, and everything that grows or is made.

Very good.

Would you not admit that both the sections of this division have different degrees of truth, and that the copy is to the original as the sphere of opinion is to the sphere of knowledge?

Most undoubtedly.

Next proceed to consider the manner in which the sphere of the intellectual is to be divided.

In what manner?

Images and hypotheses. Thus:—There are two subdivisions, in the lower of which the soul uses the figures given by the former division as images; the enquiry can only be hypothetical, and instead of going upwards to a principle descends to the other end; in the higher of the two, the soul passes out of hypotheses, and goes up to a principle which is above hypotheses, making no use of images as in the former case, but proceeding only in and through the ideas themselves.

I do not quite understand your meaning, he said.

The hypotheses of mathematics. Then I will try again; you will understand me better when I have made some preliminary remarks. You are aware that students of geometry, arithmetic, and the kindred sciences assume the odd and the even and the figures and three kinds of angles and the like in their several branches of science; these are their hypotheses, which they and every body are supposed to know, and therefore they do not deign to give any account of them either to themselves or others; but they begin with them, and go on until they arrive at last, and in a consistent manner, at their conclusion?

Yes, he said, I know.

In both spheres hypotheses are used, in the lower taking the form of images, but in the higher the soul ascends above hypotheses to the idea of good. And do you not know also that although they make use of the visible forms and reason about them, they are thinking not of these, but of the ideals which they resemble; not of the figures which they draw, but of the absolute square and the absolute diameter, and so on—the forms which they draw or make, and which have shadows and reflections in water of their own, are converted by them into images, but they are really seeking to behold the things themselves, which can only be seen with the eye of the mind?

That is true.

And of this kind I spoke as the intelligible, although in the search after it the soul is compelled to use hypotheses; not ascending to a first principle, because she is unable to rise above the region of hypothesis, but employing the objects of which the shadows below are resemblances in their turn as images, they having in relation to the shadows and reflections of them a greater distinctness, and therefore a higher value.

I understand, he said, that you are speaking of the province of geometry and the sister arts.

Dialectic by the help of hypotheses rises above hypotheses. And when I speak of the other division of the intelligible, you will understand me to speak of that other sort of knowledge which reason herself attains by the power of dialectic, using the hypotheses not as first principles, but only as hypotheses—that is to say, as steps and points of departure into a world which is above hypotheses, in order that she may soar beyond them to the first principle of the whole; and clinging to this and then to that which depends on this, by successive steps she descends again without the aid of any sensible object, from ideas, through ideas, and in ideas she ends.

I understand you, he replied; not perfectly, for you seem to me to be describing a task which is really tremendous; but, at any rate, I understand you to say that knowledge and being, which the science of dialectic contemplates, are clearer than the notions of the arts, as they are termed, which proceed from hypotheses only: these are also contemplated by the understanding, and not by the senses: yet, because they start from hypotheses and do not ascend to a principle, those who contemplate them appear to you not to exercise the higher reason upon them, although when a first principle is added to them they are cognizable by the higher reason. Return to psychology. And the habit which is concerned with geometry and the cognate sciences I suppose that you would term understanding and not reason, as being intermediate between opinion and reason.

Four faculties: Reason, understanding, faith, perception of shadows. You have quite conceived my meaning, I said; and now, corresponding to these four divisions, let there be four faculties in the soul—reason answering to the highest, understanding to the second, faith (or conviction) to the third, and perception of shadows to the last—and let there be a scale of them, and let us suppose that the several faculties have clearness in the same degree that their objects have truth.

I understand, he replied, and give my assent, and accept your arrangement.

Excerpt 5: The Cave: *Republic* Book VII 514–527c

AND now, I said, let me show in a figure how far our nature is enlightened or unenlightened:—Behold! human beings living in a underground den, which has a mouth open towards the light and reaching all along the den; here they have been from their childhood, and have their legs and necks chained so that they cannot move, and Bcan only see before them, being prevented by the chains from turning round their heads. Above and behind them a fire is blazing at a distance, and between the fire and the prisoners there is a raised way; and you will see, if you look, a low wall built along the way, like the screen which marionette players have in front of them, over which they show the puppets.

I see.

The low wall, and the moving figures of which the shadows are seen on the opposite wall of the den. And do you see, I said, men passing along the wall carrying all sorts of vessels, and statues and figures of animals made of wood and stone and various materials, which appear over the wall? Some of them are talking, others silent.

You have shown me a strange image, and they are strange prisoners.

Like ourselves, I replied; and they see only their own shadows, or the shadows of one another, which the fire throws on the opposite wall of the cave?

True, he said; how could they see anything but the shadows if they were never allowed to move their heads?

And of the objects which are being carried in like manner they would only see the shadows?

Yes, he said.

And if they were able to converse with one another, would they not suppose that they were naming what was actually before them?

Very true.

The prisoners would mistake the shadows for realities. And suppose further that the prison had an echo which came from the other side, would they not be sure to fancy when one of the passers-by spoke that the voice which they heard came from the passing shadow?

No question, he replied.

To them, I said, the truth would be literally nothing but the shadows of the images.

That is certain.

And now look again, and see what will naturally follow if the prisoners are released and disabused of their error. At first, when any of them is liberated and compelled suddenly to stand up and turn his neck round and walk and look towards the light, he will suffer sharp pains; the glare will distress him, and he will be unable to see the realities of which in his former state he had seen the shadows; and then conceive some one saying to him, that what he saw before was an illusion, but that now, when he is approaching nearer to being and his eye is turned towards more real existence, he has a clearer vision,—what will be his reply? And when released, they would still persist in maintaining the superior truth of the shadows. And you may further imagine that his instructor is pointing to the objects as they pass and requiring him to name them,—will he not be perplexed? Will he not fancy that the shadows which he formerly saw are truer than the objects which are now shown to him?

Far truer.

And if he is compelled to look straight at the light, will he not have a pain in his eyes which will make him turn away to take refuge in the objects of vision which he can see, and which he will conceive to be in reality clearer than the things which are now being shown to him?

True, he said.

When dragged upwards, they would be dazzled by excess of light. And suppose once more, that he is reluctantly dragged up a steep and rugged ascent, and held fast until he is forced into the presence of the sun himself, is he not likely to be pained and irritated? When he approaches the light his eyes will be dazzled, and he will not be able to see anything at all of what are now called realities.

Not all in a moment, he said.

He will require to grow accustomed to the sight of the upper world. And first he will see the shadows best, next the reflections of men and other objects in the water, and then the objects themselves; then he will gaze upon the light of the moon and the stars and the spangled heaven; Band he will see the sky and the stars by night better than the sun or the light of the sun by day?

Certainly.

At length they will see the sun and understand his nature. Last of all he will be able to see the sun, and not mere reflections of him in the water, but he will see him in his own proper place, and not in another; and he will contemplate him as he is.

Certainly.

He will then proceed to argue that this is he who gives the season and the years, and is the guardian of all that is in the visible world, and in a certain way the cause of all things which he and his fellows have been accustomed to behold?

Clearly, he said, he would first see the sun and then reason about him.

They would then pity their old companions of the den. And when he remembered his old habitation, and the wisdom of the den and his fellow-prisoners, do you not suppose that he would felicitate himself on the change, and pity them?

Certainly, he would.

And if they were in the habit of conferring honors among themselves on those who were quickest to observe the passing shadows and to remark which of them went before, and which followed after, and which were together; and who were therefore best able to draw conclusions as to the future, do you think that he would care for such honors and glories, or envy the possessors of them? Would he not say with Homer,

'Better to be the poor servant of a poor master,'

and to endure anything, rather than think as they do and live after their manner?

Yes, he said, I think that he would rather suffer anything than entertain these false notions and live in this miserable manner.

But when they returned to the den they would see much worse than those who had never left it. Imagine once more, I said, such an one coming suddenly out of the sun to be replaced in his old situation; would he not be certain to have his eyes full of darkness?

To be sure, he said.

And if there were a contest, and he had to compete in measuring the shadows with the prisoners who had never moved out of the den, while his sight was still weak, and before his eyes had become steady (and the time which would be needed to acquire this new habit of sight might be very considerable), would he not be ridiculous? Men would say of him that up he went and down he came without his eyes; and that it was better not even to think of ascending; and if any one tried to loose another and lead him up to the light, let them only catch the offender, and they would put him to death.

No question, he said.

The prison is the world of sight, the light of the fire is the sun. This entire allegory, I said, you may now append, dear Glaucon, to the previous argument; the prison-house is the world of sight, the light of the fire is the sun, and you will not misapprehend me if you interpret the journey upwards to be the ascent of the soul into the intellectual world according to my poor belief, which, at your desire, I have expressed—whether rightly or wrongly God knows. But, whether true or false, my opinion is that in the world of knowledge the idea of good appears last of all, and is seen only with an effort; and, when seen, is also inferred to be the universal author of all things beautiful and right, parent of light and of the lord of light in this visible world, and the immediate source of reason and truth in the intellectual; and that this is the power upon which he who would act rationally either in public or private life must have his eye fixed.

I agree, he said, as far as I am able to understand you.

Moreover, I said, you must not wonder that those who attain to this beatific vision are unwilling to descend to human affairs; for their souls are ever hastening into the upper world where they desire to dwell; which desire of theirs is very natural, if our allegory may be trusted.

Yes, very natural.

Nothing extraordinary in the philosopher being unable to see in the dark. And is there anything surprising in one who passes from divine contemplations to the evil state of man, misbehaving himself in a ridiculous manner; if, while his eyes are blinking and before he has become accustomed to the surrounding darkness, he is compelled to fight in courts of law, or in other places, about the images or the shadows of images of justice, and is endeavoring to meet the conceptions of those who have never yet seen absolute justice?

Anything but surprising, he replied.

The eyes may be blinded in two ways, by excess or by defect of light. Any one who has common sense will remember that the bewilderments of the eyes are of two kinds, and arise from two causes, either from coming out of the light or from going into the light, which is true of the mind's eye, quite as much as of the bodily eye; and he who remembers this when he sees any one whose vision is perplexed and weak, will not be too ready to laugh; he will first ask whether that soul of man has come out of the brighter life, and is unable to see because unaccustomed to the dark, or having turned from darkness to the day is dazzled by excess of light. And he will count the one happy in his condition and state of being, and he will pity the other; or, if he have a mind to laugh at the soul which comes from below into the light, there will be more reason in this than in the laugh which greets him who returns from above out of the light into the den.

That, he said, is a very just distinction.

The conversion of the soul is the turning round the eye from darkness to light. But then, if I am right, certain professors of education must be wrong when they say that they can put a knowledge into the soul which was not there before, like sight into blind eyes.

They undoubtedly say this, he replied.

Whereas, our argument shows that the power and capacity of learning exists in the soul already; and that just as the eye was unable to turn from darkness to light without the whole body, so too the instrument of knowledge can only by the movement of the whole soul be turned from the world of becoming into that of being, and learn by degrees to endure the sight of being, and of the brightest and best of being, or in other words, of the good.

Very true.

And must there not be some art which will effect conversion in the easiest and quickest manner; not implanting the faculty of sight, for that exists already, but has been turned in the wrong direction, and is looking away from the truth?

Yes, he said, such an art may be presumed.

The virtue of wisdom has a divine power which may be turned either towards good or towards evil. And whereas the other so-called virtues of the soul seem to be akin to bodily qualities, for even when they are not originally innate they can be implanted later by habit and exercise, the virtue of wisdom more than anything else contains a divine element which always remains, and by this conversion is rendered useful and profitable; or, on the other hand, hurtful and useless. Did you never observe the narrow intelligence flashing from the keen eye of a clever rogue—how eager he is, how clearly his paltry soul sees the way to his end; he is the reverse of blind, but his keen eye-sight is forced into the service of evil, and he is mischievous in proportion to his cleverness?

Very true, he said.

But what if there had been a circumcision of such natures in the days of their youth; and they had been severed from those sensual pleasures, such as eating and drinking, which, like leaden weights, were attached to them at their birth, and which drag them down and turn the vision of their souls upon the things that are below—if, I say, they had been released from these impediments and turned in the opposite direction, the very same faculty in them would have seen the truth as keenly as they see what their eyes are turned to now.

Very likely.

Neither the uneducated nor the overeducated will be good servants of the State. Yes, I said; and there is another thing which is likely, or rather a necessary inference from what has preceded, that neither the uneducated and uninformed of the truth, nor yet those who never make an end of their education, will be able ministers of State; not the former, because they have no single aim of duty which is the rule of all their actions, private as well as public; nor the latter, because they will not act at all except upon compulsion, fancying that they are already dwelling apart in the islands of the blest.

Very true, he replied.

Then, I said, the business of us who are the founders of the State will be to compel the best minds to attain that knowledge which we have already shown to be the greatest of all—they must continue to ascend until they arrive at the good; but when they have ascended and seen enough we must not allow them to do as they do now.

What do you mean?

Men should ascend to the upper world, but they should also return to the lower. I mean that they remain in the upper world: but this must not be allowed; they must be made to descend again among the prisoners in the den, and partake of their labors and honors, whether they are worth having or not.

But is not this unjust? he said; ought we to give them a worse life, when they might have a better?

You have again forgotten, my friend, I said, the intention of the legislator, who did not aim at making any one class in the State happy above the rest; the happiness was to be in the whole State, and he held the citizens together by persuasion and necessity, making them benefactors of the State, and therefore benefactors of one another; to this end he created them, not to please themselves, but to be his instruments in binding up the State.

True, he said, I had forgotten.

The duties of philosophers. Observe, Glaucon, that there will be no injustice in compelling our philosophers to have a care and providence of others; we shall explain to them that in other States, men of their class are not obliged to share in the toils of politics: and this is reasonable, for they grow up at their own sweet will, and the government would rather not have them. Being self-taught, they cannot be expected to show any gratitude for a culture which they have never received. But we have brought you into the world to be rulers of the hive, kings of yourselves and of the other citizens, and have educated you far better and more perfectly than they have been educated, and you are better able to share in the double duty. Their obligations to their country will induce them to take part in her government. Wherefore each of you, when his turn comes, must go down to the general underground abode, and get the habit of seeing in the dark. When you have acquired the habit, you will see ten thousand times better than the inhabitants of the den, and you will know what the several images are, and what they represent, because you have seen the beautiful and just and good in their truth. And thus our State, which is also yours, will be a reality, and not a dream only, and will be administered in a spirit unlike that of other States, in which men fight with one another about shadows only and are distracted in the struggle for power, which in their eyes is a great good. Whereas the truth is that the State in which the rulers are most reluctant to govern is always the best and most quietly governed, and the State in which they are most eager, the worst.

Quite true, he replied.

And will our pupils, when they hear this, refuse to take their turn at the toils of State, when they are allowed to spend the greater part of their time with one another in the heavenly light?

They will be willing but not anxious to rule. Impossible, he answered; for they are just men, and the commands which we impose upon them are just; there can be no doubt that every one of them will take office as a stern necessity, and not after the fashion of our present rulers of State.

Yes, my friend, I said; and there lies the point. You must contrive for your future rulers another and a better life than that of a ruler, and then you may have a well-ordered State; The statesman must be provided with a better life than that of a ruler; and then he will not covet office for only in the State which offers this, will they rule who are truly rich, not in silver and gold, but in virtue and wisdom, which are the true blessings of life. Whereas if they go to the administration of public affairs, poor and hungering after their own private advantage, thinking that hence they are to snatch the chief good, order there can never be; for they will be fighting about office, and the civil and domestic broils which thus arise will be the ruin of the rulers themselves and of the whole State.

Most true, he replied.

And the only life which looks down upon the life of political ambition is that of true philosophy. Do you know of any other?

Indeed, I do not, he said.

And those who govern ought not to be lovers of the task? For, if they are, there will be rival lovers, and they will fight.

No question.

Who then are those whom we shall compel to be guardians? Surely they will be the men who are wisest about affairs of State, and by whom the State is best administered, and who at the same time have other honors and another and a better life than that of politics?

They are the men, and I will choose them, he replied.

And now shall we consider in what way such guardians will be produced, and how they are to be brought from darkness to light,—as some are said to have ascended from the world below to the gods?

By all means, he replied.

The training of the guardians. The process, I said, is not the turning over of an oyster-shell, but the turning round of a soul passing from a day which is little better than night to the true day of being, that is, the ascent from below, which we affirm to be true philosophy?

Quite so.

And should we not enquire what sort of knowledge has the power of effecting such a change?

Certainly.

What knowledge will draw the soul upwards? What sort of knowledge is there which would draw the soul from becoming to being? And another consideration has just occurred to me: You will remember that our young men are to be warrior athletes?

Yes, that was said.

Then this new kind of knowledge must have an additional quality?

What quality?

Usefulness in war.

Yes, if possible.

Recapitulation. There were two parts in our former scheme of education, Ewere there not?

There were two parts in our former scheme of education, were there not? Just so.

There was gymnastic which presided over the growth and decay of the body, and may therefore be regarded as having to do with generation and corruption?

True.

Then that is not the knowledge which we are seeking to discover?

No.

But what do you say of music, which also entered to a certain extent into our former scheme?

Music, he said, as you will remember, was the counterpart of gymnastic, and trained the guardians by the influences of habit, by harmony making them harmonious, by rhythm rhythmical, but not giving them science; and the words, whether fabulous or possibly true, had kindred elements of rhythm and harmony in them. But in music there was Bnothing which tended to that good which you are now seeking.

You are most accurate, I said, in your recollection; in music there certainly was nothing of the kind. But what branch of knowledge is there, my dear Glaucon, which is of the desired nature; since all the useful arts were reckoned mean by us?

Undoubtedly; and yet if music and gymnastic are excluded, and the arts are also excluded, what remains?

Well, I said, there may be nothing left of our special subjects; and then we shall have to take something which is not special, but of universal application.

What may that be?

There remains for the second education, arithmetic; something which all arts and sciences and intelligences use in common, and which every one first has to learn among the elements of education.

What is that?

The little matter of distinguishing one, two, and three—in a word, number and calculation:—do not all arts and sciences necessarily partake of them?

Yes.

Then the art of war partakes of them?

To be sure.

Then Palamedes, whenever he appears in tragedy, proves Agamemnon ridiculously unfit to be a general. Did you never remark how he declares that he had invented number, and had numbered the ships and set in array the ranks of the army at Troy; which implies that they had never been numbered before, and Agamemnon must be supposed literally to have been incapable of counting his own feet—how could he if he was ignorant of number? And if that is true, what sort of general must he have been?

I should say a very strange one, if this was as you say.

Can we deny that a warrior should have a knowledge of arithmetic?

Certainly he should, if he is to have the smallest understanding of military tactics, or indeed, I should rather say, if he is to be a man at all.

I should like to know whether you have the same notion which I have of this study?

What is your notion?

that being a study which leads naturally to reflection, for It appears to me to be a study of the kind which we are seeking, and which leads naturally to reflection, but never to have been rightly used; for the true use of it is simply to draw the soul towards being.

Will you explain your meaning? he said.

I will try, I said; and I wish you would share the enquiry with me, and say 'yes' or 'no' when I attempt to distinguish in my own mind what branches of knowledge have this attracting power, in order that we may have clearer proof that arithmetic is, as I suspect, one of them.

Explain, he said.

reflection is aroused by contradictory impressions of sense. I mean to say that objects of sense are of two kinds; some of them do not invite thought because the sense is an adequate judge of them; while in the case of other objects sense is so untrustworthy that further enquiry is imperatively demanded.

You are clearly referring, he said, to the manner in which the senses are imposed upon by distance, and by painting in light and shade.

No, I said, that is not at all my meaning.

Then what is your meaning?

When speaking of uninviting objects, I mean those which do not pass from one sensation to the opposite; inviting objects are those which do; in this latter case the sense coming upon the object, whether at a distance or near, gives no more vivid idea of anything in particular than of its opposite. An illustration will make my meaning clearer:—here are three fingers—a little finger, a second finger, and a middle finger.

Very good.

You may suppose that they are seen quite close: And here comes the point.

What is it?

No difficulty in simple perception. Each of them equally appears a finger, whether seen in the middle or at the extremity, whether white or black, or thick or thin—it makes no difference; a finger is a finger all the same. In these cases a man is not compelled to ask of thought the question what is a finger? for the sight never intimates to the mind that a finger is other than a finger.

True.

And therefore, I said, as we might expect, there is nothing here which invites or excites intelligence.

There is not, he said.

But the same senses at the same time give different impressions which are at first indistinct and have to be distinguished by the mind. But is this equally true of the greatness and smallness of the fingers? Can sight adequately perceive them? and is no difference made by the circumstance that one of the fingers is in the middle and another at the extremity? And in like manner does the touch adequately perceive the qualities of thickness or thinness, of softness or hardness? And so of the other senses; do they give perfect intimations of such matters? Is not their mode of operation on this wise—the sense which is concerned with the quality of hardness is necessarily concerned also with the quality of softness, and only intimates to the soul that the same thing is felt to be both hard and soft?

You are quite right, he said.

And must not the soul be perplexed at this intimation which the sense gives of a hard which is also soft? What, again, is the meaning of light and heavy, if that which is light is also heavy, and that which is heavy, light?

Yes, he said, these intimations which the soul receives are very curious and require to be explained.

The aid of numbers is invoked in order to remove the confusion. Yes, I said, and in these perplexities the soul naturally summons to her aid calculation and intelligence, that she may see whether the several objects announced to her are one or two.

True.

And if they turn out to be two, is not each of them one and different?

Certainly.

And if each is one, and both are two, she will conceive the two as in a state of division, for if there were undivided they could only be conceived of as one?

True.

The eye certainly did see both small and great, but only in a confused manner; they were not distinguished.

Yes.

The chaos then begins to be defined. Whereas the thinking mind, intending to light up the chaos, was compelled to reverse the process, and look at small and great as separate and not confused.

Very true.

Was not this the beginning of the enquiry 'What is great?' and 'What is small?'

Exactly so.

The parting of the visible and intelligible. And thus arose the distinction of the visible and the intelligible.

Most true.

This was what I meant when I spoke of impressions which invited the intellect, or the reverse—those which are simultaneous with opposite impressions, invite thought; those which are not simultaneous do not.

I understand, he said, and agree with you.

And to which class do unity and number belong?

I do not know, he replied.

Thought is aroused by the contradiction of the one and many. Think a little and you will see that what has preceded will supply the answer; for if simple unity could be adequately perceived by the sight or by any other sense, then, as we were saying in the case of the finger, there would be nothing to attract towards being; but when there is some contradiction always present, and one is the reverse of one and involves the conception of plurality, then thought begins to be aroused within us, and the soul perplexed and wanting to arrive at a decision asks 'What is absolute unity?' This is the way in which the study of the one has a power of drawing and converting the mind to the contemplation of true being.

And surely, he said, this occurs notably in the case of one; for we see the same thing to be both one and infinite in multitude?

Yes, I said; and this being true of one must be equally true of all number?

Certainly.

And all arithmetic and calculation have to do with number?

Yes.

And they appear to lead the mind towards truth?

Yes, in a very remarkable manner.

Arithmetic has a practical and also a philosophical use, the latter the higher. Then this is knowledge of the kind for which we are seeking, having a double use, military and philosophical; for the man of war must learn the art of number or he will not know how to array his troops, and the philosopher also, because he has to rise out of the sea of change and lay hold of true being, and therefore he must be an arithmetician.

That is true.

And our guardian is both warrior and philosopher?

Certainly.

Then this is a kind of knowledge which legislation may fitly prescribe; and we must endeavor to persuade those who are to be the principal men of our State to go and learn arithmetic, not as amateurs, but they must carry on the study until they see the nature of numbers with the mind only; nor again, like merchants or retail-traders, with a view to buying or selling, but for the sake of their military use, and of the soul herself; and because this will be the easiest way for her to pass from becoming to truth and being.

That is excellent, he said.

Yes, I said, and now having spoken of it, I must add how charming the science is! and in how many ways it conduces to our desired end, if pursued in the spirit of a philosopher, and not of a shopkeeper!

How do you mean?

The higher arithmetic is concerned, not with visible or tangible objects, but with abstract numbers. I mean, as I was saying, that arithmetic has a very great and elevating effect, compelling the soul to reason about abstract number, and rebelling against the introduction of visible or tangible objects into the argument. You know how steadily the masters of the art repel and ridicule any one who attempts to divide absolute unity when he is calculating, and if you divide, they multiply, taking care that one shall continue one and not become lost in fractions.

Meaning either (1) that they integrate the number because they deny the possibility of fractions; or (2) that division is regarded by them as a process of multiplication, for the fractions of one continue to be units.

That is very true.

Now, suppose a person were to say to them: O my friends, what are these wonderful numbers about which you are reasoning, in which, as you say, there is a unity such as you demand, and each unit is equal, invariable, indivisible,—what would they answer?

They would answer, as I should conceive, that they were speaking of those numbers which can only be realized in thought.

Then you see that this knowledge may be truly called Bnecessary, necessitating as it clearly does the use of the pure intelligence in the attainment of pure truth?

Yes; that is a marked characteristic of it.

The arithmetician is naturally quick, and the study of arithmetic gives him still greater quickness. And have you further observed, that those who have a natural talent for calculation are generally quick at every other kind of knowledge; and even the dull, if they have had an arithmetical training, although they may derive no other advantage from it, always become much quicker than they would otherwise have been.

Very true, he said.

And indeed, you will not easily find a more difficult study, and not many as difficult.

You will not.

And, for all these reasons, arithmetic is a kind of knowledge in which the best natures should be trained, and which must not be given up.

I agree.

Let this then be made one of our subjects of education. And next, shall we enquire whether the kindred science also concerns us?

You mean geometry?

Exactly so.

Geometry has practical applications; Clearly, he said, we are concerned with that part of geometry which relates to war; for in pitching a camp, or taking up a position, or closing or extending the lines of an army, or any other military man oeuvre, whether in actual battle or on a march, it will make all the difference whether a general is or is not a geometrician.

these however are trifling in comparison with that greater part of the science which tends towards the good, Yes, I said, but for that purpose a very little of either geometry or calculation will be enough; the question relates rather to the greater and more advanced part of geometry—whether that tends in any degree to make more easy the vision of the idea of good; and thither, as I was saying, all things tend which compel the soul to turn her gaze towards that place, where is the full perfection of being, which she ought, by all means, to behold.

True, he said.

Then if geometry compels us to view being, it concerns us; if becoming only, it does not concern us?

Yes, that is what we assert.

Yet anybody who has the least acquaintance with geometry will not deny that such a conception of the science is in flat contradiction to the ordinary language of geometricians.

How so?

They have in view practice only, and are always speaking, in a narrow and ridiculous manner, of squaring and extending and applying and the like—they confuse the necessities of geometry with those of daily life; whereas knowledge is the Breal object of the whole science.

Certainly, he said.

Then must not a further admission be made?

What admission?

That the knowledge at which geometry aims is knowledge of the eternal, and not of aught perishing and transient.

That, he replied, may be readily allowed, and is true.

Then, my noble friend, geometry will draw the soul towards truth, and create the spirit of philosophy, and raise up that which is now unhappily allowed to fall down.

Nothing will be more likely to have such an effect.

Then nothing should be more sternly laid down than that the inhabitants of your fair city should by all means learn geometry. Moreover the science has indirect effects, which are not small.

Aristotle

NICOMACHEAN ETHICS EXCERPTS

Book 1

Surely then, even with reference to actual life and conduct, the knowledge of it must have great weight; and like archers, with a mark in view, we shall be more likely to hit upon what is right: and if so, we ought to try to describe, in outline at least, what it is and of which of the sciences and faculties it is the End.

Now one would naturally suppose it to be the End of that which is most commanding and most inclusive: and to this description, [politics and ethics] plainly answers: for this it is that determines which of the sciences should be in the communities, and which kind individuals are to learn, and what degree of proficiency is to be required. Again; we see also ranging under this the most highly esteemed faculties, such as the art military, and that of domestic management, and Rhetoric. Well then, since this uses all the other practical sciences, and moreover lays down rules as to what men are to do, and from what to abstain, the End of this must include the Ends of the rest, and so must be *The Good* of Man. And grant that this is the same to the individual and to the community, yet surely that of the latter is plainly greater and more perfect to discover and preserve: for to do this even for a single individual were a matter for contentment; but to do it for a whole nation, and for communities generally, were more noble and godlike.

Such then are the objects proposed by our treatise, which is of the nature of [ethics and politics]: and I conceive I shall have spoken on them satisfactorily, if they be made as distinctly clear as the nature of the subject-matter will admit: for exactness must not be looked for in all discussions alike, any more than in all works of handicraft. Now the notions of nobleness and justice, with the examination of which [ethics and politics] is concerned, admit of variation and error to such a degree, that they are supposed by some to exist conventionally only, and not in the nature of things: but then, again, the things which are allowed to be goods admit of a similar error, because harm comes to many from them: for before now some have perished through wealth, and others through valor.

We must be content then, in speaking of such things and from such data, to set forth the truth roughly and in outline; in other words, since we are speaking of general matter and from general data, to draw also conclusions merely general. And in the same spirit should each person receive what we say: for the man of education will seek exactness so far in each subject as the nature of the thing admits, it being plainly much the same absurdity to put up with a mathematician who tries to persuade instead of proving, and to demand strict demonstrative reasoning of a Rhetorician.

Now each man judges well what he knows, and of these things he is a good judge: on each particular matter then he is a good judge who has been instructed in it, and in a general way the man of general mental cultivation.

Hence the young man is not a fit student of Moral Philosophy, for he has no experience in the actions of life, while all that is said presupposes and is concerned with these: and in the next place, since he is apt to follow the impulses of his passions, he will hear as though he heard not, and to no profit, the end in view being practice and not mere knowledge.

And I draw no distinction between young in years, and youthful in temper and disposition: the defect to which I allude being no direct result of the time, but of living at the beck and call of passion, and following each object as it rises. For to them that are such the knowledge comes to be unprofitable, as to those of imperfect self-control: but, to those who form their desires and act in accordance with reason, to have knowledge on these points must be very profitable.

Let thus much suffice by way of preface on these three points, the student, the spirit in which our observations should be received, and the object which we propose.

Ch. VII

And now let us revert to the Good of which we are in search: what can it be? for manifestly it is different in different actions and arts: for it is different in the healing art and in the art military, and similarly in the rest. What then is the Chief Good in each? Is it not "that for the sake of which the other things are done?" and this in the healing art is health, and in the art military victory, and in that of house-building a house, and in any other thing something else; in short, in every action and moral choice the End, because in all cases men do everything else with a view to this. So that if there is some one End of all things which are and may be done, this must be the Good proposed by doing, or if more than one, then these.

Thus our discussion after some traversing about has come to the same point which we reached before. And this we must try yet more to clear up.

Now since the ends are plainly many, and of these we choose some with a view to others (wealth, for instance, musical instruments, and, in general, all instruments), it is clear that all are not final: but the Chief Good is manifestly something final; and so, if there is some one only which is final, this must be the object of our search: but if several, then the most final of them will be it.

Now that which is an object of pursuit in itself we call more final than that which is so with a view to something else; that again which is never an object of choice with a view to something else than those which are so both in themselves and with a view to this ulterior object: and so by the term "absolutely final," we denote that which is an object of choice always in itself, and never with a view to any other.

And of this nature Happiness is mostly thought to be, for this we choose always for its own sake, and never with a view to anything further: whereas honour, pleasure, intellect, in fact every excellence we choose for their own sakes, it is true (because we would choose each of these even if no result were to follow), but we choose them also with a view to happiness, conceiving that through their instrumentality we shall be happy: but no man chooses happiness with a view to them, nor in fact with a view to any other thing whatsoever.

The same result is seen to follow also from the notion of self-sufficiency, a quality thought to belong to the final good. Now by sufficient for Self, we mean not for a single individual living a solitary life, but for his parents also and children and wife, and, in general, friends and countrymen; for man is by nature adapted to a social existence. But of these, of course, some limit must be fixed: for if one extends it to parents and descendants and friends' friends, there is no end to it. This point, however, must be left for future investigation: for the present we define that to be self-sufficient "which taken alone makes life choice-worthy, and to be in want of nothing;" now of such kind we think Happiness to be: and further, to be most choice-worthy of all things; not being reckoned with any other thing, for if it were so reckoned, it is plain we must then allow it, with the addition of ever so small a good, to be more choice-worthy than it was before: because what is put to it becomes an addition of so much more good, and of goods the greater is ever the more choice-worthy.

So then Happiness is manifestly something final and self-sufficient, being the end of all things which are and may be done.

But, it may be, to call Happiness the Chief Good is a mere truism, and what is wanted is some clearer account of its real nature. Now this object may be easily attained, when we have discovered what is the work of man; for as in the case of flute-player, statuary, or artisan of any kind, or, more generally, all who have any work or course of action, their Chief Good and Excellence is thought to reside in their work, so it would seem to be with man, if there is any work belonging to him.

Are we then to suppose, that while carpenter and cobbler have certain works and courses of action, Man as Man has none, but is left by Nature without a work? or would not one rather hold, that as eye, hand, and foot, and generally each of his members, has manifestly some special work; so too the whole Man, as distinct from all these, has some work of his own?

What then can this be? not mere life, because that plainly is shared with him even by vegetables, and we want what is peculiar to him. We must separate off then the life of mere nourishment and growth, and next will come the life of sensation: but this again manifestly is common to horses, oxen, and every animal. There remains then a kind of life of the Rational Nature apt to act: and of this Nature there are two parts denominated Rational, the one as being obedient to Reason, the other as having and exerting it. Again, as this life is also spoken of in two ways, we must take that which is in the way of actual working, because this is thought to be most properly entitled to the name. If then the work of Man is a working of the soul in accordance with reason, or at least not independently of reason, and we say that the work of any given subject, and of that subject good of its kind, are the same in kind (as, for instance, of a harp-player and a good harp-player, and so on in every case, adding to the work eminence in the way of excellence; I mean, the work of a harp-player is to play the harp, and of a good harp-player to play it well); if, I say, this is so, and we assume the work of Man to be life of a certain kind, that is to say a working of the soul, and actions with reason, and of a good man to do these things well and nobly, and in fact everything is finished off well in the way of the excellence which peculiarly belongs to it: if all this is so, then the Good of Man comes to be "a working of the Soul in the way of Excellence," or, if Excellence admits of degrees, in the way of the best and most perfect Excellence.

And we must add, in a complete life; for as it is not one swallow or one fine day that makes a spring, so it is not one day or a short time that makes a man blessed and happy.

Let this then be taken for a rough sketch of the Chief Good: since it is probably the right way to give first the outline, and fill it in afterwards. And it would seem that any man may improve and connect what is good in the sketch, and that time is a good discoverer and co-operator in such matters: it is thus in fact that all improvements in the various arts have been brought about, for any man may fill up a deficiency.

You must remember also what has been already stated, and not seek for exactness in all matters alike, but in each according to the subject-matter, and so far as properly belongs to the system. The carpenter and geometrician, for instance, inquire into the right line in different fashion: the former so far as he wants it for his work, the latter inquires into its nature and properties, because he is concerned with the truth.

So then should one do in other matters, that the incidental matters may not exceed the direct ones.

And again, you must not demand the reason either in all things alike, because in some it is sufficient that the fact has been well demonstrated, which is the case with first principles; and the fact is the first step, i.e. starting-point or principle.

And of these first principles some are obtained by induction, some by perception, some by a course of habituation, others in other different ways. And we must try to trace up each in their own nature, and take pains to secure their being well defined, because they have great influence on what follows: it is thought, I mean, that the starting-point or principle is more than half the whole matter, and that many of the points of inquiry come simultaneously into view thereby.

Ch. XIII

Moreover, since Happiness is a kind of working of the soul in the way of perfect Excellence, we must inquire concerning Excellence: for so probably shall we have a clearer view concerning Happiness; and again, he who is really a statesman is generally thought to have spent most pains on this, for he wishes to make the citizens good and obedient to the laws. (For examples of this class we have the lawgivers of the Cretans and Lacedaemonians and whatever other such there have been.) But if this investigation belongs properly to [Greek: politikae], then clearly the inquiry will be in accordance with our original design.

Well, we are to inquire concerning Excellence, i.e. Human Excellence of course, because it was the Chief Good of Man and the Happiness of Man that we were inquiring of just now. By Human Excellence we mean not that of man's body but that of his soul; for we call Happiness a working of the Soul.

And if this is so, it is plain that some knowledge of the nature of the Soul is necessary for the statesman, just as for the Oculist a knowledge of the whole body, and the more so in proportion as [Greek: politikae] is more precious and higher than the healing art: and in fact physicians of the higher class do busy themselves much with the knowledge of the body.

So then the statesman is to consider the nature of the Soul: but he must do so with these objects in view, and so far only as may suffice for the objects of his special inquiry: for to carry his speculations to a greater exactness is perhaps a task more laborious than falls within his province.

In fact, the few statements made on the subject in my popular treatises are quite enough, and accordingly we will adopt them here: as, that the Soul consists of two parts, the Irrational and the Rational (as to whether these are actually divided, as are the parts of the body, and everything that is capable of division; or are only metaphysically speaking two, being by nature inseparable, as are convex and concave circumferences, matters not in respect of our present purpose). And of the Irrational, the one part seems common to other objects, and in fact vegetative; I mean the cause of nourishment and growth (for such a faculty of the Soul one would assume to exist in all things that receive nourishment, even in embryos, and this the same as in the perfect creatures; for this is more likely than that it should be a different one).

Now the Excellence of this manifestly is not peculiar to the human species but common to others: for this part and this faculty is thought to work most in time of sleep, and the good and bad man are least distinguishable while asleep; whence it is a common saying that during one half of life there is no difference between the happy and the wretched; and this accords with our anticipations, for sleep is an inactivity of the soul, in so far as it is denominated good or bad, except that in some wise some of its movements find their way through the veil and so the good come to have better dreams than ordinary men. But enough of this: we must forego any further mention of the nutritive part, since it is not naturally capable of the Excellence which is peculiarly human.

And there seems to be another Irrational Nature of the Soul, which yet in a way partakes of Reason. For in the man who controls his appetites, and in him who resolves to do so and fails, we praise the Reason or Rational part of the Soul, because it exhorts aright and to the best course: but clearly there is in them, beside the Reason, some other natural principle which fights with and strains against the Reason. (For in plain terms, just as paralysed limbs of the body when their owners would move them to the right are borne aside in a contrary direction to the left, so is it in the case of the Soul, for the impulses of men who cannot control their appetites are to contrary points: the difference is that in the case of the body we do see what is borne aside but in the case of the soul we do not. But, it may be, not the less on that account are we to suppose that there is in the Soul also somewhat besides the Reason, which is opposed to this and goes against it; as to how it is different, that is irrelevant.)

But of Reason this too does evidently partake, as we have said: for instance, in the man of self-control it obeys Reason: and perhaps in the man of perfected self-mastery, or the brave man, it is yet more obedient; in them it agrees entirely with the Reason.

So then the Irrational is plainly twofold: the one part, the merely vegetative, has no share of Reason, but that of desire, or appetition generally, does partake of it in a sense, in so far as it is obedient to it and capable of submitting to its rule. (So too in common phrase we say we have [Greek: logos] of our father or friends, and this in a different sense from that in which we say we have [Greek: logos] of mathematics.)

Now that the Irrational is in some way persuaded by the Reason, admonition, and every act of rebuke and exhortation indicate. If then we are to say that this also has Reason, then the Rational, as well as the Irrational, will be twofold, the one supremely and in itself, the other paying it a kind of filial regard.

The Excellence of Man then is divided in accordance with this difference: we make two classes, calling the one Intellectual, and the other Moral; pure science, intelligence, and practical wisdom–Intellectual: liberality, and perfected self-mastery–Moral: in speaking of a man's Moral character, we do not say he is a scientific or intelligent but a meek man, or one of perfected self-mastery: and we praise the man of science in right of his mental state; and of these such as are praiseworthy we call Excellences.

Book II

Well: human Excellence is of two kinds, Intellectual and Moral: now the Intellectual springs originally, and is increased subsequently, from teaching (for the most part that is), and needs therefore experience and time; whereas the Moral comes from custom, and so the Greek term denoting it is but a slight deflection from the term denoting custom in that language.

From this fact it is plain that not one of the Moral Virtues comes to be in us merely by nature: because of such things as exist by nature, none can be changed by custom: a stone, for instance, by nature gravitating downwards, could never by custom be brought to ascend, not even if one were to try and accustom it by throwing it up ten thousand times; nor could file again be brought to descend, nor in fact could anything whose nature is in one way be brought by custom to be in another. The Virtues then come to be in us neither by nature, nor in despite of nature, but we are furnished by nature with a capacity for receiving them and are perfected in them through custom.

Again, in whatever cases we get things by nature, we get the faculties first and perform the acts of working afterwards; an illustration of which is afforded by the case of our bodily senses, for it was not from having often seen or heard that we got these senses, but just the reverse: we had them and so exercised them, but did not have them because we had exercised them. But the Virtues we get by first performing single acts of working, which, again, is the case of other things, as the arts for instance; for what we have to make when we have learned how, these we learn how to make by making: men come to be builders, for instance, by building; harp-players, by playing on the harp: exactly so, by doing just actions we come to be just; by doing the actions of self-mastery we come to be perfected in self-mastery; and by doing brave actions brave.

And to the truth of this testimony is borne by what takes place in communities: because the law-givers make the individual members good men by habituation, and this is the intention certainly of every law-giver, and all who do not effect it well fail of their intent; and herein consists the difference between a good Constitution and a bad.

Again, every Virtue is either produced or destroyed from and by the very same circumstances: art too in like manner; I mean it is by playing the harp that both the good and the bad harp-players are formed: and similarly builders and all the rest; by building well men will become good builders; by doing it badly bad ones: in fact, if this had not been so, there would have been no need of instructors, but all men would have been at once good or bad in their several arts without them.

So too then is it with the Virtues: for by acting in the various relations in which we are thrown with our fellow men, we come to be, some just, some unjust: and by acting in dangerous positions and being habituated to feel fear or confidence, we come to be, some brave, others cowards.

Similarly is it also with respect to the occasions of lust and anger: for some men come to be perfected in self-mastery and mild, others destitute of all self-control and passionate; the one class by behaving in one way under them, the other by behaving in another. Or, in one word, the habits are produced from the acts of working like to them: and so what we have to do is to give a certain character to these particular acts, because the habits formed correspond to the differences of these.

So then, whether we are accustomed this way or that straight from childhood, makes not a small but an important difference, or rather I would say it makes all the difference…

First then this must be noted, that it is the nature of such things to be spoiled by defect and excess; as we see in the case of health and strength (since for the illustration of things which cannot be seen we must use those that can), for excessive training impairs the strength as well as deficient: meat and drink, in like manner, in too great or too small quantities, impair the health: while in due proportion they cause, increase, and preserve it.

Thus it is therefore with the habits of perfected Self-Mastery and Courage and the rest of the Virtues: for the man who flies from and fears all things, and never stands up against anything, comes to be a coward; and he who fears nothing, but goes at everything, comes to be rash. In like manner too, he that tastes of every pleasure and abstains from none comes to lose all self-control; while he who avoids all, as do the dull and clownish, comes as it were to lose his faculties of perception: that is to say, the habits of perfected Self-Mastery and Courage are spoiled by the excess and defect, but by the mean state are preserved.

Furthermore, not only do the origination, growth, and marring of the habits come from and by the same circumstances, but also the acts of working after the habits are formed will be exercised on the same: for so it is also with those other things which are more directly matters of sight, strength for instance: for this comes by taking plenty of food and doing plenty of work, and the man who has attained strength is best able to do these: and so it is with the Virtues, for not only do we by abstaining from pleasures come to be perfected in Self-Mastery, but when we have come to be so we can best abstain from them: similarly too with Courage: for it is by accustoming ourselves to despise objects of fear and stand up against them that we come to be brave; and [Sidenote: 1104b] after we have come to be so we shall be best able to stand up against such objects.

And for a test of the formation of the habits we must [Sidenote: III] take the pleasure or pain which succeeds the acts; for he is perfected in Self-Mastery who not only abstains from the bodily pleasures but is glad to do so; whereas he who abstains but is sorry to do it has not Self-Mastery: he again is brave who stands up against danger, either with positive pleasure or at least without any pain; whereas he who does it with pain is not brave.

For Moral Virtue has for its object-matter pleasures and pains, because by reason of pleasure we do what is bad, and by reason of pain decline doing what is right (for which cause, as Plato observes, men should have been trained straight from their childhood to receive pleasure and pain from proper objects, for this is the right education). Again: since Virtues have to do with actions and feelings, and on every feeling and every action pleasure and pain follow, here again is another proof that Virtue has for its object-matter pleasure and pain. The same is shown also by the fact that punishments are effected through the instrumentality of these; because they are of the nature of remedies, and it is the nature of remedies to be the contraries of the ills they cure. Again, to quote what we said before: every habit of the Soul by its very nature has relation to, and exerts itself upon, things of the same kind as those by which it is naturally deteriorated or improved: now such habits do come to be vicious by reason of pleasures and pains, that is, by men pursuing or avoiding respectively, either such as they ought not, or at wrong times, or in wrong manner, and so forth (for which reason, by the way, some people define the Virtues as certain states of impassibility and utter quietude, but they are wrong because they speak without modification, instead of adding "as they ought," "as they ought not," and "when," and so on). Virtue then is assumed to be that habit which is such, in relation to pleasures and pains, as to effect the best results, and Vice the contrary…

And so, viewing it in respect of its essence and definition, Virtue is a mean state; but in reference to the chief good and to excellence it is the highest state possible.

But it must not be supposed that every action or every feeling is capable of subsisting in this mean state, because some there are which are so named as immediately to convey the notion of badness, as malevolence, shamelessness, envy; or, to instance in actions, adultery, theft, homicide; for all these and suchlike are blamed because they are in themselves bad, not the having too much or too little of them.

In these then you never can go right, but must always be wrong: nor in such does the right or wrong depend on the selection of a proper person, time, or manner (take adultery for instance), but simply doing any one soever of those things is being wrong.

You might as well require that there should be determined a mean state, an excess and a defect in respect of acting unjustly, being cowardly, or giving up all control of the passions: for at this rate there will be of excess and defect a mean state; of excess, excess; and of defect, defect.

But just as of perfected self-mastery and courage there is no excess and defect, because the mean is in one point of view the highest possible state, so neither of those faulty states can you have a mean state, excess, or defect, but howsoever done they are wrong: you cannot, in short, have of excess and defect a mean state, nor of a mean state excess and defect.

Book X

VII

Now if Happiness is a Working in the way of Excellence of course that Excellence must be the highest, that is to say, the Excellence of the best Principle. Whether then this best Principle is Intellect or some other which is thought naturally to rule and to lead and to conceive of noble and divine things, whether being in its own nature divine or the most divine of all our internal Principles, the Working of this in accordance with its own proper Excellence must be the perfect Happiness.

That it is Contemplative has been already stated: and this would seem to be consistent with what we said before and with truth: for, in the first place, this Working is of the highest kind, since the Intellect is the highest of our internal Principles and the subjects with which it is conversant the highest of all which fall within the range of our knowledge.

Next, it is also most Continuous: for we are better able to contemplate than to do anything else whatever, continuously.

Again, we think Pleasure must be in some way an ingredient in Happiness, and of all Workings in accordance with Excellence that in the way of Science is confessedly most pleasant: at least the pursuit of Science is thought to contain Pleasures admirable for purity and permanence; and it is reasonable to suppose that the employment is more pleasant to those who have mastered, than to those who are yet seeking for, it.

And the Self-Sufficiency which people speak of will attach chiefly to the Contemplative Working: of course the actual necessaries of life are needed alike by the man of science, and the just man, and all the other characters; but, supposing all sufficiently supplied with these, the just man needs people towards whom, and in concert with whom, to practice his justice; and in like manner the man of perfected self-mastery, and the brave man, and so on of the rest; whereas the man of science can contemplate and speculate even when quite alone, and the more entirely he deserves the appellation the more able is he to do so: it may be he can do better for having fellow-workers but still he is certainly most Self-Sufficient.

Again, this alone would seem to be rested in for its own sake, since nothing results from it beyond the fact of having contemplated; whereas from all things which are objects of moral action we do mean to get something beside the doing them, be the same more or less.

Also, Happiness is thought to stand in perfect rest; for we toil that we may rest, and war that we may be at peace. Now all the Practical Virtues require either society or war for their Working, and the actions regarding these are thought to exclude rest; those of war entirely, because no one chooses war, nor prepares for war, for war's sake: he would indeed be thought a bloodthirsty villain who should make enemies of his friends to secure the existence of fighting and bloodshed. The Working also of the statesman excludes the idea of rest, and, beside the actual work of government, seeks for power and dignities or at least Happiness for the man himself and his fellow-citizens: a Happiness distinct the national Happiness which we evidently seek as being different and distinct.

If then of all the actions in accordance with the various virtues those of policy and war are pre-eminent in honor and greatness, and these are restless, and aim at some further End and are not choiceworthy for their own sakes, but the Working of the Intellect, being apt for contemplation, is thought to excel in earnestness, and to aim at no End beyond itself and to have Pleasure of its own which helps to increase the Working, and if the attributes of Self-Sufficiency, and capacity of rest, and unweariedness (as far as is compatible with the infirmity of human nature), and all other attributes of the highest Happiness, plainly belong to this Working, this must be perfect Happiness, if attaining a complete duration of life, which condition is added because none of the points of Happiness is incomplete.

But such a life will be higher than mere human nature, because a man will live thus, not in so far as he is man but in so far as there is in him a divine Principle: and in proportion as this Principle excels his composite nature so far does the Working thereof excel that in accordance with any other kind of Excellence: and therefore, if pure Intellect, as compared with human nature, is divine, so too will the life in accordance with it be divine compared with man's ordinary life. [Sidenote: 1178a] Yet must we not give ear to those who bid one as man to mind only man's affairs, or as mortal only mortal things; but, so far as we can, make ourselves like immortals and do all with a view to living in accordance with the highest Principle in us, for small as it may be in bulk yet in power and preciousness it far more excels all the others.

In fact this Principle would seem to constitute each man's "Self," since it is supreme and above all others in goodness it would be absurd then for a man not to choose his own life but that of some other.

And here will apply an observation made before, that whatever is proper to each is naturally best and pleasantest to him: such then is to Man the life in accordance with pure Intellect (since this Principle is most truly Man), and if so, then it is also the happiest…

And that the perfect Happiness must be a kind of Contemplative Working may appear also from the following consideration: our conception of the gods is that they are above all blessed and happy: now what kind of Moral actions are we to attribute to them? those of justice? nay, will they not be set in a ridiculous light if represented as forming contracts, and restoring deposits, and so on? well then, shall we picture them performing brave actions, withstanding objects of fear and meeting dangers, because it is noble to do so? or liberal ones? but to whom shall they be giving? and further, it is absurd to think they have money or anything of the kind. And as for actions of perfected self-mastery, what can theirs be? would it not be a degrading praise that they have no bad desires? In short, if one followed the subject into all details all the circumstances connected with Moral actions would appear trivial and unworthy of gods.

Still, every one believes that they live, and therefore that they Work because it is not supposed that they sleep their time away like Endymion: now if from a living being you take away Action, still more if Creation, what remains but Contemplation? So then the Working of the Gods, eminent in blessedness, will be one apt for Contemplative

Speculation; and of all human Workings that will have the greatest capacity for Happiness which is nearest akin to this.

A corroboration of which position is the fact that the other animals do not partake of Happiness, being completely shut out from any such Working.

To the gods then all their life is blessed; and to men in so far as there is in it some copy of such Working, but of the other animals none is happy because it in no way shares in Contemplative Speculation.

Happiness then is co-extensive with this Contemplative Speculation, and in proportion as people have the act of Contemplation so far have they also the being happy, not incidentally, but in the way of Contemplative Speculation because it is in itself precious.

So Happiness must be a kind of Contemplative Speculation...

Now he that works in accordance with, and pays observance to, Pure Intellect, and tends this, seems likely to be both in the best frame of mind and dearest to the Gods: because if, as is thought, any care is bestowed on human things by the Gods then it must be reasonable to think that they take pleasure in what is best and most akin to themselves (and this must be the Pure Intellect); and that they requite with kindness those who love and honour this most, as paying observance to what is dear to them, and as acting rightly and nobly. And it is quite obvious that the man of Science chiefly combines all these: he is therefore dearest to the Gods, and it is probable that he is at the same time most Happy.

Thus then on this view also the [philosopher] will be most Happy... The formation of a virtuous character some ascribe to Nature, some to Custom, and some to Teaching. Now Nature's part, be it what it may, obviously does not rest with us, but belongs to those who in the truest sense are fortunate, by reason of certain divine agency,

Then, as for Words and Precept, they, it is to be feared, will not avail with all; but it may be necessary for the mind of the disciple to have been previously prepared for liking and disliking as he ought; just as the soil must, to nourish the seed sown. For he that lives in obedience to passion cannot hear any advice that would dissuade him, nor, if he heard, understand: now him that is thus how can one reform? in fact, generally, passion is not thought to yield to Reason but to brute force. So then there must be, to begin with, a kind of affinity to Virtue in the disposition; which must cleave to what is honourable and loath what is disgraceful. But to get right guidance towards Virtue from the earliest youth is not easy unless one is brought up under laws of such kind; because living with self-mastery and endurance is not pleasant to the mass of men, and specially not to the young. For this reason the food, and manner of living generally, ought to be the subject of legal regulation, because things when become habitual will not be disagreeable.

[Sidenote: 1180a] Yet perhaps it is not sufficient that men while young should get right food and tendance, but, inasmuch as they will have to practise and become accustomed to certain things even after they have attained to man's estate, we shall want laws on these points as well, and, in fine, respecting one's whole life, since the mass of men are amenable to compulsion rather than Reason, and to punishment rather than to a sense of honour.

And therefore some men hold that while lawgivers should employ the sense of honour to exhort and guide men to Virtue, under the notion that they will then obey who have been well trained in habits; they should impose chastisement and penalties on those who disobey and are of less promising nature; and the incurable expel entirely: because the good man and he who lives under a sense of honour will be obedient to reason; and the baser sort, who grasp at pleasure, will be kept in check, like beasts of burthen by pain. Therefore also they say that the pains should be such as are most contrary to the pleasures which are liked…

Of course, the best thing would be that there should be a right Public System and that we should be able to carry it out: but, since as a public matter those points are neglected, the duty would seem to devolve upon each individual to contribute to the cause of Virtue with his own children and friends, or at least to make this his aim and purpose: and this, it would seem, from what has been said, he will be best able to do by making a Legislator of himself: since all public systems, it is plain, are formed by the instrumentality of laws and those are good which are formed by that of good laws: whether they are written or unwritten, whether they are applied to the training of one or many, will not, it seems, make any difference, just as it does not in music, gymnastics, or any other such accomplishments, which are gained by practice.

For just as in Communities laws and customs prevail, so too in families the express commands of the Head, and customs also: and even more in the latter, because of blood-relationship and the benefits conferred: for there you have, to begin with, people who have affection and are naturally obedient to the authority which controls them.

Then, furthermore, Private training has advantages over Public, as in the case of the healing art: for instance, as a general rule, a man who is in a fever should keep quiet, and starve; but in a particular case, perhaps, this may not hold good; or, to take a different illustration, the boxer will not use the same way of fighting with all antagonists.

It would seem then that the individual will be most exactly attended to under Private care, because so each will be more likely to obtain what is expedient for him. Of course, whether in the art of healing, or gymnastics, or any other, a man will treat individual cases the better for being acquainted with general rules; as, "that so and so is good for all, or for men in such and such cases:" because general maxims are not only said to be but are the object-matter of sciences: still this is no reason against the possibility of a man's taking excellent care of some one case, though he possesses no scientific knowledge but from experience is exactly acquainted with what happens in each point; just as some people are thought to doctor themselves best though they would be wholly unable to administer relief to others. Yet it may seem to be necessary nevertheless, for one who wishes to become a real artist and well acquainted with the theory of his profession, to have recourse to general principles and ascertain all their capacities: for we have already stated that these are the object-matter of sciences.

If then it appears that we may become good through the instrumentality of laws, of course whoso wishes to make men better by a system of care and training must try to make a Legislator of himself; for to treat skilfully just any one who may be put before you is not what any ordinary person can do, but, if any one, he who has knowledge; as in the healing art, and all others which involve careful practice and skill…

The Enchiridion

By Epictetus
Translated By Thomas W. Higginson

Introduction

The little book by Epictetus called *Enchiridion* or "manual" has played a disproportionately large role in the rise of modern attitudes and modern philosophy. As soon as it had been translated into the vernacular languages, it became a bestseller among independent intellectuals, among anti-Christian thinkers, and among philosophers of a subjective cast. Montaigne had a copy of the *Enchiridion* among his books. Pascal violently rejected the megalomaniac pride of the Stoic philosopher. Frederick the Great carried the book with him on all campaigns. It was a source of inspiration and encouragement to Anthony, Earl of Shaftesbury, in the serious illness which ended only in his death; many pages of his diaries contain passages copied from the *Enchiridion*. It has been studied and widely quoted by Scottish philosophers like Francis Hutcheson, Adam Smith, and Adam Ferguson who valued Stoic moral philosophy for its reconciliation of social dependency and personal independence.

That there was a rebirth of Stoicism in the centuries of rebirth which marked the emergence of the modern age was not mere chance. Philosophical, moral, and social conditions of the time united to cause it. Roman Stoicism had been developed in times of despotism as a philosophy of lonely and courageous souls who had recognized the redeeming power of philosophical reason in all the moral and social purposes of life. Philosophy as a way of life makes men free. It is the last ditch stand of liberty in a world of servitude. Many elements in the new age led to thought which had structural affinity with Roman Stoicism. Modern times had created the independent thinker, the free intellectual in a secular civilization. Modern times had destroyed medieval liberties and had established the new despotism of the absolute state supported by ecclesiastical authority. Modern philosophies continued the basic trend in Stoicism in making the subjective consciousness the foundation of philosophy. The Stoic emphasis on moral problems was also appealing in an era of rapid transition when all the values which had previously been taken for granted were questioned and reconsidered.

While it is interesting to observe how varied were the effects produced by this small volume, this epitome of the Stoic system of moral philosophy, these effects seem still more remarkable when we consider that it was not intended to be a philosophical treatise on Stoicism for students. It was, rather, to be a guide for the advanced student of Stoicism to show him the best roads toward the goal of becoming a true philosopher. Thus Epictetus and his *Enchiridion* have a unique position in Roman Stoicism. Seneca and Marcus Aurelius had selected Stoic philosophy as the most adequate system for expressing their existential problems of independence, solitude, and history. In this enterprise, Seneca made tremendous strides toward the insights of social psychology as a by-product of his consciousness of decadence (in this he was close to Nietzsche), but he was not primarily concerned with the unity of the Stoic system. Marcus Aurelius changed the philosophical doctrine into the regimen of the lonesome ruler. In contrast to both, Epictetus was teaching Stoic philosophy as a doctrine and as a way of life. The *Enchiridion* is a summary of theoretical and applied Stoicism.

Epictetus was the son of a woman slave, born between 50 and 60 A.D. at Hieropolis in Phrygia. We do not know how he came to Rome. He was there as slave to one of Nero's distinguished freedmen who served as the Emperor's secretary. While still in service, Epictetus took courses with Musonius Rufus, the fashionable Stoic philosopher, who was impressed by the sincere and dynamic personality of the young slave and trained him to be a Stoic philosopher. Epictetus became a free man and began teaching philosophy on street corners, in the market, but he was not successful. During the rule of Domitian, Epictetus with many other philosophers was exiled from Rome, probably between 89 and 92 A.D. He went to Nicopolis, across Actium in Epirus, where he conducted his own school. He was so well regarded and highly esteemed that he established the reputation of the place as the town of Epictetus' school. Students came from Athens and Rome to attend his classes. Private citizens came to ask his advice and guidance. Some of his students returned to their homes to enter the traditional careers to which they were socially obligated. Others assumed the philosophic way of life in order to escape into the sphere of Stoic freedom.

Among the students was a young Roman, Flavius Arrian, who took courses at Nicopolis when Epictetus was already old. Flavius, who was born in 108 A.D., was one of the intimates of Hadrian, who made him consul in 130 A.D. He probably studied with Epictetus between the years 123 and 126 A.D. The informal philosophical talks which Epictetus had with his students fascinated him. Needless to say there were also systematic courses in the fields of philosophy. But it was the informal discourses which convinced Arrian that he had finally discovered a Stoic Socrates or a Stoic Diogenes, who was not merely teaching a doctrine, but also living the truth. Arrian recorded many of the discourses and informal conversations of Epictetus with his intimate students. He took them down in shorthand in order not to lose the ineffable liveliness, grace, and wit of the beloved teacher. Arrian retired into private life after the death of Hadrian in 138 A.D. and dedicated himself to his literary work. He published his notes on Epictetus' teaching under the title: *Discourses in Four Books*. The *Enchiridion*, which was also arranged by Arrian, is a brief summary of the basic ideas of Stoic philosophy and an introduction to the techniques required to transform Stoic philosophy into a way of life.

Thus we do not have any original writings of Epictetus. Like G. H. Mead in recent times, he was completely dedicated to the human and intellectual problems of his students. He left it for them to preserve what they considered to be the lasting message of the teacher. In contrast to Seneca and Marcus Aurelius, Epictetus had no subjective approach to the Stoic doctrines. Moral philosophy was the center of his teaching, and epistemology was only instrumental. It is even permissible to say that he took physics or cosmology too lightly. If this is granted, we must admit that he is completely absorbed by the fundamentals of Stoic thought as presented in the *Enchiridion*. Epictetus' personality is totally integrated in the act of reasoning which establishes conformity with nature.

A remarkable difference between the Discourses and the *Enchiridion* should be mentioned. The Discourses are a living image of the teacher in action; they present the process of philosophizing, not the finished product. They show the enthusiastic and sober, the realistic and pathetic moralist in constantly changing perspectives determined by the changing students with their various concerns, problems, and questions; his teachings, his formulations, have direct reference to the various life situations in which the students should apply and practice the master's Stoic teaching. No human situation is omitted; as a guide to conduct, philosophy has relevance for all. Whether the students have to attend a dinner party, whether they are among competitors in a stadium or in a swimming pool, whether they have to present themselves at court or in an office, whether they are in the company of their mothers and sisters or of girl friends, in all human situations the philosopher knows the correct advice for the philosophical apprentice. Thus, in the Discourses, Arrian presents the unique individuality of the philosopher and of his applied moral method in living contact with various students in concrete situations. Epictetus as teacher anticipates very modern educational methods in his regard for the structure of situations and the changing perspectives in human relationships.

Nothing like this is revealed in the *Enchiridion*. Gone is the Stoic philosopher as living spirit. What remains is the living spirit of Stoicism. The *Enchiridion* is a manual for the combat officer. This analogy should be taken seriously. The Roman Stoics coined the formula: *Vivere militare*! (Life is being a soldier.) The student of philosophy is a private, the advancing Stoic is a non-commissioned officer, and the philosopher is the combat officer. For this reason all Roman Stoics apply metaphors and images derived from military life. Apprentice students of Stoicism are described as messengers, as scouts of God, as representatives of divine nature. The advancing student who is close to the goal of being a philosopher has the rank of an officer. He is already able to establish inner freedom and independence. He understands the basic Stoic truth of subjective consciousness, which is to distinguish what is in our power from what is not in our power. Not in our power are all the elements which constitute our environment, such as wealth, health, reputation, social prestige, power, the lives of those we love, and death. In our power are our thinking, our intentions, our desires, our decisions. These make it possible for us to control ourselves and to make of ourselves elements and parts of the universe of nature. This knowledge of ourselves makes us free in a world of dependencies. This superiority of our powers enables us to live in conformity with nature. The rational philosophy of control of Self and of adjustment to the Whole implies an asceticism of the emotional and the sensitive life. The philosopher must examine and control his passions, his love, his tenderness at all times in order always to be ready for the inevitable moment of farewell. The Stoics practiced a Jesuitism *avant la lettre*. They were able to live in the world as if they did not live in it. To the Stoic, life is a military camp, a play on the stage, a banquet to which we are invited.

The *Enchiridion* briefly indicated the techniques which the philosopher should apply in acting well the diverse roles which God might assign to those whom he loves, the Stoic philosophers. From the rules of social conduct to the recommendations of sexual asceticism before marriage, and the method of true thinking, the advanced Stoic will find all principles of perfection and all precepts for realizing philosophical principles in his conduct in this tiny volume.

Thus the *Enchiridion* was liberating for all intellectuals who learned from it that there are philosophical ways of self-redemption. From its time, the secular thinker could feel jubilant because he was not in need of a divine grace. Epictetus had taught him that philosophical reason could make him free and that he was capable of redeeming himself by sound reasoning.

In the Stoic distinctions of personality and world, of I and mine, of subjective consciousness and the world of objects, of freedom and dependence, we find implicit the basic elements of modern philosophies of rationalism and of objective idealism or pantheism. For this reason there is a continuous renascence of Stoicism from Descartes, Grotius, and Bishop Butler, to Montesquieu, Adam Smith, and Kant. In this long development in modern times, the tiny *Enchiridion* of Epictetus played a remarkable part.

The translations of Epictetus and of all other Stoics had the widest effect on philosophers, theologians, and lay thinkers. They were studied by the clergy of the various Christian denominations, by the scientists who were striving for a natural religion, and by the independent philosophers who were eager to separate philosophy from religion. There were many outstanding bishops in the Catholic and Anglican Churches who were eager to transform the traditions of Roman Stoicism into Christian Stoicism. Among the Calvinistic denominations were many thinkers who were in sympathy with Stoic moral principles because of their praise of the austerity of life and of the control of passions. Likewise the adherents of natural religion were propagating Stoicism as the ideal pattern of universally valid and intelligible religion. Renascent Stoicism had three functions in the rise of the modern world. First, it reconciled Christian traditions to modern rationalistic philosophies; secondly, it established an ideal pattern of natural religion; and, thirdly, it opened the way for the autonomy of morals.

The Enchiridion

I

There are things which are within our power, and there are things which are beyond our power. Within our power are opinion, aim, desire, aversion, and, in one word, whatever affairs are our own. Beyond our power are body, property, reputation, office, and, in one word, whatever are not properly our own affairs.

Now the things within our power are by nature free, unrestricted, unhindered; but those beyond our power are weak, dependent, restricted, alien. Remember, then, that if you attribute freedom to things by nature dependent and take what belongs to others for your own, you will be hindered, you will lament, you will be disturbed, you will find fault both with gods and men. But if you take for your own only that which is your own and view what belongs to others just as it really is, then no one will ever compel you, no one will restrict you; you will find fault with no one, you will accuse no one, you will do nothing against your will; no one will hurt you, you will not have an enemy, nor will you suffer any harm.

Aiming, therefore, at such great things, remember that you must not allow yourself any inclination, however slight, toward the attainment of the others; but that you must entirely quit some of them, and for the present postpone the rest. But if you would have these, and possess power and wealth likewise, you may miss the latter in seeking the former; and you will certainly fail of that by which alone happiness and freedom are procured.

Seek at once, therefore, to be able to say to every unpleasing semblance, "You are but a semblance and by no means the real thing." And then examine it by those rules which you have; and first and chiefly by this: whether it concerns the things which are within our own power or those which are not; and if it concerns anything beyond our power, be prepared to say that it is nothing to you.

II

Remember that desire demands the attainment of that of which you are desirous; and aversion demands the avoidance of that to which you are averse; that he who fails of the object of his desires is disappointed; and he who incurs the object of his aversion is wretched. If, then, you shun only those undesirable things which you can control, you will never incur anything which you shun; but if you shun sickness, or death, or poverty, you will run the risk of wretchedness. Remove [the habit of] aversion, then, from all things that are not within our power, and apply it to things undesirable which are within our power. But for the present, altogether restrain desire; for if you desire any of the things not within our own power, you must necessarily be disappointed; and you are not yet secure of those which are within our power, and so are legitimate objects of desire. Where it is practically necessary for you to pursue or avoid anything, do even this with discretion and gentleness and moderation.

III

With regard to whatever objects either delight the mind or contribute to use or are tenderly beloved, remind yourself of what nature they are, beginning with the merest trifles: if you have a favorite cup, that it is but a cup of which you are fond of—for thus, if it is broken, you can bear it; if you embrace your child or your wife, that you embrace a mortal—and thus, if either of them dies, you can bear it.

IV

When you set about any action, remind yourself of what nature the action is. If you are going to bathe, represent to yourself the incidents usual in the bath—some persons pouring out, others pushing in, others scolding, others pilfering. And thus you will more safely go about this action if you say to yourself, "I will now go to bathe and keep my own will in harmony with nature." And so with regard to every other action. For thus, if any impediment arises in bathing, you will be able to say, "It was not only to bathe that

I desired, but to keep my will in harmony with nature; and I shall not keep it thus if I am out of humor at things that happen."

V

Men are disturbed not by things, but by the views which they take of things. Thus death is nothing terrible, else it would have appeared so to Socrates. But the terror consists in our notion of death, that it is terrible. When, therefore, we are hindered or disturbed, or grieved, let us never impute it to others, but to ourselves—that is, to our own views. It is the action of an uninstructed person to reproach others for his own misfortunes; of one entering upon instruction, to reproach himself; and one perfectly instructed, to reproach neither others nor himself.

VI

Be not elated at any excellence not your own. If a horse should be elated, and say, "I am handsome," it might be endurable. But when you are elated and say, "I have a handsome horse," know that you are elated only on the merit of the horse. What then is your own? The use of the phenomena of existence. So that when you are in harmony with nature in this respect, you will be elated with some reason; for you will be elated at some good of your own.

VII

As in a voyage, when the ship is at anchor, if you go on shore to get water, you may amuse yourself with picking up a shellfish or a truffle in your way, but your thoughts ought to be bent toward the ship, and perpetually attentive, lest the captain should call, and then you must leave all these things, that you may not have to be carried on board the vessel, bound like a sheep; thus likewise in life, if, instead of a truffle or shellfish, such a thing as a wife or a child be granted you, there is no objection; but if the captain calls, run to the ship, leave all these things, and never look behind. But if you are old, never go far from the ship, lest you should be missing when called for.

VIII

Demand not that events should happen as you wish; but wish them to happen as they do happen, and you will go on well.

IX

Sickness is an impediment to the body, but not to the will unless itself pleases. Lameness is an impediment to the leg, but not to the will; and say this to yourself with regard to everything that happens. For you will find it to be an impediment to something else, but not truly to yourself.

X

Upon every accident, remember to turn toward yourself and inquire what faculty you have for its use. If you encounter a handsome person, you will find continence the faculty needed; if pain, then fortitude; if reviling, then patience. And when thus habituated, the phenomena of existence will not overwhelm you.

XI

Never say of anything, "I have lost it," but, "I have restored it." Has your child died? It is restored. Has your wife died? She is restored. Has your estate been taken away? That likewise is restored. "But it was a bad man who took it." What is it to you by whose hands he who gave it has demanded it again? While he permits you to possess it, hold it as something not your own, as do travelers at an inn.

XII

If you would improve, lay aside such reasonings as these: "If I neglect my affairs, I shall not have a maintenance; if I do not punish my servant, he will be good for nothing." For it were better to die of hunger, exempt from grief and fear, than to live in affluence with perturbation; and it is better that your servant should be bad than you unhappy.

Begin therefore with little things. Is a little oil spilled or a little wine stolen? Say to yourself, "This is the price paid for peace and tranquility; and nothing is to be had for nothing." And when you call your servant, consider that it is possible he may not come at your call; or, if he does, that he may not do what you wish. But it is not at all desirable for him, and very undesirable for you, that it should be in his power to cause you any disturbance.

XIII

If you would improve, be content to be thought foolish and dull with regard to externals. Do not desire to be thought to know anything; and though you should appear to others to be somebody, distrust yourself. For be assured, it is not easy at once to keep your will in harmony with nature and to secure externals; but while you are absorbed in the one, you must of necessity neglect the other.

XIV

If you wish your children and your wife and your friends to live forever, you are foolish, for you wish things to be in your power which are not so, and what belongs to others to be your own. So likewise, if you wish your servant to be without fault, you are foolish, for you wish vice not to be vice but something else. But if you wish not to be disappointed in your desires, that is in your own power. Exercise, therefore, what is in your power. A man's master is he who is able to confer or remove whatever that man seeks or shuns. Whoever then would be free, let him wish nothing, let him decline nothing, which depends on others; else he must necessarily be a slave.

XV

Remember that you must behave as at a banquet. Is anything brought round to you? Put out your hand and take a moderate share. Does it pass by you? Do not stop it. Is it not yet come? Do not yearn in desire toward it, but wait till it reaches you. So with regard to children, wife, office, riches; and you will some time or other be worthy to feast with the gods. And if you do not so much as take the things which are set before you, but are able even to forego them, then you will not only be worthy to feast with the gods, but to rule with them also. For, by thus doing, Diogenes and Heraclitus, and others like them, deservedly became divine, and were so recognized.

XVI

When you see anyone weeping for grief, either that his son has gone abroad or that he has suffered in his affairs, take care not to be overcome by the apparent evil, but discriminate and be ready to say, "What hurts this man is not this occurrence itself—for another man might not be hurt by it—but the view he chooses to take of it." As far as conversation goes, however, do not disdain to accommodate yourself to him and, if need be, to groan with him. Take heed, however, not to groan inwardly, too.

XVII

Remember that you are an actor in a drama of such sort as the Author chooses—if short, then in a short one; if long, then in a long one. If it be his pleasure that you should enact a poor man, or a cripple, or a ruler, or a private citizen, see that you act it well. For this is your business—to act well the given part, but to choose it belongs to another.

XVIII

When a raven happens to croak unluckily, be not overcome by appearances, but discriminate and say, "Nothing is portended to me, either to my paltry body, or property, or reputation, or children, or wife. But to me all portents are lucky if I will. For whatsoever happens, it belongs to me to derive advantage therefrom."

XIX

You can be unconquerable if you enter into no combat in which it is not in your own power to conquer. When, therefore, you see anyone eminent in honors or power, or in high esteem on any other account, take heed not to be bewildered by appearances and to pronounce him happy; for if the essence of good consists in things within our own power, there will be no room for envy or emulation. But, for your part, do not desire to be a general, or a senator, or a consul, but to be free; and the only way to this is a disregard of things which lie not within our own power.

XX

Remember that it is not he who gives abuse or blows, who affronts, but the view we take of these things as insulting. When, therefore, anyone provokes you, be assured that it is your own opinion which provokes you. Try, therefore, in the first place, not to be bewildered by appearances. For if you once gain time and respite, you will more easily command yourself.

XXI

Let death and exile, and all other things which appear terrible, be daily before your eyes, but death chiefly; and you will never entertain an abject thought, nor too eagerly covet anything.

XXII

If you have an earnest desire toward philosophy, prepare yourself from the very first to have the multitude laugh and sneer, and say, "He is returned to us a philosopher all at once"; and, "Whence this supercilious look?" Now, for your part, do not have a supercilious look indeed, but keep steadily to those things which appear best to you, as one appointed by God to this particular station. For remember that, if you are persistent, those very persons who at first ridiculed will afterwards admire you. But if you are conquered by them, you will incur a double ridicule.

XXIII

If you ever happen to turn your attention to externals, for the pleasure of anyone, be assured that you have ruined your scheme of life. Be content, then, in everything, with being a philosopher; and if you wish to seem so likewise to anyone, appear so to yourself, and it will suffice you.

XXIV

Let not such considerations as these distress you: "I shall live in discredit and be nobody anywhere." For if discredit be an evil, you can no more be involved in evil through another than in baseness. Is it any business of yours, then, to get power or to be admitted to an entertainment? By no means. How then, after all, is this discredit? And how it is true that you will be nobody anywhere when you ought to be somebody in those things only which are within your own power, in which you may be of the greatest consequence? "But my friends will be unassisted." What do you mean by "unassisted"? They will not have money from you, nor will you make them Roman citizens. Who told you, then, that these are among the things within our own power, and not rather the affairs of others? And who can give to another the things which he himself has not? "Well, but get them, then, that we too may have a share." If I can get them with the preservation of my own honor and fidelity and self-respect, show me the way and I will get them; but if you require me to lose my own proper good, that you may gain what is no good, consider how unreasonable and foolish you are. Besides, which would you rather have, a sum of money or a faithful and honorable friend? Rather assist me, then, to gain this character than require me to do those things by which I may lose it. Well, but my country, say you, as far as depends upon me, will be unassisted. Here, again, what assistance is this you mean? It will not have porticos nor baths of your providing? And what signifies that? Why, neither does a smith provide it with shoes, nor a shoemaker with arms. It is enough if everyone fully performs his own proper business. And were you to supply it with another faithful and honorable citizen, would not he be of use to it? Yes. Therefore neither are you yourself useless to it. "What place, then," say you, "shall I hold in the state?" Whatever you can hold with the preservation of your fidelity and honor. But if, by desiring to be useful to that, you lose these, how can you serve your country when you have become faithless and shameless?

XXV

Is anyone preferred before you at an entertainment, or in courtesies, or in confidential intercourse? If these things are good, you ought to rejoice that he has them; and if they are evil, do not be grieved that you have them not. And remember that you cannot be permitted to rival others in externals without using the same means to obtain them. For how can he who will not haunt the door of any man, will not attend him, will not praise him, have an equal share with him who does these things? You are unjust, then, and unreasonable if you are unwilling to pay the price for which these things are sold, and would have them for nothing. For how much are lettuces sold? An obulus, for instance. If another, then, paying an obulus, takes the lettuces, and you, not paying it, go without them, do not imagine that he has gained any advantage over you. For as he has the lettuces, so you have the obulus which you did not give. So, in the present case, you have not been invited to such a person's entertainment because you have not paid him the price for which a supper is sold. It is sold for praise; it is sold for attendance. Give him, then, the value if it be for your advantage. But if you would at the same time not pay the one, and yet receive the other, you are unreasonable and foolish. Have you nothing, then, in place of the supper? Yes, indeed, you have—not to praise him whom you do not like to praise; not to bear the insolence of his lackeys.

XXVI

The will of nature may be learned from things upon which we are all agreed. As when our neighbor's boy has broken a cup, or the like, we are ready at once to say, "These are casualties that will happen"; be assured, then, that when your own cup is likewise broken, you ought to be affected just as when another's cup was broken. Now apply this to greater things. Is the child or wife of another dead? There is no one who would not say, "This is an accident of mortality." But if anyone's own child happens to die, it is immediately, "Alas! how wretched am I!" It should be always remembered how we are affected on hearing the same thing concerning others.

XXVII

As a mark is not set up for the sake of missing the aim, so neither does the nature of evil exist in the world.

XXVIII

If a person had delivered up your body to some passer-by, you would certainly be angry. And do you feel no shame in delivering up your own mind to any reviler, to be disconcerted and confounded?

XXIX

In every affair consider what precedes and what follows, and then undertake it. Otherwise you will begin with spirit, indeed, careless of the consequences, and when these are developed, you will shamefully desist. "I would conquer at the Olympic Games." But consider what precedes and what follows, and then, if it be for your advantage, engage in the affair. You must conform to rules, submit to a diet, refrain from dainties; exercise your body, whether you choose it or not, at a stated hour, in heat and cold; you must drink no cold water, and sometimes no wine—in a word, you must give yourself up to your trainer as to a physician. Then, in the combat, you may be thrown into a ditch, dislocate your arm, turn your ankle, swallow an abundance of dust, receive stripes [for negligence], and, after all, lose the victory. When you have reckoned up all this, if your inclination still holds, set about the combat. Otherwise, take notice, you will behave like children who sometimes play wrestlers, sometimes gladiators, sometimes blow a trumpet, and sometimes act a tragedy, when they happen to have seen and admired these shows. Thus you too will be at one time a wrestler, and another a gladiator; now a philosopher, now an orator; but nothing in earnest. Like an ape you mimic all you see, and one thing after another is sure to please you, but is out of favor as soon as it becomes familiar. For you have never entered upon anything considerately; nor after having surveyed and tested the whole matter, but carelessly, and with a halfway zeal. Thus some, when they have seen a philosopher and heard a man speaking like Euphrates—though, indeed, who can speak like him?—have a mind to be philosophers, too. Consider first, man, what the matter is, and what your own nature is able to bear. If you would be a wrestler, consider your shoulders, your back, your thighs; for different persons are made for different things. Do you think that you can act as you do and be a philosopher, that you can eat, drink, be angry, be discontented, as you are now? You must watch, you must labor, you must get the better of certain appetites, must quit your acquaintances, be despised by your servant, be laughed at by those you meet; come off worse than others in everything—in offices, in honors, before tribunals. When you have fully considered all these things, approach, if you please—that is, if, by parting with them, you have a mind to purchase serenity, freedom, and tranquility. If not, do not come hither; do not, like children, be now a philosopher, then a publican, then an orator, and then one of Caesar's officers. These things are not consistent. You must be one man, either good or bad. You must cultivate either your own reason or else externals; apply yourself either to things within or without you—that is, be either a philosopher or one of the mob.

XXX

Duties are universally measured by relations. Is a certain man your father? In this are implied taking care of him, submitting to him in all things, patiently receiving his reproaches, his correction. But he is a bad father. Is your natural tie, then, to a good father? No, but to a father. Is a brother unjust? Well, preserve your own just relation toward him. Consider not what he does, but what you are to do to keep your own will in a state conformable to nature, for another cannot hurt you unless you please. You will then be hurt when you consent to be hurt. In this manner, therefore, if you accustom yourself to contemplate the relations of neighbor, citizen, commander, you can deduce from each the corresponding duties.

XXXI

Be assured that the essence of piety toward the gods lies in this—to form right opinions concerning them, as existing and as governing the universe justly and well. And fix yourself in this resolution, to obey them, and yield to them, and willingly follow them amidst all events, as being ruled by the most perfect wisdom. For thus you will never find fault with the gods, nor accuse them of neglecting you. And it is not possible for this to be affected in any other way than by withdrawing yourself from things which are not within our own power, and by making good or evil to consist only in those which are. For if you suppose any other things to be either good or evil, it is inevitable that, when you are disappointed of what you wish or incur what you would avoid, you should reproach and blame their authors. For every creature is naturally formed to flee and abhor things that appear hurtful and that which causes them; and to pursue and admire those which appear beneficial and that which causes them. It is impracticable, then, that one who supposes himself to be hurt should rejoice in the person who, as he thinks, hurts him, just as it is impossible to rejoice in the hurt itself. Hence, also, a father is reviled by his son when he does not impart the things which seem to be good; and this made Polynices and Eteocles mutually enemies—that empire seemed good to both. On this account the husbandman reviles the gods; [and so do] the sailor, the merchant, or those who have lost wife or child. For where our interest is, there, too, is piety directed. So that whoever is careful to regulate his desires and aversions as he ought is thus made careful of piety likewise. But it also becomes incumbent on everyone to offer libations and sacrifices and first fruits, according to the customs of his country, purely, and not heedlessly nor negligently; not avariciously, nor yet extravagantly.

XXXII

When you have recourse to divination, remember that you know not what the event will be, and you come to learn it of the diviner; but of what nature it is you knew before coming; at least, if you are of philosophic mind. For if it is among the things not within our own power, it can by no means be either good or evil. Do not, therefore, bring with you to the diviner either desire or aversion—else you will approach him trembling—but first clearly understand that every event is indifferent and nothing to you, of whatever sort it may be; for it will be in your power to make a right use of it, and this no one can hinder. Then come with confidence to the gods as your counselors; and afterwards, when any counsel is given you, remember what counselors you have assumed, and whose advice you will neglect if you disobey. Come to divination as Socrates prescribed, in cases of which the whole consideration relates to the event, and in which no opportunities are afforded by reason or any other art to discover the matter in view. When, therefore, it is our duty to share the danger of a friend or of our country, we ought not to consult the oracle as to whether we shall share it with them or not. For though the diviner should forewarn you that the auspices are unfavorable, this means no more than that either death or mutilation or exile is portended. But we have reason within us; and it directs us, even with these hazards, to stand by our friend and our country. Attend, therefore, to the greater diviner, the Pythian God, who once cast out of the temple him who neglected to save his friend.

XXXIII

Begin by prescribing to yourself some character and demeanor, such as you may preserve both alone and in company.

Be mostly silent, or speak merely what is needful, and in few words. We may, however, enter sparingly into discourse sometimes, when occasion calls for it; but let it not run on any of the common subjects, as gladiators, or horse races, or athletic champions, or food, or drink—the vulgar topics of conversation—and especially not on men, so as either to blame, or praise, or make comparisons. If you are able, then, by your own conversation, bring over that of your company to proper subjects; but if you happen to find yourself among strangers, be silent.

Let not your laughter be loud, frequent, or abundant.

Avoid taking oaths, if possible, altogether; at any rate, so far as you are able.

Avoid public and vulgar entertainments; but if ever an occasion calls you to them, keep your attention upon the stretch, that you may not imperceptibly slide into vulgarity. For be assured that if a person be ever so pure himself, yet, if his companion be corrupted, he who converses with him will be corrupted likewise.

Provide things relating to the body no further than absolute need requires, as meat, drink, clothing, house, retinue. But cut off everything that looks toward show and luxury.

Before marriage guard yourself with all your ability from unlawful intercourse with women; yet be not uncharitable or severe to those who are led into this, nor boast frequently that you yourself do otherwise.

If anyone tells you that a certain person speaks ill of you, do not make excuses about what is said of you, but answer: "He was ignorant of my other faults, else he would not have mentioned these alone."

It is not necessary for you to appear often at public spectacles; but if ever there is a proper occasion for you to be there, do not appear more solicitous for any other than for yourself—that is, wish things to be only just as they are, and only the best man to win; for thus nothing will go against you. But abstain entirely from acclamations and derision and violent emotions. And when you come away, do not discourse a great deal on what has passed and what contributes nothing to your own amendment. For it would appear by such discourse that you were dazzled by the show.

Be not prompt or ready to attend private recitations; but if you do attend, preserve your gravity and dignity, and yet avoid making yourself disagreeable.

When you are going to confer with anyone, and especially with one who seems your superior, represent to yourself how Socrates or Zeno would behave in such a case, and you will not be at a loss to meet properly whatever may occur.

When you are going before anyone in power, fancy to yourself that you may not find him at home, that you may be shut out, that the doors may not be opened to you, that he may not notice you. If, with all this, it be your duty to go, bear what happens and never say to yourself, "It was not worth so much"; for this is vulgar, and like a man bewildered by externals.

In company, avoid a frequent and excessive mention of your own actions and dangers. For however agreeable it may be to yourself to allude to the risks you have run, it is not equally agreeable to others to hear your adventures. Avoid likewise an endeavor to excite laughter, for this may readily slide you into vulgarity, and, besides, may be apt to lower you in the esteem of your acquaintance. Approaches to indecent discourse are likewise dangerous. Therefore, when anything of this sort happens, use the first fit opportunity to rebuke him who makes advances that way, or, at least, by silence and blushing and a serious look show yourself to be displeased by such talk.

XXXIV

If you are dazzled by the semblance of any promised pleasure, guard yourself against being bewildered by it; but let the affair wait your leisure, and procure yourself some delay. Then bring to your mind both points of time—that in which you shall enjoy the pleasure, and that in which you will repent and reproach yourself, after you have enjoyed it—and set before you, in opposition to these, how you will rejoice and applaud yourself if you abstain. And even though it should appear to you a seasonable gratification, take heed that its enticements and allurements and seductions may not subdue you, but set in opposition to this how much better it is to be conscious of having gained so great a victory.

XXXV

When you do anything from a clear judgment that it ought to be done, never shrink from being seen to do it, even though the world should misunderstand it; for if you are not acting rightly, shun the action itself; if you are, why fear those who wrongly censure you?

XXXVI

As the proposition, "either it is day or it is night," has much force in a disjunctive argument, but none at all in a conjunctive one, so, at a feast, to choose the largest share is very suitable to the bodily appetite, but utterly inconsistent with the social spirit of the entertainment. Remember, then, when you eat with another, not only the value to the body of those things which are set before you, but also the value of proper courtesy toward your host.

XXXVII

If you have assumed any character beyond your strength, you have both demeaned yourself ill in that and quitted one which you might have supported.

XXXVIII

As in walking you take care not to tread upon a nail, or turn your foot, so likewise take care not to hurt the ruling faculty of your mind. And if we were to guard against this in every action, we should enter upon action more safely.

XXXIX

The body is to everyone the proper measure of its possessions, as the foot is of the shoe. If, therefore, you stop at this, you will keep the measure; but if you move beyond it, you must necessarily be carried forward, as down a precipice; as in the case of a shoe, if you go beyond its fitness to the foot, it comes first to be gilded, then purple, and then studded with jewels. For to that which once exceeds the fit measure there is no bound.

XL

Women from fourteen years old are flattered by men with the title of mistresses. Therefore, perceiving that they are regarded only as qualified to give men pleasure, they begin to adorn themselves, and in that to place all their hopes. It is worth while, therefore, to try that they may perceive themselves honored only so far as they appear beautiful in their demeanor and modestly virtuous.

XLI

It is a mark of want of intellect to spend much time in things relating to the body, as to be immoderate in exercises, in eating and drinking, and in the discharge of other animal functions. These things should be done incidentally and our main strength be applied to our reason.

XLII

When any person does ill by you, or speaks ill of you, remember that he acts or speaks from an impression that it is right for him to do so. Now it is not possible that he should follow what appears right to you, but only what appears so to himself. Therefore, if he judges from false appearances, he is the person hurt, since he, too, is the person deceived. For if anyone takes a true proposition to be false, the proposition is not hurt, but only the man is deceived. Setting out, then, from these principles, you will meekly bear with a person who reviles you, for you will say upon every occasion, "It seemed so to him."

XLIII

Everything has two handles: one by which it may be borne, another by which it cannot. If your brother acts unjustly, do not lay hold on the affair by the handle of his injustice, for by that it cannot be borne, but rather by the opposite—that he is your brother, that he was brought up with you; and thus you will lay hold on it as it is to be borne.

XLIV

These reasonings have no logical connection: "I am richer than you, therefore I am your superior." "I am more eloquent than you, therefore I am your superior." The true logical connection is rather this: "I am richer than you, therefore my possessions must exceed yours." "I am more eloquent than you, therefore my style must surpass yours." But you, after all, consist neither in property nor in style.

XLV

Does anyone bathe hastily? Do not say that he does it ill, but hastily. Does anyone drink much wine? Do not say that he does ill, but that he drinks a great deal. For unless you perfectly understand his motives, how should you know if he acts ill? Thus you will not risk yielding to any appearances but such as you fully comprehend.

XLVI

Never proclaim yourself a philosopher, nor make much talk among the ignorant about your principles, but show them by actions. Thus, at an entertainment, do not discourse how people ought to eat, but eat as you ought. For remember that thus Socrates also universally avoided all ostentation. And when persons came to him and desired to be introduced by him to philosophers, he took them and introduced them; so well did he bear being overlooked. So if ever there should be among the ignorant any discussion of principles, be for the most part silent. For there is great danger in hastily throwing out what is undigested. And if anyone tells you that you know nothing, and you are not nettled at it, then you may be sure that you have really entered on your work. For sheep do not hastily throw up the grass to show the shepherds how much they have eaten, but, inwardly digesting their food, they produce it outwardly in wool and milk. Thus, therefore, do you not make an exhibition before the ignorant of your principles, but of the actions to which their digestion gives rise.

XLVII

When you have learned to nourish your body frugally, do not pique yourself upon it; nor, if you drink water, be saying upon every occasion, "I drink water." But first consider how much more frugal are the poor than we, and how much more patient of hardship. If at any time you would inure yourself by exercise to labor and privation, for your own sake and not for the public, do not attempt great feats; but when you are violently thirsty, just rinse your mouth with water, and tell nobody.

XLVIII

The condition and characteristic of a vulgar person is that he never looks for either help or harm from himself, but only from externals. The condition and characteristic of a philosopher is that he looks to himself for all help or harm. The marks of a proficient are that he censures no one, praises no one, blames no one, accuses no one; says nothing concerning himself as being anybody or knowing anything. When he is in any instance hindered or restrained, he accuses himself; and if he is praised, he smiles to himself at the person who praises him; and if he is censured, he makes no defense. But he goes about with the caution of a convalescent, careful of interference with anything that is doing well but not yet quite secure. He restrains desire; he transfers his aversion to those things only which thwart the proper use of our own will; he employs his energies moderately in all directions; if he appears stupid or ignorant, he does not care; and, in a word, he keeps watch over himself as over an enemy and one in ambush.

XLIX

When anyone shows himself vain on being able to understand and interpret the works of Chrysippus, say to yourself: "Unless Chrysippus had written obscurely, this person would have had nothing to be vain of. But what do I desire? To understand nature, and follow her. I ask, then, who interprets her; and hearing that Chrysippus does, I have recourse to him. I do not understand his writings. I seek, therefore, one to interpret them." So far there is nothing to value myself upon. And when I find an interpreter, what remains is to make use of his instructions. This alone is the valuable thing. But if I admire merely the interpretation, what do I become more than a grammarian, instead of a philosopher, except, indeed, that instead of Homer I interpret Chrysippus? When anyone, therefore, desires me to read Chrysippus to him, I rather blush when I cannot exhibit actions that are harmonious and consonant with his discourse.

L

Whatever rules you have adopted, abide by them as laws, and as if you would be impious to transgress them; and do not regard what anyone says of you, for this, after all, is no concern of yours. How long, then, will you delay to demand of yourself the noblest improvements, and in no instance to transgress the judgments of reason? You have received the philosophic principles with which you ought to be conversant; and you have been conversant with them. For what other master, then, do you wait as an excuse for this delay in self-reformation? You are no longer a boy but a grown man. If, therefore, you will be negligent and slothful, and always add procrastination to procrastination, purpose to purpose, and fix day after day in which you will attend to yourself, you will insensibly continue to accomplish nothing and, living and dying, remain of vulgar mind. This instant, then, think yourself worthy of living as a man grown up and a proficient. Let whatever appears to be the best be to you an inviolable law. And if any instance of pain or pleasure, glory or disgrace, be set before you, remember that now is the combat, now the Olympiad comes on, nor can it be put off; and that by one failure and defeat honor may be lost or—won. Thus Socrates became perfect, improving himself by everything, following reason alone. And though you are not yet a Socrates, you ought, however, to live as one seeking to be a Socrates.

LI

The first and most necessary topic in philosophy is the practical application of principles, [such] as, We ought not to lie; the second is that of demonstrations as, Why it is that we ought not to lie; the third, that which gives strength and logical connection to the other two, as, Why this is a demonstration. For what is demonstration? What is a consequence? What a contradiction? What truth? What falsehood? The third point is then necessary on account of the second; and the second on account of the first. But the most necessary, and that whereon we ought to rest, is the first. But we do just the contrary. For we spend all our time on the third point and employ all our diligence about that, and entirely neglect the first. Therefore, at the same time that we lie, we are very ready to show how it is demonstrated that lying is wrong.

Upon all occasions we ought to have these maxims ready at hand: Conduct me, Zeus, and thou, O Destiny, Wherever your decrees have fixed my lot. I follow cheerfully; and, did I not, Wicked and wretched, I must follow still. Who'er yields properly to Fate is deemed Wise among men, and knows the laws of Heaven. And this third: "O Crito, if it thus pleases the gods, thus let it be." "Anytus and Melitus may kill me indeed; but hurt me they cannot."

Discourse on The Method of Rightly Conducting The Reason, and Seeking Truth in the Sciences

Rene Descartes

Prefatory Note by The Author

If this Discourse appear too long to be read at once, it may be divided into six Parts: and, in the first, will be found various considerations touching the Sciences; in the second, the principal rules of the Method which the Author has discovered, in the third, certain of the rules of Morals which he has deduced from this Method; in the fourth, the reasonings by which he establishes the existence of God and of the Human Soul, which are the foundations of his Metaphysic; in the fifth, the order of the Physical questions which he has investigated, and, in particular, the explication of the motion of the heart and of some other difficulties pertaining to Medicine, as also the difference between the soul of man and that of the brutes; and, in the last, what the Author believes to be required in order to greater advancement in the investigation of Nature than has yet been made, with the reasons that have induced him to write.

Part I

Good sense is, of all things among men, the most equally distributed; for every one thinks himself so abundantly provided with it, that those even who are the most difficult to satisfy in everything else, do not usually desire a larger measure of this quality than they already possess. And in this it is not likely that all are mistaken the conviction is rather to be held as testifying that the power of judging aright and of distinguishing truth from error, which is properly what is called good sense or reason, is by nature equal in all men; and that the diversity of our opinions, consequently, does not arise from some being endowed with a larger share of reason than others, but solely from this, that we conduct our thoughts along different ways, and do not fix our attention on the same objects. For to be possessed of a vigorous mind is not enough; the prime requisite is rightly to apply it. The greatest minds, as they are capable of the highest excellences, are open likewise to the greatest aberrations; and those who travel very slowly may yet make far greater progress, provided they keep always to the straight road, than those who, while they run, forsake it.

For myself, I have never fancied my mind to be in any respect more perfect than those of the generality; on the contrary, I have often wished that I were equal to some others in promptitude of thought, or in clearness and distinctness of imagination, or in fullness and readiness of memory. And besides these, I know of no other qualities that contribute to the perfection of the mind; for as to the reason or sense, inasmuch as it is that alone which constitutes us men, and distinguishes us from the brutes, I am disposed to believe that it is to be found complete in each individual; and on this point to adopt the common opinion of philosophers, who say that the difference of greater and less holds only among the accidents, and not among the forms or natures of individuals of the same species.

I will not hesitate, however, to avow my belief that it has been my singular good fortune to have very early in life fallen in with certain tracks which have conducted me to considerations and maxims, of which I have formed a method that gives me the means, as I think, of gradually augmenting my knowledge, and of raising it by little and little to the highest point which the mediocrity of my talents and the brief duration of my life will permit me to reach. For I have already reaped from it such fruits that, although I have been accustomed to think lowly enough of myself, and although when I look with the eye of a philosopher at the varied courses and pursuits of mankind at large, I find scarcely one which does not appear in vain and useless, I nevertheless derive the highest satisfaction from the progress I conceive myself to have already made in the search after truth, and cannot help entertaining such expectations of the future as to believe that if, among the occupations of men as men, there is any one really excellent and important, it is that which I have chosen.

After all, it is possible I may be mistaken; and it is but a little copper and glass, perhaps, that I take for gold and diamonds. I know how very liable we are to delusion in what relates to ourselves, and also how much the judgments of our friends are to be suspected when given in our favor. But I shall endeavor in this discourse to describe the paths I have followed, and to delineate my life as in a picture, in order that each one may also be able to judge of them for himself, and that in the general opinion entertained of them, as gathered from current report, I myself may have a new help towards instruction to be added to those I have been in the habit of employing.

My present design, then, is not to teach the method which each ought to follow for the right conduct of his reason, but solely to describe the way in which I have endeavored to conduct my own. They who set themselves to give precepts must of course regard themselves as possessed of greater skill than those to whom they prescribe; and if they err in the slightest particular, they subject themselves to censure. But as this tract is put forth merely as a history, or, if you will, as a tale, in which, amid some examples worthy of imitation, there will be found, perhaps, as many more which it were advisable not to follow, I hope it will prove useful to some without being hurtful to any, and that my openness will find some favor with all.

From my childhood, I have been familiar with letters; and as I was given to believe that by their help a clear and certain knowledge of all that is useful in life might be acquired, I was ardently desirous of instruction. But as soon as I had finished the entire course of study, at the close of which it is customary to be admitted into the order of the learned, I completely changed my opinion. For I found myself involved in so many doubts and errors, that I was convinced I had advanced no farther in all my attempts at learning, than the discovery at every turn of my own ignorance. And yet I was studying in one of the most celebrated schools in Europe, in which I thought there must be learned men, if such were anywhere to be found. I had been taught all that others learned there; and not contented with the sciences actually taught us, I had, in addition, read all the books that had fallen into my hands, treating of such branches as are esteemed the most curious and rare. I knew the judgment which others had formed of me; and I did not find that I was considered inferior to my fellows, although there were among them some who were already marked out to fill the places of our instructors. And, in fine, our age appeared to me as flourishing, and as fertile in powerful minds as any preceding one. I was thus led to take the liberty of judging of all other men by myself, and of concluding that there was no science in existence that was of such a nature as I had previously been given to believe.

I still continued, however, to hold in esteem the studies of the schools. I was aware that the languages taught in them are necessary to the understanding of the writings of the ancients; that the grace of fable stirs the mind; that the memorable deeds of history elevate it; and, if read with discretion, aid in forming the judgment; that the perusal of all excellent books is, as it were, to interview with the noblest men of past ages, who have written them, and even a studied interview, in which are discovered to us only their choicest thoughts; that eloquence has incomparable force and beauty; that poesy has its ravishing graces and delights; that in the mathematics there are many refined discoveries eminently suited to gratify the inquisitive, as well as further all the arts an lessen the labor of man; that numerous highly useful precepts and exhortations to virtue are contained in treatises on morals; that theology points out the path to heaven; that philosophy affords the means of discoursing with an appearance of truth on all matters, and commands the admiration of the more simple; that jurisprudence, medicine, and the other sciences, secure for their cultivators honors and riches; and, in fine, that it is useful to bestow some attention upon all, even upon those abounding the most in superstition and error, that we may be in a position to determine their real value, and guard against being deceived.

But I believed that I had already given sufficient time to languages, and likewise to the reading of the writings of the ancients, to their histories and fables. For to hold converse with those of other ages and to travel, are almost the same thing. It is useful to know something of the manners of different nations, that we may be enabled to form a more correct judgment regarding our own, and be prevented from thinking that everything contrary to our customs is ridiculous and irrational, a conclusion usually come to by those whose experience has been limited to their own country. On the other hand, when too much time is occupied in traveling, we become strangers to our native country; and the over curious in the customs of the past are generally ignorant of those of the present. Besides, fictitious narratives lead us to imagine the possibility of many events that are impossible; and even the most faithful histories, if they do not wholly misrepresent matters, or exaggerate their importance to render the account of them more worthy of perusal, omit, at least, almost always the meanest and least striking of the attendant circumstances; hence it happens that the remainder does not represent the truth, and that such as regulate their conduct by examples drawn from this source, are apt to fall into the extravagances of the knight-errants of romance, and to entertain projects that exceed their powers.

I esteemed eloquence highly, and was in raptures with poesy; but I thought that both were gifts of nature rather than fruits of study. Those in whom the faculty of reason is predominant, and who most skillfully dispose their thoughts with a view to render them clear and intelligible, are always the best able to persuade others of the truth of what they lay down, though they should speak only in the language of Lower Brittany, and be wholly ignorant of the rules of rhetoric; and those whose minds are stored with the most agreeable fancies, and who can give expression to them with the greatest embellishment and harmony, are still the best poets, though unacquainted with the art of poetry.

I was especially delighted with the mathematics, on account of the certitude and evidence of their reasonings; but I had not as yet a precise knowledge of their true use; and thinking that they but contributed to the advancement of the mechanical arts, I was astonished that foundations, so strong and solid, should have had no loftier superstructure reared on them. On the other hand, I compared the disquisitions of the ancient moralists to very towering and magnificent palaces with no better foundation than sand and mud: they laud the virtues very highly, and exhibit them as estimable far above anything on earth; but they give us no adequate criterion of virtue, and frequently that which they designate with so fine a name is but apathy, or pride, or despair, or parricide.

I revered our theology, and aspired as much as any one to reach heaven: but being given assuredly to understand that the way is not less open to the most ignorant than to the most learned, and that the revealed truths which lead to heaven are above our comprehension, I did not presume to subject them to the impotency of my reason; and I thought that in order competently to undertake their examination, there was need of some special help from heaven, and of being more than man.

Of philosophy I will say nothing, except that when I saw that it had been cultivated for many ages by the most distinguished men, and that yet there is not a single matter within its sphere which is not still in dispute, and nothing, therefore, which is above doubt, I did not presume to anticipate that my success would be greater in it than that of others; and further, when I considered the number of conflicting opinions touching a single matter that may be upheld by learned men, while there can be but one true, I reckoned as well-nigh false all that was only probable.

As to the other sciences, inasmuch as these borrow their principles from philosophy, I judged that no solid superstructures could be reared on foundations so infirm; and neither the honor nor the gain held out by them was sufficient to determine me to their cultivation: for I was not, thank Heaven, in a condition which compelled me to make merchandise of science for the bettering of my fortune; and though I might not profess to scorn glory as a cynic, I yet made very slight account of that honor which I hoped to acquire only through fictitious titles. And, in fine, of false sciences I thought I knew the worth sufficiently to escape being deceived by the professions of an alchemist, the predictions of an astrologer, the impostures of a magician, or by the artifices and boasting of any of those who profess to know things of which they are ignorant.

For these reasons, as soon as my age permitted me to pass from under the control of my instructors, I entirely abandoned the study of letters, and resolved no longer to seek any other science than the knowledge of myself, or of the great book of the world. I spent the remainder of my youth in traveling, in visiting courts and armies, in holding intercourse with men of different dispositions and ranks, in collecting varied experience, in proving myself in the different situations into which fortune threw me, and, above all, in making such reflection on the matter of my experience as to secure my improvement. For it occurred to me that I should find much more truth in the reasonings of each individual with reference to the affairs in which he is personally interested, and the issue of which must presently punish him if he has judged amiss, than in those conducted by a man of letters in his study, regarding speculative matters that are of no practical moment, and followed by no consequences to himself, farther, perhaps, than that they foster his vanity the better the more remote they are from common sense; requiring, as they must in this case, the exercise of greater ingenuity and art to render them probable. In addition, I had always a most earnest desire to know how to distinguish the true from the false, in order that I might be able clearly to discriminate the right path in life, and proceed in it with confidence.

It is true that, while busied only in considering the manners of other men, I found here, too, scarce any ground for settled conviction, and remarked hardly less contradiction among them than in the opinions of the philosophers. So that the greatest advantage I derived from the study consisted in this, that, observing many things which, however extravagant and ridiculous to our apprehension, are yet by common consent received and approved by other great nations, I learned to entertain too decided a belief in regard to nothing of the truth of which I had been persuaded merely by example and custom; and thus I gradually extricated myself from many errors powerful enough to darken our natural intelligence, and incapacitate us in great measure from listening to reason. But after I had been occupied several years in thus studying the book of the world, and in essaying to gather some experience, I at length resolved to make myself an object of study, and to employ all the powers of my mind in choosing the paths I ought to follow, an undertaking which was accompanied with greater success than it would have been had I never quitted my country or my books.

Part II

I was then in Germany, attracted thither by the wars in that country, which have not yet been brought to a termination; and as I was returning to the army from the coronation of the emperor, the setting in of winter arrested me in a locality where, as I found no society to interest me, and was besides fortunately undisturbed by any cares or passions, I remained the whole day in seclusion, with full opportunity to occupy my attention with my own thoughts. Of these one of the very first that occurred to me was, that there is seldom so much perfection in works composed of many separate parts, upon which different hands had been employed, as in those completed by a single master. Thus it is observable that the buildings which a single architect has planned and executed, are generally more elegant and commodious than those which several have attempted to improve, by making old walls serve for purposes for which they were not originally built. Thus also, those ancient cities which, from being at first only villages, have become, in course of time, large towns, are usually but ill laid out compared with the regularity constructed towns which a professional architect has freely planned on an open plain; so that although the several buildings of the former may often equal or surpass in beauty those of the latter, yet when one observes their indiscriminate juxtaposition, there a large one and here a small, and the consequent crookedness and irregularity of the streets, one is disposed to allege that chance rather than any human will guided by reason must have led to such an arrangement. And if we consider that nevertheless there have been at all times certain officers whose duty it was to see that private buildings contributed to public ornament, the difficulty of reaching high perfection with but the materials of others to operate on, will be readily acknowledged. In the same way I fancied that those nations which, starting from a semi-barbarous state and advancing to civilization by slow degrees, have had their laws successively determined, and, as it were, forced upon them simply by experience of the hurtfulness of particular crimes and disputes, would by this process come to be possessed of less perfect institutions than those which, from the commencement of their association as communities, have followed the appointments of some wise legislator. It is thus quite certain that the constitution of the true religion, the ordinances of which are derived from God, must be incomparably superior to that of every other. And, to speak of human affairs, I believe that the pre-eminence of Sparta was due not to the goodness of each of its laws in particular, for many of these were very strange, and even opposed to good morals, but to the circumstance that, originated by a single individual, they all tended to a single end. In the same way I thought that the sciences contained in books (such of them at least as are made up of probable reasonings, without demonstrations), composed as they are of the opinions of many different individuals massed together, are farther removed from truth than the simple inferences which a man of good sense using his natural and unprejudiced judgment draws respecting the matters of his experience. And because we have all to pass through a state of infancy to manhood, and have been of necessity, for a length of time, governed by our desires and preceptors (whose dictates were frequently conflicting, while neither perhaps always counseled us for the best), I farther concluded that it is almost impossible that our judgments can be so correct or solid as they would have been, had our reason been mature from the moment of our birth, and had we always been guided by it alone.

It is true, however, that it is not customary to pull down all the houses of a town with the single design of rebuilding them differently, and thereby rendering the streets more handsome; but it often happens that a private individual takes down his own with the view of erecting it anew, and that people are even sometimes constrained to this when their houses are in danger of falling from age, or when the foundations are insecure. With this before me by way of example, I was persuaded that it would indeed be preposterous for a private individual to think of reforming a state by fundamentally changing it throughout, and overturning it in order to set it up amended; and the same I thought was true of any similar project for reforming the body of the sciences, or the order of teaching them established in the schools: but as for the opinions which up to that time I had embraced, I thought that I could not do better than resolve at once to sweep them wholly away, that I might afterwards be in a position to admit either others more correct, or even perhaps the same when they had undergone the scrutiny of reason. I firmly believed that in this way I should much better succeed in the conduct of my life, than if I built only upon old foundations, and leaned upon principles which, in my youth, I had taken upon trust. For although I recognized various difficulties in this undertaking, these were not, however, without remedy, nor once to be compared with such as attend the slightest reformation in public affairs. Large bodies, if once overthrown, are with great difficulty set up again, or even kept erect when once seriously shaken, and the fall of such is always disastrous. Then if there are any imperfections in the constitutions of states (and that many such exist the diversity of constitutions is alone sufficient to assure us), custom has without doubt materially smoothed their inconveniences, and has even managed to steer altogether clear of, or insensibly corrected a number which sagacity could not have provided against with equal effect; and, in fine, the defects are almost always more tolerable than the change necessary for their removal; in the same manner that highways which wind among mountains, by being much frequented, become gradually so smooth and commodious, that it is much better to follow them than to seek a straighter path by climbing over the tops of rocks and descending to the bottoms of precipices.

Hence it is that I cannot in any degree approve of those restless and busy meddlers who, called neither by birth nor fortune to take part in the management of public affairs, are yet always projecting reforms; and if I thought that this tract contained aught which might justify the suspicion that I was a victim of such folly, I would by no means permit its publication. I have never contemplated anything higher than the reformation of my own opinions, and basing them on a foundation wholly my own. And although my own satisfaction with my work has led me to present here a draft of it, I do not by any means therefore recommend to every one else to make a similar attempt. Those whom God has endowed with a larger measure of genius will entertain, perhaps, designs still more exalted; but for the many I am much afraid lest even the present undertaking be more than they can safely venture to imitate. The single design to strip one's self of all past beliefs is one that ought not to be taken by every one. The majority of men is composed of two classes, for neither of which would this be at all a befitting resolution: in the first place, of those who with more than a due confidence in their own powers, are precipitate in their judgments and want the patience requisite for orderly and circumspect thinking; whence it happens, that if men of this class once take the liberty to doubt of their accustomed opinions, and quit the beaten highway, they will never be able to thread the byway that would lead them by a shorter course, and will lose themselves and continue to wander for life; in the second place, of those who, possessed of sufficient sense or modesty to determine that there are others who excel them in the power of discriminating between truth and error, and by whom they may be instructed, ought rather to content themselves with the opinions of such than trust for more correct to their own reason.

For my own part, I should doubtless have belonged to the latter class, had I received instruction from but one master, or had I never known the diversities of opinion that from time immemorial have prevailed among men of the greatest learning. But I had become aware, even so early as during my college life, that no opinion, however absurd and incredible, can be imagined, which has not been maintained by some on of the philosophers; and afterwards in the course of my travels I remarked that all those whose opinions are decidedly repugnant to ours are not in that account barbarians and savages, but on the contrary that many of these nations make an equally good, if not better, use of their reason than we do. I took into account also the very different character which a person brought up from infancy in France or Germany exhibits, from that which, with the same mind originally, this individual would have possessed had he lived always among the Chinese or with savages, and the circumstance that in dress itself the fashion which pleased us ten years ago, and which may again, perhaps, be received into favor before ten years have gone, appears to us at this moment extravagant and ridiculous. I was thus led to infer that the ground of our opinions is far more custom and example than any certain knowledge. And, finally, although such be the ground of our opinions, I remarked that a plurality of suffrages is no guarantee of truth where it is at all of difficult discovery, as in such cases it is much more likely that it will be found by one than by many. I could, however, select from the crowd no one whose opinions seemed worthy of preference, and thus I found myself constrained, as it were, to use my own reason in the conduct of my life.

But like one walking alone and in the dark, I resolved to proceed so slowly and with such circumspection, that if I did not advance far, I would at least guard against falling. I did not even choose to dismiss summarily any of the opinions that had crept into my belief without having been introduced by reason, but first of all took sufficient time carefully to satisfy myself of the general nature of the task I was setting myself, and ascertain the true method by which to arrive at the knowledge of whatever lay within the compass of my powers.

Among the branches of philosophy, I had, at an earlier period, given some attention to logic, and among those of the mathematics to geometrical analysis and algebra,–three arts or sciences which ought, as I conceived, to contribute something to my design. But, on examination, I found that, as for logic, its syllogisms and the majority of its other precepts are of avail–rather in the communication of what we already know, or even as the art of Lully, in speaking without judgment of things of which we are ignorant, than in the investigation of the unknown; and although this science contains indeed a number of correct and very excellent precepts, there are, nevertheless, so many others, and these either injurious or superfluous, mingled with the former, that it is almost quite as difficult to effect a severance of the true from the false as it is to extract a Diana or a Minerva from a rough block of marble. Then as to the analysis of the ancients and the algebra of the moderns, besides that they embrace only matters highly abstract, and, to appearance, of no use, the former is so exclusively restricted to the consideration of figures, that it can exercise the understanding only on condition of greatly fatiguing the imagination; and, in the latter, there is so complete a subjection to certain rules and formulas, that there results an art full of confusion and obscurity calculated to embarrass, instead of a science fitted to cultivate the mind. By these considerations I was induced to seek some other method which would comprise the advantages of the three and be exempt from their defects. And as a multitude of laws often only hampers justice, so that a state is best governed when, with few laws, these are rigidly administered; in like manner, instead of the great number of precepts of which logic is composed, I believed that the four following would prove perfectly sufficient for me, provided I took the firm and unwavering resolution never in a single instance to fail in observing them.

The first was never to accept anything for true which I did not clearly know to be such; that is to say, carefully to avoid precipitancy and prejudice, and to comprise nothing more in my judgement than what was presented to my mind so clearly and distinctly as to exclude all ground of doubt.

The second, to divide each of the difficulties under examination into as many parts as possible, and as might be necessary for its adequate solution.

The third, to conduct my thoughts in such order that, by commencing with objects the simplest and easiest to know, I might ascend by little and little, and, as it were, step by step, to the knowledge of the more complex; assigning in thought a certain order even to those objects which in their own nature do not stand in a relation of antecedence and sequence.

And the last, in every case to make enumerations so complete, and reviews so general, that I might be assured that nothing was omitted.

The long chains of simple and easy reasonings by means of which geometers are accustomed to reach the conclusions of their most difficult demonstrations, had led me to imagine that all things, to the knowledge of which man is competent, are mutually connected in the same way, and that there is nothing so far removed from us as to be beyond our reach, or so hidden that we cannot discover it, provided only we abstain from accepting the false for the true, and always preserve in our thoughts the order necessary for the deduction of one truth from another. And I had little difficulty in determining the objects with which it was necessary to commence, for I was already persuaded that it must be with the simplest and easiest to know, and, considering that of all those who have hitherto sought truth in the sciences, the mathematicians alone have been able to find any demonstrations, that is, any certain and evident reasons, I did not doubt but that such must have been the rule of their investigations. I resolved to commence, therefore, with the examination of the simplest objects, not anticipating, however, from this any other advantage than that to be found in accustoming my mind to the love and nourishment of truth, and to a distaste for all such reasonings as were unsound. But I had no intention on that account of attempting to master all the particular sciences commonly denominated mathematics: but observing that, however different their objects, they all agree in considering only the various relations or proportions subsisting among those objects, I thought it best for my purpose to consider these proportions in the most general form possible, without referring them to any objects in particular, except such as would most facilitate the knowledge of them, and without by any means restricting them to these, that afterwards I might thus be the better able to apply them to every other class of objects to which they are legitimately applicable. Perceiving further, that in order to understand these relations I should sometimes have to consider them one by one and sometimes only to bear them in mind, or embrace them in the aggregate, I thought that, in order the better to consider them individually, I should view them as subsisting between straight lines, than which I could find no objects more simple, or capable of being more distinctly represented to my imagination and senses; and on the other hand, that in order to retain them in the memory or embrace an aggregate of many, I should express them by certain characters the briefest possible. In this way I believed that I could borrow all that was best both in geometrical analysis and in algebra, and correct all the defects of the one by help of the other.

And, in point of fact, the accurate observance of these few precepts gave me, I take the liberty of saying, such ease in unraveling all the questions embraced in these two sciences, that in the two or three months I devoted to their examination, not only did I reach solutions of questions I had formerly deemed exceedingly difficult but even as regards questions of the solution of which I continued ignorant, I was enabled, as it appeared to me, to determine the means whereby, and the extent to which a solution was possible; results attributable to the circumstance that I commenced with the simplest and most general truths, and that thus each truth discovered was a rule available in the discovery of subsequent ones Nor in this perhaps shall I appear too vain, if it be considered that, as the truth on any particular point is one whoever apprehends the truth, knows all that on that point can be known. The child, for example, who has been instructed in the elements of arithmetic, and has made a particular addition, according to rule, may be assured that he has found, with respect to the sum of the numbers before him, and that in this instance is within the reach of human genius. Now, in conclusion, the method which teaches adherence to the true order, and an exact enumeration of all the conditions of the thing sought includes all that gives certitude to the rules of arithmetic.

But the chief ground of my satisfaction with thus method, was the assurance I had of thereby exercising my reason in all matters, if not with absolute perfection, at least with the greatest attainable by me: besides, I was conscious that by its use my mind was becoming gradually habituated to clearer and more distinct conceptions of its objects; and I hoped also, from not having restricted this method to any particular matter, to apply it to the difficulties of the other sciences, with not less success than to those of algebra. I should not, however, on this account have ventured at once on the examination of all the difficulties of the sciences which presented themselves to me, for this would have been contrary to the order prescribed in the method, but observing that the knowledge of such is dependent on principles borrowed from philosophy, in which I found nothing certain, I thought it necessary first of all to endeavor to establish its principles. And because I observed, besides, that an inquiry of this kind was of all others of the greatest moment, and one in which precipitancy and anticipation in judgment were most to be dreaded, I thought that I ought not to approach it till I had reached a more mature age (being at that time but twenty-three), and had first of all employed much of my time in preparation for the work, as well by eradicating from my mind all the erroneous opinions I had up to that moment accepted, as by amassing variety of experience to afford materials for my reasonings, and by continually exercising myself in my chosen method with a view to increased skill in its application.

Part III

And finally, as it is not enough, before commencing to rebuild the house in which we live, that it be pulled down, and materials and builders provided, or that we engage in the work ourselves, according to a plan which we have beforehand carefully drawn out, but as it is likewise necessary that we be furnished with some other house in which we may live commodiously during the operations, so that I might not remain irresolute in my actions, while my reason compelled me to suspend my judgement, and that I might not be prevented from living thenceforward in the greatest possible felicity, I formed a provisory code of morals, composed of three or four maxims, with which I am desirous to make you acquainted.

The first was to obey the laws and customs of my country, adhering firmly to the faith in which, by the grace of God, I had been educated from my childhood and regulating my conduct in every other matter according to the most moderate opinions, and the farthest removed from extremes, which should happen to be adopted in practice with general consent of the most judicious of those among whom I might be living. For as I had from that time begun to hold my own opinions for nought because I wished to subject them all to examination, I was convinced that I could not do better than follow in the meantime the opinions of the most judicious; and although there are some perhaps among the Persians and Chinese as judicious as among ourselves, expediency seemed to dictate that I should regulate my practice conformably to the opinions of those with whom I should have to live; and it appeared to me that, in order to ascertain the real opinions of such, I ought rather to take cognizance of what they practiced than of what they said, not only because, in the corruption of our manners, there are few disposed to speak exactly as they believe, but also because very many are not aware of what it is that they really believe; for, as the act of mind by which a thing is believed is different from that by which we know that we believe it, the one act is often found without the other. Also, amid many opinions held in equal repute, I chose always the most moderate, as much for the reason that these are always the most convenient for practice, and probably the best (for all excess is generally vicious), as that, in the event of my falling into error, I might be at less distance from the truth than if, having chosen one of the extremes, it should turn out to be the other which I ought to have adopted. And I placed in the class of extremes especially all promises by which somewhat of our freedom is abridged; not that I disapproved of the laws which, to provide against the instability of men of feeble resolution, when what is sought to be accomplished is some good, permit engagements by vows and contracts binding the parties to persevere in it, or even, for the security of commerce, sanction similar engagements where the purpose sought to be realized is indifferent: but because I did not find anything on earth which was wholly superior to change, and because, for myself in particular, I hoped gradually to perfect my judgments, and not to suffer them to deteriorate, I would have deemed it a grave sin against good sense, if, for the reason that I approved of something at a particular time, I therefore bound myself to hold it for good at a subsequent time, when perhaps it had ceased to be so, or I had ceased to esteem it such.

My second maxim was to be as firm and resolute in my actions as I was able, and not to adhere less steadfastly to the most doubtful opinions, when once adopted, than if they had been highly certain; imitating in this the example of travelers who, when they have lost their way in a forest, ought not to wander from side to side, far less remain in one place, but proceed constantly towards the same side in as straight a line as possible, without changing their direction for slight reasons, although perhaps it might be chance alone which at first determined the selection; for in this way, if they do not exactly reach the point they desire, they will come at least in the end to some place that will probably be preferable to the middle of a forest. In the same way, since in action it frequently happens that no delay is permissible, it is very certain that, when it is not in our power to determine what is true, we ought to act according to what is most probable; and even although we should not remark a greater probability in one opinion than in another, we ought notwithstanding to choose one or the other, and afterwards consider it, in so far as it relates to practice, as no longer dubious, but manifestly true and certain, since the reason by which our choice has been determined is itself possessed of these qualities. This principle was sufficient thenceforward to rid me of all those repentings and pangs of remorse that usually disturb the consciences of such feeble and uncertain minds as, destitute of any clear and determinate principle of choice, allow themselves one day to adopt a course of action as the best, which they abandon the next, as the opposite.

My third maxim was to endeavor always to conquer myself rather than fortune, and change my desires rather than the order of the world, and in general, accustom myself to the persuasion that, except our own thoughts, there is nothing absolutely in our power; so that when we have done our best in things external to us, all wherein we fail of success is to be held, as regards us, absolutely impossible: and this single principle seemed to me sufficient to prevent me from desiring for the future anything which I could not obtain, and thus render me contented; for since our will naturally seeks those objects alone which the understanding represents as in some way possible of attainment, it is plain, that if we consider all external goods as equally beyond our power, we shall no more regret the absence of such goods as seem due to our birth, when deprived of them without any fault of ours, than our not possessing the kingdoms of China or Mexico, and thus making, so to speak, a virtue of necessity, we shall no more desire health in disease, or freedom in imprisonment, than we now do bodies incorruptible as diamonds, or the wings of birds to fly with. But I confess there is need of prolonged discipline and frequently repeated meditation to accustom the mind to view all objects in this light; and I believe that in this chiefly consisted the secret of the power of such philosophers as in former times were enabled to rise superior to the influence of fortune, and, amid suffering and poverty, enjoy a happiness which their gods might have envied. For, occupied incessantly with the consideration of the limits prescribed to their power by nature, they became so entirely convinced that nothing was at their disposal except their own thoughts, that this conviction was of itself sufficient to prevent their entertaining any desire of other objects; and over their thoughts they acquired a sway so absolute, that they had some ground on this account for esteeming themselves more rich and more powerful, more free and more happy, than other men who, whatever be the favors heaped on them by nature and fortune, if destitute of this philosophy, can never command the realization of all their desires.

In fine, to conclude this code of morals, I thought of reviewing the different occupations of men in this life, with the view of making choice of the best. And, without wishing to offer any remarks on the employments of others, I may state that it was my conviction that I could not do better than continue in that in which I was engaged, viz., in devoting my whole life to the culture of my reason, and in making the greatest progress I was able in the knowledge of truth, on the principles of the method which I had prescribed to myself. This method, from the time I had begun to apply it, had been to me the source of satisfaction so intense as to lead me to, believe that more perfect or more innocent could not be enjoyed in this life; and as by its means I daily discovered truths that appeared to me of some importance, and of which other men were generally ignorant, the gratification thence arising so occupied my mind that I was wholly indifferent to every other object. Besides, the three preceding maxims were founded singly on the design of continuing the work of self-instruction. For since God has endowed each of us with some light of reason by which to distinguish truth from error, I could not have believed that I ought for a single moment to rest satisfied with the opinions of another, unless I had resolved to exercise my own judgment in examining these whenever I should be duly qualified for the task. Nor could I have proceeded on such opinions without scruple, had I supposed that I should thereby forfeit any advantage for attaining still more accurate, should such exist. And, in fine, I could not have restrained my desires, nor remained satisfied had I not followed a path in which I thought myself certain of attaining all the knowledge to the acquisition of which I was competent, as well as the largest amount of what is truly good which I could ever hope to secure Inasmuch as we neither seek nor shun any object except in so far as our understanding represents it as good or bad, all that is necessary to right action is right judgment, and to the best action the most correct judgment, that is, to the acquisition of all the virtues with all else that is truly valuable and within our reach; and the assurance of such an acquisition cannot fail to render us contented.

Having thus provided myself with these maxims, and having placed them in reserve along with the truths of faith, which have ever occupied the first place in my belief, I came to the conclusion that I might with freedom set about ridding myself of what remained of my opinions. And, inasmuch as I hoped to be better able successfully to accomplish this work by holding intercourse with mankind, than by remaining longer shut up in the retirement where these thoughts had occurred to me, I betook me again to traveling before the winter was well ended. And, during the nine subsequent years, I did nothing but roam from one place to another, desirous of being a spectator rather than an actor in the plays exhibited on the theater of the world; and, as I made it my business in each matter to reflect particularly upon what might fairly be doubted and prove a source of error, I gradually rooted out from my mind all the errors which had hitherto crept into it. Not that in this I imitated the skeptics who doubt only that they may doubt, and seek nothing beyond uncertainty itself; for, on the contrary, my design was singly to find ground of assurance, and cast aside the loose earth and sand, that I might reach the rock or the clay. In this, as appears to me, I was successful enough; for, since I endeavored to discover the falsehood or incertitude of the propositions I examined, not by feeble conjectures, but by clear and certain reasonings, I met with nothing so doubtful as not to yield some conclusion of adequate certainty, although this were merely the inference, that the matter in question contained nothing certain. And, just as in pulling down an old house, we usually reserve the ruins to contribute towards the erection, so, in destroying such of my opinions as I judged to be Ill-founded, I made a variety of observations and acquired an amount of experience of which I availed myself in the establishment of more certain. And further, I continued to exercise myself in the method I had prescribed; for, besides taking care in general to conduct all my thoughts according to its rules, I reserved some hours from time to time which I expressly devoted to the employment of the method in the solution of mathematical difficulties, or even in the solution likewise of some questions belonging to other sciences, but which, by my having detached them from such principles of these sciences as were of inadequate certainty, were rendered almost mathematical: the truth of this will be manifest from the numerous examples contained in this volume. And thus, without in appearance living otherwise than those who, with no other occupation than that of spending their lives agreeably and innocently, study to sever pleasure from vice, and who, that they may enjoy their leisure without ennui, have recourse to such pursuits as are honorable, I was nevertheless prosecuting my design, and making greater progress in the knowledge of truth, than I might, perhaps, have made had I been engaged in the perusal of books merely, or in holding converse with men of letters.

These nine years passed away, however, before I had come to any determinate judgment respecting the difficulties which form matter of dispute among the learned, or had commenced to seek the principles of any philosophy more certain than the vulgar. And the examples of many men of the highest genius, who had, in former times, engaged in this inquiry, but, as appeared to me, without success, led me to imagine it to be a work of so much difficulty, that I would not perhaps have ventured on it so soon had I not heard it currently rumored that I had already completed the inquiry. I know not what were the grounds of this opinion; and, if my conversation contributed in any measure to its rise, this must have happened rather from my having confessed my Ignorance with greater freedom than those are accustomed to do who have studied a little, and expounded perhaps, the reasons that led me to doubt of many of those things that by others are esteemed certain, than from my having boasted of any system of philosophy. But, as I am of a disposition that makes me unwilling to be esteemed different from what I really am, I thought it necessary to endeavor by all means to render myself worthy of the reputation accorded to me; and it is now exactly eight years since this desire constrained me to remove from all those places where interruption from any of my acquaintances was possible, and betake myself to this country, in which the long duration of the war has led to the establishment of such discipline, that the armies maintained seem to be of use only in enabling the inhabitants to enjoy more securely the blessings of peace and where, in the midst of a great crowd actively engaged in business, and more careful of their own affairs than curious about those of others, I have been enabled to live without being deprived of any of the conveniences to be had in the most populous cities, and yet as solitary and as retired as in the midst of the most remote deserts.

Part IV

I am in doubt as to the propriety of making my first meditations in the place above mentioned matter of discourse; for these are so metaphysical, and so uncommon, as not, perhaps, to be acceptable to every one. And yet, that it may be determined whether the foundations that I have laid are sufficiently secure, I find myself in a measure constrained to advert to them. I had long before remarked that, in relation to practice, it is sometimes necessary to adopt, as if above doubt, opinions which we discern to be highly uncertain, as has been already said; but as I then desired to give my attention solely to the search after truth, I thought that a procedure exactly the opposite was called for, and that I ought to reject as absolutely false all opinions in regard to which I could suppose the least ground for doubt, in order to ascertain whether after that there remained aught in my belief that was wholly indubitable. Accordingly, seeing that our senses sometimes deceive us, I was willing to suppose that there existed nothing really such as they presented to us; and because some men err in reasoning, and fall into paralogisms, even on the simplest matters of geometry, I, convinced that I was as open to error as any other, rejected as false all the reasonings I had hitherto taken for demonstrations; and finally, when I considered that the very same thoughts (presentations) which we experience when awake may also be experienced when we are asleep, while there is at that time not one of them true, I supposed that all the objects (presentations) that had ever entered into my mind when awake, had in them no more truth than the illusions of my dreams. But immediately upon this I observed that, whilst I thus wished to think that all was false, it was absolutely necessary that I, who thus thought, should be somewhat; and as I observed that this truth, I think, therefore I am (COGITO ERGO SUM), was so certain and of such evidence that no ground of doubt, however extravagant, could be alleged by the skeptics capable of shaking it, I concluded that I might, without scruple, accept it as the first principle of the philosophy of which I was in search.

In the next place, I attentively examined what I was and as I observed that I could suppose that I had no body, and that there was no world nor any place in which I might be; but that I could not therefore suppose that I was not; and that, on the contrary, from the very circumstance that I thought to doubt of the truth of other things, it most clearly and certainly followed that I was; while, on the other hand, if I had only ceased to think, although all the other objects which I had ever imagined had been in reality existent, I would have had no reason to believe that I existed; I thence concluded that I was a substance whose whole essence or nature consists only in thinking, and which, that it may exist, has need of no place, nor is dependent on any material thing; so that "I," that is to say, the mind by which I am what I am, is wholly distinct from the body, and is even more easily known than the latter, and is such, that although the latter were not, it would still continue to be all that it is.

After this I inquired in general into what is essential to the truth and certainty of a proposition; for since I had discovered one which I knew to be true, I thought that I must likewise be able to discover the ground of this certitude. And as I observed that in the words I think, therefore I am, there is nothing at all which gives me assurance of their truth beyond this, that I see very clearly that in order to think it is necessary to exist, I concluded that I might take, as a general rule, the principle, that all the things which we very clearly and distinctly conceive are true, only observing, however, that there is some difficulty in rightly determining the objects which we distinctly conceive.

In the next place, from reflecting on the circumstance that I doubted, and that consequently my being was not wholly perfect (for I clearly saw that it was a greater perfection to know than to doubt), I was led to inquire whence I had learned to think of something more perfect than myself; and I clearly recognized that I must hold this notion from some nature which in reality was more perfect. As for the thoughts of many other objects external to me, as of the sky, the earth, light, heat, and a thousand more, I was less at a loss to know whence these came; for since I remarked in them nothing which seemed to render them superior to myself, I could believe that, if these were true, they were dependencies on my own nature, in so far as it possessed a certain perfection, and, if they were false, that I held them from nothing, that is to say, that they were in me because of a certain imperfection of my nature. But this could not be the case with the idea of a nature more perfect than myself; for to receive it from nothing was a thing manifestly impossible; and, because it is not less repugnant that the more perfect should be an effect of, and dependence on the less perfect, than that something should proceed from nothing, it was equally impossible that I could hold it from myself: accordingly, it but remained that it had been placed in me by a nature which was in reality more perfect than mine, and which even possessed within itself all the perfections of which I could form any idea; that is to say, in a single word, which was God. And to this I added that, since I knew some perfections which I did not possess, I was not the only being in existence (I will here, with your permission, freely use the terms of the schools); but, on the contrary, that there was of necessity some other more perfect Being upon whom I was dependent, and from whom I had received all that I possessed; for if I had existed alone, and independently of every other being, so as to have had from myself all the perfection, however little, which I actually possessed, I should have been able, for the same reason, to have had from myself the whole remainder of perfection, of the want of which I was conscious, and thus could of myself have become infinite, eternal, immutable, omniscient, all-powerful, and, in fine, have possessed all the perfections which I could recognize in God. For in order to know the nature of God (whose existence has been established by the preceding reasonings), as far as my own nature permitted, I had only to consider in reference to all the properties of which I found in my mind some idea, whether their possession was a mark of perfection; and I was assured that no one which indicated any imperfection was in him, and that none of the rest was awanting. Thus I perceived that doubt, inconstancy, sadness, and such like, could not be found in God, since I myself would have been happy to be free from them. Besides, I had ideas of many sensible and corporeal things; for although I might suppose that I was dreaming, and that all which I saw or imagined was false, I could not, nevertheless, deny that the ideas were in reality in my thoughts. But, because I had already very clearly recognized in myself that the intelligent nature is distinct from the corporeal, and as I observed that all composition is an evidence of dependency, and that a state of dependency is manifestly a state of imperfection, I therefore determined that it could not be a perfection in God to be compounded of these two natures and that consequently he was not so compounded; but that if there were any bodies in the world, or even any intelligences, or other natures that were not wholly perfect, their existence depended on his power in such a way that they could not subsist without him for a single moment.

I was disposed straightway to search for other truths and when I had represented to myself the object of the geometers, which I conceived to be a continuous body or a space indefinitely extended in length, breadth, and height or depth, divisible into divers parts which admit of different figures and sizes, and of being moved or transposed in all manner of ways (for all this the geometers suppose to be in the object they contemplate), I went over some of their simplest demonstrations. And, in the first place, I observed, that the great certitude which by common consent is accorded to these demonstrations, is founded solely upon this, that they are clearly conceived in accordance with the rules I have already laid down In the next place, I perceived that there was nothing at all in these demonstrations which could assure me of the existence of their object: thus, for example, supposing a triangle to be given, I distinctly perceived that its three angles were necessarily equal to two right angles, but I did not on that account perceive anything which could assure me that any triangle existed: while, on the contrary, recurring to the examination of the idea of a Perfect Being, I found that the existence of the Being was comprised in the idea in the same way that the equality of its three angles to two right angles is comprised in the idea of a triangle, or as in the idea of a sphere, the equidistance of all points on its surface from the center, or even still more clearly; and that consequently it is at least as certain that God, who is this Perfect Being, is, or exists, as any demonstration of geometry can be.

But the reason which leads many to persuade them selves that there is a difficulty in knowing this truth, and even also in knowing what their mind really is, is that they never raise their thoughts above sensible objects, and are so accustomed to consider nothing except by way of imagination, which is a mode of thinking limited to material objects, that all that is not imaginable seems to them not intelligible. The truth of this is sufficiently manifest from the single circumstance, that the philosophers of the schools accept as a maxim that there is nothing in the understanding which was not previously in the senses, in which however it is certain that the ideas of God and of the soul have never been; and it appears to me that they who make use of their imagination to comprehend these ideas do exactly the some thing as if, in order to hear sounds or smell odors, they strove to avail themselves of their eyes; unless indeed that there is this difference, that the sense of sight does not afford us an inferior assurance to those of smell or hearing; in place of which, neither our imagination nor our senses can give us assurance of anything unless our understanding intervene.

Finally, if there be still persons who are not sufficiently persuaded of the existence of God and of the soul, by the reasons I have adduced, I am desirous that they should know that all the other propositions, of the truth of which they deem themselves perhaps more assured, as that we have a body, and that there exist stars and an earth, and such like, are less certain; for, although we have a moral assurance of these things, which is so strong that there is an appearance of extravagance in doubting of their existence, yet at the same time no one, unless his intellect is impaired, can deny, when the question relates to a metaphysical certitude, that there is sufficient reason to exclude entire assurance, in the observation that when asleep we can in the same way imagine ourselves possessed of another body and that we see other stars and another earth, when there is nothing of the kind. For how do we know that the thoughts which occur in dreaming are false rather than those other which we experience when awake, since the former are often not less vivid and distinct than the latter? And though men of the highest genius study this question as long as they please, I do not believe that they will be able to give any reason which can be sufficient to remove this doubt, unless they presuppose the existence of God. For, in the first place even the principle which I have already taken as a rule, viz., that all the things which we clearly and distinctly conceive are true, is certain only because God is or exists and because he is a Perfect Being, and because all that we possess is derived from him: whence it follows that our ideas or notions, which to the extent of their clearness and distinctness are real, and proceed from God, must to that extent be true. Accordingly, whereas we not infrequently have ideas or notions in which some falsity is contained, this can only be the case with such as are to some extent confused and obscure, and in this proceed from nothing (participate of negation), that is, exist in us thus confused because we are not wholly perfect. And it is evident that it is not less repugnant that falsity or imperfection, in so far as it is imperfection, should proceed from God, than that truth or perfection should proceed from nothing. But if we did not know that all which we possess of real and true proceeds from a Perfect and Infinite Being, however clear and distinct our ideas might be, we should have no ground on that account for the assurance that they possessed the perfection of being true.

But after the knowledge of God and of the soul has rendered us certain of this rule, we can easily understand that the truth of the thoughts we experience when awake, ought not in the slightest degree to be called in question on account of the illusions of our dreams. For if it happened that an individual, even when asleep, had some very distinct idea, as, for example, if a geometer should discover some new demonstration, the circumstance of his being asleep would not militate against its truth; and as for the most ordinary error of our dreams, which consists in their representing to us various objects in the same way as our external senses, this is not prejudicial, since it leads us very properly to suspect the truth of the ideas of sense; for we are not infrequently deceived in the same manner when awake; as when persons in the jaundice see all objects yellow, or when the stars or bodies at a great distance appear to us much smaller than they are. For, in fine, whether awake or asleep, we ought never to allow ourselves to be persuaded of the truth of anything unless on the evidence of our reason. And it must be noted that I say of our reason, and not of our imagination or of our senses: thus, for example, although we very clearly see the sun, we ought not therefore to determine that it is only of the size which our sense of sight presents; and we may very distinctly imagine the head of a lion joined to the body of a goat, without being therefore shut up to the conclusion that a chimaera exists; for it is not a dictate of reason that what we thus see or imagine is in reality existent; but it plainly tells us that all our ideas or notions contain in them some truth; for otherwise it could not be that God, who is wholly perfect and veracious, should have placed them in us. And because our reasonings are never so clear or so complete during sleep as when we are awake, although sometimes the acts of our imagination are then as lively and distinct, if not more so than in our waking moments, reason further dictates that, since all our thoughts cannot be true because of our partial imperfection, those possessing truth must infallibly be found in the experience of our waking moments rather than in that of our dreams.

Part VI

Three years have now elapsed since I finished the treatise containing all these matters; and I was beginning to revise it, with the view to put it into the hands of a printer, when I learned that persons to whom I greatly defer, and whose authority over my actions is hardly less influential than is my own reason over my thoughts, had condemned a certain doctrine in physics, published a short time previously by another individual to which I will not say that I adhered, but only that, previously to their censure I had observed in it nothing which I could imagine to be prejudicial either to religion or to the state, and nothing therefore which would have prevented me from giving expression to it in writing, if reason had persuaded me of its truth; and this led me to fear lest among my own doctrines likewise some one might be found in which I had departed from the truth, notwithstanding the great care I have always taken not to accord belief to new opinions of which I had not the most certain demonstrations, and not to give expression to aught that might tend to the hurt of any one. This has been sufficient to make me alter my purpose of publishing them; for although the reasons by which I had been induced to take this resolution were very strong, yet my inclination, which has always been hostile to writing books, enabled me immediately to discover other considerations sufficient to excuse me for not undertaking the task. And these reasons, on one side and the other, are such, that not only is it in some measure my interest here to state them, but that of the public, perhaps, to know them.

I have never made much account of what has proceeded from my own mind; and so long as I gathered no other advantage from the method I employ beyond satisfying myself on some difficulties belonging to the speculative sciences, or endeavoring to regulate my actions according to the principles it taught me, I never thought myself bound to publish anything respecting it. For in what regards manners, every one is so full of his own wisdom, that there might be found as many reformers as heads, if any were allowed to take upon themselves the task of mending them, except those whom God has constituted the supreme rulers of his people or to whom he has given sufficient grace and zeal to be prophets; and although my speculations greatly pleased myself, I believed that others had theirs, which perhaps pleased them still more. But as soon as I had acquired some general notions respecting physics, and beginning to make trial of them in various particular difficulties, had observed how far they can carry us, and how much they differ from the principles that have been employed up to the present time, I believed that I could not keep them concealed without sinning grievously against the law by which we are bound to promote, as far as in us lies, the general good of mankind. For by them I perceived it to be possible to arrive at knowledge highly useful in life; and in room of the speculative philosophy usually taught in the schools, to discover a practical, by means of which, knowing the force and action of fire, water, air the stars, the heavens, and all the other bodies that surround us, as distinctly as we know the various crafts of our artisans, we might also apply them in the same way to all the uses to which they are adapted, and thus render ourselves the lords and possessors of nature. And this is a result to be desired, not only in order to the invention of an infinity of arts, by which we might be enabled to enjoy without any trouble the fruits of the earth, and all its comforts, but also and especially for the preservation of health, which is without doubt, of all the blessings of this life, the first and fundamental one; for the mind is so intimately dependent upon the condition and relation of the organs of the body, that if any means can ever be found to render men wiser and more ingenious than hitherto, I believe that it is in medicine they must be sought for. It is true that the science of medicine, as it now exists, contains few things whose utility is very remarkable: but without any wish to depreciate it, I am confident that there is no one, even among those whose profession it is, who does not admit that all at present known in it is almost nothing in comparison of what remains to be discovered; and that we could free ourselves from an infinity of maladies of body as well as of mind, and perhaps also even from the debility of age, if we had sufficiently ample knowledge of their causes, and of all the remedies provided for us by nature. But since I designed to employ my whole life in the search after so necessary a science, and since I had fallen in with a path which seems to me such, that if any one follow it he must inevitably reach the end desired, unless he be hindered either by the shortness of life or the want of experiments, I judged that there could be no more effectual provision against these two impediments than if I were faithfully to communicate to the public all the little I might myself have found, and incite men of superior genius to strive to proceed farther, by contributing, each according to his inclination and ability, to the experiments which it would be necessary to make, and also by informing the public of all they might discover, so that, by the last beginning where those before them had left off, and thus connecting the lives and labors of many, we might collectively proceed much farther than each by himself could do.

I remarked, moreover, with respect to experiments, that they become always more necessary the more one is advanced in knowledge; for, at the commencement, it is better to make use only of what is spontaneously presented to our senses, and of which we cannot remain ignorant, provided we bestow on it any reflection, however slight, than to concern ourselves about more uncommon and recondite phenomena: the reason of which is, that the more uncommon often only mislead us so long as the causes of the more ordinary are still unknown; and the circumstances upon which they depend are almost always so special and minute as to be highly difficult to detect. But in this I have adopted the following order: first, I have essayed to find in general the principles, or first causes of all that is or can be in the world, without taking into consideration for this end anything but God himself who has created it, and without educing them from any other source than from certain germs of truths naturally existing in our minds In the second place, I examined what were the first and most ordinary effects that could be deduced from these causes; and it appears to me that, in this way, I have found heavens, stars, an earth, and even on the earth water, air, fire, minerals, and some other things of this kind, which of all others are the most common and simple, and hence the easiest to know. Afterwards when I wished to descend to the more particular, so many diverse objects presented themselves to me, that I believed it to be impossible for the human mind to distinguish the forms or species of bodies that are upon the earth, from an infinity of others which might have been, if it had pleased God to place them there, or consequently to apply them to our use, unless we rise to causes through their effects, and avail ourselves of many particular experiments. Thereupon, turning over in my mind I the objects that had ever been presented to my senses I freely venture to state that I have never observed any which I could not satisfactorily explain by the principles had discovered. But it is necessary also to confess that the power of nature is so ample and vast, and these principles so simple and general, that I have hardly observed a single particular effect which I cannot at once recognize as capable of being deduced in man different modes from the principles, and that my greatest difficulty usually is to discover in which of these modes the effect is dependent upon them; for out of this difficulty cannot otherwise extricate myself than by again seeking certain experiments, which may be such that their result is not the same, if it is in the one of these modes at we must explain it, as it would be if it were to be explained in the other. As to what remains, I am now in a position to discern, as I think, with sufficient clearness what course must be taken to make the majority those experiments which may conduce to this end: but I perceive likewise that they are such and so numerous, that neither my hands nor my income, though it were a thousand times larger than it is, would be sufficient for them all; so that according as henceforward I shall have the means of making more or fewer experiments, I shall in the same proportion make greater or less progress in the knowledge of nature. This was what I had hoped to make known by the treatise I had written, and so clearly to exhibit the advantage that would thence accrue to the public, as to induce all who have the common good of man at heart, that is, all who are virtuous in truth, and not merely in appearance, or according to opinion, as well to communicate to me the experiments they had already made, as to assist me in those that remain to be made.

But since that time other reasons have occurred to me, by which I have been led to change my opinion, and to think that I ought indeed to go on committing to writing all the results which I deemed of any moment, as soon as I should have tested their truth, and to bestow the same care upon them as I would have done had it been my design to publish them. This course commended itself to me, as well because I thus afforded myself more ample inducement to examine them thoroughly, for doubtless that is always more narrowly scrutinized which we believe will be read by many, than that which is written merely for our private use (and frequently what has seemed to me true when I first conceived it, has appeared false when I have set about committing it to writing), as because I thus lost no opportunity of advancing the interests of the public, as far as in me lay, and since thus likewise, if my writings possess any value, those into whose hands they may fall after my death may be able to put them to what use they deem proper. But I resolved by no means to consent to their publication during my lifetime, lest either the oppositions or the controversies to which they might give rise, or even the reputation, such as it might be, which they would acquire for me, should be any occasion of my losing the time that I had set apart for my own improvement. For though it be true that every one is bound to promote to the extent of his ability the good of others, and that to be useful to no one is really to be worthless, yet it is likewise true that our cares ought to extend beyond the present, and it is good to omit doing what might perhaps bring some profit to the living, when we have in view the accomplishment of other ends that will be of much greater advantage to posterity. And in truth, I am quite willing it should be known that the little I have hitherto learned is almost nothing in comparison with that of which I am ignorant, and to the knowledge of which I do not despair of being able to attain; for it is much the same with those who gradually discover truth in the sciences, as with those who when growing rich find less difficulty in making great acquisitions, than they formerly experienced when poor in making acquisitions of much smaller amount. Or they may be compared to the commanders of armies, whose forces usually increase in proportion to their victories, and who need greater prudence to keep together the residue of their troops after a defeat than after a victory to take towns and provinces. For he truly engages in battle who endeavors to surmount all the difficulties and errors which prevent him from reaching the knowledge of truth, and he is overcome in fight who admits a false opinion touching a matter of any generality and importance, and he requires thereafter much more skill to recover his former position than to make great advances when once in possession of thoroughly ascertained principles. As for myself, if I have succeeded in discovering any truths in the sciences (and I trust that what is contained in this volume I will show that I have found some), I can declare that they are but the consequences and results of five or six principal difficulties which I have surmounted, and my encounters with which I reckoned as battles in which victory declared for me. I will not hesitate even to avow my belief that nothing further is wanting to enable me fully to realize my designs than to gain two or three similar victories; and that I am not so far advanced in years but that, according to the ordinary course of nature, I may still have sufficient leisure for this end. But I conceive myself the more bound to husband the time that remains the greater my expectation of being able to employ it aright, and I should doubtless have much to rob me of it, were I to publish the principles of my physics: for although they are almost all so evident that to assent to them no more is needed than simply to understand them, and although there is not one of them of which I do not expect to be able to give demonstration, yet, as it is impossible that they can be in accordance with all the diverse opinions of others, I foresee that I should frequently be turned aside from my grand design, on occasion of the opposition which they would be sure to awaken.

It may be said, that these oppositions would be useful both in making me aware of my errors, and, if my speculations contain anything of value, in bringing others to a fuller understanding of it; and still farther, as many can see better than one, in leading others who are now beginning to avail themselves of my principles, to assist me in turn with their discoveries. But though I recognize my extreme liability to error, and scarce ever trust to the first thoughts which occur to me, yet-the experience I have had of possible objections to my views prevents me from anticipating any profit from them. For I have already had frequent proof of the judgments, as well of those I esteemed friends, as of some others to whom I thought I was an object of indifference, and even of some whose malignancy and envy would, I knew, determine them to endeavor to discover what partiality concealed from the eyes of my friends. But it has rarely happened that anything has been objected to me which I had myself altogether overlooked, unless it were something far removed from the subject: so that I have never met with a single critic of my opinions who did not appear to me either less rigorous or less equitable than myself. And further, I have never observed that any truth before unknown has been brought to light by the disputations that are practiced in the schools; for while each strives for the victory, each is much more occupied in making the best of mere verisimilitude, than in weighing the reasons on both sides of the question; and those who have been long good advocates are not afterwards on that account the better judges.

As for the advantage that others would derive from the communication of my thoughts, it could not be very great; because I have not yet so far prosecuted them as that much does not remain to be added before they can be applied to practice. And I think I may say without vanity, that if there is any one who can carry them out that length, it must be myself rather than another: not that there may not be in the world many minds incomparably superior to mine, but because one cannot so well seize a thing and make it one's own, when it has been learned from another, as when one has himself discovered it. And so true is this of the present subject that, though I have often explained some of my opinions to persons of much acuteness, who, whilst I was speaking, appeared to understand them very distinctly, yet, when they repeated them, I have observed that they almost always changed them to such an extent that I could no longer acknowledge them as mine. I am glad, by the way, to take this opportunity of requesting posterity never to believe on hearsay that anything has proceeded from me which has not been published by myself; and I am not at all astonished at the extravagances attributed to those ancient philosophers whose own writings we do not possess; whose thoughts, however, I do not on that account suppose to have been really absurd, seeing they were among the ablest men of their times, but only that these have been falsely represented to us. It is observable, accordingly, that scarcely in a single instance has any one of their disciples surpassed them; and I am quite sure that the most devoted of the present followers of Aristotle would think themselves happy if they had as much knowledge of nature as he possessed, were it even under the condition that they should never afterwards attain to higher. In this respect they are like the ivy which never strives to rise above the tree that sustains it, and which frequently even returns downwards when it has reached the top; for it seems to me that they also sink, in other words, render themselves less wise than they would be if they gave up study, who, not contented with knowing all that is intelligibly explained in their author, desire in addition to find in him the solution of many difficulties of which he says not a word, and never perhaps so much as thought. Their fashion of philosophizing, however, is well suited to persons whose abilities fall below mediocrity; for the obscurity of the distinctions and principles of which they make use enables them to speak of all things with as much confidence as if they really knew them, and to defend all that they say on any subject against the most subtle and skillful, without its being possible for any one to convict them of error. In this they seem to me to be like a blind man, who, in order to fight on equal terms with a person that sees, should have made him descend to the bottom of an intensely dark cave: and I may say that such persons have an interest in my refraining from publishing the principles of the philosophy of which I make use; for, since these are of a kind the simplest and most evident, I should, by publishing them, do much the same as if I were to throw open the windows, and allow the light of day to enter the cave into which the combatants had descended. But even superior men have no reason for any great anxiety to know these principles, for if what they desire is to be able to speak of all things, and to acquire a reputation for learning, they will gain their end more easily by remaining satisfied with the appearance of truth, which can be found without much difficulty in all sorts of matters, than by seeking the truth itself which unfolds itself but slowly and that only in some departments, while it obliges us, when we have to speak of others, freely to confess our ignorance. If, however, they prefer the knowledge of some few truths to the vanity of appearing ignorant of none, as such knowledge is undoubtedly much to be preferred, and, if they choose to follow a course similar to mine, they do not require for this that I should say anything more than I have already said in this discourse. For if they are capable of making greater advancement than I have made, they will much more be able of themselves to discover all that I believe myself to have found; since as I have never examined aught except in order, it is certain that what yet remains to be discovered is in itself more difficult and recondite, than that which I have already been enabled to find, and the gratification would be much less in learning it from me than in discovering it for themselves. Besides this, the habit which they will acquire, by seeking first what is easy, and then passing onward slowly and step by step to the more difficult, will benefit them more than all my instructions. Thus, in my own case, I am persuaded that if I had been taught from my youth all the truths of which I have since sought out demonstrations, and had thus learned them without labor, I should never, perhaps, have known any beyond these; at least, I should never have acquired the habit and the facility which I think I possess in always discovering new truths in proportion as I give myself to the search. And, in a single word, if there is any work in the world which cannot be so well finished by another as by him who has commenced it, it is that at which I labor.

It is true, indeed, as regards the experiments which may conduce to this end, that one man is not equal to the task of making them all; but yet he can advantageously avail himself, in this work, of no hands besides his own, unless those of artisans, or parties of the same kind, whom he could pay, and whom the hope of gain (a means of great efficacy) might stimulate to accuracy in the performance of what was prescribed to them. For as to those who, through curiosity or a desire of learning, of their own accord, perhaps, offer him their services, besides that in general their promises exceed their performance, and that they sketch out fine designs of which not one is ever realized, they will, without doubt, expect to be compensated for their trouble by the explication of some difficulties, or, at least, by compliments and useless speeches, in which he cannot spend any portion of his time without loss to himself. And as for the experiments that others have already made, even although these parties should be willing of themselves to communicate them to him (which is what those who esteem them secrets will never do), the experiments are, for the most part, accompanied with so many circumstances and superfluous elements, as to make it exceedingly difficult to disentangle the truth from its adjuncts–besides, he will find almost all of them so ill described, or even so false (because those who made them have wished to see in them only such facts as they deemed conformable to their principles), that, if in the entire number there should be some of a nature suited to his purpose, still their value could not compensate for the time what would be necessary to make the selection. So that if there existed any one whom we assuredly knew to be capable of making discoveries of the highest kind, and of the greatest possible utility to the public; and if all other men were therefore eager by all means to assist him in successfully prosecuting his designs, I do not see that they could do aught else for him beyond contributing to defray the expenses of the experiments that might be necessary; and for the rest, prevent his being deprived of his leisure by the unseasonable interruptions of any one. But besides that I neither have so high an opinion of myself as to be willing to make promise of anything extraordinary, nor feed on imaginations so vain as to fancy that the public must be much interested in my designs; I do not, on the other hand, own a soul so mean as to be capable of accepting from any one a favor of which it could be supposed that I was unworthy.

These considerations taken together were the reason why, for the last three years, I have been unwilling to publish the treatise I had on hand, and why I even resolved to give publicity during my life to no other that was so general, or by which the principles of my physics might be understood. But since then, two other reasons have come into operation that have determined me here to subjoin some particular specimens, and give the public some account of my doings and designs. Of these considerations, the first is, that if I failed to do so, many who were cognizant of my previous intention to publish some writings, might have imagined that the reasons which induced me to refrain from so doing, were less to my credit than they really are; for although I am not immoderately desirous of glory, or even, if I may venture so to say, although I am averse from it in so far as I deem it hostile to repose which I hold in greater account than aught else, yet, at the same time, I have never sought to conceal my actions as if they were crimes, nor made use of many precautions that I might remain unknown; and this partly because I should have thought such a course of conduct a wrong against myself, and partly because it would have occasioned me some sort of uneasiness which would again have been contrary to the perfect mental tranquillity which I court. And forasmuch as, while thus indifferent to the thought alike of fame or of forgetfulness, I have yet been unable to prevent myself from acquiring some sort of reputation, I have thought it incumbent on me to do my best to save myself at least from being ill-spoken of. The other reason that has determined me to commit to writing these specimens of philosophy is, that I am becoming daily more and more alive to the delay which my design of self-instruction suffers, for want of the infinity of experiments I require, and which it is impossible for me to make without the assistance of others: and, without flattering myself so much as to expect the public to take a large share in my interests, I am yet unwilling to be found so far wanting in the duty I owe to myself, as to give occasion to those who shall survive me to make it matter of reproach against me some day, that I might have left them many things in a much more perfect state than I have done, had I not too much neglected to make them aware of the ways in which they could have promoted the accomplishment of my designs.

And I thought that it was easy for me to select some matters which should neither be obnoxious to much controversy, nor should compel me to expound more of my principles than I desired, and which should yet be sufficient clearly to exhibit what I can or cannot accomplish in the sciences. Whether or not I have succeeded in this it is not for me to say; and I do not wish to forestall the judgments of others by speaking myself of my writings; but it will gratify me if they be examined, and, to afford the greater inducement to this I request all who may have any objections to make to them, to take the trouble of forwarding these to my publisher, who will give me notice of them, that I may endeavor to subjoin at the same time my reply; and in this way readers seeing both at once will more easily determine where the truth lies; for I do not engage in any case to make prolix replies, but only with perfect frankness to avow my errors if I am convinced of them, or if I cannot perceive them, simply to state what I think is required for defense of the matters I have written, adding thereto no explication of any new matte that it may not be necessary to pass without end from one thing to another.

If some of the matters of which I have spoken in the beginning of the "Dioptrics" and "Meteorics" should offend at first sight, because I call them hypotheses and seem indifferent about giving proof of them, I request a patient and attentive reading of the whole, from which I hope those hesitating will derive satisfaction; for it appears to me that the reasonings are so mutually connected in these treatises, that, as the last are demonstrated by the first which are their causes, the first are in their turn demonstrated by the last which are their effects. Nor must it be imagined that I here commit the fallacy which the logicians call a circle; for since experience renders the majority of these effects most certain, the causes from which I deduce them do not serve so much to establish their reality as to explain their existence; but on the contrary, the reality of the causes is established by the reality of the effects. Nor have I called them hypotheses with any other end in view except that it may be known that I think I am able to deduce them from those first truths which I have already expounded; and yet that I have expressly determined not to do so, to prevent a certain class of minds from thence taking occasion to build some extravagant philosophy upon what they may take to be my principles, and my being blamed for it. I refer to those who imagine that they can master in a day all that another has taken twenty years to think out, as soon as he has spoken two or three words to them on the subject; or who are the more liable to error and the less capable of perceiving truth in very proportion as they are more subtle and lively. As to the opinions which are truly and wholly mine, I offer no apology for them as new,–persuaded as I am that if their reasons be well considered they will be found to be so simple and so conformed, to common sense as to appear less extraordinary and less paradoxical than any others which can be held on the same subjects; nor do I even boast of being the earliest discoverer of any of them, but only of having adopted them, neither because they had nor because they had not been held by others, but solely because reason has convinced me of their truth.

Though artisans may not be able at once to execute the invention which is explained in the "Dioptrics," I do not think that any one on that account is entitled to condemn it; for since address and practice are required in order so to make and adjust the machines described by me as not to overlook the smallest particular, I should not be less astonished if they succeeded on the first attempt than if a person were in one day to become an accomplished performer on the guitar, by merely having excellent sheets of music set up before him. And if I write in French, which is the language of my country, in preference to Latin, which is that of my preceptors, it is because I expect that those who make use of their unprejudiced natural reason will be better judges of my opinions than those who give heed to the writings of the ancients only; and as for those who unite good sense with habits of study, whom alone I desire for judges, they will not, I feel assured, be so partial to Latin as to refuse to listen to my reasonings merely because I expound them in the vulgar tongue.

In conclusion, I am unwilling here to say anything very specific of the progress which I expect to make for the future in the sciences, or to bind myself to the public by any promise which I am not certain of being able to fulfilll; but this only will I say, that I have resolved to devote what time I may still have to live to no other occupation than that of endeavoring to acquire some knowledge of Nature, which shall be of such a kind as to enable us therefrom to deduce rules in medicine of greater certainty than those at present in use; and that my inclination is so much opposed to all other pursuits, especially to such as cannot be useful to some without being hurtful to others, that if, by any circumstances, I had been constrained to engage in such, I do not believe that I should have been able to succeed. Of this I here make a public declaration, though well aware that it cannot serve to procure for me any consideration in the world, which, however, I do not in the least affect; and I shall always hold myself more obliged to those through whose favor I am permitted to enjoy my retirement without interruption than to any who might offer me the highest earthly preferments.

Kant's Spectacles
Putting man at the centre of the universe
Nicholas Fearn

Hi-fi buffs can detect differences in the clarity of musical recordings that a non-enthusiast would never notice. They devote large amounts of time and money to acquiring amplifiers and speaker systems that produce a sound as faithful as possible to the original performance. But even the most advanced hi-fi system falls short of perfection. At some point in the process from the recording to the playback, impurities creep in that keep the next generation of electronics firms in business. There may come a time, however, when audio technology is so sophisticated that the only limitations an enthusiast will have to suffer are not those of his stereo system, but of the human ear itself. At this point, philosophers will have something to say about hi-fis. Whatever the ear adds or subtracts from a crystal-clear recording will not be a difference in quality, but in kind. We hear sounds the way we do because of the particular structure our ears have. A creature with a different kind of ear – a bat, for example – might hear things quite differently because its auditory system works on a different range of frequencies to our own. Ear canals with different structures affect how things sound to their possessors – just as different kinds of cameras take different kinds of photographs. When we describe a tune we have heard, we are describing not only the sound itself, but also something about the way human ears work. We cannot help doing this, as we have no way of listening other than the one we have. Since the same goes for all our senses, the way we understand the world is partly tied to the faculties we use to arrive at that understanding.

Our perceptions are not purely passive – we do not simply sit and drink them in. Whenever we taste a flavour or hear a sound we are also actively *doing* something. It is just that our brains are so used to ordering and processing the world that we do not notice them doing it. To perceive the world is to change it. This was the central in sight of the German philosopher Immanuel Kant. The seventeenth-century English philosopher John Locke famously declared that the human mind was born *tabula rasa* – a blank slate upon which the world leaves its imprints as we learn and grow older. This thought led to the sceptical philosophy of Hume's Fork, under which the knowledge that we possess innately is trivial

---

Excerpts from *Zeno and the Tortoise*, Copyright © 2001 by Nicholas Fearn. Used by permission of Grove/Atlantic, Inc. and Atlantic Books Limited. Any third party use of this material, outside of this publication, is prohibited.

and self-referential while significant knowledge can be discovered only through experience and observation. The search for substantial knowledge that could be attained purely through thought was not yet over. Kant was the first philosopher to suspect that there might be some residual innate knowledge hidden from even Hume's gaze.

Kant was born in Königsberg in East Prussia in 1724. His father was a saddler from what Kant claimed was Scottish immigrant stock, while his mother was an uneducated but highly intelligent German woman. The family faith was the dour Lutheran pietism which prescribed the simple life under the observance of the moral law. Kant became a student of theology at the University of Königsberg in 1740 and began his first book, a work on physics, at the age of twenty. When he failed to secure an academic post six years later he was forced to work as a tutor for affluent families. This period lasted for fifteen years but was not an unhappy one. It introduced Kant to city society and provided opportunities for (by his own standards) exotic travel. His most distant excursion was to the town of Arnsdorf sixty miles away – further from his birthplace than he would ever journey again. It was wide reading rather than travel that broadened Kant's mind. Though he was weakened by a deformed chest and stood only five feet tall, he proved a sensation in the lecture room. A naturally engaging speaker, he enriched his talks with jokes and literary references and lectured on every subject from Newtonian physics to landforms and fireworks to great public acclaim. He was offered the professorship of poetry at Berlin University but declined the position in favour of the sedentary hometown life he had come to prefer. His peace and quiet were already interrupted by the droves of young philosophers and government officials who came to Königsberg to absorb his wisdom. Even so he still managed to maintain his daily regime of constitutional walks, such that people were able to set their clocks by his appearance in the streets. His favourite street was renamed 'The Philosopher's Walk' after him. Only once was his absence noted, and he explained that he had found Rousseau's *Émile* so absorbing that he had to stay at home to finish it.

In 1755, Kant returned to the University of Königsberg to complete his degree. He began teaching there the following year, spurred into creative work by reading the philosophy of David Hume, which he said woke him from his 'dogmatic slumbers'. In 1781, Kant emerged with a new philosophy that he called 'transcendental criticism'. As with so many philosophers, controversial religious beliefs got him into trouble. After the publication of *Religion Within the Boundaries of Pure Reason* in 1793 – a work expressing views which questioned traditional Christian doctrine – King Frederick William II ordered him to stop writing and teaching on religious matters. Kant obeyed his orders to the letter, at least until the king's death. But he was an old man by this time and his health was failing, and soon afterwards he retired to re-edit his works. He died in 1804. Inscribed on his tomb are the words: 'The starry heavens above me and the moral law within me' – the two things that he wrote 'fill the mind with ever new and increasing admiration and awe, the oftener and the more steadily we reflect on them'.

Kant wished to strike a new path between the two strands of eighteenth-century philosophy. The rationalists had argued that reason can comprehend the world unaided by the senses, whereas the empiricists maintained that all knowledge must be firmly grounded in experience. Both have their weaknesses – knowledge secured through pure reason may be indubitably true but says little about the way the world is. Empirical knowledge can say much about the world, on the other hand, but sacrifices certainty in payment. Kant's efforts achieved nothing short of a revolution in philosophy. Where philosophers had previously talked either of objects or our perceptions of them, Kant realized that the means by which the two meet is especially important. Metaphysics – the attempt to philosophize the nature of reality – had proceeded, Kant maintained, in entirely the wrong way, and this is what left it open to Hume's attack. Hume had argued that knowledge of the sensible world would never be attained through means other than the senses. Since Plato, the alternative suggested by philosophers was that thought could apprehend parts of reality that the senses could never reach, such as souls, the nature of God and the universe as a whole.

Kant dismissed this sort of thinking as 'mystical' and introduced a new metaphysics in its place. The fact remains that we perceive objects through the senses, he argued, but we would be mistaken in thinking that our eyes and ears deliver them as they truly are. Everything that we perceive, and thenceforth understand, is processed by the senses upon arrival. Their mediation imposes a character upon our experiences that is not itself part of the objects we are perceiving. Every object that we perceive is given to us at a certain point in space and time, but we do learn of space and time through experience because we never perceive objects that are not in space and time. With mundane objects such as apples, we might reach the general concept of 'apple' from seeing several Granny Smiths and Coxes. The concept of space, on the other hand, is not something we abstract from instances of it in the world because everything from which space might be abstracted already presupposes it. Unless we already understood space, and thought in terms of space, we would not be able to talk of anything as being 'in a certain place' or 'above' or 'below' something else. Even if I can imagine space without anything in it, I am unable to imagine anything in it without also imagining space. Such 'forms' of our experience must be built into our intuition and known to us before we open our eyes for the first time. It is as if we are wearing space-and-time tinted spectacles that we can never take off.

Kant held that there are several ways – twelve to be precise – in which the mind orders experience. The most important one is the assumption of cause and effect, according to which everything that happens is the result of a preceding event that determines its character. In Kant's view, it is the attempt to apply these general forms to objects beyond our experience that leads to the futility of traditional metaphysics. One example is the mistakes 'proof' of God's existence that identifies him as the prime mover – the cause that does not itself have a cause but to which all events can ultimately be traced. The existence of a prime mover can never be proved, but it is equally futile to attempt to disprove it. Better to be done with all such speculation and give up the hope of knowing transcendent truths. Where Plato would have us innately knowing objects (even if it is very difficult to retrieve them from the back of one's mind), Kant has us innately knowing the general form which reality will take. Empiricists claimed that any innate knowledge must be trivial or tautologous, but the kind that Kant ascribes to us is neither, because human beings might have possessed different means of processing their experiences. The nature of our eyes and ears is as contingent as the world they are used to perceive.

A further consequence of Kant's view is that the true nature of objects remains unknowable. Our knowledge may hint at things-in-themselves, or 'noumena' as Kant calls them, but the innate character of anything cannot be discerned. When we look upon a garden, for example, we do not see it as it really is but receive an impression that our eyes have filtered and made suitable for our delectation. A worker bee might see a very different vista – as its eyes can detect ultraviolet light – but this insect too would be ignorant of the garden as it is in-itself. The mediation of our faculties means that we never apprehend objects as they are in-themselves, prior to being perceived, but only a humanized version of them. Owning processing faculties makes knowledge possible, but all faculties come with this limit attached. Human knowledge has no Garden of Eden in which unalloyed truths can be known. But this does not mean that our ability to understand the world has fallen from grace, merely that all knowledge is coloured by mediation. Any other system of perception would face similar limits.

One response to these arguments is to cast aside any notion of an understanding that cuts through bias and prejudice to see the world 'as it really is'. Kant, however, did not go this far. He held that there are different grades of purity within our understanding of the world. For example, he argued that a proper apprehension of aesthetic beauty is one that is limited to an appreciation of an object's pure form – that is, one that is not tainted by any interest other than the purely aesthetic. This yields the odd conclusion that a man is not thinking primarily of a woman's beauty when he finds her sexually attractive. A morally virtuous act, meanwhile, is one that is done out of pure, cold duty rather than a feeling that it is rather nice to help old ladies across the road. Kant's preference for 'pure' motives is not made on moral grounds, however. Instead, he determines what constitutes moral behaviour by reference to what is most pure in the faculties of human beings: rationality. In our relations with one another, this means obedience to universal duties that are untarnished by personal preferences. However, to apply Ockham's Razor and make the minimum claim suggests that one method is more purely rational than the other rather than more moral.

Kant sets extremely high standards when he accuses human perception of being inherently biased. It is wrong, he argues, to hope that we can observe the world as it really, truly is, unsullied by human categories, but then it would be better not to think of it as being 'sullied' by us. This is not the language Kant uses, but it is what his account implies. Kant is often tempted to view things-in-themselves not simply as things-in-themselves, but as shining and highly desirable jewels of pure truth. There is consequently a tension in his work between the purity we can never attain and the attempt to edge ever closer to that purity. He was perhaps betraying his first principles by indulging in a detailed account of the mediation between our senses and the world. It is questionable whether our mediating faculties are not also things-in-themselves which must remain forever out of reach. In Kant's favour, the fact that our knowledge will always be coloured by the kind of creatures we are is no excuse for taking things as they come and accepting them at face value. For example, when most of us listen to a new pop Single and judge it good or bad, our verdict is influenced by the context in which we hear it, the image of the band and their previous output in addition to the quality of the song itself. We gain a clearer view by listening to it in different surroundings – since some songs are better suited to nightclubs than sitting rooms, for instance – and by disregarding the haircuts, clothes and opinions of the performers. We can never attain a perfectly objective view – because the song has to be heard in *some* context – but varying the setting can be instructive. Also, as in the case of punk and heavy metal, the accoutrements of the music may be just as important as the tunes themselves. Listening to such bands with an ear only for harmony defeats the object somewhat. When it comes to such questions of taste, Kant's essential point is as relevant as ever: pure knowledge is merely pure *human* knowledge, and the study of our faculties is at least as valid an inquiry into the nature of things as a straightforward study of the world itself.

Hegel's Dialectic
Finding truth in conflict
Nicholas Fearn

As Oscar Wilde observed, the truth is rarely pure and never simple. When two opposing views clash, it is uncommon for one or the other to be found wholly right or wholly wrong. With tedious regularity, the truth of matters in dispute contains a bit of both sides. One day there will probably be an announcement on the evening news: 'Top philosophers working at Cambridge University have found . . . THE ANSWER . . . and, well, it's a bit of both.' Learning to give and take in this way may well make us better people, but it does not satisfy the absolutist in us. When we want to learn the 'truth', we do not mean to make the best of a confused job, but hope to attain the full version in all its black-and-white glory. Sometimes, before we have realized it, this is in fact what we are left with – but only ever temporarily. Two nations might squabble over a border and eventually agree to a compromise over the disputed territory. The new border is formalized in signed treaties and appears in freshly printed atlases. Only a few years then pass, however, before that border becomes the subject of a new dispute. The process begins again, and the truth that was once clear clouds over. According to the philosopher Georg Hegel, this cycle is writ large in the history of our understanding. A belief, a system, or a way of life meets its opposite and out of their struggle comes something that combines the best elements of both. Sooner or later, this synthesis too meets its opposite, and becomes another milestone in the ongoing series of culture clashes that drives human history. Hegel named this process the 'dialectic', and its goal is perfect freedom.

Hegel was born in Stuttgart in 1770, the son of a revenue officer in the civil service. He lived a relatively quiet life. The most outrageous apocryphal story associated with him is that he planted a 'liberty' tree one Sunday morning in sympathy with the French revolutionary spirit. His sedentary existence was set among great events, however, and he once avowed that if he saw any hope of success for Napoleon he would take a rifle and join him in Paris. He did not have to travel so far, though there is no record of Hegel taking up arms when Napoleon advanced into Prussia. The philosopher was even too busy working to a deadline to celebrate his hero's victory at Jena in 1806. Hegel's greatest work, *The Phenomenology of Spirit,* had

---

Excerpts from *Zeno and the Tortoise,* Copyright © 2001 by Nicholas Fearn. Used by permission of Grove/Atlantic, Inc. and Atlantic Books Limited. Any third party use of this material, outside of this publication, is prohibited.

garnered him a substantial cash advance that came with swingeing penalty clauses should he fail to deliver the manuscript by 13 October. The French marched into Jena to occupy the city on that very day, and Hegel was lucky that the only copy of his magnum opus arrived safely amidst the chaos. He was not so fortunate when the ensuing 'Reign of Terror' in Jena forced the closure of the university and put him out of his job as a professor. Perhaps these experiences made an impact upon his political leanings, for in his later years he became a confirmed Prussian patriot. Hegel believed that Napoleon had introduced modern, rationally conceived institutions into his backward homeland, and he later insisted that Germany had changed during his lifetime. Indeed, he claimed that his country came closer to true freedom than any other state in history. Prussia's absolutist monarchy of the time was probably as surprised by this assertion as a modern historian would be, but the ruling classes were grateful for Hegel's approval and the philosopher enjoyed the patronage of several high-ranking government officials towards the end of his life. He effectively became Prussia's state philosopher and did much to kindle German nationalism.

There are students of philosophy who approach the subject with a mission to make their preconceived ideas respectable rather than to criticize them or learn new ones. Few such students do so as successfully as Hegel. A large part of his work was concerned with formalizing the mystical intuitions of his youth. These intuitions consisted in the oneness of the universe and the belief that only the world taken in its entirety can be said to be truly real. The world's component parts exist only in relation to the whole, and it is the gradual realization of this dependence that leads us to apprehend the world as a single, perfect unity. Since we are ourselves part of the universe, the human race is the instrument by which the world becomes aware of itself. The significance of humanity had been battered by the Enlightenment, and Hegel's contemporaries seized on his ideas for their promise to restore purpose to human life. Many Enlightenment thinkers wanted reason to inform, rather than replace, religion. Hegel was among them, though he deemed religion subordinate to reason. Religion, he argued, expressed the same truths, only it did so through parable rather than directly through the intellect. As we came closer to realizing the Absolute Spirit, however, we would be able to think what previously we could merely feel and would have no further need for myths, allegories or symbolism. This would be the privilege of a civilization as attuned to philosophy as the ancient Greeks were to aesthetics. Not everyone was impressed by this vision. Hegel's great contemporary, the philosopher Arthur Schopenhauer (1788–1860), described him as a 'commonplace, inane, loathsome and ignorant charlatan' and despised the hold he exercised over young disciples. To counter Hegel's influence, Schopenhauer scheduled his lectures to clash with his rival's but was forced to terminate the course when no one turned up. Although Hegel was a poor speaker – he would cough and splutter to buy time while he leafed through copious notes to find the right turn of phrase – his lectures attracted large audiences. Schopenhauer was in the minority, and it is no exaggeration to say that Hegel took the world by storm.

As his most important ideas are not difficult to grasp, the notorious impenetrability of Hegel's writings was no bar to his influence. His method, the dialectic, is a simple one in essence and can be used to interpret an individual's experience as readily as the history of a nation. The dialectic relies on the internal contradictions, or opposites, to be found in all areas of human life. Hegel argued that all progress is achieved through the conflict of opposites, with their resolution leading humanity onwards and upwards to the realization of the Absolute Spirit, which is a perfect unity. The three stages of a dialectic are: thesis, antithesis and synthesis. The thesis might be an idea, an attitude, a civilization or a movement in history. Being incomplete in itself, each of these will sooner or later meet its antithesis. The partial truths contained in both the thesis and antithesis will then come to be embodied on a higher level in the synthesis that results from their conflict.

For a thesis, take, for example, a young recruit going off to war for the first time. He can barely control his panic at the sound of gunfire as he nears the front. At the point at which his nerves are about to break, his shame overpowers his fear and the antithesis in this case is rashness: he breaks from cover in a moment of madness and charges blindly at the enemy. If he is lucky enough to survive his wounds and reflect on his experience, he may reach the synthesis, which would be a golden mean between cowardice and rashness. In a word, bravery: an ability to meet danger with a cool head and consider calmly when to advance and when to take cover. Freedom – the currency of Hegel's dialectic – will now be better realized in his actions. He will have the ability to control himself and make a rational decision in a crisis where before he was limited by his passions. The recruit had the potential for bravery all along, but it took the conflict of his fear with his shame to bring it to expression. A modern army would prefer him to sort out this particular conflict on the training ground, and many soldiers may be able to do this. Hegel would no doubt be sceptical of these cases, however, unless, perhaps, the training ground was itself a dangerous and arduous place staffed by the very fiercest of drill instructors.

The conflicts within a dialectic need not be violent ones, even though pitched battles seem to be Hegel's favourite exemplars. In many cases of self-realization, vigorous hand-wringing will do. If we take a repressed homosexual as our thesis, the antithesis is when he or she realizes that sexual desire can be suppressed by will-power. The clash between desire and self-control leads to a synthesis, since with the power to control oneself comes also the ability to liberate oneself – to express desire deliberately rather than as a response to instinct. All being well, the result is new self-respect in which sexual preferences can be acted upon without shame. This is probably not what Hegel had in mind when he conceived of the dialectic, but his method is nothing if not flexible.

For all its personal applications, the dialectic was designed primarily for the wider canvas of history. There Hegel saw the dialectic sweeping man out of the state of nature and propelling him into the nation-state. The thesis is the unfettered behaviour of the savage, who acts as the mood takes him without thought for the consequences. In time, the savage abandons his unrestrained freedom and submits before the law and the pressures of convention. This antithesis presents him with what he perceives as tyranny. In the synthesis of these opposing conditions he becomes a citizen under the rule of law. In this new environment he is capable of much that was beyond him both as a savage and a subject. He can now understand that there is more to liberty than vulgar licence and that the law is not simply a spoilsport. Admittedly, he might have found it difficult to be so understanding in Hegel's Prussia, but the philosopher himself conceded that the course of freedom may not have reached its end. This is an important caveat, because Hegel's notion of freedom is a strange one, weighted heavily towards the state over the individual. As Bertrand Russell noted, it is not the kind that would keep you out of a concentration camp.

Hegel died in Berlin during a cholera epidemic in 1831. The future for the dialectic was far from the Absolute Knowing that he dreamed of. One of his young disciples took the method and redrew it on materialist lines. In place of the progress of the spirit, this new dialectic traced the history of man and predicted his future according to his economic conditions. The disciple was, of course, Karl Marx.

Nietzsche

On the Use and Abuse of History for Life

Forward

"Incidentally, I despise everything which merely instructs me without increasing or immediately enlivening my activity." These are Goethe's words. With them, as with a heartfelt expression of *Ceterum censeo[I judge otherwise]*, our consideration of the worth and the worthlessness of history may begin. For this work is to set down why, in the spirit of Goethe's saying, we must seriously despise instruction without vitality, knowledge which enervates activity, and history as an expensive surplus of knowledge and a luxury, because we lack what is still most essential to us and because what is superfluous is hostile to what is essential. To be sure, we need history. But we need it in a manner different from the way in which the spoilt idler in the garden of knowledge uses it, no matter how elegantly he may look down on our coarse and graceless needs and distresses. That is, we need it for life and action, not for a comfortable turning away from life and action or merely for glossing over the egotistical life and the cowardly bad act. We wish to use history only insofar as it serves living. But there is a degree of doing history and a valuing of it through which life atrophies and degenerates. To bring this phenomenon to light as a remarkable symptom of our time is every bit as necessary as it may be painful.

I have tried to describe a feeling which has often enough tormented me. I take my revenge on this feeling when I expose it to the general public. Perhaps with such a description someone or other will have reason to point out to me that he also knows this particular sensation but that I have not felt it with sufficient purity and naturalness and definitely have not expressed myself with the appropriate certainty and mature experience. Perhaps one or two will respond in this way. However, most people will tell me that this feeling is totally wrong, unnatural, abominable, and absolutely forbidden, that with it, in fact, I have shown myself unworthy of the powerful historical tendency of the times, as it has been, by common knowledge, observed for the past two generations, particularly among

From http://johnstoniatexts.x10host.com/ by Nietzsche, Ian Johnston, Translator. Copyright © 1998 by Ian Johnston. Reprinted by permission.

the Germans. Whatever the reaction, now that I dare to expose myself with this natural description of my feeling, common decency will be fostered rather than shamed, because I am providing many opportunities for a contemporary tendency like the reaction just mentioned to make polite pronouncements. Moreover, I obtain for myself something of even more value to me than respectability: I become publicly instructed and set straight about our times.

This essay is also out of touch with the times because here I am trying for once to see as a contemporary disgrace, infirmity, and defect something of which our age is justifiably proud, its historical culture. For I believe, in fact, that we are all suffering from a consumptive historical fever and at the very least should recognize that we are afflicted with it. If Goethe with good reason said that with our virtues we simultaneously cultivate our faults and if, as everyone knows, a hypertrophic virtue (as the historical sense of our age appears to me to be) can serve to destroy a people just as well as a hypertrophic vice, then people may make allowance for me this once. Also in my defence I should not conceal the fact that the experiences which aroused these feelings of torment in me I have derived for the most part from myself and only from others for the purpose of comparison and that, insofar as I am a student more of ancient times, particularly the Greeks, I come as a child in these present times to such anachronistic experiences concerning myself. But I must be allowed to ascribe this much to myself on account of my profession as a classical philologue, for I would not know what sense classical philology would have in our age unless it is to be effective by its inappropriateness for the times, that is, in opposition to the age, thus working on the age, and, we hope, for the benefit of a coming time.

I

Observe the herd which is grazing beside you. It does not know what yesterday or today is. It springs around, eats, rests, digests, jumps up again, and so from morning to night and from day to day, with its likes and dislikes closely tied to the peg of the moment, and thus neither melancholy nor weary. To witness this is hard for man, because he boasts to himself that his human race is better than the beast and yet looks with jealousy at its happiness. For he wishes only to live like the beast, neither weary nor amid pains, and he wants it in vain, because he does not will it as the animal does. One day the man demands of the beast: "Why do you not talk to me about your happiness and only gaze at me?" The beast wants to answer, too, and say: "That comes about because I always immediately forget what I wanted to say." But by then the beast has already forgotten this reply and remains silent, so that the man wonders on once more.

But he also wonders about himself, that he is not able to learn to forget and that he always hangs onto past things. No matter how far or how fast he runs, this chain runs with him. It is something amazing: the moment, in one sudden motion there, in one sudden motion gone, before nothing, afterwards nothing, nevertheless comes back again as a ghost and disturbs the tranquillity of each later moment. A leaf is continuously released from the roll of time, falls out, flutters away—and suddenly flutters back again into the man's lap. For the man says, "I remember," and envies the beast, which immediately forgets and sees each moment really perish, sink back in cloud and night, and vanish forever.

Thus the beast lives *unhistorically*, for it gets up in the present like a number without any odd fraction left over; it does not know how to play a part, hides nothing, and appears in each moment exactly and entirely what it is. Thus a beast can be nothing other than honest. By contrast, the human being resists the large and ever increasing burden of the past, which pushes him down or bows him over. It makes his way difficult, like an invisible and dark burden which he can for appearances' sake even deny, and which he is only too happy to deny in his interactions with his peers, in order to awaken their envy. Thus, it moves him, as if he remembered a lost paradise, to see the grazing herd or, something more closely familiar, the child, which does not yet have a past to deny and plays in blissful blindness between the fences of the past and the future. Nonetheless this game must be upset for the child. He will be summoned all too soon out of his forgetfulness. For he learns to understand the expression "It was," that password with which struggle, suffering, and weariness come over human beings, so as to remind him what his existence basically is—a never completed past tense. If death finally brings the longed for forgetting, it nevertheless thereby destroys present existence and thus impresses its seal on the knowledge that existence is only an uninterrupted living in the past [*Gewesensein*], something which exists for the purpose of self-denial, self-destruction, and self-contradiction.

If happiness or if, in some sense or other, a reaching out for new happiness is what holds the living onto life and pushes them forward into life, then perhaps no philosopher has more justification than the cynic. For the happiness of the beast, like that of the complete cynic, is the living proof of the rightness of cynicism. The smallest happiness, if only it is uninterrupted and creates happiness, is incomparably more happiness than the greatest which comes only as an episode, as it were, like a mood, as a fantastic interruption between nothing but boredom, cupidity, and deprivation. However, with the smallest and with the greatest good fortune, happiness becomes happiness in the same way: through forgetting or, to express the matter in a more scholarly fashion, through the capacity, for as long as the happiness lasts, to sense things *unhistorically*.

The person who cannot set himself down on the crest of the moment, forgetting everything from the past, who is not capable of standing on a single point, like a goddess of victory, without dizziness or fear, will never know what happiness is. Even worse, he will never do anything to make other people happy. Imagine the most extreme example, a person who did not possess the power of forgetting at all, who would be condemned to see everywhere a coming into being. Such a person no longer believes in his own being, no longer believes in himself, sees everything in moving points flowing out of each other, and loses himself in this stream of becoming. He will, like the true pupil of Heraclitus, finally hardly dare any more to lift his finger. Forgetting belongs to all action, just as both light and darkness belong in the life of all organic things. A person who wanted to feel utterly and only historically would be like someone who was forced to abstain from sleep, or like the beast that is to continue its life only from rumination to constantly repeated rumination. For this reason, it is possible to live almost without remembering, indeed, to live happily, as the beast demonstrates; however, it is generally completely impossible to live without forgetting. Or, to explain myself more clearly concerning my thesis: *There is a degree of insomnia, of rumination, of the historical sense, through which living comes to harm and finally is destroyed, whether it is a person or a people or a culture.*

In order to determine this degree of history and, through that, the borderline at which the past must be forgotten if it is not to become the gravedigger of the present, we have to know precisely how great the *plastic force* of a person, a people, or a culture is. I mean that force of growing in a different way out of oneself, of reshaping and incorporating the past and the foreign, of healing wounds, compensating for what has been lost, rebuilding shattered forms out of one's self. There are people who possess so little of this force that they bleed to death incurably from a single experience, a single pain, often even from a single tender injustice, as from a really small bloody scratch. On the other hand, there are people whom the wildest and most horrific accidents in life and even actions of their own wickedness injure so little that right in the middle of these experiences or shortly after they bring the issue to a reasonable state of well being with a sort of quiet conscience.

The stronger the roots which the inner nature of a person has, the more he will appropriate or forcibly take from the past. And if we imagine the most powerful and immense nature, then we would recognize there that for it there would be no frontier at all beyond which the historical sense would be able to work as an injurious overseer. Everything in the past, in its own and in the most alien, this nature would draw upon, take it into itself, and, as it were, transform into blood. What such a nature does not subjugate it knows how to forget. It is there no more. The horizon is closed completely, and nothing can recall that there still are men, passions, instruction, and purposes beyond it. This is a general principle: each living being can become healthy, strong, and fertile only within a horizon. If he is incapable of drawing a horizon around himself and too egotistical to enclose his own view within an alien one, then he wastes away there, pale or weary, to an early death. Cheerfulness, good conscience, joyful action, trust in what is to come—all that depends, with the individual as with a people, on the following facts: that there is a line which divides the observable brightness from the unilluminated darkness, that we know how to forget at the right time just as well as we remember at the right time, that we feel with powerful instinct the time when we must perceive historically and when unhistorically. This is the specific principle which the reader is invited to consider: *that for the health of a single individual, a people, and a culture the unhistorical and the historical are equally essential.*

At this point everyone brings up the comment that a person's historical knowledge and feeling can be very limited, his horizon hemmed in like that of an inhabitant of an Alpine valley; in every judgement he might set down an injustice and in every experience a mistake, which he was the first to make, and nevertheless in spite of all injustice and every mistake he stands there in invincible health and vigour and fills every eye with joy, while close beside him the far more just and scholarly person grows ill and collapses, because the lines of his horizon are always being shifted about restlessly, because he cannot wriggle himself out of the much softer nets of his justices and truths to strong willing and desiring. By contrast, we saw the beast, which is completely unhistorical and which lives almost in the middle of a sort of horizon of points, and yet exists with a certain happiness, at least without weariness and pretence. Thus, we will have to assess the capacity of being able to feel to a certain degree unhistorically as more important and more basic, to the extent that in it lies the foundation above which something right, healthy, and great, something truly human, can generally first grow. The unhistorical is like an enveloping atmosphere in which life generates itself alone, only to disappear again with the destruction of this atmosphere.

The truth is that, in the process by which the human being, in thinking, reflecting, comparing, separating, and combining, first limits that unhistorical sense, the process in which inside that surrounding misty cloud a bright gleaming beam of light arises, only then, through the power of using the past for living and making history out of what has happened, does a person first become a person. But in an excess of history the human being stops once again; without that cover of the unhistorical he would never have started or dared to start. Where do the actions come from which men are capable of doing without previously having gone into that misty patch of the unhistorical? Or to set pictures to one side and to grasp an example for illustration: we picture a man whom a violent passion, for a woman or for a great idea, shakes up and draws forward. How his world is changed for him! Looking backwards, he feels blind; listening to the side he hears the strangeness like a dull sound empty of meaning. What he is generally aware of he has never yet perceived as so true, so perceptibly close, coloured, resounding, illuminated, as if he is comprehending with all the senses simultaneously. All his estimates of worth are altered and devalued. He is unable any longer to value so much, because he can hardly feel it any more. He asks himself whether he has been the fool of strange words and strange opinions for long. He is surprised that his memory turns tirelessly in a circle but is nevertheless too weak and tired to make a single leap out of this circle. It is the most unjust condition of the world, narrow, thankless with respect to the past, blind to what has passed, deaf to warnings, a small living vortex in a dead sea of night and forgetting: nevertheless this condition—unhistorical, thoroughly anti-historical—is the birthing womb not only of an unjust deed but much more of every just deed. And no artist would achieve his picture, no field marshal his victory, and no people its freedom, without previously having desired and striven for them in that sort of unhistorical condition. As the active person, according to what Goethe said, is always without conscience, so he is also always without knowledge. He forgets most things in order to do one thing; he is unjust towards what lies behind him and knows only *one* right, the right of what is to come into being now. So every active person loves his deed infinitely more than it deserves to be loved, and the best deeds happen in such a excess of love that they would certainly have to be unworthy of this love, even if their worth were otherwise incalculably great.

Should a person be in a position to catch in many examples the scent of this unhistorical atmosphere, in which every great historical event arose, and to breathe it in, then such a person might perhaps be able, as a knowledgeable being, to elevate himself up to a *superhistorical* standpoint, in the way Niebuhr once described a possible result of historical research: "In one thing at least," he says, "is history, clearly and thoroughly grasped, useful, the fact that one knows, as even the greatest and highest spirits of our human race do not know, how their eyes have acquired by chance the way in which they see and the way in which they forcefully demand that everyone see, forcefully because the intensity of their awareness is particularly great. Someone who has not, through many examples, precisely determined, known, and grasped this point is overthrown by the appearance of a mighty spirit who in a given shape presents the highest form of passionate dedication."

We could call such a standpoint superhistorical, because a person who assumes such a stance could feel no more temptation to continue living and to participate in history. For he would have recognized the *single* condition of every event, that blindness and injustice in the soul of the man of action. He himself would have been cured from now on of taking history excessively seriously. But in the process he would have learned, for every person and for every experience, among the Greeks or Turks, from a moment of the first or the nineteenth century, to answer for himself the question how and why they conducted their lives. Anyone who asks his acquaintances whether they would like to live through the last ten or twenty years again will easily perceive which of them has been previously educated for that superhistorical point of view. For they will probably all answer "No!", but they will substantiate that "No!" differently, some of them perhaps with the confident hope "But the next twenty years will be better." Those are the ones of whom David Hume mockingly says:

And from the dregs of life hope to receive,
What the first sprightly running could not give.

We will call these the historical people. The glance into the past pushes them into the future, fires their spirit to take up life for a longer time yet, kindles the hope that justice may still come and that happiness may sit behind the mountain towards which they are walking. These historical people believe that the meaning of existence will come increasingly to light in the course of its *process*. Therefore they look backwards only to understand the present by considering previous process and to learn to desire the future more keenly. In spite of all their history, they do not understand at all how unhistorically they think and act and also how their concern with history stands, not in service to pure knowledge, but to living.

But that question whose first answer we have heard can be answered again in a different way, that is, once more with a "No!" but with a "No!" that has a different grounding. The denial comes from the superhistorical person, who does not see healing in the process and for whom the world is much more complete and at its end in every moment. What could ten new years teach that the past ten years has not been able to teach!

Now, whether the meaning of the theory is happiness, resignation, virtue, or repentance, on that issue the superhistorical people have not been united. But contrary to all the historical ways of considering the past, they do come to full unanimity on the following principle: the past and the present are one and the same, that is, in all their multiplicity typically identical and, as unchanging types everywhere present, they are a motionless picture of immutable values and eternally similar meaning. As the hundreds of different languages correspond to the same typically permanent needs of people, so that someone who understood these needs could learn nothing new from all the languages, so the superhistorical thinker illuminates for himself all the histories of people and of individuals from within, guessing like a clairvoyant the original sense of the different hieroglyphics and gradually even growing tired of avoiding the constantly new streams of written signals streaming forth. For, in the endless excess of what is happening, how is he not finally to reach saturation, supersaturation, and, yes, even revulsion, so that the most daring ones are perhaps finally ready, with Giacomo Leopardi, to say to their heart

Nothing lives which would be worthy
of your striving, and the earth deserves not a sigh.
Pain and boredom is our being and the world is excrement,
—nothing else.
Calm yourself.

However, let us leave the superhistorical people to their revulsion and their wisdom. Today for once we would much rather become joyful in our hearts with our lack of wisdom and make the day happy for ourselves as active and progressive people, as men who revere the process. Let our evaluation of the historical be only a western bias, if only from within this bias we at least move forward and not do remain still, if only we always just learn better to carry on history for the purposes of *living*! For we will happily concede that the superhistorical people possess more wisdom than we do, so long, that is, as we may be confident that we possess more life than they do. For thus at any rate our lack of wisdom will have more of a future than their wisdom. Moreover, so as to remove the slightest doubt about the meaning of this contrast between living and wisdom, I will reinforce my argument with a method well established from time immemorial: I will immediately establish a few theses.

A historical phenomenon, purely and completely known and resolved into an object of knowledge, is, for the person who has recognized it, dead. In it the person perceives the delusion, the injustice, the blind suffering, and generally the entire temporal dark horizon of that phenomenon and, at the same time, in the process he perceives his own historical power. This power has now become for him, as a knower, powerless, but perhaps not yet for him as a living person.

History, conceived as pure knowledge, once it becomes sovereign, would be a kind of conclusion to living and a final reckoning for humanity. Only when historical culture is ruled and led by a higher force and does not itself govern and lead does it bring with it a powerful new stream of life, a developing culture for example, something healthy with future promise.

Insofar as history stands in the service of life, it stands in the service of an unhistorical power and will therefore, in this subordinate position, never be able to (and should never be able to) become pure science, something like mathematics. However, the problem to what degree living requires the services of history generally is one of the most important questions and concerns with respect to the health of a human being, a people, or a culture. For with a certain excess of history, living crumbles away and degenerates. Moreover, history itself also degenerates through this decay.

II

However, the fact that living requires the services of history must be just as clearly understood as the principle, which will be demonstrated later, that an excess of history harms the living person. In three respects history belongs to the living person: it belongs to him as an active and striving person; it belongs to him as a person who preserves and admires; it belongs to him as a suffering person in need of emancipation. This trinity of relationships corresponds to a trinity of methods for history, to the extent that one may make the distinctions, a *monumental* method, an *antiquarian* method, and a *critical* method

History belongs, above all, to the active and powerful man, the man who fights one great battle, who needs the exemplary men, teachers, and comforters and cannot find them among his contemporary companions. Thus, history belongs to Schiller: for our age is so bad, said Goethe, that the poet no longer encounters any useful nature in the human life surrounding him. Looking back to the active men, Polybius calls political history an example of the right preparation for ruling a state and the most outstanding teacher, something which, through the memory of other people's accidents, advises us to bear with resolution the changes in our happiness. Anyone who has learned to recognize the sense of history in this way must get annoyed to see inquisitive travellers or painstaking micrologists climbing all over the pyramids of the great things of the past. There, in the place where he finds the stimulation to breath deeply and to make things better, he does not wish to come across an idler who strolls around, greedy for distraction or stimulation, as among the accumulated art treasures of a gallery.

In order not to despair and feel disgust in the midst of weak and hopeless idlers, surrounded by apparently active, but really only agitated and fidgeting companions, the active man looks behind him and interrupts the path to his goal to take a momentary deep breath. His purpose is some happiness or other, perhaps not his own, often that of a people or of humanity collectively. He runs back away from resignation and uses history as a way of fighting resignation. For the most part, no reward beckons him on, other than fame, that is, becoming a candidate for an honoured place in the temple of history, where he himself can be, in his turn, a teacher, consoler, and advisor for those who come later.

For his orders state: whatever once was able to expand the idea of "Human being" and to define it more beautifully must constantly be present in order that it always keeps its potential. The greatest moments in the struggle of single individuals make up a chain, in which a range of mountains of humanity are joined over thousands of years. For me the loftiest thing of such a moment from the distant past is bright and great—that is the basic idea of the faith in humanity which expresses itself in the demand for a monumental history. However, with this demand that greatness should be eternal there is immediately ignited the most dreadful struggle. For everything else still living cries out no. The monumental should not be created—that is opposition's cry.

The dull habit, the small and the base, filling all corners of the world, like a heavy atmosphere clouding around everything great, casts itself as a barrier, deceiving, dampening and suffocating along the road which greatness has to go toward immortality. This way, however, leads through human minds! Through the minds of anxious and short-lived animals, who always come back to the same needs and who with difficulty postpone their destruction for a little while. As a first priority they want only one thing: to live at any price. Who might suppose among them the difficult torch race of monumental history, through which alone greatness lives once more! Nevertheless, a few of them always wake up again, those who, by a look back at past greatness and strengthened by their observation, feel so blessed, as if the life of human beings is a beautiful thing, as if it is indeed the most beautiful fruit of this bitter plant to know that in earlier times once one man went through this existence proud and strong, another with profundity, a third with pity and a desire to help—all however leaving behind *one* teaching: that the person lives most beautifully who does not reflect upon existence.

If the common man considers this time span with such melancholy seriousness and longing, those men on their way to immorality and to monumental history knew how to bring to life an Olympian laughter or at least a lofty scorn. Often they climbed with irony into their graves, for what was there of them to bury! Surely only what had always impressed them as cinders, garbage, vanity, animality and what now sinks into oblivion, long after it was exposed to their contempt. But one thing will live, the monogram of their very own essence, a work, a deed, an uncommon inspiration, a creation. That will live, because no later world can do without it. In this most blessed form fame is indeed something more that the expensive piece of our amour propre, as Schopenhauer has called it. It is the belief in the unity and continuity of the greatness of all times. It is a protest against the changes of the generations and transience!

Now, what purpose is served for contemporary man by the monumental consideration of the past, busying ourselves with the classics and rarities of earlier times? He derives from that the fact that the greatness which was once there at all events once was *possible* and therefore will really be possible once again. He goes along his path more bravely, for now the doubt which falls over him in weaker hours, that he might perhaps be wishing for the impossible, is beaten back from the field. Let us assume that somebody believes it would take no more than a hundred productive men, effective people brought up in a new spirit, to get rid of what has become trendy in German culture right now, how must it strengthen him to perceive that the culture of the Renaissance raised itself on the shoulders of such a crowd of a hundred men.

Nevertheless, to learn right away something new from the same example, how fleeting and weak, how imprecise that comparison would be! If the comparison is to carry out this powerful effect, how much of the difference will be missed in the process. How forcefully must the individuality of the past be wrenched into a general shape, with all its sharp corners and angles broken off for the sake of the correspondence! In fact, basically something that once was possible could appear possible a second time only if the Pythagoreans were correct in thinking that with the same constellations of the celestial bodies the same phenomena on the Earth had to repeat themselves, even in the small single particulars, so that when the stars have a certain position relative to each other, a Stoic and an Epicurean will, in an eternal recurrence, unite and assassinate Caesar, and with another stellar position Columbus will eternally rediscover America.

Only if the Earth were always to begin its theatrical performance once again after the fifth act, if it were certain that the same knot of motives, the same *deux ex machina*, the same catastrophe returned in the same determined interval, could the powerful man desire monumental history in complete iconic *truth*, that is, each fact in its precisely described characteristics and unity, and probably not before the time when astronomers have once again become astrologers. Until that time monumental history will not be able to produce that full truthfulness. It will always bring closer what is unlike, generalize, and finally make things equal. It will always tone down the difference in motives and events, in order to set down the monumental *effect*, that is, the exemplary effect worthy of imitation, at the cost of the *cause*. Thus, because monumental history turns away as much as possible from the cause, we can call it a collection of "effects in themselves" with less exaggeration than calling it events which will have an effect on all ages. What is celebrated in folk festivals and in religious or military remembrance days is basically such an "effect in itself." It is the thing which does not let the ambitious sleep, which for the enterprising lies like an amulet on the heart, but it is not the true historical interconnection between cause and effect, which fully recognized, would only prove that never again could anything completely the same fall out in the dice throw of future contingency.

As long as the soul of historical writing lies in the great *driving impulses* which a powerful man derives from it, as long as the past must be written about as worthy of imitation, as capable of being imitated, with the possibility of a second occurrence, history is definitely in danger of becoming something altered, reinterpreted into something more beautiful, and thus coming close to free poeticizing. Indeed, there are times which one cannot distinguish at all between a monumental history and a mythic fiction, because from a single world one of these impulses can be derived as easily as the other. Thus, if the monumental consideration of the past *rules* over the other forms of analyzing it, I mean, over the antiquarian and the critical methods, then the past itself suffers *harm*. Really large parts of it are forgotten, despised, and flow forth like an uninterrupted grey flood, and only a few embellished facts raise themselves up above, like islands. Something unnatural and miraculous strikes our vision of the remarkable person who becomes especially visible, just like the golden hips which the pupils of Pythagoras wished to attribute to their master.

Monumental history deceives through its analogies. It attracts the spirited man to daring acts with its seductive similarities and the enthusiastic man to fanaticism. If we imagine this history really in the hands and heads of the talented egoists and the wild crowds of evil rascals, then empires are destroyed, leaders assassinated, wars and revolutions instigated, and the number of the historical "effects in themselves," that is, the effects without adequate causes, increased once more. No matter how much monumental history can serve to remind us of the injuries among great and active people, whether for better or worse, that is what it first brings about when the impotent and inactive empower themselves with it and serve it.

Let us take the simplest and most frequent example. If we imagine to ourselves uncultured and weakly cultured natures energized and armed by monumental cultural history, against whom will they now direct their weapons? Against their hereditary enemies, the strong cultural spirits and also against the only ones who are able to learn truly from that history, that is, for life, and to convert what they have learned into an noble practice. For them the path will be blocked and the air darkened, if we dance around a half-understood monument of some great past or other like truly zealous idolaters, as if we wanted to state: "See, that is the true and real culture. What concern of yours is becoming and willing!" Apparently this dancing swarm possess even the privilege of good taste. The creative man always stands at a disadvantage with respect to the man who only looks on and does not play his own hand, as for example in all times the political know-it-all was wiser, more just, and more considerate than the ruling statesman.

If we want to transfer into the area of culture the customs of popular agreement and the popular majority and, as it were, to require the artist to stand in his own defence before the forum of the artistically inert types, then we can take an oath in advance that he will be condemned, not in spite of but just *because* his judges have solemnly proclaimed the canon of monumental culture (that is, in accordance with the given explanation, culture which in all ages "has had effects"). Whereas, for the judges everything which is not yet monumental, because it is contemporary, lacks, first, the need for history, second, the clear inclination toward history, and third, the very authority of history. On the other hand, their instinct tells them that culture can be struck dead by culture. The monumental is definitely not to rise up once more. And for that their instinct uses precisely what has the authority of the monumental from the past.

So they are knowledgeable about culture because they generally like to get rid of culture. They behave as if they were doctors, while basically they are only concerned with mixing poisons. Thus, they develop their languages and their taste, in order to explain in their discriminating way why they so persistently disapprove of all offerings of more nourishing cultural food. For they do not want greatness to arise. Their method is to say: "See greatness is already there!" In truth, this greatness that is already there is of as little concern to them as what arises out of it. Of that their life bears witness. Monumental history is the theatrical costume in which they pretend that their hate for the powerful and the great of their time is a fulfilling admiration for the strong and the great of past times. In this, through disguise they invert the real sense of that method of historical observation into its opposite. Whether they know it or not, they certainly act as if their motto were: let the dead bury the living.

Each of the three existing types of history is only exactly right for a *single* area and a *single* climate; on every other one it grows up into a destructive weed. If a man who wants to create greatness uses the past, then he will empower himself through monumental history. On the other hand, the man who wishes to emphasise the customary and traditionally valued cultivates the past as an antiquarian historian. Only the man whose breast is oppressed by a present need and who wants to cast off his load at any price has a need for critical history, that is, history which sits in judgement and passes judgement. From the thoughtless transplanting of plants stem many ills: the critical man without need, the antiquarian without reverence, and the student of greatness without the ability for greatness are the sort who are receptive to weeds estranged from their natural mother earth and therefore degenerate growths.

III

History belongs secondly to the man who preserves and honours, to the person who with faith and love looks back in the direction from which he has come, where he has been. Through this reverence he, as it were, gives thanks for his existence. While he nurtures with a gentle hand what has stood from time immemorial, he want to preserve the conditions under which he came into existence for those who are to come after him. And so he serves life. His possession of his ancestors' goods changes the ideas in such a soul, for those goods are far more likely to take possession of his soul. The small, limited, crumbling, and archaic keep their own worth and integrity, because the conserving and honouring soul of the antiquarian man settles on these things and there prepares for itself a secret nest. The history of his city becomes for him the history of his own self. He understands the walls, the turreted gate, the dictate of the city council, and the folk festival, like an illustrated diary of his youth, and he rediscovers for himself in all this his force, his purpose, his passion, his opinion, his foolishness, and his bad habits. He says to himself, here one could live, for here one may live, and here one can go on living, because we endure and do not collapse overnight. Thus, with this "We" he looks back over the past amazing lives of individuals and feels himself like the spirit of the house, the generation, and the city. From time to time he personally greets from the far away, obscure, and confused centuries the soul of a people as his own soul, with a feeling of completion and premonition, a scent of almost lost tracks, an instinctively correct reading even of a past which has been written over, a swift understanding of the erased and reused parchments (which have, in fact, been erased and written over many times). These are his gifts and his virtues. With them stands Goethe in front of the memorial to Erwin von Steinbach. In the storm of his feeling the veil of the historical cloud spread out between them was torn apart. He saw the German work for the first time once more, "working from the strong rough German soul."

Such a sense and attraction led the Italians of the Renaissance and reawoke in their poets the old Italian genius, to a "wonderfully renewed sound of the ancient lyre," as Jakob Burckhardt says. But that antiquarian historical sense of reverence has the highest value when it infuses into the modest, raw, even meagre conditions in which an individual or a people live a simple moving feeling of pleasure and satisfaction, in the way, for example, Niebuhr admitted with honest sincerity he could live happily on moor and heath among free farmers who had a history, without missing art. How could history better serve living than by the fact that it thus links the less favoured races and people to their home region and home traditions, keeps them settled there, and prevents them from roaming around and from competition and warfare, looking for something better in foreign places?

Sometimes it seems as if it is an obstinate lack of understanding which keeps individuals, as it were, screwed tight to these companions and surroundings, to this arduous daily routine, to these bare mountain ridges, but it is the most healthy lack of understanding, the most beneficial to the community, as anyone knows who has clearly experienced the frightening effects of an adventurous desire to wander away, sometimes even among entire hordes of people, or who sees nearby the condition of a people which has lost faith in its ancient history and has fallen into a restless cosmopolitan choice and a constant search for novelty after novelty. The opposite feeling, the sense of well being of a tree for its roots, the happiness to know oneself in a manner not entirely arbitrary and accidental, but as someone who has grown out of a past, as an heir, flower, and fruit, and thus to have one's existence excused, indeed justified, this is what people nowadays lovingly describe as the real historical sense.

Now, that is naturally not the condition in which a person would be most capable of dissolving the past into pure knowledge. Thus, also we perceive here what we discerned in connection with monumental history, that the past itself suffers, so long as history serves life and is ruled by the drive to live. To speak with some freedom in the illustration, the tree feels its roots more than it can see them. The extent of this feeling, however, is measured by the size and force of its visible branches. If the tree makes a mistake here, then how mistaken it will be about the entire forest around it! From that forest the tree only knows and feels something insofar as this hinders or helps it, but not otherwise. The antiquarian sense of a person, a civic community, an entire people always has a very highly restricted field of vision. It does not perceive most things at all, and the few things which it does perceive it looks at far too closely and in isolation. It cannot measure it and therefore takes everything as equally important. Thus, for the antiquarian sense each single thing is too important. For it assigns to the things of the past no difference in value and proportion which would distinguish things from each other fairly, but measures things by the proportions of the antiquarian individual or people looking back into the past.

Here there is always the imminent danger that at some point everything old and past, especially what still enters a particular field of vision, is taken as equally worthy of reverence but that everything which does not fit this respect for ancient things, like the new and the coming into being, is rejected and treated as hostile. So even the Greeks tolerated the hieratic style of their plastic arts alongside the free and the great styles, indeed, they not only tolerated later the pointed noses and the frosty smiles, but made them into an elegant fashion. When the sense of a people is hardened like this, when history serves the life of the past in such a way that it buries further living, especially higher living, when the historical sense no longer conserves life, but mummifies it, then the tree dies unnaturally, from the top gradually down to the roots, and at last the roots themselves are generally destroyed. Antiquarian history itself degenerates in that moment when it no longer inspires and fills with enthusiasm the fresh life of the present. Then reverence withers away. The scholarly habit lives on without it and orbits in an egotistical and self-satisfied manner around its own centre. Then we get a glimpse of the wretched drama of a blind mania for collecting, a restless compiling together of everything that ever existed. The man envelops himself in a mouldy smell. With the antiquarian style, he manages to corrupt a significant talent, a noble need, into an insatiable new lust, a desire for everything really old. Often he sinks so deep that he is finally satisfied with that nourishment and takes pleasure in gobbling up for himself the dust of biographical quisquilien [rubbish].

But even when this degeneration does not enter into it, when antiquarian history does not lose the basis upon which it alone can take root as a cure for living, enough dangers still remain, especially if it becomes too powerful and grows over the other ways of dealing with the past. Antiquarian history knows only how to preserve life, not how to generate it. Therefore, it always undervalues what is coming into being, because it has no instinctive feel for it, as, for example, monumental history has. Thus, antiquarian history hinders the powerful willing of new things; it cripples the active man, who always, as an active person, will and must set aside reverence to some extent. The fact that something has become old now gives birth to the demand that it must be immortal, for when a man reckons what every such ancient fact, an old custom of his fathers, a religious belief, an inherited political right, has undergone throughout its existence, what sum of reverence and admiration from individuals and generations ever since, then it seems presumptuous or even criminal to replace such an antiquity with something new and to set up in opposition to such a numerous cluster of revered and admired things the single fact of what is coming into being and what is present.

Here it becomes clear how a *third* method of analyzing the past is quite often necessary for human beings, alongside the monumental and the antiquarian: the *critical* method. Once again this is in the service of living. A person must have the power and from time to time use it to break a past and to dissolve it, in order to be able to live. He manages to do this by dragging the past before the court of justice, investigating it meticulously, and finally condemning it. That past is worthy of condemnation; for that is how it stands with human things: in them human force and weakness have always been strong. Here it is not righteousness which sits in the judgement seat or, even less, mercy which announces judgement, but life alone, that dark, driving, insatiable self-desiring force. Its judgement is always unmerciful, always unjust, because it never emerges from a pure spring of knowledge, but in most cases the judgement would be like that anyway, even if righteousness itself were to utter it. "For everything that arises is *worth* destroying. Therefore, it would be better that nothing arose." It requires a great deal of power to be able to live and to forget just how much life and being unjust are one and the same.

Luther himself once voiced the opinion that the world only came into being through the forgetfulness of God; if God had thought about "heavy artillery," he would never have made the world. From time to time, however, this same life, which uses forgetting, demands the temporary destruction of this forgetfulness. For it should be made quite clear how unjust the existence of something or other is, a right, a caste, a dynasty, for example, and how this thing merits destruction.

For when its past is analyzed critically, then we grasp with a knife at its roots and go cruelly beyond all reverence. It is always a dangerous process, that is, a dangerous process for life itself. And people or ages serving life in this way, by judging and destroying a past, are always dangerous and in danger. For since we are now the products of earlier generations, we are also the products of their aberrations, passions, mistakes, and even crimes. It is impossible to loose oneself from this chain entirely. When we condemn that confusion and consider ourselves released from it, then we have not overcome the fact that we are derived from it. In the best case, we bring the matter to a conflict between our inherited customary nature and our knowledge, in fact, even to a war between a new strict discipline and how we have been brought up and what we have inherited from time immemorial. We cultivate a new habit, a new instinct, a second nature, so that the first nature atrophies. It is an attempt to give oneself, as it were, a past *a posteriori [after the fact]*, out of which we may be descended in opposition to the one from which we are descended. It is always a dangerous attempt, because it is so difficult to find a borderline to the denial of the past and because the second nature usually is weaker than the first. Too often what remains is a case of someone who understands the good without doing it, because we also understand what is better without being able to do it. But here and there victory is nevertheless achieved, and for the combatants, for those who make use of critical history for their own living, there is even a remarkable consolation, namely, they know that that first nature was at one time or another once a second nature and that every victorious second nature becomes a first nature.

IV

These are the services which history can carry out for living. Every person and every people, according to its goals, forces, and needs, uses a certain knowledge of the past, sometimes as monumental history, sometimes as antiquarian history, and sometimes as critical history, but not as a crowd of pure thinkers only watching life closely, not as people eager for knowledge, individuals only satisfied by knowledge, for whom an increase of understanding is the only goal, but always only for the purpose of living and, in addition, under the command and the highest guidance of this life. This is the natural relationship to history of an age, a culture, and a people: summoned up by hunger, regulated by the degree of the need, held to limits by the plastic power within, the understanding of the past is desired at all times to serve the future and the present, not to weaken the present, not to uproot a forceful living future. That all is simple, as the truth is simple, and is also immediately convincing for anyone who does not begin by letting himself be guided by historical proof.

And now for a quick look at our time! We are frightened and run back. Where is all the clarity, all the naturalness and purity of that connection between life and history? How confusedly, excessively, and anxiously this problem now streams before our eyes! Does the fault lie with us, the observers? Or has the constellation of life and history altered, because a powerful and hostile star has interposed itself between them? Other people might point out that we have seen things incorrectly, but we want to state what we think we see. In any case, such a star has come in between, an illuminating and beautiful star. The constellation has truly changed *through science, through the demand that history is to be a science*. Now not only does life no longer rule and control knowledge about the past, but also all the border markings have been ripped up, and everything that used to exist has come crashing down onto people. As far back as there has been a coming into being, far back into the endless depths, all perspectives have also shifted. No generation ever saw such an immense spectacle as is shown now by the science of universal becoming, by history. Of course, history even shows this with the dangerous boldness of its motto: *Fiat veritas, pereat vita* [let the truth be done and let life perish].

Let us picture to ourselves the spiritual result produced by this process in the soul of the modern man. Historical knowledge streams out of invincible sources always renewing itself with more. Strange and disconnected things push forward. Memory opens all its gates and is nevertheless not open wide enough. Nature strives its utmost to receive these strange guests, to arrange and honour them. But these are at war with each other, and it appears necessary to overcome them forcibly, in order not to destroy oneself in their conflict. Habituation to such a disorderly, stormy, and warring household gradually becomes a second nature, although it is immediately beyond question that this second nature is much weaker, much more restless, and completely less healthy than the first. Modern man finally drags a huge crowd of indigestible rocks of knowledge around inside him, which then occasionally audibly bang around in his body, as it says in fairy tales. Through this noise the most characteristic property of this modern man reveals itself: the remarkable conflict on the inside, to which nothing on the outside corresponds, and an outside to which nothing inside corresponds, a conflict of which ancient peoples were ignorant.

Knowledge, taken up to excess without hunger, even in opposition to any need, now works no longer as something which reorganizes, a motivation driving outwards. It stays hidden in a certain chaotic inner world, which that modern man describes with a strange pride as an "Inwardness" peculiar to him. Thus, people say that we have the content and that only the form is lacking. But with respect to everything alive this is a totally improper contradiction. For our modern culture is not alive, simply because it does let itself be understood without that contradiction; that is, it is really no true culture, but only a way of knowing about culture. There remain in it thoughts of culture, feelings of culture, but no cultural imperatives come from it. In contrast to this, what really motivates and moves outward into action then often amounts to not much more than a trivial convention, a pathetic imitation, or even a raw grimace. At that point the inner feeling is probably asleep, like the snake which has swallowed an entire rabbit and then lies down contentedly still in the sunlight and avoids all movements other than the most essential.

The inner process, that is now the entire business, that essentially is "Culture." And everyone who wanders by has only one wish, that such a culture does not collapse from indigestion. Think, for example, of a Greek going past such a culture. He would perceive that for more recent people "educated" and "historically educated" appear to be mentioned very closely together, as if they are one and the same and are distinguished only by the number of words. If he talked of his own principle that it is possible for an individual to be very educated and nevertheless not to be historically educated at all, then people would think they had not heard him correctly and shake their heads. That famous people of a not too distant past, I mean those very Greeks, had in the period of their greatest power an unhistorical sense tried and tested in rough times. A contemporary man magically taken back into that world would presumably find the Greeks very uneducated. In that reaction, of course, the secret of modern education, so painstakingly disguised, would be exposed to public laughter. For we modern people have nothing at all which comes from us. Only because we fill and overfill ourselves with foreign ages, customs, arts, philosophies, religions, and discoveries do we become something worthy of consideration, that is, like wandering encyclopaedias, as some ancient Greek lost our time would put it.

However, people come across all the value of encyclopaedias only in what is inside, in the contents, not in what is on the outside or in the binding and on the cover. Thus, all modern education is essentially inner. The bookbinder has printed on the outside something to this effect: Handbook of inner education for external barbarians. In fact, this contrast between inner and outer makes the outer even more barbaric than it would have to be, if a rough people were evolving out of it only according to their basic needs. For what means does nature still have at its disposal to deal with the super-abundance forcing itself outward? Only one means, to take it as lightly as possible in order to shove it aside again quickly and dispose of it. From that arises a habit of not taking real things seriously any more. From that arises the "weak personality," as a result of which reality and existence make only an insignificant impression. Finally people become constantly more venial and more comfortable and widen the disturbing gulf between content and form until they are insensitive to the barbarism, so long as the memory is always newly stimulated, so long as constantly new things worthy of knowledge flow by, which can be neatly packaged in the compartments of memory.

The culture of a people, in contrast to that barbarism, was once described (and correctly so, in my view) as a unity of the artistic style in all expressions of the life of the people. This description must not be misunderstood, as if the issue were an opposition between barbarism and a *beautiful* style. The people to whom we ascribe a culture should be only in a really vital unity and not so miserably split apart into inner and outer, into content and form. Anyone who wants to strive after and foster the culture of a people strives after and fosters this higher unity and, for the sake of a true education, works to destroy the modern notion of being educated. He dares to consider how the health of a people which has been disturbed by history could be restored, how the people could find their instinct once again and with that their integrity.

Now I want to speak directly about us Germans of the present day. It is our lot to suffer more than any other people from this weakness of the personality and from the contradiction between content and form. Form is commonly accepted by us Germans as a convention, as a disguise and a pretence, and is thus, when not hated, then at any rate not particularly loved. It would be even more just to say that we have an extraordinary anxiety with the word convention and also with the fact of convention. In this anxiety, the German abandoned the French school, for he wanted to become more natural and thereby more German. Now, however, he appears to have included in this "thereby" a running away from the school of convention. Now he lets himself go how and where he has the mere desire to go, and basically imitates nervously whatever he wants in semi-forgetfulness of what in earlier times he imitated painstakingly and often happily.

Thus, measured against earlier times, people still live according to a slipshod, incorrect French convention, as all our moving, standing, conversing, clothing, and dwelling demonstrate. While people believe they are escaping back to the natural, they only think about letting themselves go, about comfort, and about the smallest possible amount of self-control. Wander through a German city: everything is conventional, compared to the particular national characteristics of foreign cities. This shows itself in negatives: all is colourless, worn out, badly copied, apathetic. Each man goes about as he wishes, but not with a forceful desire rich in ideas, but following the laws which the general haste, along with the general desire for comfort, establishes for the time being. A piece of clothing, whose invention required no brain power, whose manufacture took no time, one derived from foreigners and imitated as casually as possible, instantly counts among the Germans as a contribution to German national dress. The sense of form is disavowed with complete irony, for people have indeed *the sense of the content*. After all, they are the renowned people of the inward life.

However, there is a well known danger with this inwardness: the content itself, which people assume they cannot see at all from the outside, may one day happen to disappear. From the outside people would not notice either its absence or its earlier presence. But even if people think that, in any case, the German people are as far as possible from this danger; the foreigner will always have a certain justification when he levels the accusation at us that our inner life is too weak and unorganized to be effective on the outside and to give itself a shape. This inward life can to a rare degree prove delicately sensitive, serious, strong, and sincere, and perhaps even richer than the inward lives of other peoples. But as a totality it remains weak, because all the beautiful threads are not tied together into a powerful knot. Thus, the visible act is not the total action and self-revelation of this inner life, but only a weak or crude attempt of a few strands or other to will something whose appearance might pass muster as the totality. Thus, one cannot judge the German according to a single action. As an individual he is still completely hidden after the action. As is well known, he must be measured by his thoughts and feelings, and they speak out nowadays in his books. If only these books did not awaken, in recent times more than ever, a doubt about whether the famous inner life is really still sitting in its inaccessible little temple. It would be a horrible idea that one day it may have disappeared and now the only thing left behind is the externality, that arrogant, clumsy, and respectfully unkempt German externality. Almost as terrible as if that inner life, without people being able to see it, sat inside, counterfeit, coloured, painted over, and had become an actress, if not something worse, as, for example, Grillparzer, who stood on the sidelines as a quiet observer, appears to assume about his experience as a dramatist in the theatre: "We feel with abstractions," he says, "we hardly know any more how feeling expresses itself among our contemporaries. We let our feelings jump about in ways they do not affect us any more. Shakespeare has destroyed everything new for us."

This is a single example, perhaps too quickly generalized. But how fearful would his justified generalization be if the individual cases should force themselves upon the observer far too frequently, how despairingly the statement would echo: We Germans feel abstractedly; we have all been corrupted by history. This statement would destroy at the root every hope for a future national culture. For that kind of hope grows out of the faith in the authenticity and the immediacy of German feeling, from the belief in the undamaged inner life. What is there still to be hoped for or to be believed, if the inner life has learned to leap about, to dance, to put on make up, and to express itself outwardly with abstraction and calculation and gradually to lose itself! And how is the great productive spirit to maintain himself among a people no longer sure of its unified inner life, which falls apart into sections, with a miseducated and seduced inner life among the cultured, and an inadequate inner life among the uneducated? How is he to keep going if the unity of the people's feeling gets lost, if, in addition, he knows that the very part which calls itself the educated portion of the people and which arrogates to itself the national artistic spirit is false and biased. Here and there the judgement and taste of individuals may themselves have become finer and more sublimated, but that is no compensation for him. It pains the productive spirit to have to speak, as it were, to one class and no longer to be necessary within his own people. Perhaps he would sooner bury his treasure, since it disgusts him to be exquisitely patronized by one class, while his heart is full of pity for all. The instinct of the people no longer comes to meet him. It is useless to stretch out one's arms toward it in yearning. What still remains for him, other than to turn his enthusiastic hate against that restricting prohibition, against the barriers erected in the so-called education of his people, in order at least, as a judge, to condemn what for him, the living and the producer of life, is destruction and degradation? Thus, he exchanges the deep understanding of his own fate for the divine pleasure of the creator and helper and finishes up a lonely philosopher, a supersaturated wise man.

It is the most painful spectacle. Generally whoever sees it will recognize a holy need here. He tells himself: here it is necessary to give assistance; that higher unity in the nature and soul of a people must be established once more; that gulf between the inner and the outer must disappear again under the hammer blows of need. What means should he now reach for? What remains for him now other than his deep understanding? By speaking out on this and spreading awareness of it, by sowing from his full hands, he hopes to plant a need. And out of the strong need will one day arise the strong deed. And so that I leave no doubt where I derive the example of that need, that necessity, that knowledge, here my testimony should stand, that it is *German unity* in that highest sense which we are striving for and more passionately for that than for political reunification, *the unity of the German spirit and life after the destruction of the opposition of form and content, of the inner life and convention.*

V

In five ways the supersaturation of an age in history seems to me hostile and dangerous. Through such an excess, first, that hitherto mentioned contrast between inner and outer is produced; second, the personality is weakened; an age is caught up in the fantasy that it possesses the rarest virtue, righteousness, in a higher degree than any other time; third, the instincts of a people are disrupted, and the individual no less than the totality is hindered from developing maturely; fourth, through this excess the always dangerous belief in the old age of humanity takes root, the belief that we are late arrivals and epigones; fifth, an age attains the dangerous mood of irony about itself and, beyond that, an even more dangerous cynicism. In this, however, it increasingly ripens towards a cleverly egotistical practice, through which the forces of life are crippled and finally destroyed.

And now back to our first statement: modern man suffers from a weakened personality. Just as the Roman in the time of the Caesars became un-Roman with regard to the area of the earth standing at his disposal, as he lost himself among the foreigners streaming in and degenerated with the cosmopolitan carnival of gods, customs, and arts, so matters must go with the modern person who continually allows his historical artists to prepare the celebration of a world market fair. He has become a spectator, enjoying and wandering around, converted into a condition in which even great wars and huge revolutions are hardly able to change anything momentarily. The war has not yet ended, and already it is transformed on printed paper a hundred thousand times over; soon it will be promoted as the newest stimulant for the palate of those greedy for history. It appears almost impossible that a strong and full tone will be produced by the most powerful plucking of the strings. As soon as the sound appears again, already in the next moment it dies away, softly evaporating without force into history. To state the matter in moral terms: you do not manage to hold onto what is noble any more; your deeds are sudden bangs, not rolling thunder. If the very greatest and most wonderful thing is accomplished, it must nevertheless move to Hades without any fuss. For art runs away, when you instantly throw over your actions the roof of the historical marquee. The person there who wants to understand immediately, to calculate and grasp, where he should in an enduring oscillation hang onto the unknowable as something sublime, may be called intelligent, but only in the sense in which Schiller speaks of the understanding of the intelligent person: he does not see some things which even the child sees; he does not hear some things which the child hears; these "some things" are precisely the most important thing. Because he does not understand this, his understanding is more childish than the child's and more simplistic than simple mindedness, in spite of the many shrewd wrinkles on his parchment-like features and the virtuoso practice of his fingers unravelling all complexities. This amounts to the fact that he has destroyed and lost his instinct. Now he can no longer let the reins hang loose, trusting the "divine animal," when his understanding wavers and his road leads through deserts. Thus, individuality becomes timid and unsure and can no longer believe in itself. It sinks into itself, into the inner life. That means here only into the piled up mass of scholarly data which does not work towards the outside, instruction which does not become living. If we look for a moment out to the exterior, then we notice how the expulsion of instinct by history has converted people almost into nothing but *abstraction* and shadows. A man no longer gambles his identity on that instinct. Instead he masks himself as educated man, as scholar, as poet, as politician.

If we seize such masks because we believe the matter is something serious and not merely a marionette play (for they all paper themselves over with seriousness), then we suddenly have only rags and bright patches in our hands. Therefore, we should no longer allow ourselves to be deceived and should shout out, "Strip off your jackets or be what you seem." No longer should each serious person turn into a Don Quixote, for he has something better to do than to keep getting into fights with such illusory realities. In any case, however, he must keenly inspect each mask, cry "Halt! Who goes there?" and pull the mask down onto their necks. Strange! We should have thought that history encouraged human beings above all to be *honest*, even if only an honest fool. This has always been its effect. But nowadays it is no longer that! Historical education and the common uniform of the middle class together both rule. While never before has there been such sonorous talk of the "free personality," we never once see personalities, to say nothing of free people, but only anxiously disguised universal people. Individuality has drawn itself back into the inner life: on the outside we no longer observe any of it. This being the case, we could doubt whether, in general, there could be causes without effects. Or should a race of eunuchs be necessary as a guard over the great historical harem of the world? For them, of course, pure objectivity is well and truly established on their faces. However, it does seem almost as if it was their assignment to stand guardian over history, so that nothing comes out of it other than just histories without events, to ensure that through it no personalities become "free," that is, true to themselves and true with respect to others in word and deed. First through this truthfulness will the need, the inner misery of the modern man, see the light of day, and art and religion will be able to enter as true helpers in place of that anxiously concealed convention and masquerade, in order to cultivate a common culture corresponding to real needs, culture which does not, like the present universal education, just teach one to lie to oneself about these needs and thus to become a wandering lie.

In what an unnatural, artificial, and definitely unworthy position must the truly naked goddess Philosophy, the most sincere of all sciences, be in a time which suffers from universal education. She remains in such a world of compulsory external uniformity the learned monologue of a solitary stroller, an individual's accidental hunting trophy, a hidden parlour secret, or a harmless prattle between academic old men and children. No one is allowed to venture on fulfilling the law of philosophy on his own. No one lives philosophically, with that simple manly truth, which acted forcefully on a man in ancient times, wherever he was, and which thus drove him to behave as Stoic if he had once promised to be true to the Stoa.

All modern philosophy is political and police-like, restricted to the appearance of learning through the ruling powers, churches, academies, customs, and human cowardice. It sticks around with sighs of "If only" or with the knowledge "There was once." Philosophy is wrong to be at the heart of historical education, if it wants to be more than an inner repressed knowledge without effect. If the modern human being were, in general, only courageous and decisive, if he were in even his hostility not just an inner being, he would banish philosophy. Thus, he contents himself by modestly covering up her nudity. Yes, people think, write, print, speak, and learn philosophically; to this extent almost everything is allowed. Only in action, in so-called living, are things otherwise. There only one thing is always allowed, and everything else is simply impossible. So historical education wills it. Are they still human beings, we ask ourselves then, or perhaps only thinking, writing, and speaking machines?

Of Shakespeare Goethe once said, "No one hated the material costume more than he. He understood really well the inner costume of human beings, and here all people are alike. People say he presented the Romans excellently. I do not find that. They are nothing but inveterate Englishmen, but naturally they are human beings, people from the ground up, and the Roman toga suits them well enough." Now, I ask if it might be possible to lead out our contemporary men of letters, men of the people, officials, and politicians as Romans. It will not work, because they are not human beings, but only physical compendia and, as it were, concrete abstractions. If they should have character and their own style, this is buried so deep that it has no power at all to struggle out into the daylight. If they should be human beings, then they are that only for the man "who tests the kidneys." For everyone else they are something other, not human beings, not gods, not animals, but historically educated pictures, completely and utterly education, picture, form, without demonstrable content, unfortunately only bad form and, in addition, uniform. And in this sense may my claim may be understood and considered: *History is borne only by strong personalities; the weak personalities it obliterates completely*. It comes down to this: history bewilders feeling and sensing where these are not strong enough to measure the past against themselves.

Anyone who does not dare any longer to trust himself but who involuntarily turns to history for his feeling and seeks advice by asking "What should I feel here?" in his timidity gradually becomes an actor and plays a role, usually in fact many roles. Therefore, he plays each badly and superficially. Gradually the congruence between the man and his historical sphere fails. We see no forward young men associating with the Romans, as if they were their equals. They rummage around and dig away in the remnants of the Greek poets, as if these bodies were also ready for their post-mortem examination and were worthless things, whatever their own literary bodies might be. If we assume there is a concern with Democritus, then the question always on my lips is this: Why then just Democritus? Why not Heraclitus? Or Philo? Or Bacon? Or Descartes? and so on to one's heart's content. And in that case, why then just a philosopher? Why not a poet, an orator? And why particularly a Greek? Why not an Englishman, a Turk? Is the past then not large enough to find something, so that you do not make yourself so ridiculous on your own. But, as I have mentioned, it is a race of eunuchs; for a eunuch one woman is like another, in effect, one woman, the woman-in-itself, the eternally unapproachable, and so what drives them is something indifferent, so long as history itself remains splendidly objective and protected by precisely the sort of people who could never create history themselves. And since the eternally feminine is never attracted to you, then you pull it down to yourselves and assume, since you are neuters, that history is also a neuter.

However, so that people do not think that I am serious in comparing history with the eternally feminine, I will express myself much more clearly: I consider that history is the opposite of the eternally masculine and that it must be quite unimportant for those who are through and through "historically educated." But whatever the case, such people are themselves neither male nor female, not something common to both, but always only neutral or, to express myself in a more educated way, they are just the eternally objective.

If the personalities are, first of all, as has been described, inflated to an eternal loss of subjectivity or, as people say, to objectivity, then nothing more can work on them. Let something good and right come about, in action, poetry, or music. Immediately the person emptied out by his education looks out over the world and asks about the history of the author. If this author has already created a number of things, immediately the critic must allow himself to point out the earlier and the presumed future progress of the author's development; right away he will bring in others for comparative purposes, he will dissect and rip apart the choice of the author's material and his treatment, and will, in his wisdom, fit the work together again anew, giving him advice and setting him right about everything. Let the most astonishing thing occur; the crowd of historical neutrals is always in place ready to assess the author from a great distance. Momentarily the echo resounds, but always as "Criticism." A short time before, however, the critic did not permit himself to dream that such an event was possible.

The work never achieves an influence, but only more "Criticism," and the criticism itself, in its turn, has no influence, but leads only to further criticism. In this business people have agreed to consider a lot of critics as an influence and a few critics or none as a failure. Basically, however, everything remains as in the past, even with this "influence." True, people chat for a while about something new, and then about something else new, and in between do what they always do. The historical education of our critics no longer permits an influence on our real understanding, namely, an influence on life and action. On the blackest writing they impress immediately their blotting paper, to the most delightful drawing they apply their thick brush strokes, which are to be considered corrections. And then everything is over once again. However, their critical pens never cease flying, for they have lost power over them and are led by them rather than leading them. In this excess of their critical ejaculations, in the lack of control over themselves, in what the Romans call impotence, the weakness of the modern personality reveals itself.

VI

But let us leave this weakness. Let us rather turn to a much praised strength of the modern person, with the truly awkward question whether, on account of his well known "Objectivity," he has a right to call himself strong, that is, *just*, and just to a higher degree than the people of other times. Is it true that this objectivity originates from a heightened need and demand for justice? Or does it, as an effect with quite different causes, merely create the appearance that justice might be its real cause? Does this objectivity perhaps tempt one to a detrimental and too flattering bias concerning the virtues of modern man? Socrates considered it an illness close to insanity to imagine oneself in possession of a virtue and not to possess it. Certainly such conceit is more dangerous than the opposite delusion, suffering from a mistake or vice. For through the latter delusion it is perhaps still possible to become better. The former conceit, however, makes a person or a time daily worse, and, in this case, less just.

True, no one has a higher claim on our admiration than the man who possesses the drive and the power for justice. For in such people are united and hidden the highest and rarest virtues, as in a bottomless sea that receives streams from all sides and absorbs them into itself. The hand of the just man authorized to sit in judgement no longer trembles when it holds the scales. Unsparingly he puts on weight after weight against himself. His eye does not become dim if he sees the pan in the scales rise and fall, and his voice rings out neither hard nor broken when he delivers the verdict. If he were a cold demon of knowledge, then he would spread out around him the ice cold atmosphere of a terrifyingly superhuman majesty, which we would have to fear and not to revere. But since he is a human being and yet has tried to rise above venial doubt to a strong certainty, above a patient leniency to an imperative "You must," above the rare virtue of magnanimity to the rarest virtue of all justice, since he now is like this demon, but from the very beginning without being anything other than a poor human being, and above all, since in each moment he has to atone for his humanity and be tragically consumed by an impossible virtue, all this places him on a lonely height, as the example of the human race most worthy of reverence. For he wills truth, not as cold knowledge without consequences, but as the ordering and punishing judge, truth not as a selfish possession of the individual but as the sacred entitlement to shift all the boundary stones of egotistical possessions, in a word, truth as the Last Judgement and not at all something like the captured trophy desired by the individual hunter.

Only insofar as the truthful man has the unconditional will to be just is the striving after truth, which is so thoughtlessly glorified, something great. In the vision of the duller person a large number of different sorts of drives (like curiosity, the flight from boredom, resentment, vanity, playfulness), which have nothing at all to do with the truth, blend in with that striving for truth which has its roots in justice. In fact, the world seems to be full of people who "serve the truth." But the virtue of justice is very seldom present, even more rarely recognized, and almost always hated to the death; whereas, the crowd of the apparently virtuous are honoured as they march in with a great public display. Few people serve truthfulness, because only a few have the purity of will to be just. Moreover, even of these, the fewest have the strength to be able to be just. It is certainly not enough only to have the will for justice. And the most horrible sufferings have come directly from the drive for justice without the power of judgement among human beings. For this reason the general welfare would require nothing *more* than to scatter the seeds of the power of judgement as widely as possible, so that the fanatic remained distinguishable from the judge and blind desire to be a judge distinguishable from the conscious power to be able to judge. But where would one find a means of cultivating the power of judgement! Thus, when there is talk of truth and justice, people remain in an eternal wavering hesitation whether a fanatic or a judge is talking. Hence, we should forgive those who welcome benevolently the "servers of the truth" who possess neither the will nor the power to judge and who set themselves the task of searching for pure knowledge with no attention to consequences or, more clearly, of searching for a barren truth. There are many trivial truths; there are problems that never require effort, let alone any self-sacrifice, in order for one to judge them correctly. In this field of the trivial and the safe, a person indeed succeeds in becoming a cold demon of knowledge nonetheless. When, especially in favourable times, whole cohorts of learned people and researchers are turned into such demons, it always remains unfortunately possible that the time in question suffers from a lack of strong and great righteousness, in short, of the most noble kernel of the so-called drive to the truth.

Let us now place before our eyes the historical virtuoso of the present times. Is he the most just man of his time? It is true that he has cultivated in himself such a tenderness and sensitivity of feeling that for him nothing human is far distant. The most different times and people ring out at once from his lyre in harmonious tones. He has become a tuneful passive thing, which through its resounding tone works on other passive things of the same type, until finally the entire air of an age is full of such delicate reverberations, twanging away in concord. But, in my view, we hear that original historical major chord only as an overtone, so to speak: the sturdiness and power of the original can no longer be sensed in the thin shrill sound of the strings. Whereas the original tone usually aroused actions, needs, and terrors, this lulls us to sleep and makes us weak hedonists. It is as if we have arranged the Eroica Symphony for two flutes and use it for dreamy opium smoking. By that we may now measure, among the virtuosi, how things stand with the highest demands of modern man for a loftier and purer justice, a virtue which never has anything pleasant, knows no attractive feelings, but is hard and terrifying.

Measured by that, how low magnanimity stands now on the ladder of virtues, magnanimity characteristic of a few rare historians! But for many more it is a matter only of tolerance, of leaving aside all consideration of what cannot be once and for all denied, of editing and glossing over in a moderate and benevolent way, of an intelligent acceptance of the fact that the inexperienced man interprets it as a virtue of justice if the past is generally explained without hard accents and without the expression of hate. But only the superior power can judge. Weakness must tolerate, unless it wishes to feign strength and turn justice on the judgement seat into a performing actress.

There is just one fearful species of historian still remaining: efficient, strong, and honest characters, but with narrow heads. Here good will to be just is present, together with the strong feeling in the judgements. But all the pronouncements of the judges are false, roughly for the same reasons that the judgements of the ordinary sworn jury are false.

How unlikely the frequency of historical talent is! To say nothing at all here about the disguised egoists and fellow travellers, who adopt a thoroughly objective demeanour for the insidious games they play; and by the same token to say nothing of the unthinking people who write as historians in the naive belief that their own age is right in all its popular views and that to write by the standards of the time generally amounts to being right, a faith in which each and every religion lives and about which, in the case of religion, there is nothing more to say. Those naive historians call "Objectivity" the process of measuring past opinions and deeds by the universal public opinion of the moment. Here they find the canon of all truths. Their work is to adapt the past to contemporary triviality. By contrast, they call "subjective" that way of writing history which does not take popular opinion as canonical.

And might not an illusion have occurred in the highest interpretation of the word objectivity? With this word, people understand a condition in the historian in which he looks at an event with such purity in all his motives and consequences that they have no effect at all on his subject. People mean that aesthetic phenomenon, that state of being detached from one's personal interests, with which the painter in a stormy landscape, under lightning and thunder, or on the moving sea looks at his inner picture and, in the process, forgets his own person. Thus, people also demand from the historian the artistic tranquillity and the full immersion in the thing. However, it is a myth that the picture which shows things in a person constituted in this way reflects the empirical essence of things. Or is it the case that, by some inner capacity at these times things depict themselves and, as it were, draw a good likeness of themselves or photograph themselves on a purely passive medium?

This would be a mythology and on top of that a bad one. In addition, people might forget that that very moment is the most artistic and most spontaneous creative moment in the inner life of the artist, a moment of composition of the very highest order, whose result will be an artistically really true picture, not a historically true one. To think of history as objective in this way is the secret work of the dramatist, that is, to think of everything one after the other, to weave the isolated details into a totality, always on the condition that a unity of the plan in the material has to be established, if it is not inherent in it. Thus, man spins a web over the past and tames it; in this way the artistic impulse itself expresses its drive for justice, but not its drive for truth. Objectivity and Justice have nothing to do with each other.

One might imagine a way of writing history which has no drop of the common empirical truth in it and yet which might be able to claim the highest rating on an objective scale. Indeed, Grillparzer ventures to clarify this point. "What is history then other than the way in which the spirit of man takes in the *events which are impenetrable* to him, something in which only God knows whether there is a relationship holding it together, in which that spirit replaces an incomprehensible thing with something comprehensible, underwrites with its ideas of external purposes a totality which really can only be known from within, and assumes chance events, where a thousand small causes were at work. At any one time everyone has his own individual necessity so that millions of trends run next to each other in parallel, crooked, and straight lines, intersect each other, help, hinder, flow forward and backwards, thus taking on in relation to each other the character of chance and, to say nothing of the effects of natural events, render it impossible to prove a compelling, all-encompassing necessity for events."

However, this necessary conclusion about that "objective" look at the matter in hand should be exposed right away. This is an assumption which, when it is voiced as a statement of belief by historians, can only assume an odd form. Schiller, in fact, is completely clear concerning the essential subjectivity of this assumption, when he says of historians: "One phenomenon after another begins to liberate itself from accidentaland lawless freedom and, as a coordinated link, to become part of a harmonious totality, *which naturally is present only in its depiction.*" But how should we consider the claim (made in good faith) of a famous historical virtuoso, a claim hovering artificially between tautology and absurdity: "The fact is that that all human action and striving are subordinate to the light and often unremarked but powerful and irresistible progress of things"? In such a statement we do not feel any mysterious wisdom expressing itself as clear illogic, like the saying of Goethe's gardener, "Nature lets itself be forced but not compelled", or in the inscription of a booth in a fair ground, as Swift tells it, "Here you can see the largest elephant in the world except itself." For what is, in fact, the opposition between the actions and the drives of men and the progress of things? In particular, it strikes me that such historians, like that one from whom we quoted a sentence, cease to instruct as soon as they become general and then, in their darkness, show a sense of weakness. In other sciences generalizations are the most important thing, insofar as they contain laws. However, if statements like the one we quoted were to serve as valid laws, one would have to reply that then the work of the writer of history is changed, for what remains particularly true in such statements, once we remove the above-mentioned irreconcilably dark remainder, is well known and totally trivial. For it is apparent to everyone's eye in the smallest area of experience.

However, for that reason to inconvenience entire peoples and to spend wearisome years of work on the subject amounts to nothing more than, as in the natural sciences, to pile experiment on experiment a long time after the law can be inferred from the present store of experiments. Incidentally, according to Zoellner, natural science nowadays may suffer from an excess of experimentation. If the value of a drama is to lie only in the main ideas of the conclusion, then drama itself would be the furthest possible route to the goal, crooked and laborious. And thus I hope that history can realize that its significance is not in universal ideas, like some sort of blossom or fruit, but that its worth is directly one which indicates a known, perhaps a habitual theme, a daily melody, in an elegant way, elevates it, intensifies it to an inclusive symbol, and thus allows one to make out in the original theme an entire world of profundity, power, and beauty. What is appropriate, however, in this process, before everything else, is a great artistic potential, a creative hovering above and a loving immersion in the empirical data, a further poetical composing on the given types—to this process objectivity certainly belongs, but as a positive quality.

However, too often objectivity is only a phrase. Instead of that innerly flashing, externally unmoving and mysterious composure in the artist's eyes, the affectation of composure emerges, just as the lack of pathos and moral power cultivates the disguise of a biting coldness of expression. In certain cases, the banality of the conviction ventures to appear, that wisdom of every man, which creates the impression of composure for unexcited people only through its tediousness, in order to pass muster as that artistic condition in which the subject is silent and becomes completely imperceptible. So everything which generally does not rouse emotion is sought out, and the driest expression is immediately the right one. Indeed, people go as far as to assume that the person whom a moment in the past does *not affect in the slightest* is competent to present it. Philologues and Greeks frequently behave towards each other in this way. They do not concern themselves with each other in the slightest. People call this real "objectivity," as well. Now, in those places where the highest and rarest matter is to be directly presented, it is absolutely outrageous to find the deliberate state of indifference, something put on for show, the acquired flat and sober art of seeking out motives, especially when the *vanity* of the historian drives toward this objectively indifferent behaviour. Incidentally, with such authors people should base their judgement more closely on the principle that each man's vanity is inversely proportional to his understanding. No, at least be honest! Do not seek the appearance of that artistic power truly called objectivity, and do not seek the appearance of justice, if you have not been ordained in the fearful vocation of the just. As if it also were the work of every age to have to be just in relation to everything that once was! As a matter of fact, times and generations never have the right to be the judges of all earlier times and generations. Such an uncomfortable task always falls to only a few, indeed, to the rarest people. Who compels you then to judge? And so, just test yourselves, whether you could be just, if you wanted to! As judges you must stand higher than what is being assessed, whereas, you have only come later. The guests who come last to the table should in all fairness receive the last places. And you wish to have the first places? Then at least do something of the highest and best order. Perhaps people will then really make a place for you, even if you come at the end.

You can interpret the past only on the basis of the highest power of the present. Only in the strongest tension of your noblest characteristics will you surmise what from the past is great and worth knowing and preserving. Like by like! Otherwise you reduce the past down to your level. Do not believe a piece of historical writing if it does not spring out of the head of the rarest of spirits. You will always perceive the quality of its spirit if it is forced to express something universal or to repeat once more something universally known. The true historian must have the power of reshaping the universally known into what has never been heard and to announce what is universal so simply and deeply that people overlook the simplicity in the profundity and the profundity in the simplicity. No person can be simultaneously a great historian, an artistic person, and a numskull. On the other hand, people should not rate as insignificant the workers who go around with a cart, piling things up and sifting through them, because they will certainly not be able to become great historians. Even less should we exchange them for numskulls. We should see them as the necessary colleagues and manual labourers in the service of the master, just as the French, with greater naïveté than is possible among the Germans, were accustomed to speak of the *historiens de M. Thiers [historians of Monsieur Thiers].* These workers should gradually become very learned men, but for that reason cannot ever become masters. An eminently learned man and a great numskull—those go together very easily under a single hat.

Thus, the person of experience and reflection writes history. Anyone who has not experienced life on a greater and higher level than everyone else will not know how to interpret the greatness and loftiness of the past. The utterance of the past is always an oracular pronouncement. You will understand it only as builders of the future and as people who know about the present. People now explain the extraordinarily deep and far-reaching effect of Delphi by the particular fact that the Delphic priests had precise knowledge about the past. It is appropriate now to understand that only the man who builds the future has a right to judge the past. In order to look ahead, set yourselves an important goal, and at the same time control that voluptuous analytical drive with which you now lay waste the present and render almost impossible all tranquillity, all peaceful growth and maturing. Draw around yourself the fence of a large and extensive hope, an optimistic striving. Create in yourselves a picture to which the future is to correspond, and forget the myth that you are epigones. You have enough to plan and to invent when you imagine that future life for yourselves. But in considering history do not ask that she show you the "How?" and the "With what?" If, however, you live your life in the history of great men, then you will learn from history the highest command: to become mature and to flee away from that paralyzing and prohibiting upbringing of the age, which sees advantages for itself in not allowing you to become mature, in order to rule and exploit you, the immature. And when you ask after biographies, then do not ask for those with the refrain "Mr. Soandso and His Age" but for those whose title page must read "A Fighter Against His Age." Fill your souls with Plutarch, and dare to believe in yourselves when you have faith in his heroes. With a hundred people raised in such an unmodern way, that is, people who have become mature and familiar with the heroic, one could permanently silence the entire noisy pseudo-education of this age.

VII

When the historical sense reigns *unchecked* and drags with it all its consequences, it uproots the future, because it destroys illusions and takes from existing things the atmosphere in which they alone can live. Historical justice, even if it is practised truly and with a purity of conviction, is therefore a fearful virtue, because it always undermines living and brings about its downfall. Its judgement is always an annihilation. If behind the historical drive no constructive urge is at work, if things are not destroyed and cleared away so that a future, something already alive in hope, builds its dwelling on the liberated ground, if justice alone rules, then the creative instinct is enfeebled and disheartened.

For example, a religion which is to be turned into historical knowledge under the power of pure justice, a religion which is to be scientifically understood through and through, is by the end of this process immediately destroyed. The reason for this is that in the historical method of reckoning so many false, crude, inhuman, absurd, and violent things always emerge that the fully pious atmosphere of illusion in which alone everything that wants to live can live necessarily disappears. But only in love, only in a love overshadowed by illusion, does a person create, that is, only in unconditional belief in perfection and righteousness. Anything which compels a person no longer to love unconditionally cuts away the roots of his power. He must wither up, that is, become dishonest.

In effects like this, history is opposed by art. And only when history takes it upon itself to turn itself into an art work and thus to become a purely artistic picture can it perhaps maintain the instincts or even arouse them. Such historical writing, however, would thoroughly go against the analytical and inartistic trends of our time; indeed, they would consider it counterfeit. But history which only destroys, without an inner drive to build guiding it, makes its implements permanently blasé and unnatural. For such people destroy illusions, and "whoever destroys illusions in himself and others is punished by the strongest tyrant, nature." True, for a fairly long time one can keep oneself really busy with history completely harmlessly and thoughtlessly, as if it were an occupation as good as any other. The newer Theology, in particular, seems to have become involved with history purely harmlessly, and now it will hardly notice that, in doing so, it stands, probably very much against its will, in the service of Voltaire's *écrasez* [*i.e., Voltaire's extreme hostility to the church*].

Let no one assume from this a new powerfully constructive instinct. For that we would have to let the so-called Protestant Union be considered the maternal womb of a new religion and someone like Judge Holtzendorf (the editor of and chief spokesman for the even more questionable Protestant Bible) as John at the River Jordan. For some time perhaps the Hegelian philosophy still clouding the brains of older people will help to promote that harmlessness, somewhat in the way that people differentiate the "Idea of Christianity" from its manifold incomplete "apparent forms" and convince themselves it is really just a matter of the "tendency of the idea" toreveal itself in ever purer forms, and finally as certainly the purest, most transparent, that is, the hardly visible form in the brain of the present *theologus liberalis vulgis [liberal theologian for the rabble]*.

However, if we listen to this purest of all Christianities expressing itself concerning the earlier impure forms of Christianity, then the uninvolved listener often has the impression that the talk is not at all about Christianity, but of—now, what are we to think if we find Christianity described by the "greatest Theologian of the century" as the religion which makes the claim that "it can be found in all true and even in a few other barely possible religions" and when the "true church" is to be the one which "becomes a flowing mass, where there is no outline, where each part finds itself sometimes here, sometimes there, and everything mingles freely with everything else." Once again, what are we to think?

What we can learn from Christianity, how under the effect of a historicising treatment it has become blasé and unnatural, until finally a fully historical, that is, an impartial treatment, dissolves it in pure knowledge about Christianity and thereby destroys it, that fact we can study in everything which has life. It ceases to live when it is completely dissected and exists in pain and sickness, if we start to practice historical dissection on it. There are people who believe in a revolutionary and reforming art of healing in German music among German people. They get angry and consider it an injustice committed against the most living aspect of our culture when even such men as Mozart and Beethoven are inundated nowadays with the entire scholarly welter of biographical detail and are compelled through the systematic torture of the historical critic to answer to a thousand importunate questions. Through this method, is it not the case that something which has definitely not yet exhausted its living effects is dismissed as irrelevant or at least paralyzed, because we direct our curiosity at countless microscopic details of the life and work and seek intellectual problems in places where we should learn to live and to forget all problems? Set a pair of such modern biographers to thinking about the birth place of Christianity or Luther's Reformation. Their dispassionate pragmatic curiosity would immediately manage to make every spiritual action at a distance impossible, just as the most wretched animal can prevent the origin of the most powerful oak by gobbling down the acorn. All living things need an atmosphere around them, a secret circle of darkness. If this veil is taken from them, if people condemn a religion, an art, a genius to orbit like a star without an atmosphere, then we should no longer wonder about their rapid decay and the way they become hard and barren. That is the way it is now with all great things

> which never succeed without some delusion

as Hans Sachs says in the *Meistersinger*.

But every people, indeed every person, who wishes to become *mature* needs such an enveloping delusion, such a protecting and veiling cloud. But today people generally despise becoming mature, because they honour history more than living. Indeed, people exult over the fact that now "science is beginning to rule over living." It is possible that people will attain that goal but it is certain that a life so governed is not worth much, because it is much less *living* and it establishes a life for the future far less than does the previous life governed not by knowledge but by instinct and powerful illusory images. But, as stated, it is clearly not to be the era of fully developed and mature people, of harmonious personalities, but the era of common work which is as useful as possible. That, however, amounts only to the fact that people are to be trained for the purposes of the time, in order to get to work with their hands as promptly as possible. They are to labour in the factories of the universal utilities before they are mature, that is, so that they really no longer become mature, because this would be a luxury, which would deprive the "labour market" of a lot of power. We blind some birds, so that they sing more beautifully. I do not think that today's people sing more beautifully than their grandfathers, but I do know this: we blind them early. But the method, the disreputable method, which people use to blind them is *excessively bright, excessively sudden, and excessively changing light*. The young person is lashed through all the centuries. Youngsters who understand nothing about a war, a diplomatic action, or a trade policy are found fit to be introduced to political history. But then, just as the young person races through history, so we moderns race through the store rooms of art and listen to concerts. We really feel that something sounds different from something else, that something has a different effect than something else. Constantly losing more of this feeling of surprise and dislike, becoming excessively astonished no longer, or finally allowing oneself to enjoy everything—people really call that historical sense historical education.

Without saying anything to gloss over the expression: the mass of stuff streaming in is so great that what is surprising, shocking, barbarous, and powerful, "concentrated in a dreadful cluster," presses so overpoweringly on the young soul that it knows how to rescue itself only with a deliberate apathy. Where a keener and stronger consciousness is firmly established, then a very different feeling appears: disgust. The young man has become homeless and has doubts about all customs and ideas. Now he knows this fact: that at all times things were different, and they do not depend upon the way you are. In melancholy absence of feeling he lets opinion on opinion flow past him and understands Holderlein's pointed words in response to his reading of Laertius Diogenes concerning the life and teaching of the Greek philosophers: "Here I have also experienced more of what I have already come across sometimes, that what passes temporarily by and what comes and goes in human thoughts and systems strike me as almost more tragic than the fates which we usually call the only realities."

No, such an overwhelming, anaesthetizing, and powerful historicising is certainly not required for the young, as ancient times demonstrate, and is, indeed, dangerous in the highest degree, as newer ages demonstrate. But let us really look at the historical student, the inheritor of a blasé attitude, already apparent all too early, almost in childhood. Now the "method" in his own work, the right grip and the elegant tone of the master's manner, have become his own. An entirely isolated small chapter of the past has fallen victim to his keen mind and the method he has learned. He has already produced, indeed, in prouder language, he has "created." He has now become a servant of truth in action and master in the world empire of history. If, as a child, he was already "ready," now he is already over-ready. One only needs to shake him for wisdom to fall into one's lap with a rattle. But the wisdom is rotten, and each apple has its own worm. Believe me on this point: when people work in the scientific factory and are to become useful before they are mature, then science itself is ruined in the process, just like the slaves used these days in this factory. I regret that people even find it necessary to use the verbal jargon of the slave holder and employer to describe such relationships which should be thought of as free from utility, free from life's needs, but the words "Factory, labour market, bargain, exploitation," uttered like all the words assisting egoism, spontaneously press themselves on the lips when we want to describe the youngest generation of scholars. The stolid mediocrity becomes ever more mediocre, science becomes ever more practical economically. Essentially all the most recent scholars are wise in only *a single* point, and in that naturally wiser than all people of the past. In all other points they are, to speak with care, only infinitely different from all the scholars of the old school. Nevertheless they demand respect and perquisites for themselves, as if the state and official opinion were under an obligation to consider the new coins just as valuable as the old. The labourers have made a working compact among themselves and decreed that genius is superfluous because each labourer is stamped as a genius. Presumably a later time will consider the structure they have cobbled together, not built together.

To those who tirelessly proclaim the modern cry of combat and sacrifice "Division of labour! In rows and tiers!" we can once and for all say clearly and firmly: "Do you want to destroy science as quickly as possible, just as you destroy hens, which you artificially compel to lay eggs too quickly." Well, in the last century science has been promoted at an astonishing rate. But take a look now at the scholars, the exhausted hens. There are in truth no "harmonious" natures. They can only cackle more than before, because they lay eggs more often. Naturally, however, the eggs have become constantly smaller (although the books have become constantly thicker). As the final natural result, things resign themselves to the commonly loved "Popularizing" of science (in addition to the "Feminization" and "Infantization"), that is, the notorious tailoring of the scientific coat to the body of the "motley public" (I am attempting here to cultivate a moderately tailored German to describe a moderately tailored activity). Goethe saw an abuse in this and demanded that sciences should have an effect on the external world only through a *higher praxis*. Besides, to the older generation of scholars such an abuse appeared (for good reasons) difficult and tiresome. For similarly good reasons it comes easily to the younger scholars, because they themselves, with the exception of a really small corner of knowledge, are the motley public and carry its needs in themselves. They only need once to settle themselves down comfortably in order for them to succeed in opening up the small study area to that popular need for the variously curious. People pretend that below this action of making themselves comfortable stands the title "the modest condescension of the scholar for his people"; while at bottom the scholar, to the extent that he is not a scholar but a member of the rabble, is only descending into himself. If you create for yourself the idea of a "people" then you can never think sufficiently nobly and highly of it. If you thought highly of a people, then you would be also compassionate towards them and would be on your guard against offering them your historical *aqua fortis[nitric acid]* as a living and refreshing drink. But deep down you think little of the people, because you are permitted to have no true and confidently based respect for its future, and you operate as practical pessimists, I mean as people led by the premonition of destruction, people who thus become indifferent and permissive towards what is strange, even towards your very own welfare. If only the soil still supported *us*! And if it no longer carries us, then that is also all right. Thus they feel and live an *ironic* existence.

VIII

In fact, it must seem odd, although it is not contradictory, when to the age which so audibly and insistently is in the habit of bursting out in the most carefree exulting over its historical culture, I nevertheless ascribe an *ironical self-consciousness*, a presentiment which hovers all around it that this is not a matter for rejoicing, a fear that soon all the celebrations over historical knowledge will be over. Goethe proposed to us a similar enigma with respect to a single personality in his remarkable characterization of Newton. He found at bottom (or more correctly, at the top) of Newton's being "a dark premonition of his own error," as it were, the expression (noticeable in solitary moments) of a consciousness with a superior power of judgement, something which a certain ironical perspective had gained over the essential nature dwelling inside him. Thus we find particularly in the greater people with a higher historical development a consciousness, often toned down to a universal scepticism, of how much folly and superstition are in the belief that the education of a people must be so overwhelmingly historical as it is now. For the most powerful people, that is, powerful in deeds and works, have lived very differently and have raised their young people differently. But that folly and that superstition suit us—so runs the sceptical objection—us, the late comers, the faded last shoots of more powerful and more happily courageous generations, us, in whom one can see realized Herod's prophecy that one day people would be born with instant grey beards and that Zeus would destroy this generation as soon as that sign became visible to him. Historical culture is really a kind of congenital grey haired condition, and those who bear its mark from childhood on would have to come to the instinctive belief in the *old age of humanity*. An old person's occupation, however, is appropriate to old age, that is, looking back, tallying the accounts, balancing the books, seeing consolation in what used to be through memories, in short, a historical culture.

The human race, however, is a tough and persistent thing and will not have its steps forward and backwards viewed according to millennia, indeed hardly according to hundreds of thousands of years. That is, it will not be viewed *at all* as a totality from the infinitely small point of an atomic individual person. Then what will a couple of thousand years signify (or, put another way, the time period of thirty-four consecutive human lives, reckoned at sixty years each) so that we can speak of the beginning of such a time as still the "Youth of Mankind" and the end of it as already the "Old Age of Mankind." Is it not much more that case that in this paralyzing belief in an already faded humanity there sticks the misunderstanding of an idea of Christian theology inherited from the Middle Ages, the idea of the imminent end of the world, of the nervously awaited judgement? Has this idea, in fact, changed through the intensified need of history to judge, as if our time, the last of all possible, has been authorized to consider itself the universal judge of everything in the past, something which Christian belief awaits, not in any way from human beings, but from the "Son of Man." In earlier times this was, for humanity as well as for the individual, a loudly proclaimed "*memento mori*," *[reminder of death]* an always tormenting barb and, so to speak, the summit of medieval knowledge and conscience. The phrase of more recent times, called out in a contrasting response, "*memento vivere*" *[a reminder of living]* sounds, to speak openly, still quite timid, is not a full throated cry, and has something almost dishonest about it. For human beings still sit firmly on the *memento mori* and betray the fact through their universal need for history.

In spite of the most powerful beating of its wings, knowledge cannot tear itself loose in freedom. A deep feeling of hopelessness is left over and has taken on that historical colouring, because of which all higher training and education are now melancholy and dark. A religion which of all the hours of a person's life considers the last the most important, which generally predicts the end of earthy life and condemns all living people to live in the fifth act of the tragedy, certainly arouses the deepest and noblest forces, but it is hostile to all new cultivation, daring undertakings, and free desiring. It resists that flight into the unknown, because there it does not love and does not hope. It lets what is coming into being push forward only unwillingly so that at the right time it can push it to the side or sacrifice it as a seducer of being or as a liar about the worth of existence. What the Florentines did when, under the influence of Savonarola's sermons calling for repentance, they organized those famous sacrificial fires of paintings, manuscripts, mirrors, and masks, Christianity would like to do with every culture which rouses one to renewed striving and which leads to that slogan *memento vivere*. If it is not possible to achieve this directly, without a digression (that is, through superior force), then it attains its goal nonetheless if it unites itself with historical education, usually even with its knowledge. Now, speaking out through historical knowledge, with a shrug of its shoulders, Christianity rejects all becoming and thus disseminates the feeling of the person who has come much too late and is unoriginal, in short, of the person born with grey hair.

The stringent and profoundly serious consideration of the worthlessness of everything which has happened, of the way in which the world in its maturity is ready for judgement, has subsided to a sceptical consciousness that it is in any case good to know everything that has happened, because it is too late to do anything better. Thus the historical sense makes its servants passive and retrospective. Only in momentary forgetfulness, when that sense is intermittent, does the patient suffering from the historical fever become active, so that, as soon as the action is over and done with, he may seize his deed, through analytical consideration prevent any further effects, and finally flay it for "History." In this sense, we are still living in the Middle Ages, and history is always still a disguised theology, in exactly the same way that the reverence with which the unscientific laity treat the scientific caste is a reverence inherited from the clergy. What people in earlier times gave the church, people now give, although in scantier amounts, to science. However, the fact that people give was something the church achieved in earlier times, not something first done by the modern spirit, which, along with its other good characteristics, much rather has something stingy about it, as is well known, and is, so far as the pre-eminent virtue of generosity is concerned, a piker.

Perhaps this observation is not pleasant, perhaps no more pleasant than that derivation of the excess of history from the medieval *memento mori* and from the hopelessness which Christianity carried in its heart concerning all future ages of earthly existence. But at any rate people should replace the explanation which I have put down only hesitantly with better explanations. For the origin of historical education and its inherent and totally radical opposition to the spirit of a "new age," of a "modern consciousness"—this origin *must* itself be once again recognized historically. History *must* itself resolve the problem of history. Knowledge *must* turn its barbs against itself. This triple *Must* is the spiritual imperative of the "new age," if there is in it truly something new, powerful, vital, and original. Or if, to leave the Romance peoples out of consideration, it should be the case that we Germans, in all higher matters of culture, always have to be only the "followers" just because that is the only thing we could be, as William Wackernagel once expressed it all too convincingly: "We Germans are a people of followers. With all our higher knowledge and even with our faith, we are always still followers of the old world. Even those who are hostile to that and certainly do not wish it breathe in the spirit of Christianity together with the immortal spirit of the old classical culture, and if anyone were to succeed in separating out these two elements from the living air which envelops the inner man, then not much would be left over with which one might still eke out a spiritual life."

But even if we wanted to reassure ourselves happily about this calling to be the followers of antiquity, if we would only make up our minds to take the calling as something right, urgent, serious, and great, and would recognize in this urgency our designated and unique privilege, nonetheless we would find it necessary to ask whether it must always be our purpose to be *pupils of a declining antiquity*. At some time or other we might be permitted to aim our goal somewhat higher and further, at some time or other we might permit ourselves to praise ourselves for having reworked so fruitfully and splendidly the Alexandrian-Roman culture in ourselves also through our universal history, so that now, as the most noble reward we might set ourselves the still more monumental task of getting back behind and above this Alexandrian world and seeking out our models of the courageous gaze in the ancient Greek original world of the great, the natural, and the human. *But there we find also the reality of an essentially unhistorical education, an education nevertheless (or rather therefore) unspeakably rich and vital.* If we Germans were nothing but followers, then by looking at such a culture as a legacy appropriately ours, there could be nothing greater or prouder for us than to be its followers.

As a result we should say only this and nothing but this: that the often unpleasantly strange thought that we are epigones, nobly thought out, can guarantee important effects and a richly hopeful desire for the future, both for the individual and for a people, to the extent that we understand ourselves as the heirs and followers of an astonishing classical force and see in that our legacy and our spur, but not as pale and withered late arrivals of powerful races, who scrape out a cold living as the antiquarians and gravediggers of those races. Such late arrivals naturally live an ironic existence. Destruction follows closely on the heels of their limping passage through life. They shudder in the face of that, when they derive enjoyment from the past, for they are living memorials, and yet their thoughts are senseless without someone to inherit them. So the dark premonition envelops them that their life may be an injustice, for no future life can set it right. However, if we were to imagine such antiquarian late comers suddenly exchanging that painfully ironic moderation for impudence, and if we imagine them to ourselves as if they were reporting with a ringing voice: "The race is at its peak, because now for the first time it has the knowledge of itself and has become clear to itself," then we would have a performance in which, as in an allegory, the enigmatic meaning of a certain very famous philosophy is deciphered for German culture.

I believe that there has been no dangerous variation or change in German culture in this century which has not become more dangerous through the monstrous influence of the philosophy of Hegel, an influence which continues to flow right up to the present. The belief that one is a late comer of the age is truly crippling and disorienting; but it must appear fearful and destructive when such a belief one day with a bold reversal idolizes this late comer as the true meaning and purpose of all earlier events, when his knowledgeable misery is equated to the completion of world history. Such a way of considering things has made the Germans accustomed to talking of the "World Process" and to justify their own time as the necessary result of the world process. Such a way of thinking about things has made history the single sovereign, in the place of the other spiritual powers, culture and religion, insofar as history is "the self-realizing idea" and "the dialectic of the spirits of peoples" and the "last judgement."

People have scornfully called this Hegelian understanding of history the earthly changes of God; but this God for His part was first created by history. However, this God became intelligible and comprehensible inside Hegelian brain cases and has already ascended all the dialectically possible steps of His being right up to that self-revelation. Thus, for Hegel the summit and end point of the world process coincided with his own individual existence in Berlin. In fact, strictly speaking he should have said that everything coming after him should be valued really only as a musical coda of the world historical rondo, or even more truly, as superfluous. He did not say that. Thus, he planted in the generations leavened by him that admiration for the "Power of History", which transforms practically every moment into a naked admiration of success and leads to idolatrous worship of the factual. For this service people nowadays commonly repeat the very mythological and, in addition, the truly German expression "to carry the bill of facts" But the person who has first learned to stoop down and to bow his head before the "Power of History", finally nods his agreement mechanically, in the Chinese fashion, to that power, whether it is a government or public opinion or a numerical majority, and moves his limbs precisely to the beat of strings plucked by some "power" or other.

If every success contains within itself a rational necessity, if every event is the victory of the logical or the "Idea", then get down quickly now and kneel before the entire hierarchy of "success." What? Do you claim there are no ruling mythologies any more and religions are dying out? Only look at the religion of the power of history; pay attention to the priests of the mythology of the Idea and their knees all covered in cuts! Surely all the virtues come only in the wake of this new faith. Is it not unselfishness when the historical person lets himself be blown into an objective glass mirror? Is it not generosity to do without all the force of heaven and earth so that in this power people worship pure force in itself? Is it not justice to have a scale balance always in one's hands and to watch closely what sinks down as the stronger and heavier? And what a respectable school such a consideration of history is! To take everything objectively, to get angry about nothing, to love nothing, to understand everything, how gentle and flexible that makes things. And even if one man brought up in this school becomes publicly angry at some point and gets annoyed, people can then enjoy that, for they know it is really only intended as an artistic expression; it is *ira [anger]* and *studium [study]*. However, it is entirely *sine ira et studio [without anger and study]*.

What antiquated thoughts I have in my heart about such a complex of mythology and virtue! But they should come out for once, even if people should just go on laughing. I would also say: history constantly impresses on us "It was once" and the moral "You should not" or "You should not have." So history turns into a compendium of the really immoral. How seriously mistaken would the person be who at the same time considered history as the judge of this factual immorality! For example, it is offensive to morality that a Raphael had to die at thirty-six years of age; such a being should not have died. Now, if you want history, as the apologist for the factual, to provide assistance, then you will say that Raphael expressed everything that was in him; with a longer life he would have been able to create something beautiful only as a similar beauty, and not as something beautifully new, and so on. In so doing, you are the devil's advocate for the very reason that you make success, the fact, your idol; whereas, the fact is always dumb and at all times has looked upon something like a calf as a god. Moreover, as apologists for history, you prompt each other by whispering this ignorance. Because you do not know what such a *natura naturans [essential creative force]* like Raphael is, it does not make you make you hot to hear that such a person was and will never be again. In Goethe's case, recently someone wanted to teach us that with his eighty-two years he had reached his limit, and yet I would happily trade a couple of years of the "washed up" Goethe for an entire cart full of fresh ultra-modern lives, in order to share in conversations like the ones Goethe conducted with Eckermann and in this way to remain protected from all the contemporary teachings of the legionaries of the moment.

In comparison with such dead people, how few living people generally have a right to live! That the many live and that those few no longer live is nothing more than a brutal truth, that is, an incorrigible stupidity, a blatant "That is the case" in contrast to the moral "It should not have been so." Yes, in contrast to the moral! For let people speak about whatever virtue they want, about righteousness, generosity, courage, wisdom and human sympathy—a person is always virtuous just because he rebels against that blind power of the factual, against the tyranny of the real and submits himself to laws which are not the laws of that historical fluctuation. He constantly swims against the historical waves, whether he fights his passions as the closest mute facts of his existence or whether he commits himself to truthfulness, while the lies spin around him their glittering webs. If history were in general nothing more than "the world system of passion and error," then human beings would have to read it in the way Goethe summoned us to read Werther, exactly as if it cried out "Be a man and do not follow me!" Fortunately history also preserves the secret of the great fighters *against history*, that is, against the blind force of the real, and thus puts itself right in the pillory, because it brings out directly as the essential historical natures those who worried so little about the "Thus it was," in order rather to follow with a more cheerful pride a "So it should be." Not to drag their race to the grave but to found a new race—that drove them ceaselessly forwards; and if they themselves were born as latecomers, there is an art of living which makes one forget this. The generations to come will know them only as first comers.

IX

Is our age perhaps such a first comer? In fact, the vehemence of its historical sense is so great and expresses itself in such a universal and simply unlimited way that at least in this the coming ages will assess its quality as a first comer, if in fact there are going to be *coming ages* at all, understood in the sense of culture. But right here there remains a serious doubt. Close by the pride of the modern man stands his irony about his very self, his consciousness that he must live in a historicising and, as it were, a twilight mood, and his fear that in future he will be totally unable to rescue any more of his youthful hopes and powers. Here and there people go even further, into *cynicism*, and justify the passage of history, indeed, of the whole development of the world as essentially for the use of modern man, according to the cynical rule that things must turn out just as they are going right now, that man must be nothing other than what people now are, and that against this Must no one may rebel. In the sense of well being of such a cynicism a person who cannot maintain that view with irony curses himself. In addition, the last decade offers him as a gift one of its most beautiful inventions, a rounded and sonorous phrase for such cynicism: it calls his style of living mindlessly with the times, "the full dedication of the personality to the world process." The personality and the world process! The world process and the personality of the turnip flea! If only people did not have to hear the eternal hyperbole of all hyperboles, the word World, World, World, when really each person should speak in all honesty only of Men, Men, Men. Heirs of the Greeks and Romans? Of Christianity? That all appears as nothing to this cynic. But heirs of the world process! The high points and targets of the world process! High points and targets of the world process! Sense and solution of all riddles of becoming in general, expressed in the modern man, the ripest fruit of the tree of knowledge—I call that a swollen feeling of elation. By this symbol are the first comers of all ages known, even if they have come along right at the end.

Historical considerations have never flown so far afield, not even in dreams. For now the history of human beings is only the continuation of the history of animals and plants. Indeed, even in the furthest depths of the sea the historical universalist finds the traces of himself, as living mucus; he gazes in astonishment (as if at a miracle) at the immense route which human beings have already passed through and trembles at the sight of the even more astonishing miracle, modern man himself, who has the ability to survey this route. He stands high and proud on the pyramid of the world process. As he sets down on the top of it the final stone of his knowledge, he appears to call out to nature listening all around, "We are at the goal, we are the goal, we are the perfection of nature."

Arrogant European of the nineteenth century, you are raving! Your knowledge does not complete nature, but only kills your own. For once measure your height as a knower against your depth as a person who can do something. Of course, you clamber on the solar rays of knowledge upward towards heaven, but you also climb downward to chaos. Your way of going, that is, clambering about as a knower, is your fate. The ground and floor move back away from you into the unknown; for your life there are no supports any more, but only spider's threads, which every new idea of your knowledge rips apart.

But no more serious talk about this, for it is possible to say something more cheerful.

The incredibly thoughtless fragmenting and fraying of all the fundamentals, their disintegration into a constantly flowing and dissolving becoming, the inexhaustible spinning away and historicising of all that has come into being because of modern men, the great garden spiders in the knots of the world net, that may keep the moralists, the artists, the devout, as well as the statesman, busy and worried. Today it should for once cheer us up, because we see all this in the gleaming magical mirror of a *philosophical writer of parodies*, in whose head the age has come to an ironical consciousness of itself, a consciousness clear all the way to lunacy (to speak in Goethe's style). Hegel once taught us, "when the spirit makes a sudden turn, then we philosophers are still there." Our age has made a turn into self-irony, and, lo and behold, E. von Hartmann was also at hand and had written his famous Philosophy of the Unconscious, or, to speak more clearly, his philosophy of unconscious irony. Rarely have we read a more amusing invention and a more philosophically roguish prank than Hartmann's. Anyone who is not enlightened by him concerning *Becoming*, who is not really set right on the inside, is truly ripe for the state of existing in the past. The start and the goal of the world process, from the first motions of consciousness right to the state of being hurled back into nothingness, together with the precisely defined task of our generation for the world process, all presented from such a wittily inventive font of inspiration of the unconscious and illuminated with an apocalyptic light, with everything so deceptively imitative of a unsophisticated seriousness, as if it were really serious philosophy and not playful philosophy, such a totality makes its creator one of the pre-eminent writers of philosophical parodies of all times. Let us sacrifice on an altar, sacrifice to him, the inventor of a truly universal medicine, a lock of hair, to steal an expression of admiration from Schleiermacher. For what medicine would be healthier against the excess of historical culture than Hartmann's parody of all world history?

If we want a correct matter-of-fact account of what Hartmann is telling us about the noxious tri-legged stool of unconscious irony, then we would say that he is telling us that our age would have to be just the way it is if humanity is to ever get seriously fed up with this existence. That is what we believe in our hearts. That frightening fossilizing of the age, that anxious rattling of the bones, which David Strauss has described for us in his naive way as the most beautiful reality, is justified in Hartmann not only retrospectively *ex causis efficientibus* [*from efficient causes, i.e., as the result of certain mechanical causes*], but even looking ahead, *ex causa finali* [*from a final cause, i.e., as having a higher purpose*]. The joker lets his light stream over the most recent periods of our time, and there finds that our age is very good, especially for the person who wants to endure as strongly as possible the indigestible nature of life and who cannot wish that doomsday comes quickly enough. Indeed, Hartmann calls the age which humanity is now approaching the "maturity of humanity." But that maturity is, according to his own description, the fortunate condition where there is still only " pure mediocrity" and culture is "some evening farce for the Berlin stockbroker," where "geniuses are no longer a requirement of the age, because that means casting pearls before swine or also because the age has progressed to a more important level, beyond the stage for which geniuses are appropriate," that is, to that stage of social development in which each worker "with a period of work which allows him sufficient leisure for his intellectual development leads a comfortable existence." You rogue of all rogues, you speak of the yearning of contemporary humanity; but you also know what sort of ghost will stand at the end of this maturity of humanity as the result of that intellectual development—disgust. Things stand in a state of visible wretchedness, but they will get even more wretched, "before our eyes the Antichrist reaches out further and further around him"—but things *must* be so, thing *must* come about this way, because for all that we are on the best route to disgust with all existing things. "Thus, go forward vigorously into the world process as a worker in the vineyard of the Lord, for the process is the only thing which can lead to redemption."

The vineyard of the Lord! The process! For redemption! Who does not see and hear the historical culture which knows the word "becoming" only as it intentionally disguises itself in a misshapen parody, as it expresses through the grotesque grimacing mask held up in front of its face the most wilful things about itself! For what does this last mischievous summons to the workers in the vineyard essentially want from them? In what work are they to strive vigorously forwards? Or, to ask the question another way, what has the historically educated man, the modern fanatic swimming and drowning in the flood of becoming, still left to do, in order to reap that disgust, the expensive grapes of that vineyard? He has to do nothing other than continue to live as he has been living, to continue loving what he has loved, to continue to hate what he has hated, and to continue reading the newspapers which he has been reading. For him there is only *one* sin, to live differently from the way he has been living. But we are told the way he has been living with the excessive clarity of something written in stone by that famous page with the sentences in large print, in which the entire contemporary cultural rabble kingdom is caught up in a blind rapture and a frenzy of delight, because they believe they read their own justification, indeed, their own justification in the light of the apocalypse. For the unconscious writer of parody has required of each one of them "the complete dedication of his personality to the world process in pursuit of its goal, for the sake of the world's redemption," or still more pellucid, "the approval of the will to live is proclaimed as right only provisionally, for only in the full dedication to life and its pains, not in cowardly renunciation and drawing back, is there something to achieve for the world process," "the striving for individual denial of the will is just as foolish and useless, even more foolish, than suicide." "The thinking reader will also understand without further suggestions how a practical philosophy built on these principles would look and that such a philosophy cannot contain any falling apart but only the full reconciliation with life."

The thinking reader will understand it. And people could misunderstand Hartmann! How unspeakably amusing it is that people misunderstand him! Should contemporary Germans be very sensitive? A trusty Englishman noticed their lack of a Delicacy of Perception, and even dared to say "in the German mind there does seem to be something splay, something blunt-edged, unhandy and infelicitous" Would the great German writer of parodies really contradict him? In fact, according to Hartmann's explanation, we are approaching "that ideal condition, where the race of mankind consciously makes his own history." But obviously we are quite far from that state, perhaps even more ideal, where humanity reads Hartmann's book with awareness. If that state ever arrives, then no person will let the word

"World process" pass his lips any more, without these lips breaking into a smile. For with that phrase people will remember the time when Hartmann's parodying gospel with its stolidly middle-class notion of that "German mind," and with "the distorted seriousness of the owl," as Goethe puts it, was listened to, absorbed, disputed, honoured, publicized, and canonized.

But the world must go forward. The ideal condition cannot be dreamed up; it must be fought for and won. Only through joy does the way go to redemption, to redemption from that misunderstood owl-like seriousness. The time will come in which people wisely refrain from all constructions of the world process or even of human history, a time in which people in general no longer consider the masses but once again think about individuals who construct a sort of bridge over the chaotic storm of becoming. These people do not set out some sort of process, but live timelessly and contemporaneously, thanks to history which permits such a combination. They live like the republic of geniuses, about which Schopenhauer once explained that one giant shouts out to another across the barren intervals of time, and undisturbed by the wanton and noisy midgets who creeparound them, the giants continue their lofty spiritual conversation. The task of history is to be a mediator between them and thus to provide an opportunity and the energies for the development of greatness. No, the *goal of humanity* cannot finally be anywhere but in *its greatest examples*.

By contrast, our comic person naturally states with that wonderful dialectic, just as worthy of admiration as its admirers, "With the idea of this development it would be inconsistent to ascribe to the world process an infinite length of time in the past, because then each and every imaginable development must have already been gone through; that, however, is not the case (O you rascal). And we are no more able to assign to the process an infinite future period. Both of these raise the idea of development to a final goal (o, once again, you rascal) and makes the world process like the water drawing of the Danaids. The complete victory of the logical over the illogical (O, you rascal of all rascals), however, must coincide with the temporal end of the world process, the day of judgement." No, you lucidly mocking spirit, as long as the illogical still prevails to the extent it does today, for example, as long as people can still talk of the "world process" with a common understanding, in the way you talk, judgement day is still a long way off. For it is still too joyful on this earth; many illusions are still blooming (for example, the illusion of your contemporaries about you). We are not yet sufficiently ripe to be flung back into your nothingness. For we believe that things here will get even more amusing when people first begin to understand you, you misunderstood unconscious man. However, if in spite of this, disgust should come with power, just as you have predicted to your readers, if you should be right in your description of your present and future (and no one has hated both with such disgust as you have) then I am happily prepared to vote with the majority, in the way you have proposed, that next Saturday evening at twelve o'clock precisely your world will go under, and our decree may conclude that from tomorrow on there will be no more time and no newspaper will appear any more. However, perhaps the result will fail to materialize, and we have made our decree in vain.

Bit then at any rate we will not lack the time for a beautiful experiment. We take a balance scale and put in one scale pan Hartmann's unconsciousness and in the other Hartmann's world process. There are people who think that they will both weigh the same, for in each scale pan would lie an equally poor quotation and an equally good jest. When people first come to understand Hartmann's jest, then no one will use Hartmann's talk of "world process" as anything but a joke. In fact, it is high time we moved forward to proclaim satirical malice against the dissipation of the historical sense, against the excessive pleasure in the process at the expense of being and living, against the senseless shifting of all perspectives. And in praise of the author of the Philosophy of the Unconscious it should always be repeated that he was the first to succeed in registering keenly the ridiculousness of the idea of the "world process" and to allow an even keener appreciation of that ridiculousness through the particular seriousness of his treatment. Why the "world" is there, why "humanity" is there—these should not concern us at all for the time being. For it may be that we want to make a joke. The presumptuousness of the small human worm is simultaneously the funniest and the most joyful thing on this earthly stage. But why you, as an individual, are there, that is something I am asking you. And if no one else can say it for you, then at least try once to justify the sense of your existence, as it were, *a posteriori* by establishing for yourself a purpose, a final goal, a "To this end," and a high and noble "To this end." If you are destroyed by this, well, I know no better purpose for life than to die in service of the great and the impossible, *animae magnae prodigus [a generous man with a great spirit]*.

If by contrast the doctrine of the sovereign becoming, of the fluidity of all ideas, types, and styles, of the lack of all cardinal differences between man and animal (doctrines which I consider true but deadly) are foisted on people for another generation with the frenzied instruction which is now customary, then it should take no one by surprise if people destroy themselves in egotistical trifles and misery, ossifying themselves in their self-absorption, initially falling apart and ceasing to be a people. Then, in place of this condition, perhaps systems of individual egotism, alliances for the systematic larcenous exploitation of those non-members of the alliance and similar creations of utilitarian nastiness will step forward onto the future scene. Let people just proceed to prepare these creations, to write history from the standpoint of the *masses* and to seek for those laws in it which are to be inferred from the needs of these masses, and for the laws of motion of the lowest clay and loam layers of society. To me, the masses seem to be worth a glance in only in three respects: first as blurred copies of great men, presented on bad paper with worn out printing plates, then as the resistance against the great men, and finally as working implements of the great. For the rest, let the devil and statistics carry them off! How might statistics demonstrate that there could be laws in history? Laws? Yes, statistics prove how coarse and disgustingly uniform the masses are. Are we to call the effects of the powerful forces of stupidity, mimicry, love, and hunger laws?

Now, we are willing to concede that point, but by the same token the principle then is established that as far as there are laws in history, they are worth nothing and history is worth nothing. However, precisely this sort of history nowadays is generally esteemed, the history which takes the large mass tendencies as the important and principal thing in history and considers all great men only like the clearest examples of bubbles which become visible in the watery flood. Thus, the mass is to produce greatness out of itself, and chaos is to produce order from itself. At the end, of course, the hymn is sung to the productive masses. Everything which has preoccupied such masses for a long time is then called "Great" and, as people say, "a historical power" has come into being. But is that not a case of quite deliberately exchanging quantity and quality? When the podgy masses have found some idea or other (for example, a religious idea) quite adequate, has tenaciously defended it, and dragged it along for centuries, then, and only then, the discoverer and founder of that idea is to be great. But why? The most noble and highest things have no effect at all on the masses. The historical success of Christianity, its historical power, tenacity, and duration, all that fortunately proves nothing with respect to the greatness of its founder. Basically, that would act as a proof against him. But between him and that historical success lies a very earthly and dark layer of passion, error, greed for power and honour, the persisting powers of the *imperium romanum*, a layer from which Christianity acquired that earthy taste and scrap of ground which made possible its perseverance in this world and, as it were, gave it its durability.

Greatness should not depend upon success. Demosthenes had greatness, although at the same time he had no success. The purest and most genuine followers of Christianity were always more likely to put their worldly success, their so-called "historical power," into question and to restrict it rather than to promote it. For they trained themselves to stand outside "the world" and did not worry themselves about the "progress of the Christian idea." For this reason, for the most part they are also unknown to history and have remained unnamed. To express this in a Christian manner: in this way the devil is the regent of the world and the master of success and progress. He is in all historical powers the essential power, and so it will substantially remain, although it may for some time sound quite painful to ears which have become accustomed to the idolatry of success and historical power. For in this matter these people have practised giving things new names and have rechristened even the devil. It is certainly a time of great danger: human beings seem to be close to discovering that the egotism of the individual, the group, or the masses was the lever of historical movements at all times. However, at the same time, people are not at all worried by this discovery. On the contrary, people declaim: Egotism is to be our God. With this new faith people are on the point of erecting, with the clearest of intentions, future history on egotism. But it is only to be a clever egotism subject to a few limitations, in order that it may consolidate itself in an enduring way. It is the sort of egotism which studies history just in order to acquaint itself with unclever egotism.

Through this study people have learned that the state has received a very special mission in the established world system of egotism: the state is to become the patron of all clever egotism, so that, with its military and police forces, it may protect against the frightening outbreak of the unintelligent egotism. For the same purpose history, that is, the history of animals and human beings, is also stirred into the popular masses and working classes, who are dangerous because they are unintelligent, for people know that a small grain of historical education is capable of breaking the rough and stupefied instincts and desires or to divert them into the path of improved egotism. *In summa*: people are paying attention now, to express oneself with E. von Hartmann, " to a deliberate looking into the future for a practical homely structure in their earthly home region." The same writer calls such a period the "full maturity of mankind" and makes fun about what is now called "Man," as if with that term one is to understand only the sober selfish person; in the same way he also prophecies that after such a period of full maturity there comes to this "Man" an appropriate old age, but apparently only with this idea to vent his ridicule on our contemporary old men. For he speaks of the mature peacefulness with which they "review all the chaotic stormy suffering of their past lives and understand the vanity of the previously assumed goals of their striving." No, a maturity of this sly egotism of a historical culture is appropriate for an old age of hostile craving and disgraceful clinging to life and then a final act, with its

last scene of all
That ends this strange eventful history,
Is second childhood and mere oblivion,
Sans teeth, sans eyes, sans taste, sans everything.

Whether the dangers of our life and our culture now come from these desolate, toothless and tasteless old men, whether they come from those so-called "Men" of Hartmann's, in opposition to both we wish to hold on with our teeth to our right to our *youth* and not to grow tired of defending, in our youth, the future against these forceful portrayers of the future. In this fight, however, we would have to acknowledge a particularly unpleasant perception: *that people intentionally promote the excesses of the historical sense from which the present time suffers, they encourage them, and they use them.*

However, people use history against the young, in order to train them for that maturity of egotism which is striven for everywhere; people use it to break the natural aversion of youth through a transfiguring, that is to say, a magically scientific illumination of that manly-effeminate egotism. Yes, people know what a certain predominance of history is capable of; people know it only too well: to uproot the strongest instincts of youth, fire, defiance, forgetting of the self, to dampen down the heat of their sense of right and wrong, to hold back or repress the desire to mature slowly with the contrary desire to be finished quickly, to be useful and productive, to infect the honesty and boldness of the feelings with doubts. Indeed, history is itself capable of deceiving the young about their most beautiful privilege, about their power to cultivate in themselves with complete conviction a great idea and to allow an even greater idea to grow forth out of it. A certain excess of history is capable of all this. We have seen it. And this is the reason: through its incessant shifting of the horizons of significance, through the elimination of a surrounding atmosphere, it no longer allows a person to perceive and to act *unhistorically*. He then draws himself from the infinity of his horizon back into himself, into the smallest egotistical region and there must wither away and dry up. He probably achieves cleverness in this, but never wisdom. He permits himself inner conversations, calculates, and gets along well with the facts, does not boil over, winks, and understands how to seek out his own advantage or that of his party amid the advantages and disadvantages of strangers; he forgets superfluous modesty and thus step by step becomes a "Man" and an "Old Man" on the Hartmann model. But he *should* become this—that is the precise sense of the cynical demand nowadays for "the complete dedication of the personality to the world process," so far as his goal is concerned, for the sake of the redemption of the world, as that rascal E. Hartmann assures us. Now, the will and goal of these Hartmann "men" and "old men" is indeed hardly the redemption of the world. Certainly the world would be more redeemed if it were redeemed from these men and old men. For then the kingdom of youth would come.

X

Imagining this reign of *youth*, I cry out "Land, land! Enough and more than enough of the passionate seeking and the wandering passage on the dark alien seas!" Now finally a coast reveals itself. Whatever it may be, we must land on it. The worst emergency port is better than returning to staggering in hopeless infinite scepticism. If now we only hold on to the land, we will later find the good havens and ease the approach for those who come later. This journey was dangerous and exciting. How far we are now from the calm contemplation with which we first saw our ship set out to sea. By investigating the dangers of history, we have found ourselves exposed to all these dangers as strongly as possible. We ourselves bear the traces of that illness which has come over humanity in recent times as a result of an excess of history. For example, this very treatise shows its modern character, the character of the weak personality (which I will not conceal from myself) in the intemperance of its criticism, the immaturity of its humanity, the frequent transitions from irony to cynicism, from pride to scepticism. Nevertheless I trust in the inspiring power which, rather than my genius, controls the vessel: I trust in *youth*, that it has led me correctly when it requires from me now a *protest against the historical education of young modern people* and if the protester demands that human beings above all learn to live and to use history only in *the service of the life which he has learned*. People must be young to understand this protest. In fact, among the contemporary grey-haired types of our present youth, one can hardly be young enough still to feel what is here essentially being protested against.

To help people understand this point I will use an example. In Germany it is not much longer than a hundred years ago that a natural instinct for what people call poetry arose in a few young people. Do people think that the previous generations up to that time would never have spoken of that art, inwardly strange and unnatural to them? We know the opposite is true: they thought about "poetry" with loving passion, wrote and argued about it with words, words, and more words. The appearance of that revival of words for living was not the immediate death of those word makers. In a certain sense they are still alive, because if, as Gibbon says, for a world to go under takes not just time but plenty of time, then in Germany, the "land of gradual change," for a false idea to be destroyed takes more than time; it takes a great deal of time. Today there are perhaps a hundred people more than a hundred years ago who know what poetry is; perhaps one hundred years from now there will be another hundred people more who in the meantime have also learned what culture is and that the Germans up to this point have had no culture, no matter how much they may talk and boast about it. For them the very general contentment of the Germans with their "culture" would seem just as incredible and stupid as the formerly acknowledged classicism of Gottsched or the appraisal of Ramler as a German Pindar seem to us. They will perhaps judge that this culture has been only a sort of knowledge about culture and, in addition, a completely false and superficial knowledge. I say false and superficial because people endured the contradiction of life and knowledge, for they did not see anything characteristic of a truly cultured people: that the culture can only grow up and blossom forth out of living. By contrast, with the Germans culture is put up like a paper flower or poured out like a sugar drink. Therefore it must always remain untruthful and infertile.

The German education of the young, however, begins directly from this false and barren idea of culture. Its end goal, imagined in all purity and loftiness, is not at all the freely educated man, but the scholar, the scientific person, indeed, the scientific person who is useful as early as possible, the person who sets himself apart from life in order to recognize it clearly. The product of this education, considered in a correct empirically general way, is the historically and aesthetically educated Philistine, the precocious and freshly wise chatterer about state, church, and art, the sensorium for thousands of sensations, the inexhaustible stomach which nevertheless does not know what an honest hunger and thirst are. The fact that an education with this goal and result is an unnatural education is felt only by the person who has not yet completed it; it is felt only by the instinct of the young, because they still have the instinct of nature, which is first artificially and powerfully broken through that education. But the person who wants to break this education in its turn must assist the young in expressing themselves. He must shine the bright light of ideas to illuminate their unconscious resistance and turn that into a conscious and loudly uttered consciousness. How is he to reach such a strange goal?

Above all through the fact that he destroys a superstition, the faith in the *necessity* of that method of education. People think that there would be no other possibility than our contemporary highly tiresome reality. Just let someone examine the essential literature of the higher schooling and education system in the last decades exactly on this point. For all the varieties of proposals and for all the intensity of the opposition, the examiner will to his astonishment realize how uniform the thinking is about the entire purpose of education, how thoughtlessly people assume that the present result, the "educated person," as the term is now understood, is a necessary and reasonable fundamental basis for that wider education. That monotonous orthodoxy would sound something like this: the young person has to begin with a knowledge of culture, not at first with a knowledge of life, and even less with life and experience themselves. Moreover, this knowledge about culture as historical knowledge is poured over or stirred into the youth; that is, his head is filled up with a monstrous number of ideas derived from extremely indirect knowledge of past times and peoples, not from the immediate contemplation of living. His desire to experience something for himself and to feel growing in him a coordinated and living system of his own experiences—such a desire is narcotized and, as it were, made drunk through the opulent deceptions about matters of fact, as if it were possible in a few years to sum up in oneself the highest and most remarkable experiences of all times, especially of the greatest ages. It is precisely this insane procedure which leads our young developing artists into the halls of culture and galleries instead of into the workshop of a master and, above all, into the extraordinary workshops of the extraordinary master craftswoman Nature. Yes, as if people were able to predict their ideas and arts, their actual life's work, as cursory strollers in the history of past times. Yes, as if life itself were not a craft which must be learned continuously from the basic material and practised without special treatment, if it is not to allow bunglers and chatterers to be produced

Plato considered it necessary that the first generation of his new society (in the perfect state) would be brought up with the help of a powerful *necessary lie*. The children were to learn to believe that they had all already lived a long time dreaming under the earth, where they had been properly kneaded and formed by nature's master worker. It was impossible to have any effect against this work of the gods. It is to stand as an inviolable law of nature that the person who is born a philosopher has gold in his body, the person who is born as a guard has only silver, and the person who is born as a worker has iron and bronze. Since it is not possible to mix these metals, Plato explains, then it should not be possible to overthrow or mix up the order of classes. The faith in the *aeterna veritas* [*eternal truth*] of this order is the basis of the new education and thus of the new state. The modern German similarly believes now in the *aeterna veritas* of his education, of his style of culture. Nevertheless, this faith would collapse, as the Platonic state would have collapsed, if in opposition to the necessary lie there was set up a *necessary truth*: the German has no culture, because he can have nothing whatsoever on the basis of his education. He wants the flowers without roots and stalk. So he wants them in vain. That is the simple truth, unpleasant and gross, a correct necessary truth.

In this necessary truth, however, *our first generation* must be educated. Certainly they suffer from it with the greatest difficulty, for they must educate themselves through it, in fact, divided against themselves, to new habits and a new nature derived out of old and previous nature and habits, so that they might be able to say with the ancient Spaniards: "Efienda me Dios de my," God, defend me from myself, that is, from the nature already instilled into me. They must taste that truth drop by drop, as if sampling a bitter and powerful medicine. Each individual of this generation must overcome himself, to judge for himself what he might more easily endure as a general judgement concerning an entire age: we are without education, even more, we are ruined for living, for correct and simple seeing and hearing, for the fortunate grasping of what is closest at hand and natural, and we have up to this moment not yet even the basis of a culture, because we ourselves are not convinced that we have a genuine life within us. Fractured and fallen apart, in everything carved up mechanically into an inner and an outer half, saturated with ideas like dragons' teeth producing dragon ideas, thus suffering from the sickness of words and without trust in any unique sensation which is not yet franked with words, as such a non-living and yet uncannily lively factory of ideas and words, I still perhaps have the right to say about myself *cogito, ergo sum* [*I am thinking; therefore, I am*], but not *vivo, ergo cogito* [*I am living; therefore, I am thinking*]. That empty "Being", not that full and green "Living" is ensured for me. My original feeling only guarantees me that I am a thinking thing, not that I am a living essence, that I am not *animal*, but at most a *cogital*. First give me life; then I will make a culture out of it for you!—so shouts each individual of this first generation, and all these individuals will recognize each other from this call. Who will present this life to them?

No god and no human being: only their own *youth* unleashes this life, and with it you will liberate life for yourself. For it only lay hidden in a prison. It has not yet withered away and died—inquire of yourself!

But this unbridled life is sick and must be healed. It is ailing from many ills. Not only does it suffer from the memory of its fetters; it suffers from what is here our principal concern, from the *historical sickness*. The excess of history has seized the plastic force of life. It understands no more to make use of the past as a powerful nourishment. The evil is fearsome, and nevertheless if youth did not have the clairvoyant gift of nature, then no one would know that that is an evil and that a paradise of health has been lost. This same youth surmises, however, also with the powerful healing instinct of this same nature, how this paradise can be won back. It knows the juices for wounds and the medicines to combat the historical sickness, to combat the excess of the historical. What are they called?

Now, people should not be surprised: they are the names of poisons: the antidotes against the historical are called *the unhistorical and the super-historical*. With these names we turn back to the start of our examination and to its close.

With the phrase "the unhistorical" I designate the art and the power of being able *to forget* and to enclose oneself in a horizon with borders; "super-historical" I call the powers which divert the gaze from what is developing back to what gives existence an eternal and unchanging character, to *art* and *religion*. *Science* (for it is science which would talk about poisons) sees in that force, in these powers opposing forces, for it maintains that only the observation of things is true and right, the scientific way of considering things, which everywhere sees what has come into being as something historical and never as something eternally living. Science lives in an inner contradiction against the eternalizing powers of art and religion just as much as it hates forgetfulness, the death of knowledge, when it seeks to remove all limitations of horizons and to hurl human beings into an infinite sea without frontiers, a sea of light waves of acknowledged becoming.

If he only could live there! As the cities collapse in an earthquake and become desolate and the human being, trembling and in haste, erects his house on volcanic ground, so life breaks apart and becomes weak and dispirited when the *earthquake of ideas* which science arouses takes from a person the basis of all his certainty and rest, his faith in the eternally permanent. Is life to rule over knowledge now, over science, or is knowledge to rule over life? Which of the two forces is the higher and the decisive one? No one will have any doubt: life is the higher, the ruling power, for knowledge which destroyed life would in the process have destroyed itself. Knowledge presupposes life and has the same interest in preserving life which every being has in its own continuing existence. So science needs a higher supervision and control. A *doctrine of a healthy life* is positioned close beside science, and a principle of this doctrine of health would sound like this: the unhistorical and the super-historical are the natural counter-measures against the excess cancerous growth of history on life, against the historical sickness. It is probable that we, the historically ill, also have to suffer from the counter measures. But the fact that we suffer from them is no proof against the correctness of the course of treatment we have chosen.

And here I recognize the mission of that *youth*, that first generation of fighters and dragon slayers, which brings forth a more fortunate and more beautiful culture and humanity, without having more of this future happiness and future beauty than a promise-filled premonition. These youth will suffer from the evil and the counter-measures simultaneously, and nevertheless they believe they may boast of a more powerful health and in general a more natural nature than their previous generations, the educated "Men" and "Old Men" of the present. However, their mission is to shake the ideas which this present holds about "health" and "culture" and to develop contempt and hatred against such hybrid monstrous ideas. The most strongly guaranteed mark of their own stronger health is to be precisely the fact that they, I mean these youth, themselves can use no idea, no party slogan from the presently circulating currency of words and ideas, as a designation of their being, but are convinced only by a power acting in it, a power which fights, eliminates, and cuts into pieces, and by an always heightened sense of life in every good hour. People may dispute the fact that these youth already have culture, but for what young person would this be a reproach? People may speak against their crudeness and immoderation, but they are not yet old and wise enough to be content; above all they do not need to feign any ready-made culture to defend and enjoy all the comforts and rights of youth, especially the privilege of a braver spontaneous honesty and the rousing consolation of hope.

Of these hopeful people I know that they understand all these generalities at close hand and in their own most personal experience will translate them into a personally thought-out teaching for themselves. The others may for the time being perceive nothing but covered over bowls, which could also really be empty, until, surprised one day, they see with their own eyes that the bowls are full and that attacks, demands, living impulses, passions lay mixed in and impressed into these generalities, which could not lie hidden in this way for a long time. I refer these doubters to time, which brings all things to light, and, in conclusion, I turn my attention to that society of those who hope, in order to explain to them in an allegory the progress and outcome of their healing, their salvation from the historical sickness, and thus their own history, up to the point where they will be again healthy enough to undertake a new history and to make use of the past under the mastery of life in a threefold sense, that is, monumental, or antiquarian, or critical. At that point of time they will be less knowledgeable than the "educated" of the present, for they will have forgotten a good deal and even have lost the pleasure of looking for what those educated ones above all wish to know, in general still in order to look back. Their distinguishing marks, from the point of view of those educated ones, are precisely their "lack of education," their indifference and reserve with respect to many famous men, even with respect to many good things. But they have become, at this final point of their healing, once again *men* and have ceased to be human-like aggregates—that is something! There are still hopes! Are you not laughing at that in your hearts, you hopeful ones!

And, you will ask, How do we come to that end point? The Delphic god shouts out to you, at the very start of your trek to that goal, his aphorism: "Know thyself." It is a difficult saying; for that god "hides nothing and announces nothing, but only points the way," as Heraclitus has said. But what direction is he indicating to you?

There were centuries when the Greeks found themselves in a danger similar to the one in which we find ourselves, that is, the danger of destruction from being swamped by what is foreign and past, from "history." The Greeks never lived in proud isolation; their "culture" was for a long time much more a chaos of foreign, Semitic, Babylonian, Lydian, and Egyptian forms and ideas, and their religion a real divine struggle of the entire Orient, something similar to the way "German culture" and religion are now a self-struggling chaos of all foreign lands and all prehistory. Nevertheless Hellenic culture did not become an aggregate, thanks to that Apollonian saying. The Greeks learned gradually *to organize the chaos* because, in accordance with the Delphic teaching, they directed their thoughts back to themselves, that is, to their real needs, and let the apparent needs die off. So they seized possession of themselves again. They did not remain long the over-endowed heirs and epigones of the entire Orient. After an arduous battle with themselves, through the practical interpretation of that saying, they became the most fortunate enrichers and increasers of the treasure they had inherited and the firstlings and models for all future national cultures.

This is a parable for every individual among us. He must organize the chaos in himself by recalling in himself his own real needs. His honesty, his better and more genuine character must now and then struggle against what will be constantly repeated, relearned, and imitated. He begins then to grasp that culture can still be something other than *a decoration of life*, that is, basically always only pretence and disguise; for all ornamentation covers over what is decorated. So the Greek idea of culture reveals itself to him, in opposition to the Roman, the idea of culture as a new and improved nature, without inner and outer, without pretence and convention, culture as a unanimity of living, thinking, appearing, and willing. Thus, he learns out of his own experience that it was the higher power of *moral* nature through which the Greeks attained their victory over all other cultures and that each increase of truthfulness must also be a demand in preparation for *true* culture. This truthfulness may also occasionally seriously harm the idea of culture esteemed at the time; it even may be able to assist a totally decorative culture to collapse.

The Question Concerning Technology

Martin Heidegger

In what follows we shall be *questioning* concerning technology. Questioning builds a way. We would be advised, therefore, above all to pay heed to the way, and not to fix our attention on isolated sentences and topics. The way is a way of thinking. All ways of thinking, more or less perceptibly, lead through language in a manner that is extraordinary. We shall be questioning concerning *technology*, and in so doing we should like to prepare a free relationship to it. The relationship will be free, if it opens our human existence to the essence of technology.[1] When we can respond to this essence, we shall be able to experience the technological within its own bounds.

Technology is not equivalent to the essence of technology. When we are seeking the essence of "tree," we have to become aware that That which pervades every tree, as tree, is not itself a tree that can be encountered among all the other trees.

---

1   "Essence" is the traditional translation of the German noun *Wesen*. One of Heidegger's principal aims in this essay is to seek the true meaning of essence through or by way of the "correct" meaning. He will later show that *Wesen* does not simply mean *what* something is, but that it means, further, the way in which something pursues its course, the way in which it remains through time as what it is. Heidegger writes elsewhere that the noun *Wesen* does not mean *quidditas* originally, but rather "enduring as presence" *(das Währen als Gegenwart)*. (See *An Introduction to Metaphysics*, trans. Ralph Manheim [New York: Doubleday, 1961], p. 59.) *Wesen* as a noun derives from the verb *wesen*, which is seldom used as such in modern German. The verb survives primarily in inflected forms of the verb *sein* (to be) and in such words as the adjective *anwesend* (present). The old verbal forms from which *wesen* stems meant to tarry or dwell. Heidegger repeatedly identifies *wesen* as "the same as *währen* [to last or endure]." (See p. 30 below and SR 161.) As a verb, *wesen* will usually be translated here with "to come to presence," a rendering wherein the meaning "endure" should be strongly heard. Occasionally it will be translated "to essence," and its gerund will be rendered with "essencing." The noun *Wesen* will regularly be translated "essence" until Heidegger's explanatory discussion is reached. Thereafter, in this and the succeeding essays, it will often be translated with "coming to presence." In relation to all these renderings, the reader should bear in mind a point that is of fundamental importance to Heidegger, namely, that the root of *wesen*, with its meaning "to dwell," provides one integral component in the meaning of the verb *sein* (to be). (CL *An Introduction to Metaphysics*, p. 59.)

"The Question Concerning Technology" [pp. 3–35] from *The Question Concerning Technology and Other Essays* by Martin Heidegger. Translated and with an Introduction by William Lovitt. English translation copyright © 1977 by Harper & Row, Publishers, Inc. Reprinted by permission of HarperCollins Publishers.

Likewise, the essence of technology is by no means anything technological. Thus we shall never experience our relationship to the essence of technology so long as we merely conceive and push forward the technological, put up with it, or evade it. Everywhere we remain unfree and chained to technology, whether we passionately affirm or deny it. But we are delivered over to it in the worst possible way when we regard it as something neutral; for this conception of it,[2] to which today we particularly like to do homage, makes us utterly blind to the essence of technology.

According to ancient doctrine, the essence of a thing is considered to be *what* the thing is. We ask the question concerning technology when we ask what it is. Everyone knows the two statements that answer our question. One says: Technology is a means to an end. The other says: Technology is a human activity. The two definitions of technology belong together. For to posit ends and procure and utilize the means to them is a human activity. The manufacture and utilization of equipment, tools, and machines, the manufactured and used things themselves, and the needs and ends that they serve, all belong to what technology is. The whole complex of these contrivances is technology. Technology itself is a contrivance, or, in Latin, an *instrumentum*.[3]

The current conception of technology, according to which it is a means and a human activity, can therefore be called the instrumental and anthropological definition of technology.

Who would ever deny that it is correct? It is in obvious conformity with what we are envisioning when we talk about technology. The instrumental definition of technology is indeed so uncannily correct that it even holds for modern technology, of which, in other respects, we maintain with some justification that it is, in contrast to the older handwork technology, something completely different and therefore new. Even the power plant with its turbines and generators is a man-made means to an end established by man. Even the jet aircraft and the high frequency apparatus are means to ends. A radar station is of course less simple than a weather vane. To be sure, the construction of a high-frequency apparatus requires the interlocking of various processes of technical-industrial production. And certainly a sawmill in a secluded valley of the Black Forest is a primitive means compared with the hydroelectric plant in the Rhine River.

But this much remains correct: modern technology too is a means to an end. That is why the instrumental conception of technology conditions every attempt to bring man into the right relation to technology. Everything depends on our manipulating technology in the proper manner as a means. We will, as we say "get" technology "spiritually in hand."

---

2   "Conception" here translates the noun *Vorstellung*. Elsewhere in this volume, *Vorstellung* will usually he translated by "representation," and its related verb *vorstellen* by "to represent." Both "conception" and "representation" should suggest a placing or setting-up-before. Cf. the discussion of *Vorstellung* in AWP 131–132.

3   *Instrumentum* signifies that which functions to heap or build up or to arrange. Heidegger here equates it with the noun *Einrichtung*, translated "contrivance," which can also mean arrangement, adjustment, furnishing, or equipment. In accordance with his dictum that the true must be sought by way of the correct, Heidegger here anticipates with his identification of technology as an *instrumentum* and an *Einrichtung* his later "true" characterization of technology in terms of setting-in-place, ordering, Enframing, and standing-reserve.

We will master it. The will to mastery becomes all the more urgent the more technology threatens to slip from human control.

But suppose now that technology were no mere means, how would it stand with the will to master it? Yet we said, did we not, that the instrumental definition of technology is correct? To be sure. The correct always fixes upon something pertinent in whatever is under consideration. However, in order to be correct, this fixing by no means need to uncover the thing in question in its essence. Only at the point where such an uncovering happens does the true come to pass.[4] For that reason the merely correct is not yet the true. Only the true brings us into a free relationship with that which concerns us from out of its essence. Accordingly, the correct instrumental definition of technology still does not show us technology's essence. In order that we may arrive at this, or at least come close to it, we must seek the true by way of the correct. We must ask: What is the instrumental itself? Within what do such things as means and end belong? A means is that whereby something is effected and thus attained. Whatever has an effect as its consequence is called a cause. But not only that by means of which something else is effected is a cause. The end in keeping with which the kind of means to be used is determined is also considered a cause. Wherever ends are pursued and means are employed, wherever instrumentality reigns, there reigns causality.

For centuries philosophy has taught that there are four causes: (1) the *causa materialis*, the material, the matter out of which, for example, a silver chalice is made; (2) the *causa formalis*, the form, the shape into which the material enters; (3) the *causa finalis*, the end, for example, the sacrificial rite in relation to which the chalice required is determined as to its form and matter; (4) the *causa efficiens*, which brings about the effect that is the finished, actual chalice, in this instance, the silversmith. What technology is, when represented as a means, discloses itself when we trace instrumentality back to fourfold causality.

But suppose that causality, for its part, is veiled in darkness with respect to what it is? Certainly for centuries we have acted as though the doctrine of the four causes had fallen from heaven as a truth as clear as daylight. But it might be that the time has come to ask, Why are there just four causes? In relation to the aforementioned four, what does "cause" really mean? From whence does it come that the causal *character* of the four causes is so unifiedly determined that they belong together?

So long as we do not allow ourselves to go into these questions, causality, and with it instrumentality, and with the latter the accepted definition of technology, remain obscure and groundless.

For a long time we have been accustomed to representing cause as that which brings something about. In this connection, to bring about means to obtain results, effects. The *causa efficiens*, but one among the four causes, sets the standard for all causality. This goes so far that we no longer even count the *causa finalis*, telic finality, as causality. *Causa, casus*, belongs to the verb *cadere*, "to fall," and means that which brings it about that something falls out as a result in such and such a way. The doctrine of the four causes goes back to Aristotle. But everything that later ages seek in Greek thought under the conception and rubric "causality," in the realm of Greek thought and for Greek thought per se has simply

---

4 "Come to pass" translates *sich ereignet*. For a discussion of the fuller meaning of the verb *ereignen*, see T 38 n. 4, 45.

nothing at all to do with bringing about and effecting. What we call cause [*Ursache*] and the Romans call *causa* is called *aition* by the Greeks, that to which something else is indebted [*das, was ein anderes verschuldet*].[5] The four causes are the ways, all belonging at once to each other, of being responsible for something else. An example can clarify this.

Silver is that out of which the silver chalice is made. As this matter (*hyle*), it is co-responsible for the chalice. The chalice is indebted to, i.e., owes thanks to, the silver for that out of which it consists. But the sacrificial vessel is indebted not only to the silver. As a chalice, that which is indebted to the silver appears in the aspect of a chalice and not in that of a brooch or a ring. Thus the sacrificial vessel is at the same time indebted to the aspect (*eidos*) of chaliceness. Both the silver into which the aspect is admitted as chalice and the aspect in which the silver appears are in their respective ways co-responsible for the sacrificial vessel.

But there remains yet a third that is above all responsible for the sacrificial vessel. It is that which in advance confines the chalice within the realm of consecration and bestowal.[6] Through this the chalice is circumscribed as sacrificial vessel. Circumscribing gives bounds to the thing. With the bounds the thing does not stop; rather from out of them it begins to be what, after production, it will be. That which gives bounds, that which completes, in this sense is called in Greek *telos*, which is all too often translated as "aim" or "purpose," and so misinterpreted. The *telos* is responsible for what as matter and for what as aspect are together co-responsible for the sacrificial vessel.

Finally there is a fourth participant in the responsibility for the finished sacrificial vessel's lying before us ready for use, i.e., the silversmith—but not at all because he, in working, brings about the finished sacrificial chalice as if it were the effect of a making; the silversmith is not a *causa efficiens*.

The Aristotelian doctrine neither knows the cause that is named by this term nor uses a Greek word that would correspond to it.

The silversmith considers carefully and gathers together the three aforementioned ways of being responsible and indebted. To consider carefully [*überlegen*] is in Greek *legein, logos*. *Legein* is rooted in *apophainesthai*, to bring forward into appearance. The silversmith is co-responsible as that from whence the sacrificial vessel's bringing forth and resting-in-self take and retain their first departure. The three previously mentioned ways of being responsible owe thanks to the pondering of the silversmith for the "that" and the "how" of their coming into appearance and into play for the production of the sacrificial vessel.

Thus four ways of being responsible hold sway in the sacrificial vessel that lies ready before us. They differ from one another, yet they belong together. What unites them from the

---

5 *Das, was ein anderes verschuldet* is a quite idomatic expression that here would mean to many German readers "that which is the cause of something else." The verb *verschulden* actually has a wide range of meanings—to be indebted, to owe, to be guilty, to be responsible for or to, to cause. Heidegger intends to awaken all these meanings and to have connotations of mutual interdependence sound throughout this passage.

6 Literally, "confines into"—the German preposition *in* with the accusative. Heidegger often uses this construction in ways that are unusual in German, as they would be in English. It will ordinarily be translated here by "within" so as to distinguish it from "in" used to translate *in* with the dative.

beginning? In what does this playing in unison of the four ways of being responsible play? What is the source of the unity of the four causes? What, after all, does this owing and being responsible mean, thought as the Greeks thought it?

Today we are too easily inclined either to understand being responsible and being indebted moralistically as a lapse, or else to construe them in terms of effecting. In either case we bar to ourselves the way to the primal meaning of that which is later called causality. So long as this way is not opened up to us we shall also fail to see what instrumentality, which is based on causality, actually is.

In order to guard against such misinterpretations of being responsible and being indebted, let us clarify the four ways of being responsible in terms of that for which they are responsible. According to our example, they are responsible for the silver chalice's lying ready before us as a sacrificial vessel. Lying before and lying ready (*hypokeisthai*) characterize the presencing of something that presences. The four ways of being responsible bring something into appearance. They let it come forth into presencing [*An-wesen*].[7] They set it free to that place and so start it on its way, namely, into its complete arrival. The principal characteristic of being responsible is this starting something on its way into arrival. It is in the sense of such a starting something on its way into arrival that being responsible is an occasioning or an inducing to go forward [*Ver-an-lassen*].[8] On the basis of a look at what the Greeks experienced in being responsible, in *aitia*, we now give this verb "to occasion" a more inclusive meaning, so that it now is the name for the essence of causality thought as the Greeks thought it. The common and narrower meaning of "occasion" in contrast is nothing more than striking against and releasing, and means a kind of secondary cause within the whole of causality.

But in what, then, does the playing in unison of the four ways of occasioning play? They let what is not yet present arrive into presencing. Accordingly, they are unifiedly ruled over by a bringing that brings what presences into appearance. Plato tells us what this bringing is in a sentence from the *Symposium* (205b): *hē gar toi ek tou mē onton eis to on ionti hotōioun aitia pasa esti poiēsis*. "Every occasion for whatever passes over and goes forward into presencing from that which is not presencing is *poiēsis*, is bringing-forth [*Her-vor-bringen*]."[9]

---

7   By writing *An-wesen*, Heidegger stresses the composition of the verb *anwesen*, translated as "to presence." The verb consists of *wesen* (literally, to continue or endure) with the prepositional prefix *an-* (at, to, toward). It is man who must receive presencing, man *to* whom it comes as endurmg. Cf. *On Time and Being*, trans. Joan Stambaugh (New York: Harper & Row, 1972), p. 12.

8   *Ver-an-Iassen* is Heidegger's writing of the verb *veranlassen* in noun form, now hyphenated to being out its meaning. *Veranlassen* ordinarily means to occasion, to cause, to bring about, to call forth. Its use here relates back to the use of *anlassen* (to leave [something] on, to let loose, to set going), here translated "to start something on its way." *Anlassen* has just been similarly written as *an-lassen* so as to emphasize its composition from *lassen* (to let or leave) and *an* (to or toward). One of the functions, of the German prefix *ver-* is to intensify the force of a verb. André Préau quotes Heidegger as saying: "*Ver-an-Iassen* is more active than *an-lassen*. The *ver-*, as it were, pushes the latter toward a doing [*vers un faire*]. Cf. Martin Heidegger, *Essais et Conférences* (Paris: Gallimard, 1958), p. 16 n.

9   The full gamut of meaning for the verb *hervorbringen*, here functioning as a noun, includes to bring forth or produce, to generate or beget, to utter, to elicit. Heidegger intends that all of these nuances be heard. He

It is of utmost importance that we think bringing-forth in its full scope and at the same time in the sense in which the Greeks thought it. Not only handcraft manufacture, not only artistic and poetical bringing into appearance and concrete imagery, is a bringing-forth, *poiēsis*. *Physis* also, the arising of something from out of itself, is a bringing-forth, *poiēsis*. *Physis* is indeed *poiēsis* in the highest sense. For what presences by means of *physis* has the bursting open belonging to bringing-forth, e.g., the bursting of a blossom into bloom, in itself (*en heautōi*). In contrast, what is brought forth by the artisan or the artist, e.g., the silver chalice, has the bursting open belonging to bringing-forth not in itself, but in another (*en allōi*), in the craftsman or artist.

The modes of occasioning, the four causes, are at play, then, within bringing-forth. Through bringing-forth, the growing things of nature as well as whatever is completed through the crafts and the arts come at any given time to their appearance.

But how does bringing-forth happen, be It in nature or in handwork and art? What is the bringing-forth in which the fourfold way of occasioning plays? Occasioning has to do with the presencing [*Anwesen*] of that which at any given time comes to appearance in bringing-forth. Bringing-forth brings hither out of concealment forth into unconcealment. Bringing-forth comes to pass only insofar as something concealed comes into unconcealment. This coming rests and moves freely within what we call revealing [*das Entbergen*].¹⁰ The Greeks have the word *alētheia* for revealing. The Romans translate this with *veritas*. We say "truth" and usually understand it as the correctness of an idea.

---

hyphenates the word in order to emphasize its adverbial prefixes, *her-* (here or hither) and *vor-* (forward or forth). Heidegger elsewhere makes specific the meaning resident in *Her-vor-bringen* for him by utilizing those prefixes independently. Thus he says (translating literally), "Bringing-forthhither brings hither out of concealment, forth into unconcealment" (cf. below, p. 11); and—after identifying working (*wirken*) and *her-vor-bringen*—he says that working must be understood as "bringing *hither*—into unconcealment, *forth*—into presencing" (SR 161). Because of the awkwardness of the English phrase "to bring forth hither," it has not been possible to include in the translation of *her-vor-bringen* the nuance of meaning that *her-* provides.

10 The verb *entbergen* (to reveal) and the allied noun *Entbergung* (revealing) are unique to Heidegger. Because of the exigencies of translation, *entbergen* must usually be translated with "revealing," and the presence of *Entbergung*, which is rather infrequently used, has therefore regrettably been obscured for want of an appropriate English noun as alternative that would be sufficiently active in meaning. *Entbergen* and *Entbergung* are formed from the verb *bergen* and the verbal prefix *ent-*. Bergen means to rescue, to recover, to secure, to harbor, to conceal. *Ent-* is used in German verbs to connote in one way or another a change from an existing situation. It can mean "forth" or "out" or can connote a change that is the negating of a former condition. *Entbergen* connotes an opening out from protective concealing, a harbouring forth. For a presentation of Heidegger's central tenet that it is only as protected and preserved—and that means as that which it is, i.e., to be, see "Building Dwelling Thinking" in *Poetry, Language, Thought*, trans. Albert Hofstadter (New York: Harper & Row, 1971), p. 149, and cf. p. 25 below.

Entbergen and *Entbergung* join a family of words all formed from *bergen—verbergen* (to conceal), *Verborgenheit* (concealment), *das Verborgene* (the concealed), *Unverborgenheit* (unconcealment), *das Unverborgene* (the unconcealed)—of which Heidegger makes frequent use. The lack of viable English words sufficiently numerous to permit a similar use of but one fundamental stem has made it necessary to obscure, through the use of "reveal," the close relationship among all the words just mentioned. None of the English words used—"reveal," "conceal," "unconceal"—evinces with any adequacy the meaning resident in *bergen* itself; yet the reader should be constantly aware that the full range of connotation present in *bergen* sounds for Heidegger within all these, its derivatives

But where have we strayed to? We are questioning concerning technology, and we have arrived now at *alētheia*, at revealing. What has the essence of technology to do with revealing? The answer: everything. For every bringing-forth is grounded in revealing. Bringing-forth, indeed, gathers within itself the four modes of occasioning—causality—and rules them throughout. Within its domain belong end and means, belongs instrumentality.[11] Instrumentality is considered to be the fundamental characteristic of technology. If we inquire, step by step, into what technology, represented as means, actually is, then we shall arrive at revealing. The possibility of all productive manufacturing lies in revealing.

Technology is therefore no mere means. Technology is a way of revealing. If we give heed to this, then another whole realm for the essence of technology will open itself up to us. It is the realm of revealing, i.e., of truth.[12]

This prospect strikes us as strange. Indeed, it should do so, should do so as persistently as possible and with so much urgency that we will finally take seriously the simple question of what the name "technology" means. The word stems from the Greek. *Technikon* means that which belongs to *technē*. We must observe two things with respect to the meaning of this word. One is that *technē* is the name not only for the activities and skills of the craftsman, but also for the arts of the mind and the fine arts. *Technē* belongs to bringing-forth, to *poiēsis*; it is something poietic.

The other point that we should observe with regard to *technē* is even more important. From earliest times until Plato the word *technē* is linked with the word *epistēmē*. Both words are names for knowing in the widest sense. They mean to be entirely at home in something, to understand and be expert in it. Such knowing provides an opening up. As an opening up it is a revealing. Aristotle, in a discussion of special importance (*Nicomachean Ethics*, Bk. VI, chaps. 3 and 4), distinguishes between *epistēmē* and *technē* and indeed with respect to what and how they reveal. *Technē* is a mode of *alētheuein*. It reveals whatever does not bring itself forth and does not yet lie here before us, whatever can look and turn out now one way and now another. Whoever builds a house or a ship or forges a sacrificial chalice reveals what is to be brought forth, according to the perspectives of the four modes of occasioning. This revealing gathers together in advance the aspect and the matter of ship or house, with a view to the finished thing envisioned as completed, and from this gathering determines the manner of its construction. Thus what is decisive in *technē* does not lie at all in making and manipulating nor in the

---

11 Here and elsewhere "belongs within" translates the German *gehört in* with the accusative (literally, belongs into), an unusual usage that Heidegger often employs. The regular German construction is *gehört zu* (belongs to). With the use of "belongs into," Heidegger intends to suggest a relationship involving origin.

12 Heidegger here hyphenates the word *Wahrheit* (truth) so as to expose its stem, *wahr*. He points out elsewhere that words with this stem have a Common derivation and underlying meaning (SR 165). Such words often show .the connotations of attentive watchfulness and guarding that he there finds in their Greek cognates, *horaō, ōra*, e.g., *wahren* (to watch over and keep safe) and *bewahren* (to preserve). Hyphenating *Wahrheit* draws it overtly into this circle of meaning. It points to the fact that in truth, which is unconcealment *(Unverborgenheit)*, a safekeeping carries itself out *Wahrheit* thus offer here a very close parallel to its companion noun *Entbergung* (revealing; literally, harboring forth), built on *bergen* (to rescue, to harbor, to conceal). See n. 10, above. For a further discussion of words built around *wahr*, see T 42, n. 9.

using of means, but rather in the aforementioned revealing. It is as revealing, and not as manufacturing, that *technē* is a bringing-forth.

Thus the clue to what the word *technē* means and to how the Greeks defined it leads us into the same context that opened itself to us when we pursued the question of what instrumentality as such in truth might be.

Technology is a mode of revealing. Technology to presence [*West*] in the realm where revealing and unconcealment take place, where *alētheia*, truth, happens.

In opposition to this definition of the essential domain of technology, one can object that it indeed holds for Greek thought and that at best it might apply to the techniques of the handcraftsman, but that it simply does not fit modern machine-powered technology. And it is precisely the latter and it alone that is the disturbing thing, that moves us to ask the question concerning technology per se. It is said that modern technology is something incomparably different from all earlier technologies because it is based on modern physics as an exact science. Meanwhile we have come to understand more clearly that the reverse holds true as well: Modern physics, as experimental, is dependent upon technical apparatus and upon progress in the building of apparatus. The establishing of this mutual relationship between technology and physics is correct. But it remains a merely historiographical establishing of facts and says nothing about that in which this mutual relationship is grounded. The decisive question still remains: Of what essence is modern technology that it happens to think of putting exact science to use?

What is modern technology? It too is a revealing. Only when we allow our attention to rest on this fundamental characteristic does that which is new in modern technology show itself to us.

And yet the revealing that holds sway throughout modern technology does not unfold into a bringing-forth in the sense of *poiēsis*. The revealing that rules in modern technology is a challenging [*Herausfordern*],[13] which puts to nature the unreasonable demand that it supply energy that can be extracted and stored as such. But does this not hold true for the old windmill as well? No. Its sails do indeed turn in the wind; they are left entirely to the wind's blowing. But the windmill does not unlock energy from the air currents in order to store it.

In contrast, a tract of land is challenged into the putting out of coal and ore. The earth now reveals itself as a coal mining district, the soil as a mineral deposit. The field that the peasant formerly cultivated and set in order [*bestellte*] appears differently than it did when to set in order still meant to take care of and to maintain. The work of the peasant does not challenge the soil of the field. In the sowing of the grain it places the seed in the keeping of the forces of growth and watches over its increase. But meanwhile even the cultivation of

---

13 *Herausfordern* means to challenge, to call forth or summon to action, to demand positively, to provoke. It is composed of the verb *fordern* (to demand, to summon, to challenge) and the adverbial prefixes *her-* (hither) and *aus-* (out). The verb might be rendered very literally as "to demand out hither." The structural similarity between *herausfordern* and *her-vorbringen* (to bring forth hither) is readily apparent. It serves of itself to point up the relation subsisting between the two modes of revealing of which the verbs speak—modes that, in the very distinctive ways peculiar to them, occasion a coming forth into unconcealment and presencing. See below, 29–30.

the field has come under the grip of another kind of setting-in-order, which *sets* upon [*stellt*] nature.[14] It sets upon it in the sense of challenging it. Agriculture is now the mechanized food industry. Air is now set upon to yield nitrogen, the earth to yield ore, ore to yield uranium, for example; uranium is set upon to yield atomic energy, which can be released either for destruction or for peaceful use.

This setting-upon that challenges forth the energies of nature is an expediting [*Fördern*], and in two ways. It expedites in that it unlocks and exposes. Yet that expediting is always itself directed from the beginning toward furthering something else, i.e., toward driving on to the maximum yield at the minimum expense. The coal that has been hauled out in some mining district has not been supplied in order that it may simply be present somewhere or other. It is stockpiled; that is, it is on call, ready to deliver the sun's warmth that is stored in it. The sun's warmth is challenged forth for heat, which in turn is ordered to deliver steam whose pressure turns the wheels that keep a factory running.

The hydroelectric plant is set into the current of the Rhine. It sets the Rhine to supplying its hydraulic pressure, which then sets the turbines turning. This turning sets those machines in motion whose thrust sets going the electric current for which the long-distance power station and its network of cables are set up to dispatch electricity.[15] In the context of the interlocking processes pertaining to the orderly disposition of electrical energy, even the Rhine itself appears as something at our command. The hydroelectric plant is not built into the Rhine River as was the old wooden bridge that joined bank with bank for hundreds of years. Rather the river is dammed up into the power plant. What the river is now, namely, a water power supplier, derives from out of the essence of the power station. In order that we may even remotely consider the monstrousness that reigns here, let us ponder for a moment the contrast that speaks out of the two titles, "The Rhine" as dammed up into the *power* works, and "The Rhine" as uttered out of the *art* work, in Hölderlin's hymn by that name. But, it will be replied, the Rhine is still a river in the landscape is it not? Perhaps. But how? In no other way than as an object on call for inspection by a tour group ordered there by the vacation industry.

---

14 The verb *stellen* (to place or set) has a wide variety of uses. It can mean to put in place, to order, to arrange, to furnish or supply, and, in a military context, to challenge or engage. Here Heidegger sees the connotations of *herausfordern* (to challenge, to call forth, to demand out hither) as fundamentally determinative of the meaning of *stellen*, and this remains true throughout his ensuing discussion. The translation of *stellen* with "to set upon" is intended to carry this meaning. The connotations of setting in place and of supplying that lie within the word *stellen* remain strongly present in Heidegger's repeated use of the verb hereafter, however, since the "setting-upon" of which it speaks is inherently a setting in place so as to supply. Where these latter meanings come decisively to the fore, *stellen* has been translated with "to set" or "to set up," or, rarely, with "to supply."

    Stellen embraces the meanings of a whole family of verbs: *bestellell* (to order, command; to set in order), *vorstellen* (to represent), *sicherstellen* (to secure), *nachstellen* (to entrap), *verstellen* (to block or disguise), *herstellen* (to produce, to set here), *darstellen* (to present or exhibit), and so on. In these verbs the various nuances within *stellen* are reinforced and made specific. All these meanings are gathered together in Heidegger's unique use of the word that is pivotal for him, *Ge-stell* (Enframing). Cf. pp. 19 ff. See also the opening paragraph of "The Turning," pp. 36–37.

15 In these two sentences, in order to show something of the manner in which Heidegger gathers together a family of meanings, a series of *stellen* verbs—*stellen* (three times), *herstellen*, *bestellell*—have been translated with verbal expressions formed around "set." For the usual meanings of these verbs, see n. 14.

The revealing that rules throughout modern technology has the character of a setting-upon, in the sense of a challenging-forth. That challenging happens in that the energy concealed in nature is unlocked, what is unlocked is transformed, what is transformed is stored up, what is stored up is, in turn, distributed, and what is distributed is switched about ever anew. Unlocking, transforming, storing, distributing, and switching about are ways of revealing. But the revealing never simply comes to an end. Neither does it run off into the indeterminate. The revealing reveals to itself its own manifoldly interlocking paths, through regulating their course. This regulating itself is, for its part, everywhere secured. Regulating and securing even become the chief characteristics of the challenging revealing.

What kind of unconcealment is it, then, that is peculiar to that which comes to stand forth through this setting-upon that challenges? Everywhere everything is ordered to stand by, to be immediately at hand, indeed to stand there just so that it may be on call for a further ordering. Whatever is ordered about in this way has its own standing. We call it the standing-reserve [*Bestand*].[16] The word expresses here something more, and something more essential, than mere "stock." The name "standing-reserve" assumes the rank of an inclusive rubric. It designates nothing less than the way in which everything presences that is wrought upon by the challenging revealing. Whatever stands by in the sense of standing-reserve no longer stands over against us as object.

Yet an airliner that stands on the runway is surely an object. Certainly. We can represent the machine so. But then it conceals itself as to what and how it is. Revealed, it stands on the taxi strip only as standing-reserve, inasmuch as it is ordered to ensure the possibility of transportation. For this it must be in its whole structure and in every one of its constituent parts, on call for duty, i.e., ready for takeoff. (Here it would be appropriate to discuss Hegel's definition of the machine as an autonomous tool. When applied to the tools of the craftsman, his characterization is correct. Characterized in this way, however, the machine is not thought at all from out of the essence of technology within which it belongs. Seen in terms of the standing-reserve, the machine is completely unautonomous, for it has its standing only from the ordering of the orderable.)

The fact that now, wherever we try to point to modern technology as the challenging revealing, the words "setting-upon," "ordering," "standing-reserve," obtrude and accumulate in a dry, monotonous, and therefore oppressive way, has its basis in what is now coming to utterance.

Who accomplishes the challenging setting-upon through which what we call the real is revealed as standing-reserve? Obviously, man. To what extent is man capable of such a revealing? Man can indeed conceive, fashion, and carry through this or that in one way or another. But man does not have control over unconcealment itself, in which at any given time the real shows itself or withdraws. The fact that the real has been showing itself in

---

16 *Bestand* ordinarily denotes a store or supply as "standing by." It carries the connotation of the verb *bestehen* with its dual meaning of to last and to undergo. Heidegger uses the word to characterize the manner in which everything commanded into place and ordered according to the challenging demand ruling in modern technology presences as revealed. He wishes to s tress here not the permanency, but the orderability and substitutability of objects. *Bestand* contrasts with *Gegenstand* (object; that which stands over against). Objects indeed lose their character as objects when they are caught up in the "standing-reserve." Cf. Introduction, p. xxix.

the light of Ideas ever since the time of Plato, Plato did not bring about. The thinker only responded to what addressed itself to him.

Only to the extent that man for his part is already challenged to exploit the energies of nature can this ordering revealing happen. If man is challenged, ordered, to do this, then does not man himself belong even more originally than nature within the standing-reserve? The current talk about human resources, about the supply of patients for a clinic, gives evidence of this. The forester who, in the wood, measures the felled timber and to all appearances walks the same forest path in the same way as did his grandfather is today commanded by profit-making in the lumber industry, whether he knows it or not. He is made subordinate to the orderability of cellulose, which for its part is challenged forth by the need for paper, which is then delivered to newspapers and illustrated magazines. The latter, in their turn, set public opinion to swallowing what is printed, so that a set configuration of opinion becomes available on demand. Yet precisely because man is challenged more originally than are the energies of nature, i.e., into the process of ordering, he never is transformed into mere standing-reserve. Since man drives technology forward, he takes part in ordering as a way of revealing. But the unconcealment itself, within which ordering unfolds, is never a human handiwork, any more than is the realm through which man is already passing every time he as a subject relates to an object.

Where and how does this revealing happen if it is no mere handiwork of man? We need not look far. We need only apprehend in an unbiased way That which has already claimed man and has done so, so decisively that he can only be man at any given time as the one so claimed. Wherever man opens his eyes and ears, unlocks his heart, and gives himself over to meditating and striving, shaping and working, entreating and thanking, he finds himself everywhere already brought into the unconcealed. The unconcealrnent of the unconcealed has already come to pass whenever it calls man forth into the modes of revealing allotted to him. When man, in his way, from within unconceahnent reveals that which presences, he merely responds to the call of unconcealment even when he contradicts it. Thus when man, investigating, observing, ensnares nature as an area of his own conceiving, he has already been claimed by a way of revealing that challenges him to approach nature as an object of research, until even the object disappears into the objectlessness of standing-reserve.

Modern technology as an ordering revealing is, then, no merely human doing. Therefore we must take that challenging that sets upon man to order the real as standing-reserve in accordance with the way in which it shows itself. That challenging gathers man into ordering. This gathering concentrates man upon ordering the real as standing-reserve.

That which primordially unfolds the mountains into mountain ranges and courses through them in their folded togetherness is the gathering that we call "*Gebirg*" [mountain chain].

That original gathering from which unfold the ways in which we have feelings of one kind or another we name "*Gemiit*" [disposition].

We now name that challenging claim which gathers man thither to order the self-revealing as standing-reserve: "*Ge-stell*" [Enframing].[17]

---

[17] The translation "Enframing" for *Ge-stell* is intended to suggest, through the use of the prefix "en-," something of the active meaning that Heidegger here gives to the German word. While following the

We dare to use this word in a sense that has been thoroughly unfamiliar up to now.

According to ordinary usage, the word *Gestell* [frame] means some kind of apparatus, e.g., a bookrack. *Gestell* is also the name for a skeleton. And the employment of the word *Ge-stell* [Enframing] that is now required of us seems equally eerie, not to speak of the arbitrariness with which words of a mature language are thus misused. Can anything be more strange? Surely not. Yet this strangeness is an old usage of thinking. And indeed thinkers accord with this usage precisely at the point where it is a matter of thinking that which is highest. We, late born, are no longer in a position to appreciate the significance of Plato's daring to use the word *eidos* for that which in everything and in each particular thing endures as present. For *eidos*, in the common speech, meant the outward aspect [*Ansicht*] that a visible thing offers to the physical eye. Plato exacts of this word, however, something utterly extraordinary: that it name what precisely is not and never will be perceivable with physical eyes. But even this is by no means the full extent of what is extraordinary here. For *idea* names not only the nonsensuous aspect of what is physically visible.[18] Aspect (*idea*) names and is, also, that which constitutes the essence in the audible, the tasteable, the tactile, in everything that is in any way accessible. Compared with the demands that Plato makes on language and thought in this and other instances, the use of the word *Gestell* as the name for the essence of modern technology, which we now venture here, is almost harmless. Even so, the usage now required remains something exacting and is open to misinterpretation.

Enframing means the gathering together of that setting-upon which sets upon man, i.e., challenges him forth, to reveal the real, in the mode of ordering, as standing-reserve. Enframing means that way of revealing which holds sway in the essence of modern technology and which is itself nothing technological. On the other hand, all those things that are so familiar to us and are standard parts of an assembly, such as rods, pistons, and chassis, belong to the technological. The assembly itself, however, together with the aforementioned stockparts, falls within the sphere of technological activity; and this activity always merely responds to the challenge of Enframing, but it never comprises Enframing itself or brings it about.

The word *stellen* [to set upon] in the name *Ge-stell* [Enframing] not only means challenging. At the same time it should preserve the suggestion of another *Stellen* from which it stems, namely, that producing and presenting [*Her- und Dar-stellen*] which, in the sense of *poiēsis*, lets what presences come forth into unconcealment. This producing that brings forth—e.g., the erecting of a statue in the temple precinct—and the challenging ordering now under consideration are indeed fundamentally different, and yet they remain related in their essence. Both are ways of revealing, of *alētheia*. In Enframing, that unconcealment comes to pass in conformity with which the work of modern technology

---

discussion that now ensues, in which Enframing assumes a central role, the reader should be careful not to interpret the word as though it simply meant a framework of some sort. Instead he should constantly remember that Enframing is fundamentally a calling-forth. It is a "challenging claim," a demanding summons, that "gathers" so as to reveal. This claim *enframes* in that it assembles and orders. It puts into a framework or configuration everything that it summons forth, through an ordering for use that it is forever restructuring anew. Cf. Introduction, pp. xxix ff.

18 Where *idea* is italicized it is not the English word but a transliteration of the Greek.

reveals the real as standing-reserve. This work is therefore neither only a human activity nor a mere means within such activity. The merely instrumental, merely anthropological definition of technology is therefore in principle untenable. And it cannot be rounded out by being referred back to some metaphysical or religious explanation that undergirds it.

It remains true, nonetheless, that man in the technological age is, in a particularly striking way, challenged forth into revealing. That revealing concerns nature, above all, as the chief storehouse of the standing energy reserve. Accordingly, man's ordering attitude and behavior display themselves first in the rise of modern physics as an exact science. Modern science's way of representing pursues and entraps nature as a calculable coherence of forces. Modern physics is not experimental physics because it applies apparatus to the questioning of nature. Rather the reverse is true. Because physics, indeed already as pure theory, sets nature up to exhibit itself as a coherence of forces calculable in advance, it therefore orders its experiments precisely for the purpose of asking whether and how nature reports itself when set up in this way.

But after all, mathematical physics arose almost two centuries before technology. How, then, could it have already been set upon by modern technology and placed in its service? The facts testify to the contrary. Surely technology got under way only when it could be supported by exact physical science. Reckoned chronologically, this is correct. Thought historically, it does not hit upon the truth.

The modern physical theory of nature prepares the way first not simply for technology but for the essence of modern technology. For already in physics the challenging gathering-together into ordering revealing holds sway. But in it that gathering does not yet come expressly to appearance. Modern physics is the herald of Enframing, a herald whose origin is still unknown. The essence of modern technology has for a long time been concealing itself, even where power machinery has been invented, where electrical technology is in full swing, and where atomic technology is well under way.

All coming to presence, not only modern technology, keeps itself everywhere concealed to the last.[19] Nevertheless, it remains, with respect to its holding sway, that which precedes all: the earliest. The Greek thinkers already knew of this when they said: That which is earlier with regard to the arising that holds sway becomes manifest to us men only later. That which is primally early shows itself only ultimately to men.[20] Therefore, in the realm of thinking, a painstaking effort to think through still more primally what was primally thought is not the absurd wish to revive what is past, but rather the sober readiness to be astounded before the coming of what is early.

Chronologically speaking, modern physical science begins in the seventeenth century. In contrast, machine-power technology develops only in the second half of the eighteenth

---

19 "Coming to presence" here translates the gerund *Wesende*, a verbal form that appears, in this volume, only in this essay. With the introduction into the discussion of "coming to presence" as an alternate translation of the noun *Wesen* (essence), subsequent to Heidegger's consideration of the meaning of essence below (pp. 30 ff.), occasionally the presence of *das Wesende* is regrettably but unavoidably obscured.

20 "That which is primally early" translates *die anfängliche Frühe*. For a discussion of that which "is to all present and absent beings . . . the earliest and most ancient at once"— i.e., *Ereignen, das Ereignis*—see "The Way to Language" in *On the Way to Language*, trans. Peter D. Hertz (New York: Harper & Row, 1971), p. 127.

century. But modern technology, which for chronological reckoning is the later, is, from the point of view of the essence holding sway within it, the historically earlier.

If modern physics must resign itself ever increasingly to the fact that its realm of representation remains inscrutable and incapable of being visualized, this resignation is not dictated by any committee of researchers. It is challenged forth by the rule of Enframing, which demands that nature be orderable as standing-reserve. Hence physics, in all its retreating from the representation turned only toward objects that has alone been standard till recently, will never be able to renounce this one thing: that nature reports itself in some way or other that is identifiable through calculation and that it remains orderable as a system of information. This system is determined, then, out of a causality that has changed once again. Causality now displays neither the character of the occasioning that brings forth nor the nature of the *causa efficiens*, let a one that of the *causa formalis*. It seems as though causality is shrinking into a reporting—a reporting challenged forth—of standing-reserves that must be guaranteed either simultaneously or in sequence. To this shrinking would correspond the process of growing resignation that Heisenberg's lecture depicts in so impressive a manner.*

Because the essence of modern technology lies in Enframing, modern technology must employ exact physical science. Through its so doing, the deceptive illusion arises that modern technology is applied physical science. This illusion can maintain itself only so long as neither the essential origin of modern science nor indeed the essence of modern technology is adequately found out through questioning.

We are questioning concerning technology in order to bring to light our relationship to its essence. The essence of modern technology shows itself in what we call Enframing. But simply to point to this is still in no way to answer the question concerning technology, if to answer means to respond, in the sense of correspond, to the essence of what is being asked about.

Where do we find ourselves brought to, if now we think one step further regarding what Enframing itself actually is? It is nothing technological nothing on the order of a machine. It is the way in which the real reveals itself as standing-reserve. Again we ask: Does this revealing happen somewhere beyond all human doing? No. But neither does it happen exclusively *in* man, or decisively *through* man.

Enframing is the gathering together that belongs to that setting-upon which sets upon man and puts him in position to reveal the real in the mode of ordering, as standing-reserve. As the one who is challenged forth in this way, man stands within the essential realm of Enframing. He can never take up a relationship to it only subsequently. Thus the question as to how we are to arrive at a relationship to the essence of technology, asked in this way, always comes too late. But never too late comes the question as to whether we actually experience ourselves as the ones whose activities everywhere, public and private, are challenged forth by Enframing. Above all, never too late comes the question as to whether and how we actually admit ourselves into that wherein Enframing itself comes to presence.

---

* W. Heisenberg, "Das Naturbild in der heutigen Physik," in *Die Künste im technischen Zeitalter* (Munich, 1954), pp. 43 ff.

The essence of modern technology starts man upon the way of that revealing through which the real everywhere, more or less distinctly, becomes standing-reserve. "To start upon a way" means "to send" in our ordinary language. We shall call that sending-that-gathers [*versammelde Schicken*] which first starts man upon a way of revealing, *destining* [*Geschick*].[21] It is from out of this destining that the essence of all history [*Geschichte*] is determined. History is neither simply the object of written chronicle nor simply the fulfillment of human activity. That activity first becomes history as something destined.* And it is only the destining into objectifying representation that makes the historical accessible as an object for historiography, i.e., for a science, and on this basis makes possible the current equating of the historical with that which is chronicled.

Enframing, as a challenging-forth into ordering, sends into a way of revealing. Enframing is an ordaining of destining, as is every way of revealing. Bringing-forth, *poiēsis*, is also a destining in this sense.

Always the unconcealment of that which is[22] goes upon a way of revealing. Always the destining of revealing holds complete sway over man. But that destining is never a fate that compels. For man becomes truly free only insofar as he belongs to the realm of destining and so becomes one who listens and hears [*Hörender*], and not one who is simply constrained to obey [*Höriger*].

The essence of freedom is *originally* not connected with the will or even with the causality of human willing.

Freedom governs the open in the sense of the cleared and lighted up, i.e., of the revealed?[23] It is to the happening of revealing, i.e., of truth, that freedom stands in the closest and most intimate kinship. All revealing belongs within a harboring and a concealing. But that which frees—the mystery—is concealed and always concealing itself. All revealing comes out of the open, goes into the open, and brings into the open. The freedom of the open consists neither in unfettered arbitrariness nor in the constraint of mere laws. Freedom is that which conceals in a way that opens to light, in whose clearing there shimmers that veil that covers what comes to presence of all truth and lets the veil appear as what veils. Freedom is the realm of the destining that, any given time starts a revealing upon its way.

The essence of modern technology lies in Enframing. Enframing belongs within the destining of revealing. These sentences express something different from the talk that we hear more frequently, to the effect that technology is the fate of our age, where "fate" means the inevitableness of an unalterable course.

But when we consider the essence of technology, then we experience Enframing as a destining of revealing. In this way we are already sojourning within the open space of

---

21 For a further presentation of the meaning resident in *Geschick* and the related verb *schicken*, cf. T 38 ff., and Introduction, pp. xxviii ff.
* See *Vom Wesen dey Wahrheit*, 1930; 1st ed., 1943, pp. 16 ff. [English translation, "On the Essence of Truth," in *Existence and Being*, ed. Werner Brock (Chicago: Regnery, 1949), pp. 308 ff.]
22 *dessen was ist*. On the peculiar significance of *das was ist* (that which is), see T 44 n. 12.
23 "The open" here translates *das Freie*, cognate with *Freiheit*, freedom. Unfortunately the repetitive stress of the German phrasing cannot be reproduced in English, since the basic meaning of *Freie*—open air, open space—is scarcely heard in the English "free."

destining, a destining that in no way confines us to a stultified compulsion to push on blindly with technology or, what comes to the same thing to rebel helplessly against it and curse it as the work of the devil. Quite to the contrary, when we once open ourselves expressly to the *essence* of technology, we find ourselves unexpectedly taken into a freeing claim.

The essence of technology lies in Enframing. Its holding sway belongs within destining. Since destining at any given time starts man on a way of revealing, man, thus under way, is continually approaching the brink of the possibility of pursuing and pushing forward nothing but what is revealed in ordering, and of deriving all his standards on this basis. Through this the other possibility is blocked, that man might be admitted more and sooner and ever more primally to the essence of that which is unconcealed and to its unconcealment, in order that he might experience as his essence his needed belonging to revealing.

Placed between these possibilities, man is endangered from out of destining. The destining of revealing is as such, in everyone of its modes, and therefore necessarily, *danger*.

In whatever way the destining of revealing may hold sway, the unconcealment in which everything that is shows itself at any given time harbors the danger that man may quail at the unconcealed and may misinterpret it. Thus where everything that presences exhibits itself in the light of a cause-effect coherence, even God can, for representational thinking, lose all that is exalted and holy, the mysteriousness of his distance. In the light of causality, God can sink to the level of a cause, of *causa efficiens*. He then becomes, even in theology, the god of the philosophers, namely, of those who define the unconcealed and the concealed in terms of the causality of making, without ever considering the essential origin of this causality.

In a similar way the unconcealment in accordance with which nature presents itself as a calculable complex of the effects of forces can indeed permit correct determinations; but precisely through these successes the danger can remain that in the midst of all that is correct the true will withdraw.

The destining of revealing is in itself not just any danger, but danger as such.

Yet when destining reigns in the mode of Enframing, it is the supreme danger. This danger attests itself to us in two ways. soon as what is unconcealed no longer concerns man even as object, but does so, rather, exclusively as standing-reserve, and man in the midst of objectlessness is nothing but the orderer of the standing-reserve, then he comes to the very brink of a precipitous fall; that is, he comes to the point where he himself will have to be taken as standing-reserve. Meanwhile man, precisely as the one so threatened, exalts himself to the posture of lord of the earth. In this way the impression comes to prevail that everything man encounters exists only insofar as it is his construct. This illusion gives rise in turn to one final delusion: It seems as though man everywhere and always encounters only himself. Heisenberg has with complete correctness pointed out that the real must present itself to contemporary man in this way.* *In truth, however, precisely nowhere does man today any longer encounter himself, i.e., his essence.* Man stands so decisively in attendance

---

* "Das Naturbild," pp. 60 ff.

on the challenging-forth of Enframing that he does not apprehend Enframing as a claim, that he fails to see himself as the one spoken to, and hence also fails in every way to hear in what respect he ek-sists, from out of his essence, in the realm of an exhortation or address, and thus *can never* encounter only himself.

But Enframing does not simply endanger man in his relationship to himself and to everything that is. As a destining, it banishes man into that kind of revealing which is an ordering. Where this ordering holds sway, it drives out every other possibility of revealing. Above all, Enframing conceals that revealing which, in the sense of *poiēsis*, lets what presences come forth into appearance. As compared with that other revealing, the setting-upon that challenges forth thrusts man into a relation to that which is, that is at once antithetical and rigorously ordered. Where Enframing holds sway, regulating and securing of the standing-reserve mark all revealing. They no longer even let their own fundamental characteristic appear, namely, this revealing as such.

Thus the challenging Enframing not only conceals a former way of revealing, bringing-forth, but it conceals revealing itself and with it That wherein unconcealment, i.e., truth, comes to pass.

Enframing blocks the shining-forth and holding-sway of truth. The destining that sends into ordering is consequently the extreme danger. What is dangerous is not technology. There is no demonry of technology, but rather there is the mystery of its essence. The essence of technology, as a destining of revealing, is the danger. The transformed meaning of the word "Enframing" will perhaps become somewhat more familiar to us now if we think Enframing in the sense of destining and danger.

The threat to man does not come in the first instance from the potentially lethal machines and apparatus of technology. The actual threat has already affected man in his essence. The rule of Enframing threatens man with the possibility that it could be denied to him to enter into a more original revealing and hence to experience the call of a more primal truth.

Thus, where Enframing reigns, there is *danger* in the highest sense.

> *But where danger is, grows*
>
> *The saving power also.*

Let us think carefully about these words of Hölderlin. What does it mean "to save"? Usually we think that it means only to seize hold of a thing threatened by ruin, in order to secure it in its former continuance. But the verb "to save" says more. "To save" is to fetch something home into its essence, in order to bring the essence for the first time into its genuine appearing. If the essence of technology, Enframing, is the extreme danger, and if there is truth in Hölderlin's words, then the rule of Enframing cannot exhaust itself solely in blocking all lighting-up of every revealing, all appearing of truth. Rather, precisely the essence of technology must harbor in itself the growth of the saving power. But in that case, might not an adequate look into what Enframing is as a destining of revealing bring into appearance the saving power in its arising?

In what respect does the saving power grow there also where the danger is? Where something grows, there it takes root, from thence it thrives. Both happen concealedly and quietly and in their own time. But according to the words of the poet we have no right whatsoever to expect that there where the danger is we should be able to lay hold of the saving power immediately and without preparation. Therefore we must consider now, in advance, in what respect the saving power does most profoundly take root and thence thrive even in that wherein the extreme danger lies, in the holding sway of Enframing. In order to consider this, it is necessary, as a last step upon our way, to look with yet clearer eyes into the danger. Accordingly, we must once more question concerning technology. For we have said that in technology's essence roots and thrives the saving power.

But how shall we behold the saving power in the essence of technology so long as we do not consider in what sense of "essence" it is that Enframing is actually the essence of technology?

Thus far we have understood "essence" in its current meaning. In the academic language of philosophy, "essence" means *what* something is; in Latin, *quid*. *Quidditas*, whatness, provides the answer to the question concerning essence. For example, what pertains to all kinds of trees—oaks, beeches, birches, firs—is the same "treeness." Under this inclusive genus—the "universal"—fall all real and possible trees. Is then the essence of technology, Enframing, the common genus for, everything technological? If that were the case then the steam turbine, the radio transmitter, and the cyclotron would each be an Enframing. But the word "Enframing" does not mean here a tool or any kind of apparatus. Still less does it mean the general concept of such resources. The machines and apparatus are no more cases and kinds of Enframing than are the man at the switchboard and the engineer in the drafting room. Each of these in its own way indeed belongs as stockpart, available resource, or executer, within Enframing; but Enframing is never the essence of technology in the sense of a genus. Enframing is a way of revealing having the character of destining, namely, the way that challenges forth. The revealing that brings forth (*poiēsis*) is also a way that has the character of destining. But these ways are not kinds that, arrayed beside one another, fall under the concept of revealing. Revealing is that destining which, ever suddenly and inexplicably to all thinking, apportions itself into the revealing that brings forth and that also challenges, and which allots itself to man. The challenging revealing has its origin as a destining in bringing-forth. But at the same time Enframing, in a way characteristic of a destining, blocks *poiēsis*.

Thus Enframing, as a destining of revealing, is indeed the essence of technology, but never in the sense of genus and *essentia*. If we pay heed to this, something astounding strikes us: It is technology itself that makes the demand on us to think in another way what is usually understood by "essence," But in what way?

If we speak of the "essence of a house" and the "essence of a state," we do not mean a generic type; rather we mean the ways in which house and state hold sway, administer themselves, develop and decay—the way in which they "essence" [*Wesen*]. Johann Peter Hebel in a poem, "Ghost on Kanderer Street," for which Goethe had a special fondness, uses the old word *die Weserei*. It means the city hall inasmuch as there the life of the community gathers and village existence is constantly in play, i.e., comes to presence. It is from the verb *wesen* that the noun is derived. *Wesen* understood as a verb is the same as *währen* [to last or endure], not only in terms of meaning, but also in terms of the phonetic formation of the word. Socrates and Plato already think the essence of something as what essences, what comes to presence, in the sense of what endures. But they think what endures as what remains permanently [*das Fortwährende*] (*aei on*). And they find what endures permanently in what, as that which remains, tenaciously persists throughout all that happens. That which remains they discover, in turn, in the aspect [*Aussehen*] (*eidos, idea*), for example, the Idea "house."

The Idea "house" displays what anything is that is fashioned as a house. Particular, real, and possible houses, in contrast, are changing and transitory derivatives of the Idea and thus belong to what does not endure.

But it can never in any way be established that enduring is based solely on what Plato thinks as *idea* and Aristotle thinks as *to ti ēn einai* (that which any particular thing has always been), or what metaphysics in its most varied interpretations thinks as *essentia*.

All essencing endures. But is enduring only permanent enduring? Does the essence of technology endure in the sense of the permanent enduring of an Idea that hovers over everything technological, thus making it seem that by technology we mean some mythological abstraction? The way in which technology essences lets itself be seen only from out of that permanent enduring in which Enframing comes to pass as a destining of revealing. Goethe once uses the mysterious word *fortgewähren* [to grant permanently] in place of *fortwähren* [to endure permanently].* He hears *währen* [to endure] and *gewähren* [to grant] here in one unarticulated accord.[24] And if we now ponder more carefully than we did before what it is that actually endures and perhaps alone endures, we may venture to say: *Only what is granted endures. That which endures primally out of the earliest beginning is what grants.*[25]

As the essencing of technology, Enframing is that which endures. Does Enframing hold sway at all in the sense of granting? No doubt the question seems a horrendous blunder. For according to everything that has been said, Enframing is, rather, a destining that gathers together into the revealing that challenges forth. Challenging is anything but a granting. So it seems, so long as we do not notice that the challenging-forth into the ordering of the real as standing-reserve still remains a destining that starts man upon a way of revealing. As this destining, the coming to presence of technology gives man entry into That which, of himself, he can neither invent nor in any way make. For there is no such thing as a man who, solely of himself is only man.

But if this destining, Enframing, is the extreme anger, not only for man's coming to presence, but for all revealing as such, should this destining still be called a granting? Yes, most emphatically, if in this destining the saving power is said to grow. Every destining of revealing comes to pass from out of a granting and as such a granting. For it is granting that first

---

* "Die Wahlverwandtschaften" [Congeniality], pt. II, chap. 10, in the novelette *Die wunderlichen Nachbarskinder* [The strange neighbor's children].

24 The verb *gewähren* is closely allied to the verbs *währen* (to endure) and *wahren* (to watch over, to keep safe, to preserve). *Gewähren* ordinarily means to be surety for, to warrant, to vouchsafe, to grant. In the discussion that follows, the verb will be translated simply with "to grant." But the reader should keep in mind also the connotations of safeguarding and guaranteeing that are present in it as well.

25 *Nur das Gewährte währt. Das anfänglich aus der Frühe Währende ist das Gewährende.* A literal translation of the second sentence would be, "That which endures primally from out of the early...." On the meaning of "the early," see n. 20 above.

conveys to man that share in revealing which the coming-to-pass of revealing needs.[26] As the one so needed and used, man is given to belong to the coming-to-pass of truth. The granting that sends in one way or another into revealing is as such the saving power. For the saving power its man see and enter into the highest dignity of his essence. This dignity lies in keeping watch over the unconcealment—and with it, from the first, the concealment—of all coming to presence on this earth. It is precisely in Enframing which threatens to sweep man away into ordering as the supposed single way of revealing, and so thrusts man into the danger of the surrender of his free essence—it is precisely in this extreme danger that the innermost indestructible belongingness of man within granting may come to light, provided that we, for our part, begin to pay heed to the coming to presence of technology.

Thus the coming to presence of technology harbors in itself what we least suspect, the possible arising of the saving power.

Everything, then, depends upon this: that we ponder this arising and that, recollecting, we watch over it. How can this happen? Above all through our catching sight of what comes to presence in technology, instead of merely staring at the technological. So long as we represent technology as an instrument we remain held fast in the will to master it. We press on past the essence of technology.

When, however, we ask how the instrumental comes to presence as a kind of causality, then we experience this coming to presence as the destining of a revealing.

When we consider, finally, that the coming to presence of the essence of technology comes to pass in the granting that needs and uses man so that he may share in revealing, then the following becomes clear:

The essence of technology is in a lofty sense ambiguous. Such ambiguity points to the mystery of all revealing, i.e., of truth.

On the one hand, Enframing challenges forth into the frenziedness of ordering that blocks every view into the coming-to-pass of revealing and so radically endangers the relation to the essence of truth.

On the other hand, Enframing comes to pass for its part in the granting that lets man endure—as yet unexperienced, but perhaps more experienced in the future—that he may be the one who is needed and used for the safekeeping of the coming to presence of truth.[27] Thus does the arising of the saving power appear.

The irresistibility of ordering and the restraint of the saving power draw past each other like the paths of two stars in the course of the heavens. But precisely this, their passing by, is the hidden side of their nearness.

---

26 Here and subsequently in this essay, "coming-to-pass" translates the noun *Ereignis*. Elsewhere, in "The Turning," this word in accordance with deeper meaning that Heidegger there finds for it, will be translated with disclosing that brings into its own." See T 45; see also Introduction pp. xxxvi–xxxvii.

27 "Safekeeping" translates the noun *Wahrnis*, which is unique to Heidegger. *Wahrnis* is closely related to the verb *wahren* (to watch over, to keep safe, to preserve), integrally related to *Wahrheit* (truth), and closely akin to *währen* (to endure) and *gewähren* (to be surety for, to grant). On the meaning of *Wahrnis*, see T 42, n. 9 and n, 12 above.

When we look into the ambiguous essence of technology, we behold the constellation, the stellar course of the mystery.

The question concerning technology is the question concerning the constellation in which revealing and concealing, in which the coming to presence of truth, comes to pass.

But what help is it to us to look into the constellation of truth? We look into the danger and see the growth of the saving power.

Through this we are not yet saved. But we are thereupon summoned to hope in the growing light of the saving power. How can this happen? Here and now and in little things, that we may foster the saving power in its increase. This includes holding always before our eyes the extreme danger.

The coming to presence of technology threatens revealing, threatens it with the possibility that all revealing will be consumed in ordering and that everything will present itself only in the unconcealedness of standing-reserve. Human activity can never directly counter this danger. Human achievement alone can never banish it. But human reflection can ponder the fact that all saving power must be of a higher essence than what is endangered, though at the same time kindred to it.

But might there not perhaps be a more primally granted revealing that could bring the saving power into its first shining forth in the midst of the danger, a revealing that in the techno: logical age rather conceals than shows itself?

There was a time when it was not technology alone that bore the name *technē*. Once that revealing that brings forth truth into the splendor of radiant appearing also was called *technē*.

Once there was a time when the bringing-forth of the true into the beautiful was called *technē*. And the *poiēsis* of the fine arts also was called *technē*.

In Greece, at the outset of the destining of the West, the arts soared to the supreme height of the revealing granted them. They brought the presence [*Gegenwart*] of the gods, brought the dialogue of divine and human destinings, to radiance. And art was simply called *technē*. It was a single, manifold revealing. It was pious, *promos*, i.e., yielding to the holding-sway and the safekeeping of truth.

The arts were not derived from the artistic. Art works were not enjoyed aesthetically. Art was not a sector of cultural activity.

What, then, was art—perhaps only for that brief but magnificent time? Why did art bear the modest name *teehnē*? Because it was a revealing that brought forth and hither, and therefore belonged within *poiēsis*. It was finally that revealing which holds complete sway in all the fine arts, in poetry, and in everything poetical that obtained *poiēsis* as its proper name.

The same poet from whom we heard the words

> *But where danger is, grows*
> *The saving power also.*

says to us:

> *... poetically dwells man upon this earth.*

The poetical brings the true into the splendor of what Plato in the *Phaedrus* calls *to ekphanestaton*, that which shines forth most purely. The poetical thoroughly pervades every art, every revealing of coming to presence into the beautiful.

Could it be that the fine arts are called to poetic revealing? Could it be that revealing lays claim to the arts most primally, so that they for their part may expressly foster the growth of the saving power, may awaken and found anew our look into that which grants and our trust in it?

Whether art may be granted this highest possibility of its essence in the midst of the extreme danger, no one can tell. Yet we can be astounded. Before what? Before this other possibility: that the frenziedness of technology may entrench itself everywhere to such an extent that someday, throughout everything technological the essence of technology may come to presence in the coming-to-pass of truth.

Because the essence of technology is nothing technological, essential reflection upon technology and decisive confrontation with it must happen in a realm that is, on the one hand, akin to the essence of technology and, on the other, fundamentally different from it.

Such a realm is art. But certainly only if reflection on art, for its part, does not shut its eyes to the, constellation of truth after which we are *questioning*.

Thus questioning, we bear witness to the crisis that in our sheer preoccupation with technology we do not yet experience the coming to presence of technology, that in our sheer aesthetic-mindedness we no longer guard and preserve the coming to presence of art. Yet the more questioningly we ponder the essence of technology, the more mysterious the essence of art becomes.

The closer we come to the danger, the more brightly do the ways into the saving power begin to shine and the more questioning we become. For questioning is the piety of thought.

The Ideology of Machines
Computer Technology
Neil Postman

That American Technopoly has now embraced the computer in the same hurried and mindless way it embraced medical technology is undeniable, was perhaps inevitable, and is certainly most unfortunate. This is not to say that the computer is a blight on the symbolic landscape; only that, like medical technology, it has usurped powers and enforced mind-sets that a fully attentive culture might have wished to deny it. Thus, an examination of the ideas embedded in computer technology is worth attempting. Others, of course, have done this, especially Joseph Weizenbaum in his great and indispensable book *Computer Power and Human Reason*. Weizenbaum, however, ran into some difficulties, as everyone else has, because of the "universality" of computers, meaning (a) that their uses are infinitely various, and (b) that computers are commonly integrated into the structure of other machines. It is, therefore, hard to isolate specific ideas promoted by computer technology. The computer, for example, is quite unlike the stethoscope, which has a limited function in a limited context. Except for safecrackers, who, I am told, use stethoscopes to hear the tumblers of locks click into place, stethoscopes are used only by doctors. But everyone uses or is used by computers, and for purposes that seem to know no boundaries.

Putting aside such well-known functions as electronic filing, spreadsheets, and word-processing, one can make a fascinating list of the innovative, even bizarre, uses of computers. I have before me a report from *The New York Times* that tells us how computers are enabling aquatic designers to create giant water slides that mimic roller coasters and eight-foot-high artificial waves. In my modest collection, I have another article about the uses of personal computers for making presentations at corporate board meetings. Another tells of how computer graphics help jurors to remember testimony better. Gregory Mazares, president of the graphics unit of Litigation Sciences, is quoted as saying, "We're a switched-on, tuned-in, visually oriented society, and jurors tend to believe what they see. This technology keeps the jury's attention by simplifying the material and by giving them little bursts of information." While Mr. Mazares is helping

---

"The Ideology of Machines: Computer Technology" from *Technopoly: The Surrender of Culture to Technology* by Neil Postman, Copyright © 1992 by Neil Postman. Used by permission of Alfred A. Knopf, an imprint of the Knopf Doubleday Publishing Group, a division of Penguin Random House LLC. All rights reserved.

switched-on people to remember things, Morton David, chief executive officer of Franklin Computer, is helping them find any word in the Bible with lightning speed by producing electronic Bibles. (The word "lightning," by the way, appears forty-two times in the New International version and eight times in the King James version. Were you so inclined, you could discover this for yourself in a matter of seconds.) This fact so dominates Mr. David's imagination that he is quoted as saying, "Our technology may have made a change as momentous as the Gutenberg invention of movable type." And then there is an article that reports a computer's use to make investment decisions, which helps you, among other things, to create "what-if" scenarios, although with how much accuracy we are not told. In *Technology Review,* we find a description of how computers are used to help the police locate the addresses of callers in distress; a prophecy is made that in time police officers will have so much instantly available information about any caller that they will know how seriously to regard the caller's appeal for help.

One may well wonder if Charles Babbage had any of this in mind when he announced in 1822 (only six years after the appearance of Laënnec's stethoscope) that he had invented a machine capable of performing simple arithmetical calculations. Perhaps he did, for he never finished his invention and started work on a more ambitious machine, capable of doing more complex tasks. He abandoned that as well, and in 1833 put aside his calculator project completely in favor of a programmable machine that became the forerunner of the modern computer. His first such machine, which he characteristically never finished, was to be controlled by punch cards adapted from devices French weavers used to control thread sequences in their looms.

Babbage kept improving his programmable machine over the next thirty-seven years, each design being more complex than the last. At some point, he realized that the mechanization of numerical operations gave him the means to manipulate non-numerical symbols. It is not farfetched to say that Babbage's insight was comparable to the discovery by the Greeks in the third century B. C. of the principle of alphabetization—that is, the realization that the symbols of the alphabet could be separated from their phonetic function and used as a system for the classification, storage, and retrieval of information. In any case, armed with his insight, Babbage was able to speculate about the possibility of designing "intelligent" information machinery, though the mechanical technology of his time was inadequate to allow the fulfillment of his ideas. The computer as we know it today had to await a variety of further discoveries and inventions, including the telegraph, the telephone, and the application of Boolean algebra to relay-based circuitry, resulting in Claude Shannon's creation of digital logic circuitry. Today, when the word "computer" is used without a modifier before it, it normally refers to some version of the machine invented by John von Neumann in the 1940s. Before that, the word "computer" referred to a person (similarly to the early use of the word "typewriter") who performed some kind of mechanical calculation. As calculation shifted from people to machines, so did the word, especially because of the power of von Neumann's machine.

Certainly, after the invention of the digital computer, it was abundantly clear that the computer was capable of performing functions that could in some sense be called "intelligent." In 1936, the great English mathematician Alan Turing showed that it was possible to build a machine that would, for many practical purposes, behave like a problem-solving human being. Turing claimed that he would call a machine "intelligent" if, through typed messages, it could exchange thoughts with a human being—that is, hold up its end of a conversation. In the early days of MIT's Artificial Intelligence Laboratory, Joseph Weizenbaum wrote a program called ELIZA, which showed how easy it was to meet Turing's test for intelligence. When asked a question with a proper noun in it, ELIZA's program could respond with "Why are you interested in," followed by the proper noun and a question mark. That is, it could invert statements and seek more information about one of the nouns in the statement. Thus, ELIZA acted much like a Rogerian psychologist, or at least a friendly and inexpensive therapist. Some people who used ELIZA refused to believe that they were conversing with a mere machine. Having, in effect, created a Turing machine, Weizenbaum eventually pulled the program off the computer network and was stimulated to write *Computer Power and Human Reason,* in which, among other things, he raised questions about the research programs of those working in artificial intelligence; the assumption that whatever a computer *can* do, it *should* do; and the effects of computer technology on the way people construe the world—that is, the ideology of the computer, to which I now turn.

The most comprehensive idea conveyed by the computer is suggested by the title of J. David Bolter's book, *Turing's Man.* His title is a metaphor, of course, similar to what would be suggested by saying that from the sixteenth century until recently we were "Gutenberg's Men." Although Bolter's main practical interest in the computer is in its function as a new kind of book, he argues that it is the dominant metaphor of our age; it defines our age by suggesting a new relationship to information, to work, to power, and to nature itself. That relationship can best be described by saying that the computer redefines humans as "information processors" and nature itself as information to be processed. The fundamental metaphorical message of the computer, in short, is that we are machines—thinking machines, to be sure, but machines nonetheless. It is for this reason that the computer is the quintessential, incomparable, near-perfect machine for Technopoly. It subordinates the claims of our nature, our biology, our emotions, our spirituality. The computer claims sovereignty over the whole range of human experience, and supports its claim by showing that it "thinks" better than we can. Indeed, in his almost hysterical enthusiasm for artificial intelligence, Marvin Minsky has been quoted as saying that the thinking power of silicon "brains" will be so formidable that "If we are lucky, they will keep us as pets." An even giddier remark, although more dangerous, was offered by John McCarthy, the inventor of the term "artificial intelligence." McCarthy claims that "even machines as simple as thermostats can be said to have beliefs." To the obvious question, posed by the philosopher John Searle, "What beliefs does your thermostat have?," McCarthy replied, "My thermostat has three beliefs—it's too hot in here, it's too cold in here, and it's just right in here."

What is significant about this response is that it has redefined the meaning of the word "belief." The remark rejects the view that humans have internal states of mind that are the foundation of belief and argues instead that "belief" means only what someone or something does. The remark also implies that simulating an idea is synonymous with duplicating the idea. And, most important, the remark rejects the idea that mind is a biological phenomenon.

In other words, what we have here is a case of metaphor gone mad. From the proposition that humans are in some respects like machines, we move to the proposition that humans are little else but machines and, finally, that human beings *are* machines. And then, inevitably, as McCarthy's remark suggests, to the proposition that machines are human beings. It follows that machines can be made that duplicate human intelligence, and thus research in the field known as artificial intelligence was inevitable. What is most significant about this line of thinking is the dangerous reductionism it represents. Human intelligence, as Weizenbaum has tried energetically to remind everyone, is not transferable. The plain fact is that humans have a unique, biologically rooted, intangible mental life which in some limited respects can be simulated by a machine but can never be duplicated. Machines cannot feel and, just as important, cannot *understand*. Eliza can ask, "Why are you worried about your mother?," which might be exactly the question a therapist would ask. But the machine does not know what the question means or even *that* the question means. (Of course, there may be some therapists who do not know what the question means either, who ask it routinely, ritualistically, inattentively. In that case we may say they are acting like a machine.) It is meaning, not utterance, that makes mind unique. I use "meaning" here to refer to something more than the result of putting together symbols the denotations of which are commonly shared by at least two people. As I understand it, meaning also includes those things we call feelings, experiences, and sensations that do not have to be, and sometimes cannot be, put into symbols. They "mean" nonetheless. Without concrete symbols, a computer is merely a pile of junk. Although the quest for a machine that duplicates mind has ancient roots, and although digital logic circuitry has given that quest a scientific structure, artificial intelligence does not and cannot lead to a meaning-making, understanding, and feeling creature, which is what a human being is.

All of this may seem obvious enough, but the metaphor of the machine as human (or the human as machine) is sufficiently powerful to have made serious inroads in everyday language. People now commonly speak of "programming" or "deprogramming" themselves. They speak of their brains as a piece of "hard wiring," capable of "retrieving data," and it has become common to think about thinking as a mere matter of processing and decoding.

Perhaps the most chilling case of how deeply our language is absorbing the "machine as human" metaphor began on November 4, 1988, when the computers around the Arpanet network became sluggish, filled with extraneous data, and then clogged completely. The problem spread fairly quickly to six thousand computers across the United States and overseas. The early hypothesis was that a software program had attached itself to other programs, a situation which is called (in another human-machine metaphor) a "virus." As it happened, the intruder was a self-contained program explicitly designed to disable computers, which is called a "worm." But the technically incorrect term "virus" stuck, no doubt because of its familiarity and its human connections. As Raymond Gozzi, Jr., discovered in his analysis of how the mass media described the event, newspapers noted that the computers were "infected," that the virus was "virulent" and "contagious," that attempts were made to "quarantine" the infected computers, that attempts were also being made to "sterilize" the network, and that programmers hoped to develop a "vaccine" so that computers could be "inoculated" against new attacks;

This kind of language is not merely picturesque anthropomorphism. It reflects a profound shift in perception about the relationship of computers to humans. If computers can become ill, then they can become healthy. Once healthy, they can think clearly and make decisions. The computer, it is implied, has a will, has intentions, has reasons—which means that humans are relieved of responsibility for the computer's decisions. Through a curious form of grammatical alchemy, the sentence "We use the computer to calculate" comes to mean "The computer calculates." If a computer calculates, then it may decide to miscalculate or not calculate at all. That is what bank tellers mean when they tell you that they cannot say how much money is in your checking account because "the computers are down." The implication, of course, is that no person at the bank is responsible. Computers make mistakes or get tired or become ill. Why blame people? We may call this line of thinking an "agentic shift," a term I borrow from Stanley Milgram to name the process whereby humans transfer responsibility for an outcome from themselves to a more abstract agent. When this happens, we have relinquished control, which in the case of the computer means that we may, without excessive remorse, pursue ill-advised or even inhuman goals because the computer can accomplish them or be imagined to accomplish them.

Machines of various kinds will sometimes assume a human or, more likely, a superhuman aspect. Perhaps the most absurd case I know of is in a remark a student of mine once made on a sultry summer day in a room without air conditioning. On being told the thermometer read ninety-eight degrees Fahrenheit, he replied, "No wonder it's so hot!" Nature was off the hook. If only the thermometers would behave themselves, we could be comfortable. But computers are far more "human" than thermometers or almost any other kind of technology. Unlike most machines, computers do no work; they direct work. They are, as Norbert Wiener said, the technology of "command and control" and have little value without something to control. This is why they are of such importance to bureaucracies.

Naturally, bureaucrats can be expected to embrace a technology that helps to create the illusion that decisions are not under their control. Because of its seeming intelligence and impartiality, a computer has an almost magical tendency to direct attention away from the people in charge of bureaucratic functions and toward itself, as if the computer were the true source of authority. A bureaucrat armed with a computer is the unacknowledged legislator of our age, and a terrible burden to bear. We cannot dismiss the possibility that, if Adolf Eichmann had been able to say that it was not he but a battery of computers that directed the Jews to the appropriate crematoria, he might never have been asked to answer for his actions.

Although (or perhaps because) I came to "administration" late in my academic career, I am constantly amazed at how obediently people accept explanations that begin with the words "The computer shows . . ." or "The computer has determined . . ." It is Technopoly's equivalent of the sentence "It is God's will," and the effect is roughly the same. You will not be surprised to know that I rarely resort to such humbug. But on occasion, when pressed to the wall, I have yielded. No one has as yet replied, "Garbage in, garbage out." Their defenselessness has something Kafkaesque about it. In *The Trial,* Josef K. is charged with a crime—of what nature, and by whom the charge is made, he does not know. The computer turns too many of us into Josef Ks. It often functions as a kind of impersonal accuser which does not reveal, and is not required to reveal, the sources of the judgments made against us. It is apparently sufficient that the computer has pronounced. Who has put the data in, for what purpose, for whose convenience, based on what assumptions are questions left unasked.

This is the case not only in personal matters but in public decisions as well. Large institutions such as the Pentagon, the Internal Revenue Service, and multinational corporations tell us that their decisions are made on the basis of solutions generated by computers, and this is usually good enough to put our minds at ease or, rather, to sleep. In any case, it constrains us from making complaints or accusations. In part for this reason, the computer has strengthened bureaucratic institutions and suppressed the impulse toward significant social change. "The arrival of the Computer Revolution and the founding of the Computer Age have been announced many times," Weizenbaum has written. "But if the triumph of a revolution is to be measured in terms of the social revision it entrained, then there has been no computer revolution."

In automating the operation of political, social, and commercial enterprises, computers may or may not have made them more efficient but they have certainly diverted attention from the question whether or not such enterprises are necessary or how they might be improved. A university, a political party, a religious denomination, a judicial proceeding, even corporate board meetings are not improved by automating their operations. They are made more imposing, more technical, perhaps more authoritative, but defects in their assumptions, ideas, and theories will remain untouched. Computer technology, in other words, has not yet come close to the printing press in its power to generate radical and substantive social, political, and religious thought. If the press was, as David Riesman called it, "the gunpowder of the mind," the computer, in its capacity to smooth over unsatisfactory institutions and ideas, is the talcum powder of the mind.

I do not wish to go as far as Weizenbaum in saying that computers are merely ingenious devices to fulfill unimportant functions and that the computer revolution is an explosion of nonsense. Perhaps that judgment will be in need of amendment in the future, for the computer is a technology of a thousand uses—the Proteus of machines, to use Seymour Papert's phrase. One must note, for example, the use of computer-generated images in the phenomenon known as Virtual Reality. Putting on a set of miniature goggle-mounted screens, one may block out the real world and move through a simulated three-dimensional world which changes its components with every movement of one's head. That Timothy Leary is an enthusiastic proponent of Virtual Reality does not suggest that there is a constructive future for this device. But who knows? Perhaps, for those who can no longer cope with the real world, Virtual Reality will provide better therapy than Eliza.

What is clear is that, to date, computer technology has served to strengthen Technopoly's hold, to make people believe that technological innovation is synonymous with human progress. And it has done so by advancing several interconnected ideas.

It has, as already noted, amplified beyond all reason the metaphor of machines as humans and humans as machines. I do not claim, by the way, that computer technology originated this metaphor. One can detect it in medicine, too: doctors and patients have come to believe that, like a machine, a human being is made up of parts which when defective can be replaced by mechanical parts that function as the original did without impairing or even affecting any other part of the machine. Of course, to some degree that assumption works, but since a human being is in fad not a machine but a biological organism all of whose organs are interrelated and profoundly affected by mental states, the human-as-machine metaphor has serious medical limitations and can have devastating effects. Something similar may be said of the mechanistic metaphor when applied to workers. Modem industrial techniques are made possible by the idea that a machine is made up of isolatable and interchangeable parts. But in organizing factories so that workers are also conceived of as isolatable and interchangeable parts, industry has engendered deep alienation and bitterness. This was the point of Charlie Chaplin's *Modern Times,* in which he tried to show the psychic damage of the metaphor carried too far. But because the computer "thinks" rather than works, its power to energize mechanistic metaphors is unparalleled and of enormous value to Technopoly, which depends on our believing that we are at our best when acting like machines, and that in significant ways machines may be trusted to act as our surrogates. Among the implications of these beliefs is a loss of confidence in human judgment and subjectivity. We have devalued the singular human capacity to see things whole in all their psychic, emotional and moral dimensions, and we have replaced this with faith in the powers of technical calculation.

Because of what computers commonly do, they place an inordinate emphasis on the technical processes of communication and offer very little in the way of substance. With the exception of the electric light, there never has been a technology that better exemplifies Marshall McLuhan's aphorism "The medium is the message." The computer is almost all process. There are, for example, no "great computerers," as there are great writers, painters, or musicians. There are "great programs" and "great programmers," but their greatness lies in their ingenuity either in simulating a human function or in creating new possibilities of calculation, speed, and volume. Of course, if J. David Bolter is right, it is possible that in the future computers will emerge as a new kind of book, expanding and enriching the tradition of writing technologies. Since printing created new forms of literature when it replaced the handwritten manuscript, it is possible that electronic writing will do the same. But for the moment, computer technology functions more as a new mode of transportation than as a new means of substantive communication. It moves information—lots of it, fast, and mostly in a calculating mode. The computer, in fact, makes possible the fulfillment of Descartes' dream of the mathematization of the world. Computers make it easy to convert facts into statistics and to translate problems into equations. And whereas this can be useful (as when the process reveals a pattern that would otherwise go unnoticed), it is diversionary and dangerous when applied indiscriminately to human affairs. So is the computer's emphasis on speed and especially its capacity to generate and store unprecedented quantities of information. In specialized contexts, the value of calculation, speed, and voluminous information may go uncontested. But the "message" of computer technology is comprehensive and domineering. The computer argues, to put it baldly, that the most serious problems confronting us at both personal and public levels require technical solutions through fast access to information otherwise unavailable. I would argue that this is, on the face of it, nonsense. Our most serious problems are not technical, nor do they arise from inadequate information. If a nuclear catastrophe occurs, it shall not be because of inadequate information. Where people are dying of starvation, it does not occur because of inadequate information. If families break up, children are mistreated, crime terrorizes a city, education is impotent, it does not happen because of inadequate information. Mathematical equations, instantaneous communication, and vast quantities of information have nothing whatever to do with any of these problems. And the computer is useless in addressing them.

And yet, because of its "universality," the computer compels respect, even devotion, and argues for a comprehensive role in all fields of human activity. Those who insist that it is foolish to deny the computer vast sovereignty are singularly devoid of what Paul Goodman once called "technological modesty"—that is, having a sense of the whole and not claiming or obtruding more than a particular function warrants. Norbert Wiener warned about lack of modesty when he remarked that, if digital computers had been in common use before the atomic bomb was invented, people would have said that the bomb could not have been invented without computers. But it was. And it is important to remind ourselves of how many things are quite possible to do without the use of computers.

Seymour Papert, for example, wishes students to be epistemologists, to think critically, and to learn how to create knowledge. In his book *Mindstorms,* he gives the impression that his computer program known as LOGO now makes this possible. But good teachers have been doing this for centuries without the benefit of LOGO. I do not say that LOGO, when used properly by a skilled teacher, will not help, but I doubt that it can do better than pencil and paper, or speech itself, when used properly by a skilled teacher.

When the Dallas Cowboys were consistently winning football championships, their success was attributed to the fact that computers were used to evaluate and select team members. During the past several years, when Dallas has been hard put to win more than a few games, not much has been said about the computers, perhaps because people have realized that computers have nothing to do with winning football games, and never did. One might say the same about writing lucid, economical, stylish prose, which has nothing to do with word-processors. Although my students don't believe it, it is actually possible to write well without a processor and, I should say, to write poorly with one.

Technological immodesty is always an acute danger in Technopoly, which encourages it. Technopoly also encourages insensitivity to what skills may be lost in the acquisition of new ones. It is important to remember what can be done without computers, and it is also important to remind ourselves of what may be lost when we do use them.

I have before me an essay by Sir Bernard Lovell, founder of Britain's Jodrell Bank Observatory, in which he claims that computers have stifled scientific creativity. After writing of his awe at the ease with which computerized operations provide amazing details of distant galaxies, Sir Bernard expresses concern that "literal-minded, narrowly focused computerized research is proving antithetical to the free exercise of that happy faculty known as serendipity—that is, the knack of achieving favorable results more or less by chance." He proceeds to give several examples of monumental but serendipitous discoveries, contends that there has been a dramatic cessation of such discoveries, and worries that computers are too narrow as filters of information and therefore may be antiserendipitous. He is, of course, not "against" computers, but is merely raising questions about their costs.

Dr. Clay Forishee, the chief FAA scientist for human performance issues, did the same when he wondered whether the automated operation of commercial aircraft has not disabled pilots from creatively responding when something goes wrong. Robert Buley, flight-standards manager of Northwest Airlines, goes further. He is quoted as saying, "If we have human operators subordinated to technology then we're going to lose creativity [in emergencies]." He is not "against" computers. He is worried about what we lose by using them.

M. Ethan Katsch, in his book *The Electronic Media and the Transformation of Law,* worries as well. He writes, "The replacement of print by computerized systems is promoted to the legal profession simply as a means to increase efficiency." But he goes on to say that, in fact, the almost unlimited capacity of computers to store and retrieve information threatens the authority of precedent, and he adds that the threat is completely unrecognized. As he notes, "a system of precedent is unnecessary when there are very few accessible cases, and unworkable when there are too many." If this is true, or even partly true, what exactly does it mean? Will lawyers become incapable of choosing relevant precedents? Will judges be in constant confusion from "precedent overload"?

We know that doctors who rely entirely on machinery have lost skill in making diagnoses based on observation. We may well wonder what other human skills and traditions are being lost by our immersion in a computer culture. Technopolists do not worry about such things. Those who do are called technological pessimists, Jeremiahs, and worse. I rather think they are imbued with technological modesty, like King Thamus.

Focal Things and Practices

Albert Borgmann

To see that the force of nature can be encountered analogously in many other places, we must develop the general notions of focal things and practices This is the first point of this chapter. The Latin word *focus*, its meaning and etymology, are our best guides to this task. But once we have learned tentatively to recognize the instances of focal things and practices in our midst, we must acknowledge their scattered and inconspicuous character too. Their hidden splendor comes to light when we consider Heidegger's reflections on simple and eminent things. But an inappropriate nostalgia clings to Heidegger's account. It can be dispelled, so I will argue, when we remember and realize more fully that the technological environment heightens rather than denies the radiance of genuine focal things and when we learn to understand that focal things require a practice to prosper within. These points I will try to give substance in the subsequent parts of this chapter by calling attention to the focal concerns of running and of the culture of the table.

The Latin word *focus* mean hearth. We came upon it in Chapter 9 where the device paradigm was first delineated and where the hearth or fireplace, a thing, was seen as the counterpart to the central heating plant a device. It was pointed out that in a pretechnological house the fireplace constituted a center of warmth, of light, and of daily practices. For the Roman the *focus* was holy, the place where the housegods resided. In ancient Greece, a baby was truly joined to the family and household when it was carried about the hearth and placed before it. The union of a Roman marriage was sanctified at the hearth. And at least in the early periods the dead were buried by the hearth. The family ate by the hearth and made sacrifices to the housegods before and after the meal. The hearth sustained ordered and centered house and family. Reflections of the hearth's significance can yet be seen in the fireplace of many American homes. The fireplace often has a central location in the house. Its fire is now symbolical since it rarely furnishes sufficient warmth. But the radiance, the sounds, and the fragrance of living fire consuming logs that are split, stacked, and felt in their grain have retained their force. There are no longer images of the ancestral gods placed by the fire; but there often are pictures of loved ones on or above the mantel, precious things of the family's history or a clock, measuring time.

From *Technology and the Character of Contemporary Life* by Albert Borgmann. Copyright © 1987 by University of Chicago Press. Reprinted by permission.

The symbolical center of the house, the living room with the fireplace, often seems forbidding in comparison with the real center, the kitchen with its inviting smells and sounds. Accordingly, the architect Jeremiah Eck has rearranged homes to give them back a hearth, "a place of warmth and activity" that encompasses cooking, eating, and living and so is central to the house whether it literally has a fireplace or not. Thus we can satisfy, he says, "the need for a place of focus in our family lives."

"Focus," in English, is now a technical term of geometry and optics. Johannes Kepler was the first so to use it, and he probably drew on the then already current sense of focus as the "burning point of lens or mirror." Correspondingly, an optic or geometric focus is a point where lines or rays converge or from which they diverge in a regular or lawful way. Hence "focus" is used as a verb in optics to denote moving an object in relation to a lens or modifying a combination of lenses in relation to an object so that a clear and well-defined image is produced.

These technical senses of "focus" have happily converged with the original one in ordinary language. Figuratively they suggest that a focus gathers the relations of its context and radiates into its surroundings and informs them. To focus on something or to bring it into focus is to make it central, clear, and articulate. It is in the context of these historical and living senses of "focus" that I want to speak of focal things and practices. Wilderness on this continent, it now appears, is a focal thing. It provides a center of orientation; when we bring the surrounding technology into it, our relations to technology become clarified and well-defined. But just how strong its gathering and radiating force is requires further reflection. And surely there will be other focal things and practices: music, gardening, the culture of the table, or running.

We might in a tentative way be able to see these things as focal; what we see more clearly and readily is how inconspicuous, homely, and dispersed they are. This is in stark contrast to the focal things of pretechnological times, the Greek temple or the medieval cathedral that we have mentioned before. Martin Heidegger was deeply impressed by the orienting force of the Greek temple. For him, the temple not only gave a center of meaning to its world but had orienting power in the strong sense of first originating or establishing the world, of disclosing the world's essential dimensions and criteria. Whether the thesis so extremely put is defensible or not, the Greek temple was certainly more than a self-sufficient architectural sculpture, more than a jewel of well-articulated and harmoniously balanced elements, more, even, than a shrine for the image of the goddess or the god. As Vincent Scully has shown, a temple or a temple precinct gathered and disclosed the land in which they were situated. The divinity of land and sea was focused in the temple.

To see the work of art as the focus and origin of the world's meaning was a pivotal discovery for Heidegger. He had begun in the modem tradition of Western philosophy where, as suggested in the first chapter of this book, the sense of reality is to be grasped by determining the antecedent and controlling conditions of all there is (the *Bedingungen der Möglichkeit* as Immanuel Kant has it). Heidegger wanted to outdo this tradition in the radicality of his search for the fundamental conditions of being. Perhaps it was the relentlessness of his pursuit that disclosed the ultimate futility of it. At any rate, when the universal conditions are explicated in a suitably general and encompassing way, what truly matters still hangs in the balance because everything depends on how the conditions come to be actualized and instantiated. The preoccupation with antecedent conditions not only leaves this question unanswered; it may even make it inaccessible by leaving the impression that, once the general and fundamental matters are determined, nothing of consequence remains to be considered. Heidegger's early work, however, already contained the seeds of its overcoming. In his determination to grasp reality in its concreteness, Heidegger had found and stressed the inexorable and unsurpassable givenness of human existence, and he had provided analyses of its pretechnological wholeness and its technological distraction though the significance of these descriptions for technology had remained concealed to him. And then he discovered that the unique event of significance in the singular work of art, in the prophet's proclamation, and in the political deed was crucial. This insight was worked out in detail with regard to the artwork. But in an epilogue to the essay that develops this point, Heidegger recognized that the insight comes too late. To be sure, our time has brought forth admirable works of art. "But," Heidegger insists, "the question remains: is art still an essential and necessary way in which that truth happens which is decisive for historical existence, or is art no longer of this character?"

Heidegger began to see technology (in his more or less substantive sense) as the force that has eclipsed the focusing powers of pretechnological times. Technology becomes for him, as mentioned at (the end of Chapter 8, the final phase of a long metaphysical development. The philosophical concern with the conditions of the possibility of whatever is now itself seen as a move into the oblivion of what finally matters. But how are we to recover orientation in the oblivious and distracted era of technology when the great embodiments of meaning, the works of art, have lost their focusing power? Amidst the complication of conditions, of the *Bedingungen*, we must uncover the simplicity of things, of the *Dinge*. A jug, an earthen vessel from which we pour wine, is such a thing. It teaches us what it is to hold, to offer, to pour, and to give. In its clay, it gathers for us the earth as it does in containing the wine that has grown from the soil. It gathers the sky whose rain and sun are present in the wine. It refreshes and animates us in our mortality. And in the libation it acknowledges and calls on the divinities. In these ways the thing (in agreement with its etymologically original meaning) gathers and discloses what Heidegger calls the fourfold, the interplay of the crucial dimensions of earth and sky, mortals and divinities. A thing, in Heidegger's eminent sense, is a focus; to speak of focal things is to emphasize the central point twice.

Still, Heidegger's account is but a suggestion fraught with difficulties. When Heidegger described the focusing power of the jug, he might have been thinking of a rural setting where wine jugs embody in their material, form, and craft a long and local tradition; where at noon one goes down to the cellar to draw a jug of table wine whose vintage one knows well; where at the noon meal the wine is thoughtfully poured and gratefully received. Under such circumstances, there might be a gathering and disclosure of the fourfold, one that is for the most part understood and in the background and may come to the fore on festive occasions. But all of this seems as remote to most of us and as muted in its focusing power as the Parthenon or the Cathedral of Chartres. How can so simple a thing as a jug provide that turning point in our relation to technology to which Heidegger is looking forward? Heidegger's proposal for a reform of technology is even more programmatic and terse than his analysis of technology. Both, however, are capable of fruitful development. Two points in Heidegger's consideration of the turn of technology must particularly be noted.

The first serves to remind us of arguments already developed which must be kept in mind if we are to make room for focal things and practices. Heidegger says, broadly paraphrased, that the orienting force of simple things will come to the fore only as the rule of technology is raised from its anonymity, is disclosed as the orthodoxy that heretofore has been taken for granted and allowed to remain invisible. As long as we overlook the tightly patterned character of technology believe that we live in a world of endlessly open and rich opportunities, as long as we ignore the definite ways in which we, acting technologically, have worked out the promise of technology and remain vaguely enthralled by that promise, so long simple things and practices will seem burdensome, confining, and drab. But if we recognize the central vacuity of advanced technology, that emptiness can become the opening for focal things. It works both ways, of course. When we see a focal concern of ours threatened by technology, our sight for the liabilities of mature technology is sharpened.

A second point of Heidegger's is one that we must develop now. The things that gather the fourfold, Heidegger says, are inconspicuous and humble. And when we look at his litany of things, we also see that they are scattered and of yesterday: jug and bench, footbridge and plow, tree and pond, brook and hill, heron and deer, horse and bull, mirror and clasp, book and picture, crown and cross. That focal things and practices are inconspicuous is certainly true; they flourish at the margins of public attention. And they have suffered a diaspora; this too must be accepted, at least for now. That is not to say that a hidden center of these dispersed focuses may not emerge some day to unite them and bring them home. But it would clearly be a forced growth to proclaim such a unity now. A reform of technology that issues from focal concerns will be radical not in imposing a new and unified master plan on the technological universe but in discovering those sources of strength that will nourish principled and confident beginnings, measures, i.e., which will neither rival nor deny technology.

But there are two ways in which we must go beyond Heidegger. One step in the first direction has already been taken. It led us to see in the preceding chapter that the simple things of yesterday attain a new splendor in today's technological context. The suggestion in Heidegger's reflections that we have to seek out pretechnological enclaves to encounter focal things is misleading and dispiriting. Rather we must see any such enclave itself as a focal thing heightened by its technological context. The turn to things cannot be a setting aside and even less an escape from technology but a kind of affirmation of it. The second move beyond Heidegger is in the direction of practice, into the social and, later, the political situation of focal things. Though Heidegger assigns humans their place in the fourfold when he depicts the jug in which the fourfold is focused, we scarcely see the hand that holds the jug, and far less do we see of the social setting in which the pouring of the wine comes to pass. In his consideration of another thing, a bridge, Heidegger notes the human ways and works that are gathered and directed by the bridge. But these remarks too present practices from the viewpoint of the focal thing. What must be shown is that focal things can prosper in human practices only. Before we can build a bridge, Heidegger suggests, we must be able to dwell. But what does that mean concretely?

The consideration of the wilderness has disclosed a center that stands in a fruitful counterposition to technology. The wilderness is beyond the procurement of technology, and our response to it takes us past consumption. But it also teaches us to accept and to appropriate technology. We must now try to discover if such centers of orientation can be found in greater proximity and intimacy to the technological everyday life. And I believe they can be found if we follow up the hints that we have gathered from and against Heidegger, the suggestions that focal things seem humble and scattered but attain splendor in technology if we grasp technology properly, and that focal things require a practice for their welfare. Running and the culture of the table are such focal things and practices. We have all been touched by them in one way or another. If we have not participated in a vigorous or competitive run, we have certainly taken walks; we have felt with surprise, perhaps, the pleasure of touching the earth, of feeling the wind, smelling the rain, of having the blood course through our bodies more steadily. In the preparation of a meal we have enjoyed the simple tasks of washing leaves and cutting bread; we have felt the force and generosity of being served a good wine and homemade bread. Such experiences have been particularly vivid when we came upon them after much sitting and watching indoors after a surfeit of readily available snacks and drinks. To encounter a few simple things was liberating and invigorating. The normal clutter and distraction fall away when, as the poet says,

> there, in limpid brightness shine,
> on the table, bread and wine.

If such experiences are deeply touching, they are fleeting as well. There seems to be no thought or discourse that would shelter and nurture such events; not in politics certainly, nor in philosophy where the prevailing idiom sanctions and applies equally to lounging and walking, to Twinkies, and to bread, the staff of life. But the reflective care of the good life has not withered away. It has left the profession of philosophy and sprung up among practical people. In fact, there is a tradition in this country of persons who are engaged by life in its concreteness and simplicity and who are so filled with this engagement that they have reached for the pen to become witnesses and teachers, speakers of deictic discourse. Melville and Thoreau are among the great prophets of this tradition. Its present health and extent are evident from the fact that it now has no overpowering heroes but many and various more or less eminent practitioners. Their work embraces a spectrum between down-to-earth instruction and soaring speculation. The span and center of their concerns vary greatly. But they all have their mooring in the attention to tangible and bodily things and practices, and they speak with an enthusiasm that is nourished by these focal concerns. Pirsig's book is an impressive and troubling monument in this tradition, impressive in the freshness of its observations and its pedagogical skill, troubling in its ambitious and failing efforts to deal with the large philosophical issues. Norman Maclean's *A River Runs through It* can be taken as a fly-fishing manual, a virtue that pleases its author. But it is a literary work of art most of all and a reflection on technology inasmuch as it presents the engaging life, both dark and bright, from which we have so recently emerged. Colin Fletcher's treatise of *The Complete Walker* is most narrowly a book of instruction about hiking and backpacking. The focal significance of these things is found in the interstices of equipment and technique; and when the author explicitly engages in deictic discourse he has "an unholy awful time" with it. Roger B. Swain's contemplation of gardening in *Earthly Pleasures* enlightens us in cool and graceful prose about the scientific basic and background of what we witness and undertake in our gardens. Philosophical significance enters unbidden and easily in the reflections on time, purposiveness, and the familiar. Looking at these books, I see a stretch of water that extends beyond my vision, disappearing in the distance. But I can see that it is a strong and steady stream, and it may well have parts that are more magnificent than the ones I know.

To discover more clearly the currents and features of this, the other and more concealed, American mainstream, I take as witnesses two books where enthusiasm suffuses instruction vigorously, Robert Farrar Capon's *The Supper of the Lamb* and George Sheehan's *Running and Being*. Both are centered on focal events, the great run and the great meal. The great run, where one exults in the strength of one's body, in the ease and the length of the stride, where nature speaks powerfully in the hills, the wind, the heat, where one takes endurance to the breaking point, and where one is finally engulfed by the good will of the spectators and the fellow runners. The great meal, the long session as Capon calls it, where the guests are thoughtfully invited, the table has been carefully set, where the food is the culmination of tradition, patience, and skill and the presence of the earth's most delectable textures and tastes, where there is an invocation of divinity at the beginning and memorable conversation throughout.

Such focal events are compact, and if seen only in their immediate temporal and spatial extent they are easily mistaken. They are more mistakable still when they are thought of as experiences in the subjective sense, events that have their real meaning in transporting a person into a certain mental or emotional state. Focal events, so conceived, fall under the rule of technology. For when a subjective state becomes decisive, the search for a machinery that is functionally equivalent to the traditional enactment of that state begins, and it is spurred by endeavors to find machineries that will procure the state more instantaneously, ubiquitously, more assuredly and easily. If, on the other hand, we guard focal things in their depth and integrity, then, to see them fully and truly, we must see them in context. Things that are deprived of their context become ambiguous. The letter "a" by itself means nothing in particular. In the context of "table" it conveys or helps to convey a more definite meaning. But "table" in turn can mean many things. It means something more powerful in the text of Capon's book where he speaks of "The Vesting of the Table." But that text must finally be seen in the context and texture of the world. To say that something becomes ambiguous is to say that it is made to say less, little, or nothing. Thus to elaborate the context of focal events is to grant them their proper eloquence.

"The distance runner," Sheehan says, "is the least of all athletes. His sport the least of all sports." Running is simply to move through time and space, step-by-step. But there is splendor in that simplicity. In a car we move of course much faster, farther, and more comfortably. But we are not moving on our own power and in our own right. We cash in prior labor for present motion. Being beneficiaries of science and engineering and having worked to be able to pay for a car, gasoline, and roads, we now release what has been earned and stored and use it for transportation. But when these past efforts are consumed and consummated in my driving, I can at best take credit for what I have done. What I am doing now, driving, requires no effort, and little or no skill or discipline. I am a divided person; my achievement lies in the past, my enjoyment in the present. But in the runner, effort and joy are one; the split between means and ends, labor and leisure is healed. To be sure, if I have trained conscientiously, my past effort will bear fruit in a race. But they are not just cashed in. My strength must be risked and enacted in the race which is itself a supreme effort and an occasion to expand my skill.

This unity of achievement and enjoyment, of competence and consumption, is just one aspect of a central wholeness to which running restores us. Good running engages mind and body. Here the mind is more than an intelligence that happens to be housed in a body. Rather the mind is the sensitivity and the endurance of the body. Hence running in its fullness, as Sheehan stresses over and over again is in principle different from exercise designed to procure physical health. The difference between running and physical exercise is strikingly exhibited in one and the same issue of the *New York Times Magazine*. It contains an account by Peter Wood of how, running the New York City Marathon, he took in the city with body and mind, and it has an account by Alexandra Penney of corporate fitness programs where executives, concerned about their Coronary Risk Factor Profile, run nowhere on treadmills or ride stationary bicycles. In another issue, the *Magazine* shows executives exercising their bodies while busying their dissociated minds with reading. To be sure, unless a runner concentrates on bodily performance, often in an effort to run the best possible race, the mind wanders as the body runs. But as in free association we range about the future and the past, the actual and the possible, our mind, like our breathing, rhythmically gathers itself to the here and now, having spread itself to distant times and faraway places.

It is clear from these reflections that the runner is mindful of the body because the body is intimate with the world. The mind becomes relatively disembodied when the body is severed from the depth of the world, i.e., when the world is split into commodious surfaces and inaccessible machineries. Thus the unity of ends and mean, of mind and body, and of body and world is one and the same. It makes itself felt in the vividness with which the runner experiences reality. "Somehow you feel more in touch," Wood says, "with the realities of a massive inner-city housing problem when you are running through it slowly enough to take in the grim details, and, surprisingly, cheered on by the remaining occupants." As this last remark suggests, the wholeness that running establishes embraces the human family too. The experience of that simple event releases an equally simple and profound sympathy. It is a natural goodwill, not in need of drugs nor dependent on a common enemy. It wells up from depths that have been forgotten, and it overwhelms the runners ever and again. As Wood recounts his running through streets normally besieged by crime and violence, he remarks: "But we can only be amazed today at the warmth that emanates from streets usually better known for violent crime." And his response to the spectators' enthusiasm is this: "I feel a great proximity to the crowd, rushing past at all of nine miles per hour; a great affection for them individually; a commitment to run as well as I possibly can, to acknowledge their support." For George Sheehan, finally, running discloses the divine. When he runs, he wrestles with God. Serious running takes us to the limits of our being. We run into threatening and seemingly unbearable pain. Sometimes, of course, the plunge into that experience gets arrested in ambition and vanity. But it can take us further to the point where in suffering our limits we experience our greatness too. This, surely, is a hopeful place to escape technology, metaphysics, and the God of the philosophers and reach out to the God of Abraham, Isaac, and Jacob.

If running allows us to center our lives by taking in the world through vigor and simplicity, the culture of the table does so by joining simplicity with cosmic wealth. Humans are such complex and capable beings that they can fairly comprehend the world and, containing it, constitute a cosmos in their own right. Because we are standing so eminently over against the world, to come in touch with the world becomes for us a challenge and a momentous event. In one sense, of course, we are always already in the world, breathing the air, touching the ground, feeling the sun. But as we can in another sense withdraw from the actual and present world, contemplating what is past and to come, what is possible and remote, 'we celebrate correspondingly our intimacy with the world. This we do most fundamentally when in eating we take in the world in its palpable, colorful, nourishing immediacy. Truly human eating is the union of the primal and the cosmic. In the simplicity of bread and wine, of meat and vegetable, the world is gathered.

The great meal of the day, be it at noon or in the evening, is a focal event par excellence. It gathers the scattered family around the table. And on the table it gathers the most delectable things nature has brought forth. But it also recollects and presents a tradition, the immemorial experiences of the race in identifying and cultivating edible plants, in domesticating and butchering animals; it brings into focus closer relations of national or regional customs, and more intimate traditions still of family recipes and dishes. It is evident from the preceding chapters how this living texture is being rent through the procurement of food as a commodity and the replacement of the culture of the table by the food industry. Once food has become freely available, it is only consistent that the gathering of the meal is shattered and disintegrates into snacks, T.V. dinners, bites that are grabbed to be eaten; and eating itself is scattered around television shows, late and early meetings, activities, overtime work, and other business. This is increasingly the normal condition of technological eating. But it is within our power to clear a central space amid the clutter and distraction. We can begin with the simplicity of a meal that has a beginning, a middle, and an end and that breaks through the superficiality of convenience food in the simple steps of beginning with raw ingredients, preparing and transforming them, and bringing them to the table. In this way we can again become freeholder of our culture. We are disfranchised from world citizenship when the foods we eat are mere commodities. Being essentially opaque surfaces, they repel all efforts at extending our sensibility and competence into the deeper reaches of the world. A Big Mac and a Coke can overwhelm our tastebuds and accommodate our hunger. Technology is not, after all, a children's crusade but a principled and skillful enterprise of defining and satisfying human needs. Through the diversion and busyness of consumption we may have unlearned to feel constrained by the shallowness of commodities. But having gotten along for a time and quite well, it seemed, on institutional or convenience food, scales fall from our eyes when we step up to a festively set family table. The foods stand out more clearly, the fragrances are stronger, eating has once more become an occasion that engages and accepts us fully.

To understand the radiance and wealth of a festive meal we must be alive to the interplay of thing and humans, of ends and means. At first a meal, once it on the table, appears to have commodity character since it is now available before us, ready to be consumed without effort or merit. But though there is of course in any eating a moment of mere consuming, in a festive meal eating is one with an order and discipline that challenges and ennobles the participants. The great meal has its structure. It begins with a moment of reflection in which we place ourselves in the presence of the first and last things. It has a sequence of courses; it requires and sponsors memorable conversation; and all this is enacted in the discipline called table manners. They are warranted when they constitute the respectful and skilled response to the great things that are coming to pass in the meal. We can see how order and discipline have collapsed when we eat a Big Mac. In consumption there is the pointlike and inconsequential conflation of a sharply delimited human need with an equally contextless and closely fitting commodity. In a Big Mac the sequence of courses has been compacted into one object and the discipline of table manners has been reduced to grabbing and eating. The social context reaches no further than the pleasant faces and quick hands of the people who run the fast-food outlet. In a festive meal, however, the food is served, one of the most generous gestures human beings are capable of. The serving is of a piece with garnishing; garnishing is the final phase of cooking, and cooking is one with preparing the food. And if we are blessed with rural circumstances, the preparation of food draws near the harvesting and the raising of the vegetables in the garden close by. This context of activities is embodied in persons. The dish and the cook, the vegetable and the gardener tell of one another. Especially when we are guests, much of the meal's deeper context is socially and conversationally mediated. But that mediation has translucence and intelligibility because it extends into the farther and deeper recesses without break and with a bodily immediacy that we too have enacted or at least witnessed firsthand. And what seems to be a mere receiving and consuming of food is in fact the enactment of generosity and gratitude, the affirmation of mutual and perhaps religious obligations. Thus eating in a focal setting differs sharply from the social and cultural anonymity of a fast-food outlet.

The pretechnological world was engaging through and through, and not always positively. There also was ignorance, to be sure, of the final workings of God and king; but even the unknown engaged one through mystery and awe. In this web of engagement, meals already had focal character, certainly as soon as there was anything like a culture of the table. Today, however, the great meal does not gather and order a web of thoroughgoing relations of engagement; within the technological setting it stands out as a place of profound calm, one in which we can leave behind the narrow concentration and one-sided strain of labor and the tiring and elusive diversity of consumption. In the technological setting, the culture of the table not only focuses our life; it is also distinguished as a place of healing, one that restores us to the depth of the world and to the wholeness of our being.

As said before we all have had occasion to experience the profound pleasure of an invigorating walk or a festive meal. And on such occasions we may have regretted the scarcity of such events; we might have been ready to allow such events a more regular and central place in our lives. But for the most part these events remain occasional, and indeed the ones that still grace us may be slipping from our grasp. In Chapter 18 we have seen various aspects of this malaise, especially its connection with television. But why are we acting against our better insights and aspirations? This at first seems all the more puzzling as the engagement in a focal activity is for most citizens of the technological society an instantaneous and ubiquitous possibility. On any day I can decide to run or to prepare a meal after work. Everyone has some sort of suitable equipment. At worst one has to stop on the way home to pick up this or that. It is of course technology that has opened up these very possibilities. But why are they lying fallow for the most part? There is a convergence of several factors. Labor is exhausting, especially when it is divided. When we come home, we often feel drained and crippled. Diversion and pleasurable consumption appear to be consonant with this sort of disability. They promise to untie the knots and to soothe the aches. And so they do at a shallow level of our existence. At any rate, the call for exertion and engagement seems like a cruel and unjust demand. We have sat in the easy chair, beer at hand and television before us; when we felt stirrings of ambition, we found it easy to ignore our superego. But we also may have had our alibi refuted on occasion when someone to whom we could not say no prevailed on us to put on our coat and to step out into cold and windy weather to take a walk. At first our indignation grew. The discomfort was worse than we had thought. But gradually a transformation set in. Our gait became steady, our blood began to flow vigorously and wash away our tension, we smelled the rain, began thoughtfully to speak with our companion, and finally returned home settled, alert, and with a fatigue that was capable of restful sleep.

But why did such occurrences remain episodes also? The reason lies in the mistaken assumption that the shaping of our lives can be left to a series of individual decisions. Whatever goal in life we entrust to this kind of implementation we in fact surrender to erosion. Such a policy ignores both the frailty and strength of human nature. On the spur of the moment, we normally act out what has been nurtured in our daily practices as they have been shaped by the norms of our time. When we sit in our easy chair and contemplate what to do, we are firmly enmeshed in the framework of technology with our labor behind us and the blessings of our labor about us, the diversions and enrichments of consumption. This arrangement has had our lifelong allegiance, and we know it to have the approval and support of our fellows. It would take superhuman strength to stand up to this order ever and again. If we are to challenge *the rule of technology*, we can do so only through *the practice of engagement*.

The human ability to establish and commit oneself to a practice reflects our capacity to comprehend the world, to harbor it in its expanse as a context that is oriented by its focal points. To found a practice is to guard a focal concern, to shelter it against the vicissitudes of fate and our frailty. John Rawls has pointed out that there is decisive difference between the justification of a practice and of a particular action falling under it. Analogously, it is one thing to decide for a focal practice and quite another to decide for a particular action that appears to have focal character. Putting the matter more clearly, we must say that without a practice an engaging action or event can momentarily light up our life, but it cannot order and orient it focally. Competence, excellence, or virtue, as Aristotle first saw, come into being as an *éthos*, a settled disposition and a way of life. Through a practice, Alasdaire MacIntyre says accordingly, "human powers to achieve excellence, and human conceptions of the ends and goods involved, are systematically extended." Through a practice we are able to accomplish what remains unattainable when aimed at in a series of individual decisions and acts.

How can a practice be established today? Here, as in the case focal things, it is helpful to consider the foundation of pretechnological practices. In mythic times the latter were often established through the founding and consecrating act of a divine power or mythic ancestor. Such an act, as mentioned in Chapter 22, set up a sacred precinct and center that gave order to a violent and hostile world. A sacred practice, then, consisted in the regular reenactment of the founding act, and so it renewed and sustained the order of the world. Christianity came into being this way; the eucharistic meal, the Supper of the Lamb, is its central event, established with the instruction that it be reenacted. Clearly a focal practice today should have centering and orienting force as well. But it differs in important regards from its grand precursors. A mythic focal practice derived much force from the power of its opposition. The alternative to the preservation of the cosmos was chaos, social and physical disorder and collapse. It is a reduction to see mythic practices merely as coping behavior of high survival value. A myth does not just aid survival; it defines what truly human life is. Still, as in the case of pretechnological morality, economic and social factors were interwoven with mythic practices. Thus the force of brute necessity supported, though it did not define, mythic focal practices. Since a mythic focal practice united in itself the social, the economic, and the cosmic, it was naturally a prominent and public affair. It rested securely in collective memory and in the mutual expectations of the people.

This sketch, of course, fails to consider many other kinds of pretechnological practices. But it does present one important aspect of them and more particularly one that serves well as a backdrop for focal practices in a technological setting. It is evident that technology is itself a sort of practice, and it procures its own kind of order and security. Its history contains great moments of innovation, but it did not arise out of a founding event that would have focal character; nor has it, as argued in Chapter 20, produced focal things. Thus it is not a *focal* practice, and it has indeed, so I have urged, a debilitating tendency to scatter our attention and to clutter our surroundings. A focal practice today, then, meets no tangible or overtly hostile opposition from its context and is so deprived of the wholesome vigor that derives from such opposition. But there is of course an opposition at a more profound and more subtle level. To feel the support of that opposing force one must have experienced the subtly debilitating character of technology, and above all one must understand, explicitly or implicitly, that the peril of technology lies not in this or that of its manifestations but in *the pervasiveness and consistency of its pattern*. There are always occasions where a Big Mac, an exercycle, or a television program are unobjectionable and truly helpful answers to human needs. This makes a case-by-case appraisal of technology so inconclusive. It is when we attempt to take the measure of technologial life in its normal totality that we are distressed by its shallowness. And I believe that the more strongly we sense and the more clearly we understand the coherence and the character of technology, the more evident it becomes to us that technology must be countered by an equally patterned and social commitment, i.e., by a practice.

At this level the opposition of technology does become fruitful to focal practices. They can now be seen as restoring a depth and integrity to our lives that are in principle excluded within the paradigm of technology. MacIntyre, though his foil is the Enlightenment more than technology, captures this point by including in his definition of practice the notion of "goods internal to a practice." These are one with the practice and can only be obtained through that practice. The split between means and ends is healed. In contrast "there are those goods externally and contingently attached" to a practice; and in that case there "are always alternative ways for achieving such goods, and their achievement is never to be had *only* by engaging in some particular kind of practice." Thus practices (in a looser sense) that serve external goods are subvertible by technology. But MacIntyre's point needs to be clarified and extended to include or emphasize not only the essential unity of human being and a particular sort of doing but also the tangible things in which the world comes to be focused. The importance of this point has been suggested by the consideration of running and the culture of the table. There are objections to this suggestion that will be examined in the next chapter. Here I want to advance the thesis by considering Rawls's contention that a practice is defined by rules. We can take a rule as an instruction for a particular domain of life to act in a certain way under specified circumstances. How important is the particular character of the tangible setting of the rules? Though Rawls does not address this question directly he suggests in using baseball for illustration that "a peculiarly shaped piece of wood" and a kind of bag become a bat and base only within the confines defined by the rules of baseball. Rules and the practice they define, we might argue in analogy to what Rawls says about their relation to particular cases, are logically prior to their tangible setting. But the opposite contention seems stronger to me. Clearly the possibilities and challenges of baseball are crucially determined by the layout and the surface of the field, the weight and resilience of the ball, the shape and size of the bat, etc. One might of course reply that there are rules that define the physical circumstances of the game. But this is to take "rule" in broader sense. Moreover it would be more accurate to say that the rules of this latter sort reflect and protect the identity of the original tangible circumstances in which the game grew up. The rules, too, that circumscribe the actions of the players can be taken as ways of securing and ordering the playful challenges that arise in the human interplay with reality. To be sure there are developments and innovations in sporting equipment. But either they quite change the nature of the sport as in pole vaulting, or they are restrained to preserve the identity of the game as in baseball.

It is certainly the purpose of a focal practice to guard in its undiminished depth and identity the thing that is central to the practice, to shield it against the technological diremption into means and end. Like values, rules and practices are recollections, anticipations, and, we can now say, guardians of the concrete things and events that finally matter. Practices protect focal things not only from technological subversion but also against human frailty. It was emphasized in Chapter 21 that the ultimately significant thing to which we respond in deictic discourse cannot be possessed or controlled. Hence when we reach out for them, we miss them occasionally and sometimes for quite some time. Running becomes unrelieved pain and cooking a thankless chore. If in the technological mode we insisted on assured results or if more generally we estimated the value of future efforts on the basis of recent experience, focal things would vanish from our lives. A practice keeps faith with focal things and saves for them an opening in our lives. To be sure, eventually the practice needs to be empowered again by the reemergence of the great thing in its splendor. A practice that is not so revived degenerates into an empty and perhaps deadening ritual.

We can now summarize the significance of a focal practice and say that such a practice is required to counter technology in its patterned pervasiveness and to guard focal things in their depth and integrity. Countering technology through a practice is to take account of our susceptibility to technological distraction, and it is also to engage the peculiarly human strength of comprehension, i.e., the power to take in the world in its extent and significance and to respond through an enduring commitment. Practically a focal practice comes into being through resoluteness, either an explicit resolution where one vows regularly to engage in a focal activity from this day on or in a more implicit resolve that is nurtured by a focal thing in favorable circumstances and matures into a settled custom.

In considering these practical circumstances we must acknowledge a final difference between focal practices today and their eminent pretechnological predecessors. The latter, being public and prominent, commanded elaborate social and physical settings: hierarchies, offices, ceremonies, and choirs; edifices, altars, implements, and vestments. In comparison our focal practices are humble and scattered. Sometimes they can hardly be called practices, being private and limited. Often they begin as a personal regimen and mature into a routine without ever attaining the social richness that distinguishes a practice. Given the often precarious and inchoate nature of focal practices evidently focal things and practices, for all the splendor of their simplicity and their fruitful opposition to technology, must be further clarified in their relation to our everyday world if they are to be seen as a foundation for the reform of technology.

Appendix 1 Images

The Taking of Christ by Caravaggio

The Taking of Christ (oil on canvas), Caravaggio, Michelangelo (1571–1610) (follower of)/Private Collection/© Lawrence Steigrad Fine Arts, New York/Bridgeman Images

323

Appendix 1 Images

The School of Athens by Raphael

© Viacheslav Lopatin/Shutterstock.com

Appendix 2 Timeline

Chronological order of major philosophers

Appendix 2 Timeline

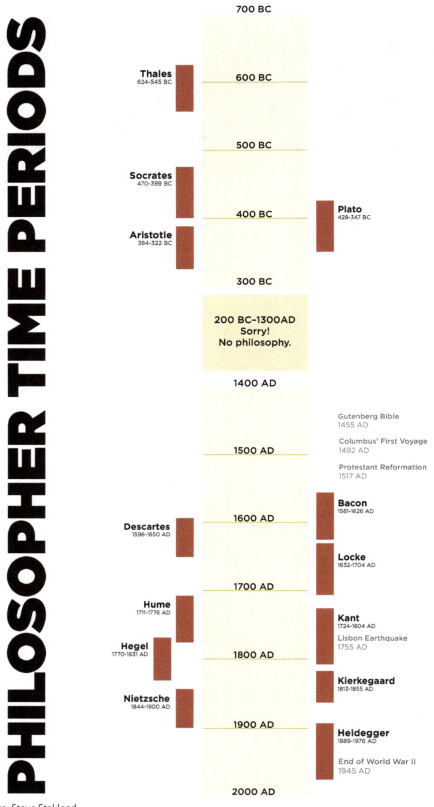

Source: Steve Stakland

Appendix 3
Why Major in Philosophy

A $75 MILLION BET ON THE HUMANITIES

Heather H. Murren

At a time when algorithms and quants rule Wall Street, one of America's legendary investors is placing a $75-million wager on a group of students seldom lauded for their arithmetic agility: philosophy majors. Bill Miller—who beat the market for 15 straight years while at Legg Mason—is betting humanities students have the critical thinking skills and global perspective needed to lead in the digital age.

Mr. Miller recently donated $75 million to fund the study of philosophy at Johns Hopkins University. His decision may come as a surprise to some, as financial firms scramble to hire computer scientists and mathematicians, not philosophers. But when Mr. Miller approached the Johns Hopkins board, on which I sit, the thesis behind his decision was clear: Philosophy is the best tool to hone the essential human skills needed in our rapidly changing world.

While Mr. Miller is renowned for his historic streak at Legg Mason, few know that he applies the tools of a scholar to the problems of an investor. He is totally absorbed not only in the analytical process but also in learning new and disparate information across the impossibly broad spectrum of topics that inform his genius. In fact, he studied philosophy in the PhD program at Hopkins himself. This enables him to find the far-sighted investments that algorithms fail to spot, often delivering the huge payouts that built his towering reputation.

Now, he is taking another contrarian position. Contrary to conventional wisdom, a deep grounding in the humanities is becoming more important as globalization and technological change accelerate. Engaging intensely with great thoughts and ideas provides the critical thinking skills, ethical base and philosophical framework to navigate unprecedented

---

First published in the Baltimore Sun, January 30, 2018. Copyright © by Heather H. Murren. Reprinted by permission.

disruption. While global information flows and new technologies allow us to access more data than ever, humans—not advanced algorithms—must decide how these tools are used to create value.

As many educational institutions redirect funds to science and technology, Mr. Miller's gift is a bold outlier and a vote of confidence in the staying power of timeless human skills. It recognizes that while STEM education is important at providing technical know-how, tomorrow's leaders need philosophy to sharpen and amplify the quintessentially human qualities that guide long-term strategy and direct science and technology to worthwhile ends.

The board and Mr. Miller expect that the donation will equip students to have an impact in both business and the broader world. As Mr. Miller has shown, the lifelong pursuit of knowledge embodied by philosophy can help its students to see hidden connections and the implications for companies and industries. This leads to the unconventional strategies, original thinking, and nuanced insights that are the hallmarks of true human advancement. They don't hurt when it comes to beating the market either.

Of course, many students will choose to make their mark outside of business, in a world that seems to include more looming challenges every day. The current tally of potential global crises ranges from climate change and terrorism to pandemics and cyber warfare. Again, philosophy is unique because it focuses on the intrinsic human abilities needed to solve these complex, interdisciplinary problems. With Mr. Miller's help, students at Johns Hopkins will take on these challenges, using the skills learned in philosophy courses to delve into new subjects, perceive overlooked solutions, and balance competing values and goals.

In short, the gift's aim is to provide students at Johns Hopkins—one of the world's intellectual leaders in the sciences and engineering—with the humane instincts and rigorous analytical framework to succeed, even amid seismic transformations. With this gift, Mr. Miller is betting that as our world advances, holding close to our humanity will be ever more important.

I wouldn't bet against him.

CPSIA information can be obtained
at www.ICGtesting.com
Printed in the USA
LVHW020440210819
628248LV00004B/12/P